D0880737

Hedge Fund
Market Wizards

Other Books by Jack D. Schwager

A Complete Guide to the Futures Markets: Fundamental Analysis, Technical Analysis, Trading, Spreads, and Options

Getting Started in Technical Analysis

Market Wizards: Interviews with Top Traders

The New Market Wizards: Conversations with America's Top Traders

Stock Market Wizards: Interviews with America's Top Stock Traders

Schwager on Futures: Fundamental Analysis

Schwager on Futures: Managed Trading Myths & Truths

Schwager on Futures: Technical Analysis

Study Guide to Accompany Fundamental Analysis (with Steven C. Turner)

Study Guide to Accompany Technical Analysis (with Thomas A. Bierovic and Steven C. Turner)

Hedge Fund Market Wizards

How Winning Traders Win

Jack D. Schwager

WILEY

John Wiley & Sons, Inc.

Copyright © 2012 by Jack D. Schwager. All rights reserved.

Published by John Wiley & Sons, Inc., Hoboken, New Jersey.
Published simultaneously in Canada.

No part of this publication may be reproduced, stored in a retrieval system, or transmitted in any form or by any means, electronic, mechanical, photocopying, recording, scanning, or otherwise, except as permitted under Section 107 or 108 of the 1976 United States Copyright Act, without either the prior written permission of the Publisher, or authorization through payment of the appropriate per-copy fee to the Copyright Clearance Center, Inc., 222 Rosewood Drive, Danvers, MA 01923, (978) 750-8400, fax (978) 646-8600, or on the Web at www.copyright.com. Requests to the Publisher for permission should be addressed to the Permissions Department, John Wiley & Sons, Inc., 111 River Street, Hoboken, NJ 07030, (201) 748-6011, fax (201) 748-6008, or online at http://www.wiley.com/go/permissions.

Limit of Liability/Disclaimer of Warranty: While the publisher and author have used their best efforts in preparing this book, they make no representations or warranties with respect to the accuracy or completeness of the contents of this book and specifically disclaim any implied warranties of merchantability or fitness for a particular purpose. No warranty may be created or extended by sales representatives or written sales materials. The advice and strategies contained herein may not be suitable for your situation. You should consult with a professional where appropriate. Neither the publisher nor author shall be liable for any loss of profit or any other commercial damages, including but not limited to special, incidental, consequential, or other damages.

For general information on our other products and services or for technical support, please contact our Customer Care Department within the United States at (800) 762-2974, outside the United States at (317) 572-3993 or fax (317) 572-4002.

Wiley also publishes its books in a variety of electronic formats. Some content that appears in print may not be available in electronic books. For more information about Wiley products, visit our web site at www.wiley.com.

Library of Congress Cataloging-in-Publication Data

Schwager, Jack D., 1948–
    Hedge fund market wizards : how winning traders win / Jack D. Schwager.
        p. cm.
    Includes index.
    ISBN 978-1-118-27304-3 (hardback)
        1. Floor traders (Finance).   2. Hedge funds.   I. Title.
    HG4621.H27   2012
    332.64'524—dc23

                                                                    2012004861

Printed in the United States of America

10 9 8 7 6 5 4 3 2 1

With love to my wife, Jo Ann,
the best thing that ever happened to me
(I know because she tells me so, and she has never been wrong)

Lara Logan: Do you feel the adrenaline at all?

Alex Honnold: There is no adrenaline rush. . . . If I get a rush, it means that something has gone horribly wrong. . . . The whole thing should be pretty slow and controlled. . . .

> —Excerpt of *60 Minutes* interview (October 10, 2011) with Alex Honnold, acknowledged to be the best free-soloing climber in the world, whose extraordinary feats include the first free-solo climb up the northwest face of Half Dome, a 2,000-foot wall in Yosemite National Park

To do my vacuum cleaner, I built 5,127 prototypes. That means I had 5,126 failures. But as I went through those failures, I made discoveries.

> —*James Dyson*

Contents

Foreword   ix

Preface   xiii

Acknowledgments   xvii

Part One   Macro Men   1

Chapter 1   **Colm O'Shea: Knowing When It's Raining**   3

Chapter 2   **Ray Dalio: The Man Who Loves Mistakes**   47

Chapter 3   **Larry Benedict: Beyond Three Strikes**   77

Chapter 4   **Scott Ramsey: Low-Risk Futures Trader**   103

Chapter 5   **Jaffray Woodriff: The Third Way**   129

Part Two   Multistrategy Players   159

Chapter 6   **Edward Thorp: The Innovator**   161

Chapter 7   **Jamie Mai: Seeking Asymmetry**   223

Chapter 8   **Michael Platt: The Art and Science
              of Risk Control**   261

              Part Three   Equity Traders   285

Chapter 9   **Steve Clark: Do More of What Works
              and Less of What Doesn't**   287

Chapter 10   **Martin Taylor: The Tsar Has No Clothes**   323

Chapter 11   **Tom Claugus: A Change of Plans**   359

Chapter 12   **Joe Vidich: Harvesting Losses**   385

Chapter 13   **Kevin Daly: Who Is Warren Buffett?**   405

Chapter 14   **Jimmy Balodimas: Stepping in Front
              of Freight Trains**   423

Chapter 15   **Joel Greenblatt: The Magic Formula**   451

Conclusion   40 Market Wizard Lessons   489
Epilogue   507
Appendix A   The Gain to Pain Ratio   513
Appendix B   Options—Understanding the Basics   515
About the Author   519
Index   521

Foreword

Once upon a time, a drought comes over the land and the wheat crop fails. Naturally, the price of wheat goes up. Some people cut back and bake less bread while others speculate and buy as much wheat as they can get and hoard it in hopes of higher prices to come.

The king hears about all the speculation and high prices and promptly sends his soldiers from town to town to proclaim that speculation is now a crime against the state—and that severe punishment is to befall speculators.

The new law, like oh so many laws against the free market, only compounds the problem. Soon, some towns have no wheat at all—while rumor has it that others still have ample, even excess, supplies.

The king keeps raising the penalty for speculation, while the price of wheat, if you can find any, keeps going higher and higher.

One day, the court jester approaches the king and, in an entertaining sort of way, tells the king of a plan to end the famine—and to emerge as a wise and gracious ruler.

The next day, the soldiers again ride from town to town, this time to proclaim the end of all laws against speculation—and to suggest that each town prominently post the local price for wheat at its central marketplace.

The towns take the suggestion and post the prices. At first, the prices are surprisingly high in some towns and surprisingly low in others. During the next few days, the roads between the towns become virtual rivers of wheat as speculators rush to discount the spreads. By the end of the week, the price of wheat is mostly the same everywhere and everyone has enough to eat.

The court jester, having a keen sense for his own survival, makes sure all the credit goes directly to the king.

I like this story.

The loose end, of course, is how the court jester happens to know so much about how markets work—and how he happens to know how to express what he knows in an effective way.

While we may never know the answer for sure, my personal hunch is that the court jester makes frequent visits to the royal library and reads *Reminiscences of a Stock Operator* by Edwin Lefèvre, *The Crowd* by Gustav LeBon, *Extraordinary Popular Delusions and the Madness of Crowds* by Charles Mackay, and the entire *Market Wizards* series by Jack Schwager.

Trading, it turns out, is the solution to most economic problems; *free markets*, *sanctity of trading*, and *healthy economy* are all ways to say the same thing. In this sense, our traders are champions and the men and women in Jack Schwager's books are our heroes.

Schwager's books define trading by vividly portraying traders. He finds the best examples, he makes them human and accessible, and he allows them to express, in their own ways, what they do and how they do it. He gives us a gut feel for the struggles, challenges, joys, and sorrows all of them face over their entire careers. We wind up knowing each of his subjects intimately—and also as a uniquely complete expression of repeating themes, such as: be humble; go with the flow; manage risk; do it your own way.

Schwager's books are essential reading for anyone who trades, wants to trade, or wants to pick a trader.

I go back a ways with Jack. I recall meeting him while we were both starting out as traders, long on enthusiasm and short on experience. Over the years, I watched him grow, mature, and develop his talent, evolving to become our Chronicler-General.

Schwager's contribution to the industry is enormous. His original *Market Wizards* inspired a whole new generation of traders, many of whom subsequently appeared in *The New Market Wizards*, and then, in turn, in *Stock Market Wizards*. Jack's *Wizards* series becomes the torch that traders pass from one generation to the next. Now *Hedge Fund Market Wizards* extends, enhances, and perfects the tradition. Traders regularly use passages and chapters from Schwager's books as a reference for their own methods and to guide their own trading. His work is an inseparable part of the consciousness and language of trading itself.

Some 30 years ago, Jack reads *Reminiscences of a Stock Operator* and notices its meaningfulness and relevance, even 60 years after its publication. He adopts that standard for his own writing.

I notice that books that actually meet that standard tend to wind up in the libraries of traders and court jesters alike, on the same shelf with *Reminiscences*, *The Crowd*, and *Extraordinary Popular Delusions and the Madness of Crowds*.

That's exactly where you find Jack's books in my library.

Ed Seykota
Bastrop, Texas
February 25, 2012

Preface

This volume is part of my continuing effort to meet with exceptional traders to better understand the elements underlying their success and what differentiates them from the multitude of pedestrian market participants. The traders interviewed range from the founder of the largest hedge fund in the world, managing $120 billion in assets with 1,400 employees, to a manager running a solo operation with only $50 million in assets. Some of the managers trade from a long-term perspective, holding positions for many months and even years, while others focus on trading horizons as short as a single day. Some managers utilize only fundamental data, others only technical input, and still others combine both. Some of the managers have very high average returns with substantial volatility, while other managers have far more moderate returns, but with much lower volatility.

The one characteristic that all the managers share is that they have demonstrated an ability to generate superior return/risk performance. Because so much of what passes for high returns merely reflects a willingness to take more risk rather than being an indication of skill, I believe that return/risk is a far more meaningful measure than return alone. In fact, the fixation of investors on return without the appropriate consideration of risk is one of the great investment mistakes—but that is a story for another book. One return/risk measure that I have found particularly useful is the Gain to Pain ratio—a statistic that is explained in Appendix A.

There were three key criteria for selecting interviews to be included in this book:

1. The managers had superior return/risk track records for significant length periods—usually (but not always) 10 or more years and often much longer.
2. The managers were open enough to provide valuable advice about trading.
3. The interviews provided sufficient color to allow for a readable chapter.

A half dozen of the interviews I did for this volume were not used because they fell short in one or more of these categories.

Over longer-term intervals (e.g., 10 years, 15 years), hedge funds consistently outperform equity indexes and mutual funds.[1] The typical pattern is that hedge funds, as a group, will have modestly higher returns, but far lower volatility and equity drawdowns. It is ironic that in terms of any type of risk measure, hedge funds, which are widely viewed as highly speculative, are actually much more conservative than traditional investments, such as mutual funds. It is primarily as a consequence of lower risk that hedge funds tend to exhibit much better return/risk performance than mutual funds or equity indexes. Moreover, with rare exception, the best managers are invariably found within the hedge fund world. This fact is not surprising because one would expect the incentive fee structure of hedge funds to draw the best talent.

When I conducted the interviews for my first two *Market Wizard* books (1988–1991), hedge funds were still a minor player in the world investment scene.[2] Based on estimates by Van Hedge Fund Advisors,

---

[1] All the performance statements made in reference to hedge funds as an investment category implicitly assume hedge fund of funds data. Indexes based on fund of funds returns largely avoid the significant statistical biases inherent in hedge fund indexes that are based on individual manager returns.

[2] *Market Wizards*, New York Institute of Finance, 1989. *New Market Wizards*, New York, HarperBusiness, 1991.

total industry assets under management during that period were in the approximate $50 billion to $100 billion range. Since that time, however, hedge fund growth has exploded, expanding more than twentyfold, with the industry currently managing in excess of $2 trillion. The impact of hedge fund trading activity far exceeds its nominal size because hedge fund managers trade far more actively than traditional fund managers. The enhanced role of hedge funds has itself influenced market behavior.

With hedge funds accounting for a much larger percentage of trading activity, trading has become more difficult. In some strategies, the effect can clearly be seen. For example, systematic trend-followers did enormously well in the 1970s and 1980s when they accounted for a minority of futures trading activity, but their return/risk performance declined dramatically in subsequent decades, as they became a larger and larger part of the pool. Too many big fish make it more difficult for other big fish to thrive.

Even if one does not accept the argument that the greater role of hedge funds has made the game more difficult, at the very least, it has made the game different. Markets change and good traders adapt. As hedge fund manager Colm O'Shea states in his interview, "Traders who are successful over the long run adapt. If they do use rules, and you meet them 10 years later, they will have broken those rules. Why? Because the world changed." Part of that change has been brought about by the increasing prominence of hedge funds themselves.

Not surprisingly, virtually all of the traders interviewed in this volume are hedge fund managers (or ex–hedge fund managers). The one exception, Jimmy Balodimas, a highly successful proprietary trader with First New York Securities, had to adapt to the presence of hedge funds. In his interview, he describes how hedge fund activity changed the nature of equity price movements and how he had to adjust his own approach accordingly.

Markets have changed in the generation since I wrote the first *Market Wizards* book, but in another sense, they have not. A bit of perspective is useful. When I asked Ed Seykota in *Market Wizards* whether the increasing role of professionals had changed the markets (a shift that the intervening years have demonstrated was then only in its infancy), he replied, "No. The markets are the same now as they were 5 to 10 years ago because they keep changing—just like they did then."

In many of the interviews, traders made reference to one or more of my earlier books. I did not include all such references, but I included more than I was comfortable doing. I am quite cognizant how self-serving this may appear to be. My guideline whether to include such references was to ask myself the following question: Would I include this comment if the reference were to another book, rather than my own? If the answer was yes, I included it.

Readers who are looking for some secret formula that will provide them with an easy way to beat the markets are looking in the wrong place. Readers who are seeking to improve their own trading abilities, however, should find much that is useful in the following interviews. I believe the trading lessons and insights shared by the traders are timeless. I believe that although markets are always changing, because of constancies in human nature, in some sense, they are also always the same. I remember, when first reading *Reminiscences of a Stock Operator* by Edwin Lefèvre nearly 30 years ago, being struck by how relevant the book remained more than 60 years after it was written. I do not mean or intend to draw any comparisons between this volume and *Reminiscences*, but merely to define the goal I had in mind in writing this book—that it still be meaningful and useful to readers trading the market 60 years from now.

Acknowledgments

First and foremost, I would like to thank my son Zachary for being my sounding board for this book. He had three essential qualifications for fulfilling this role: He understands the subject matter; he can write; and most importantly, he can be brutally honest in his opinions. His comments about one chapter: "Sorry, Dad, but I think you should pull it." Although reluctant to see two weeks of work go to waste, on reflection, I realized he was right, and I did. Zachary provided many useful suggestions (besides "ax it"), most of which were incorporated. Whatever defects remain, I can assure the reader they would have been worse without Zachary's assistance.

Four of the interviews in this book were suggested and arranged through the help of others. In this regard, I am deeply grateful to the following, each of whom was the catalyst responsible for one of the interviews in this volume: John Apperson, Jayraj Chokshi, Esther Healer, and Zachary Schwager. I also want to acknowledge that Michael Lewis's terrific book, *The Big Short*, was the source for one of the interview ideas for this book. I would also like to thank Jeff Feig for his efforts.

Finally, I would like to thank the traders who agreed to participate in the interviews and share their insights, and without whom there would be no book.

Part One

MACRO MEN

Chapter 1

Colm O'Shea

Knowing When It's Raining

When I asked Colm O'Shea to recall mistakes that were learning experiences, he struggled to come up with an example. At last, the best he was able to do was describe a trade that was a missed profit opportunity. It is not that O'Shea doesn't make mistakes. He makes lots of them. As he freely acknowledges, he is wrong on at least 50 percent of his trades. However, he never lets a mistake get remotely close to the point where it would provide a good story. Large trading losses are simply incompatible with his methodology.

O'Shea is a global macro trader—a strategy style that seeks to profit from correctly anticipating directional trends in global currency, interest rate, equity and commodity markets. At surface consideration, a strategy that requires participating in directional moves in major global markets may not sound like it would be well suited to maintaining tightly constrained losses, but the way O'Shea trades, it is. O'Shea views his trading ideas as hypotheses. A market move counter to the expected direction is proof that his hypothesis for that trade is wrong, and O'Shea then has no reluctance in liquidating the position. O'Shea defines the price point that would invalidate his hypothesis before he places a trade. He sizes his position so that the loss from a move to that price level is limited to a small percentage of assets. Hence, the lack of any good war stories of trades gone awry.

O'Shea's interest in politics came first, economics second, and markets third. His early teen years coincided with the advent of Thatcherism and the national debate over reducing the government's role in the economy—a conflict that sparked O'Shea's interest in politics and soon after economics. O'Shea educated himself so well in economics that he was able to land a job as an economist for a consulting firm before he began university. The firm had an abrupt opening for an economist position because of the unexpected departure of an employee. At one point in his interview for the position, he was asked to explain the seeming paradox of the Keynesian multiplier. The interviewer asked, "How does taking money from people by selling bonds and giving that same amount of money back to people through fiscal spending create stimulus?" O'Shea replied, "That is a really good question. I never thought about it." Apparently, the firm liked that he was willing to admit what he did not know rather than trying to bluff his way through, and he was hired.

O'Shea had picked up a good working knowledge of econometrics through independent reading, so the firm made him the economist for the Belgian economy. He was sufficiently well prepared to be able to use the firm's econometric models to derive forecasts. O'Shea, however, was kept behind closed doors. He was not allowed to speak to any clients. The firm couldn't exactly acknowledge that a 19-year-old was generating the forecasts and writing the reports. But they were happy to let O'Shea do the whole task with just enough supervision to make sure he didn't mess up.

At the time, the general consensus among economists was that the outlook for Belgium was negative. But after he had gone through the data and done his own modeling, O'Shea came to the conclusion that the growth outlook for Belgium was actually pretty good. He wanted to come up with a forecast that was at least 2 percent higher than the forecast of any other economist. "You can't do that," he was told. "This is not how things work. We will allow you to have one of the highest forecasts, and if growth is really strong as you expect, we will still be right by having a forecast near the high end of the range. There is nothing to be gained by having a forecast outside the range, in which case if you are wrong, we would look ridiculous." As it turned out, O'Shea's forecast turned out to be right, but no one cared.

His one-year stint as an economist before he attended university taught O'Shea one important lesson: He did not want to be an economic consultant. "As an economic consultant," he says, "how you package your work is more important than what you have actually done. There is massive herding in economic forecasting. By staying near the benchmark or the prevailing range, you get all the upside of being right without the downside. Once I understood the rules of the game, I became quite cynical about it."

After graduating from Cambridge in 1992, O'Shea landed a job as a trader for Citigroup. He was profitable every year, and his trading line and responsibilities steadily increased. By the time O'Shea left Citigroup in 2003 to become a portfolio manager for Soros's Quantum Fund, he was trading an exposure level equivalent to a multibillion-dollar hedge fund. After two successful years at Soros, O'Shea left to become a global macro strategy manager for the multimanager fund at Balyasny, a portfolio that was to be the precursor for his own hedge fund, COMAC, formed two years later.

O'Shea has never had a losing year. The majority of his track record, spanning his years at Citigroup and Soros, is not available for public disclosure, so no precise statements about performance can be made. The only portion of this track record that is available is for the period at Balyasny, which began in December 2004, and his current hedge fund portfolio, which launched in June 2006. For the combined period, as of end of 2011, the average annual compounded net return was 11.3 percent with an annualized volatility of 8.1 percent and a worst monthly loss of 3.7 percent. If your first thought as you read this is "only 11.3 percent," a digression into performance evaluation is necessary.

Return is a function of both skill (in selecting, implementing, and liquidating trades) and the degree of risk taken. Doubling the risk will double the return. In this light, the true measure of performance is return/risk, not return. This performance evaluation perspective is especially true for global macro, a strategy in which only a fraction of assets under management are typically required to establish and maintain portfolio positions.[1] Thus, if desired, a global macro manager could increase exposure by many multiples with existing assets under management (i.e., without any borrowing). The choice of exposure will drive the level of both returns and risk. O'Shea has chosen to run his fund at a relatively low risk level. Whether measured by volatility (8.2 percent), worst monthly loss (3.7 percent), or maximum drawdown (10.2 percent), his risk metrics are about half that of the average for global macro managers. If run at an exposure level more in line with the majority of global macro managers, or equivalently, at a volatility level equal to the S&P 500, the average annual compounded net return on O'Shea's fund would have been about 23 percent. Alternatively, if O'Shea had still been managing the portfolio as a proprietary account, an account type in which exposure is run at a much higher level relative to assets, the returns would have been many times higher for the exact same trading results. These discrepancies disappear if performance is measured in return/risk terms, which is invariant to the exposure level. O'Shea's Gain to Pain ratio (a return/risk measure detailed in Appendix A) is a strong 1.76.

I interviewed O'Shea in London on the day of the royal wedding. Because of related street closures, we met at a club at which O'Shea was a member, instead of at his office. O'Shea explained that he had chosen to join this particular club because they had an informal dress code. We conducted the interview in the club's drawing room, a pleasant space, which fortunately was sparsely populated, presumably because most people were watching the wedding. O'Shea spoke enthusiastically as he expressed his views on economics, markets, and trading. At one point in our conversation, a man came over and asked O'Shea if he could speak more quietly as his voice was disrupting the tranquility of the

---

[1]The derivatives normally used to express directional and relative value exposure in global macro (e.g., futures, FX, options, swaps) require only a small capital outlay (as margin or premium) relative to the face value exposure.

room. O'Shea apologized and subsequently dropped his voice level to library standards. Since I was recording the conversation, as I do for all interviews—I am such a poor note taker that I don't even make the attempt—I became paranoid that the recorder might not clearly pick up the now softly speaking O'Shea. My concerns were heightened anytime there was an increase in background noise, which included other conversations, piped-in music, and the occasional disruptive barking of some dogs one of the members had brought with him. I finally asked O'Shea to raise his voice to some compromise level between his natural speech and the subdued tone he had assumed. The member with the barking dogs finally left, and as he passed us, I was surprised to see—although I really shouldn't have been—that it was the same man who had complained to O'Shea that he was speaking too loudly.

■ ■ ■

When did you first become interested in markets?

It was one of those incredible chance occurrences. When I was 17, I was backpacking across Europe. I was in Rome and had run out of books to read. I went to a local open market where there was a book vendor, and, literally, the only book they had in English was *Reminiscences of a Stock Operator*. It was an old, tattered copy. I still have it. It's the only possession in the world that I care about. The book was amazing. It brought everything in my life together.

What hooked you?

What hooked me early about macro was…

No, I meant what hooked you about the book? The book has nothing to do with macro.

I disagree. It's all there. It starts off with the protagonist just reading the tape, but that isn't what he developed into. Everyone gives him tips, but the character Mr. Partridge tells him all that matters, "It's a bull market."[2]

That's a fundamental macro person. Partridge teaches him that there is a much bigger picture. It's not just random noise making the numbers go up and down. There is something else going on that makes it a bull or bear market. As the book's narrator goes through his career, he becomes increasingly fundamental. He starts talking about demand and supply, which is what global macro is all about.

People get all excited about the price movements, but they completely misunderstand that there is a bigger picture in which those price movements happen. Price movements only have meaning in the context of the fundamental landscape. To use a sailing analogy, the wind matters, but the tide matters, too. If you don't know what the tide is, and you plan everything just based on the wind, you are going to end up crashing into the rocks. That is how I see fundamentals and technicals. You need to pay attention to both to make sense of the picture.

Reminiscences is a brilliant book about the journey. The narrator starts out with an interest in watching numbers go up and down. I started out with an interest in politics and economics. But we both end up in a place that is not that far apart. You need to develop your own market experience. You are only going to fully understand what the traders in your books were saying after you have done it yourself. Then you realize, "Oh, that's what they meant." It seems really obvious. But before you experience it and learn it, it's hard to understand.

What was the next step in your journey to becoming a trader after reading *Reminiscences*?

I went to Cambridge to study economics. I knew I wanted to study economics from the age of 12, well before my interest in markets. I wanted

---

[2]The passage that O'Shea refers to is the following:

I think it was a long step forward in my education when I realized at last that when old Mr. Partridge kept on telling the other customers, "Well, you know this is a bull market!" he really meant to tell them that the big money was not in the individual fluctuations but in the main movement—that is, not in reading the tape but in sizing up the entire market and its trend.

to do it because I loved economics, not because I thought that was a pathway to the markets. Too many people do things for other reasons.

What did you learn in college about economics that was important?

I was very lucky that I went to college when I did. If I went now, I think I would be really disappointed because the way economics is currently taught is terrible.

Tell me what you mean by that.

When I went to university, economics was taught more like philosophy than engineering. Since then, economics has become all about mathematical rigor and modeling. The thing about mathematical modeling is that in order to make problems tractable, you need to make assumptions. Assumptions then become axiomatic for the entire subject—not because they are true, but because they are necessary to get a solution. So, it is easier to assume efficient markets because without that assumption, you can't do the math. The problem is that markets aren't efficient, but that fact is just conveniently ignored.

And the mathematical models can't include the unpredictable impact of speculators, either.

That's right. Because once you introduce them, you have a mathematical model that can't be solved. In the current world of economics, mathematical rigor is valued above all else. It's the only way you will get your PhD; it's the only way you will get a career in academia; it's the only way you will get tenure. As a consequence, anyone I would call an economist has been moved out of the economics department and into history, political science, or sociology. The mathematization of economics has been a disaster because it has greatly narrowed the scope of the field.

Do you have a favorite economist?

Keynes. It's a shame that Keynesianism in the United States has become this weird word whose meaning is barely recognizable.

That's because in the United States, people apply the word Keynesianism to refer to deficit spending, regardless of whether it occurs in an economic expansion or contraction.

That's not what he said.

I know that. Although he certainly would have favored deficit spending in 2008 and 2009, he would have had a very different perspective about deficit spending in the expanding economy that prevailed in previous years.

Yes, Keynes was a fiscal conservative.

I'm curious as to your views regarding the critical dilemma that currently faces the United States. On one hand, if deficits are allowed to go on, it could well lead to a catastrophic outcome. On the other hand, if you begin substantially cutting spending with current unemployment still very high, it could trigger a severe economic contraction, leading to lower revenues and upward pressure on the deficit.

The argument for fiscal stimulus is a perfectly coherent, logical case. The counterargument that we should cut spending now is also a perfectly rational case. But both sides are often expressed in totally irrational ways. I think the biggest mistake people make is to assume there is an answer when, in fact, there may not be a good answer.

I actually had the same perception after the 2008 presidential election. I thought the economy had been so mismanaged between the combination of exploding debt and a postbubble collapse in economic activity that there might not be any solution. The American humor newspaper, the *Onion*, captured the situation perfectly. Their headline after Obama was elected was, "Black Man Given Nation's Worst Job."

All solutions that will work in the real world have to embrace the fact that the U.S. is not as rich as Americans think it is. Most political solutions will be in denial of that fact. The relevant question is: Which difficult choice do you want to make?

Did you know what you wanted to do when you were in university?

Yes, become a trader. Although looking back at it, at the time, I didn't quite know what that meant.

What was your first job after graduating?

I got a job as a junior trader at Citigroup in the foreign exchange department. My first week at work was the week when the pound was kicked out of the ERM.

The Exchange Rate Mechanism (ERM), which was operative in the decades prior to the implementation of the euro, linked the exchange rates of European currencies within defined price bands. The U.K. was forced to withdraw from the ERM in 1992 when the pound declined below the low end of its band.

The week when George Soros in the popular vernacular "broke the Bank of England"?

Yes. As you may know, I worked for George Soros before starting my own fund. My favorite George Soros story concerns an interview with Chancellor Norman Lamont, who stated that the Bank of England had £10 billion in reserve to defend the pound against speculators. George apparently was reading an account of this interview in the next morning's paper and thought to himself, "£10 billion. What a remarkable coincidence!—that's exactly the size of the position I was thinking of taking."

At the time, I remember explaining to the head of the trading floor why the pound would not leave the ERM. I argued that it would be political suicide for the conservative government to drop out of the ERM; hence they would make sure it didn't happen.

What was your boss's response?

He just smiled and nodded at me. He said, "Okay, we'll see." About three hours later, the pound crashed out of the European ERM. I felt like a complete idiot.

I had absolutely no comprehension of the power of markets versus politics. The policy makers didn't understand that either. I think, as is often the case, policy makers don't understand that they are not in control. It's not that speculators are in control, either, but rather that fundamentals actually matter. Fundamentally, the U.K. remaining in the ERM was untenable. The U.K. was in a recession with a greatly overvalued currency. Germany needed high interest rates to constrain the high inflation of the postunification period with East Germany. Because the currencies were linked, the U.K. was also forced to maintain a high interest rate, even though its ongoing recession dictated a need for the exact opposite policy. All that Soros did was to recognize that the situation was untenable. The Bank of England's effort to support the pound was the equivalent of trying to fight gravity.

You were lucky to make your first big mistake when you didn't have any money on the line. Did that episode make an impression on you?

It made a huge impression. I learned that markets matter more than policy. You have to look at real fundamentals, not at what policy makers want to happen. The willing disbelief of people can carry on for a long time, but eventually it is overwhelmed by the market. The genius of Soros was recognizing the turning point when things change—the ability to not only know that a position was right, but that it was right *now*, and that now was the time to have a big risk on the trade.

[A long discussion ensues about the current (2011) European debt crisis. O'Shea provides a fairly pessimistic assessment of the long-term prospects for the euro.]

You are a macro trader. You see the problem. How do you play it?

I don't. That is why it's a bit of a distraction.

You don't because the timing is so uncertain?

Because no one cares. As long as no one cares about it, there is no trend. Would you be short Nasdaq in 1999? You can't be short just because you think fundamentally something is overpriced.

What can you do?

You can wait until people start to care. Taking Nasdaq as an example, you want to be selling Nasdaq at 4,000, but only after it has gone to 5,000. So you are selling the market on the way down, not on the way up. Because in a bubble, who is to say how far a market can go. Even though something might be a good idea, you need to wait for and recognize the right time. I am not particularly original. If you read the *Financial Times*, it's all there. You don't have to be a brilliant economist; you just have to recognize when something matters. The financial crisis is another example of the need to wait for the right time. During 2006 to 2007, I was thinking the markets were in a completely unsustainable bubble. It was ridiculous. You saw insanity everywhere.

What was your perception of the insanity at the time?

Risk premium was too low in everything. Credit was trading at ludicrous spreads, and no one cared about quality. What is the one thing you know about a company that posts smooth earnings every single quarter?

They are manipulating the numbers.

Yes. You know nothing beyond that. They may or may not have a good business, but you know they are manipulating numbers. People love stable earnings. Isn't that great? I hate stable earnings. It just tells me the company is not being truthful. And what I knew about the whole system in 2006 and 2007 was that the true facts were being obscured. The problem was most obvious in the credit markets. But you can't be short because you lose carry [the interest rate payments on the credit instrument], and at the same time, the spreads get lower and lower. [A decline in the credit spread—that is, the difference between the credit instrument interest rate and the equivalent maturity T-note rate—implies an increase in the credit instrument price.] So you not only have to pay to hold the position, but the position is also going against you. Being short credit in 2006 and 2007 was exactly the same as being short Nasdaq in 1999. You just have to make money going the other way.

How then did you position yourself during 2006 and 2007?

We recognized that we would underperform the bulls by quite a bit because in a bubble the true believers will always win. That's fine. You just need to make decent returns and wait until the market turns. Then you can make great returns. What I believe in is compounding and not losing money. We were quite happy to be part of the bubble, but to do it in positions that were highly liquid, so that we could exit the market quickly if we wanted to. One of the biggest mistakes people made was to join in the bubble, but to do it in positions for which there was no exit. All markets look liquid during the bubble, but it's the liquidity after the bubble ends that matters. We did a lot of our trades through options—positions like buying calls in currencies with a carry because the positive carry paid for your option.

Carry currencies are currencies with higher interest rates. For example, if Australian short-term rates are 5 percent and U.S. rates are 1 percent, the Australian dollar would be a carry currency. U.S. investors could convert U.S. dollars into Australian dollars and earn an extra 4 percent interest income. The risk, of course, is that the Australian dollar could decline versus the U.S. dollar in the interim. Although this risk could be hedged by selling Australian dollars in the forward market, arbitrage will assure that the forward rates in the Australian dollar are discounted by the same amount as the interest rate differential. (Otherwise, there would be a risk-free trade in buying spot Australian dollars, investing the proceeds in Australian T-bills, and hedging with a short Australian dollar position in the forward market.) If the spot exchange rate is unchanged, over time, the forward rate will climb by the amount of this differential (i.e., the carry). The strike price on an at-the-money call on a forward contract in the Australian dollar will be lower than the current spot price by the same differential.[3] If the spot price remains unchanged, the call will move in the money by this differential by expiration, serving as an offset to the premium paid for the option. Moreover, in a risk-seeking market, carry currencies will also tend to gain in the spot market as well.

---

[3]Readers unfamiliar with options may wish to first review Appendix B, which provides a brief summary of option basics.

Since the underlying currencies are also very liquid, I assume the reason you preferred buying calls to being long carry currencies was to avoid the gap risk in the event of a sudden market reversal?

Yes, by being long options, you can never have a major drawdown. If the bubble continues, you make nice returns; if it collapses, you just lose the premium. You are never short that horrible tail. But there were also structural reasons for preferring long option positions at the time. One of the aspects of risk premiums being very low was that option prices were generally too cheap. I like buying options when they are cheap. It was a low-volatility bubble, which meant that options worked. That's not always the case.

What other types of trades were you doing during the financial bubble?

What were central banks doing at the time? They were hiking rates. So I did a lot of trades related to monetary policy. During the entire Fed hiking cycle of 2005 to 2006, the futures market kept on being priced on the premise that it was about to stop. The market kept paying you over and over again to take the trade that said maybe it won't stop. It's extremely unlikely that the Fed would go from hiking to cutting immediately. Also, monetary policy was still pretty accommodative considering you had all the signs of a bubble. It was quite obvious that you needed higher rates when everything about the economy was signaling that you were in a bubble. So you had a great risk/reward trade that in six months they would still be hiking. As the months rolled on, they kept on hiking, and the market kept on saying, "I'm sure they'll stop soon." You could keep on repeating the trade.

Why was the market at the time expecting monetary policy to ease?

I try to avoid conceptualizing the market in anthropomorphic terms. Markets don't think. Just like mobs don't think. Why did the mob decide to attack that building? Well, the mob didn't actually think that. The market simply provides a price that comes about through a collection of human beings.

Okay then, rephrase the question in your own words.

What you are asking is, "Why wasn't the market priced efficiently?" There are very few market forces to make macro markets priced efficiently. Hedge funds are tiny in the macro space. If you are talking about tech stocks, then sure, hedge funds are massive. But if you are talking about the foreign exchange (FX) market or Treasuries, hedge funds are tiny compared to real money. In comparison, PIMCO or the Chinese are enormous. There are trillions of dollars moving in these markets, which make the little people like me quite irrelevant. We are not a force in pricing. One reason I like macro so much is because I am a small fish swimming in a sea of real money. Fundamentals matter. I am not playing a game against people like me. That would be a zero-sum, difficult game.

Does there have to be an identifiable reason for every trade?

Not necessarily. For example, before the 1998 financial crisis began, I didn't even know who LTCM was.

Long Term Capital Management (LTCM) was the most famous hedge fund failure in history. (Madoff may have been even more prominent, but his operation was a Ponzi scheme rather than a hedge fund. Madoff simply made up performance results and never did any trading.) In its first four years of operation, LTCM generated steady profits, quadrupling the starting net asset value. Then in a five-month period (May to September 1998), it all unraveled, with the net asset value of the fund plunging a staggering 92 percent. LTCM's positions had been enormously leveraged, placing the banks and brokerage firms that had provided credit to them at enormous risk. Fears that LTCM's failure could have a domino effect throughout the financial system prompted the Federal Reserve to orchestrate (but not pay for) a bailout for the firm. LTCM's liquidation of its enormously leveraged positions caused havoc in many financial markets. What made LTCM such a compelling story was not merely the magnitude of the failure and its threat to the financial system, but also the firm's impressive roster of brainpower, which included two Nobel Prize winners.

At the time, I was doing my own prop trading with no contacts. At the start of the crisis, there was nothing about LTCM in the press, either. I had no idea of any reason for what was going on in the markets, and I had no way of finding out. All I knew was that T-bond futures were going up limit every day. That told me there was something going on. I didn't need to know why. Once you realize something is happening, you can trade accordingly. Trades don't have to start based on fundamentals. If you wait until you can find out the reason for the price move, it can be too late. A great Soros quote is "Invest first; investigate later." You don't want to get fixated on always needing a nice story for the trade. I am an empiricist at heart. The unfolding reality trumps everything.

I believe in hypothesis testing. The hypothesis is that something big is happening. I don't know what it is, but it is so powerful that it will carry on for a long time. I should participate in this. But I will do it in a way that is liquid so that if it turns around again, I can get out quickly. If I am wrong, I will have a limited loss. If I am right, who knows what could happen.

Going back to the housing and financial bubble of 2005 to 2007, you originally participated in the bubble. How did you handle the transition to the subsequent market collapse?

I'll ask you a question: "When did the financial crisis start?"

That's a difficult question to answer. There are multiple possible starting points. You could say it was the beginning of the housing price decline in 2006, although there was no market response to that at the time. In fact, even Countrywide, who was the poster child for toxic mortgage issuers, went on to set new stock price highs well after that point. Alternatively, you could say it was the collapse of Bear Stearns, although the market rebounded after that event as well.

So, I'll ask you again: "When did it start?"

Well, that's a squishy question.

Well, since you're refusing to give me any kind of answer [he laughs], I'll give you my answer. Fundamentally, housing prices started to go down in 2006, which didn't start the crisis, but provided a reason for one. The subprime credit indexes started going down in January 2007. Subprime credit is a niche market, and the equity market was ignoring it. Then in July 2007, there was a broad selloff in the credit markets, but it still was considered a contained credit market issue. Equity people tend to trace the start of the financial crisis to the collapse of Bear Stearns in March 2008. For me, the true start of the financial crisis was in August 2007 when money markets stopped working. Basically, banks didn't trust other banks. That was the month the world broke, and no one noticed.

How did you see the money markets breaking down?

The most obvious way was that LIBOR rates spiked. [LIBOR is the rate at which banks lend to other banks.] It was an indicator that the underlying assumption that money would flow smoothly was no longer true. If you spoke to money market desks to find out what was going on, they told you that liquidity had dried up. They had never seen anything like it. If a similar event happened in any other market, it would be front-page news. But the fact that it happened in the most important market—the money market, which is at the heart of capitalism—was largely ignored.

Wasn't the stress in money markets reported in the financial press?

It was reported. It was all public information, but the point is that no one thought it mattered. Even more than three years later, we are sitting here, and you are saying, "Really, money markets broke down in August 2007? Really?"

Well, I have to admit, when I think of money markets breaking down in the financial crises, I think of the breaking of the buck by some money market funds in the aftermath of the failure of Lehman Brothers and the subsequent freezing up of the commercial paper market. But these events occurred more than a year later in September 2008.

That's my point. No one seemed to think it was important. The S&P actually went on to make new highs in the next two months.

But you made your transition from bullish positions to bearish in August 2007?

Yes, I turned bearish when money market liquidity dried up in August 2007. Declining housing prices were the impending storm clouds, but it started raining when money markets stopped working. Most people, however, didn't notice. Fundamentals are not about forecasting the weather for tomorrow, but rather noticing that it is raining today.

The great trades don't require predictions. The Soros trade of going short the pound in 1992 was based on something that had already happened—an ongoing deep recession that made it inevitable that the U.K. would not maintain the high interest rates required by remaining in the ERM. Afterward, everyone said, "That was incredibly obvious." Most of the great trades are incredibly obvious. It was the same in late 2007. In my mind, it was clear that the financial system was imploding and that most market participants hadn't noticed.

Did you go short equities then?

Equity markets would eventually notice, but being short equities is a hard trade because they might still keep going up for a long time. After a bull market that goes on for years, who is managing most of the money? The bears are all unemployed; they're not managing any money at all. You have a few very flexible smart people, but they run relatively small amounts of money; so they don't matter, either. The managers who are relentlessly bullish and who buy more every time the market goes down will be the ones who end up managing most of the money. So, you shouldn't expect a big bull market to end in any rational fashion.

The smart managers will be managing less because they don't look as good as the bulls, since they're going to have lower net long exposure?

Right. Because the bulls control most of the money, you should expect the transition to a bear market to be quite slow, but then for the move to be enormous when the turn does happen. Then the bulls will say, "This makes no sense. This was unforeseeable." Well, it clearly wasn't unforeseeable.

I have to laugh when I hear people say it was unforeseeable that housing prices could go down. I think, "Did you ever look at a housing price chart?" If you look at a long-term inflation-adjusted chart of housing prices, you can see that excluding the postdepression bust, since the 19th century, housing prices consistently moved in a sideways range, until the mid-2000s when inflation-adjusted prices nearly doubled in a few years. It sticks out like a mountain in a plateau. Yet people can claim with a straight face that they were shocked that housing prices could go down after that abnormal surge.

If you live in a world where everyone assumes that everything goes up forever, then it is inconceivable that prices might go down. Big price changes occur when market participants are forced to reevaluate their prejudices, not necessarily because the world changes that much. The world really didn't change that much in 2008. It was just that people finally noticed there was a problem.

Consider the current U.S. debt problem. A lot of people say there is apparently no inflationary threat from the growing U.S. debt because bond yields are low. But that's not true. Bond yields will only signal that there is a problem when it is too late to fix it. You have to believe in market efficiency to believe that the market will adequately price fiscal risk. Could there be a crisis in five years? Sure. Why? Because people start to care. Currently, it's not in the price. But one day, it might be. If a major financial catastrophe happens, people will talk about how it was caused by this event or that event. If it happens, though, it will be because there were fundamental reasons that were there all along.

There will always be something that happens at the same time. Calling it a catalyst isn't very helpful in explaining anything. Did World War I start because the Archduke was assassinated? Well, kind of, but mainly not. I don't subscribe to the catalyst theory of history. But most people love it, especially in markets, because they can point to that one cause and say, "Who knew that could happen?"

When you have tremendous fundamental imbalances, the change can occur anywhere along the way. Nasdaq topped above 5,000, but it could just as well have been 3,000 or 7,000. It just happened to top above 5,000. Predicting the top of a bubble is like trying to predict the weather one year out—the same set of conditions can lead to wildly different outcomes if replayed multiple times.

Absolutely right, and I can't predict that turnaround. It's very difficult. But you can notice when things have changed. Most people, though, don't. When Nasdaq is at 4,000 after having been at 5,000, there are lots of people buying it because it is cheap. They reason, "It used to be 5,000. Now it's only 4,000. I am getting a bargain." People are very poorly attuned to making decisions when there is uncertainty. Do you know the difference between risk and uncertainty?

Do you mean that in the realm of risk, you know the odds, but with uncertainty, you don't know the odds?

Right. If you play roulette, you are in the world of risk. If you are dealing with possible economic events, you are in the world of uncertainty. If you don't know the odds, putting a number on something makes no sense. What are the odds of Germany leaving the euro in the next five years? There is no way of assigning a probability. If you try to force it by saying something like "6.2 percent," it is a meaningless number because you would have to behave as if you believed it, and that would be a poor bet.

Going back to August 2007, recognizing that there was a change, how did you respond? You already explained why you didn't go short equity, but what did you do instead? Did you cover all your bullish positions right away?

Yes, getting out of everything was an easy decision. Then you look for trades that have great reward to risk. Since volatility was cheap, one trade we did was buying FX volatility.

When you say you bought volatility, does that imply that you were not playing for any directional move in currencies?

Yes, our assumption was only that it would move somewhere.

So you put on positions like long straddles and strangles in currencies?

Yes. Another big position was related to monetary policy. What did Greenspan do after the 1987 crash?

He injected liquidity.

Right. Add liquidity and cut rates. That was the policy response we expected. So that was our trade at the time: Rates would go lower and the yield curve would steepen.

So you put on long positions in short-term rate instruments?

Yes, but we coupled it with short positions on the long end because it was a better risk/reward trade. The yield curve was flat at the time and priced to stay flat. The market wasn't pricing in any risk that there would be a major problem.

So you bet on lower short-term rates through a yield curve spread rather than a long position in short-term rate instruments because you felt it was a safer way to do the trade.

Yes, because what I am trying to do is find trades that won't lose much money even if I am wrong.

Your reasoning was that if you were wrong, long rates would go up about as much as short rates, so you wouldn't lose much

money, but if you were right most of the rate decline would occur in short rates.

Yes, exactly.

So, you are not only looking for the right trade, but also for the best way to express it.

Yes, I think implementation is the key in everything. Implementation is more important than the trade idea behind it. Having a beautiful idea doesn't get you very far if you don't do it the right way. The point is that I tried to do the trade in a way so that my timing didn't have to be perfect.

Were there other trades you did at the time?

There were a lot. We were bearish on corporate credit, so we bought CDS protection. Since credit spreads were very narrow, if we were wrong, we would only lose a little bit of carry, but if we were right, the spreads could widen a lot. It was an asymmetric trade.

Corporate bonds pay a higher interest rate than U.S. Treasury notes to compensate investors for the higher risk. The yield difference is called the credit spread. *The lower the individual bond rating, the wider the spread. Overall credit spread levels will widen during times of financial crisis when investors will demand higher interest rate differentials for accepting the greater risk implicit in holding corporate bonds instead of Treasuries. There are several ways to initiate a trade that will profit if credit spreads widen. The most direct trade is shorting the corporate bond. The equivalent trade can also be implemented through derivatives by buying credit default swap (CDS) protection on the bond. A CDS is essentially an insurance policy that pays off if the bond defaults. The buyer of CDS protection, however, does not need to own the underlying bond—that is, the transaction can be made strictly as a speculative trade (one that profits from a deterioration in credit quality). The CDS price is quoted as an annual spread— the per annum amount the buyer of protection pays the seller (in quarterly payments). (The CDS spread is the "carry" on the trade.) If a bond's credit-worthiness deteriorates (an event associated with the credit spread widening), the*

CDS spread will widen as well. A third way of placing a trade that will profit from widening credit spreads, and the one employed by O'Shea, is to buy a CDS on an index based on a basket of corporate bonds. Note that buying CDS protection has an option-like payoff: The maximum risk is limited (to the per annum spread paid, which is analogous to an option premium), while the gain can be much larger (up to a theoretical maximum of the amount protected).

Why did you consider buying CDS protection a better trade than buying equity puts?

Actually, they are very similar trades. If the equity market stayed strong, the loss in both positions would be limited—to the option premium for the puts and to the carry for the CDS position. If the equity markets fell, credit spreads would widen, and both long puts and long CDS protection positions would have large profits. The advantage of CDS was that it was a cheaper way of doing the trade. One problem with buying equity puts is that equity volatility tends to be very expensive. Who is the natural seller of equity puts? No one. Who is the natural buyer of equity puts? Everyone. The world is long equities, and people like owning insurance, so there is an excess of natural buyers for equity puts. That is why equity option prices are structurally expensive.

After you turned bearish in August 2007, did you maintain that view all the way through the collapse of markets in late 2008?

Maintaining the same long-term view doesn't mean I kept the same positions. My typical time horizon for trades is one to three months. When prices change, the risk/reward on positions change.

I understand that your specific positions changed, but did you maintain an unwavering commitment to the bearish side, even during the significant rebound in the second quarter of 2008?

The reason the market bounced in the second quarter of 2008 was that people felt that the Bear Stearns bailout in March 2008 had solved the problem.

What did you think?

I thought that was clearly wrong. The big mistake people were making, and still make, was to confuse liquidity with solvency. People were acting on the premise that Bear Stearns and the banking system were solvent. They thought there was a liquidity crisis, which was just a matter of lack of confidence. The reality was that the banking system didn't have a liquidity problem; it had a liquidity problem because it had a solvency problem. You can't fix a solvency problem by adding more liquidity. If you have a house worth $100,000 with a $200,000 mortgage, I can lend you another $100,000, but it won't solve the underlying problem. You'll just end up with more debt. As long as housing prices kept going down, the solvency problem was getting worse and worse. The market, however, was behaving as if there was no problem.

Where does that leave you in terms of a trading stance when the market is acting as if everything is okay, but you think it's not?

Well, that happens all the time. In regards to the second quarter of 2008, we found better risk/reward trades to express our view. We had been very negative on credit at the start of the year. But by the second quarter, corporate and bank credit spreads had already widened sharply. Although the TED spread had also widened sharply, in the forward market, it was priced to narrow dramatically over the next few months.

The TED spread is the difference between the three-month LIBOR rate, the rate at which banks lend to other banks, and the three-month T-bill rate. The LIBOR rate is always higher than the T-bill rate because there is a small counterparty risk in interbank loans, while T-bills are considered to be risk-free. During most times, the TED spread tends to be relatively modest (roughly around 25 basis points). The TED spread, however, can widen significantly during periods of "flight-to-quality" when counterparty and liquidity concerns are heightened. It widened to more than 200 basis points in the money market liquidity freeze-up in August 2007 that O'Shea talked about earlier and to a record 485 basis points in the post-Lehman failure financial market meltdown in late 2008. The types of conditions that are conducive to a widening of the TED spread often occur during steep equity market declines. In this sense, a long TED spread is a bearish position.

In contrast, corporate and bank credit spreads were priced to stay wide in the forward market. So we rotated out of our short credit trades into TED spreads because the risk/reward was much better. During the second quarter of 2008, both corporate credit spreads and TED spreads narrowed. The TED spread, however, had been priced to narrow in the forward market, so the trade was near breakeven. If we had stayed with the short corporate credit positions during the second quarter of 2008, we would have lost a lot of money. The trade we had switched into to express our negative long-term view didn't have much downside. So when everybody got optimistic again in the second quarter of 2008, our bearish position [the TED spread] didn't change that much.

What about the second half of 2008, which was when markets collapsed?

If you started with the premise that there was a solvency issue, then everything that happened was straightforward. To begin, the banking system was underwater. Therefore, there was no reason for anyone to lend them money, unless the government was going to step in with more capital. The politics in Washington at the time, however, was for no more bailouts. [Treasury Secretary] Paulson had made multiple statements in which he was very clear that there would be no government bailout of Lehman. Once you know that Lehman has negative value and the government is not coming to the rescue, that means they're bankrupt. There isn't anything else that can happen. There is no sophisticated analysis involved. The odd thing is that Lehman going under was not a surprise. Most people knew it was going to happen, but they failed to understand what it meant.

So what were you doing at the time?

The main thing was to make sure our business was as safe as possible. We avoided counterparty exposure to Lehman. We simplified the book. We reduced leverage a lot during 2008. We restricted our trading to highly liquid positions, which meant avoiding OTC trades with lots of counterparties. Insofar as we had to have counterparty risk, we confined it to the strongest counterparties.

Okay, those are measures to reduce business risk, but what trades did you put on to take advantage of the situation you saw?

We had very similar trades to the ones we had on at the start of 2008. We were long volatility, short credit, long the TED spread, and long the dollar because of an expected flight to quality. All of these trades had one thing in common: They were all the-world-is-going-to-get-scary trades.

These were all trades that you put back on in the third quarter of 2008 prior to the Lehman failure?

Yes.

As the markets collapsed in the ensuing months, at what point did you decide it was a good time to take money off the table?

April 2009.

So you stayed with all these bearish positions all the way through the entire decline?

Yes, until we started to lose money.

What changed in April 2009 that prompted you to get out of your positions?

Two things changed: The economy stopped getting worse, and markets started going up. The underlying problems had not gone away, but that isn't the market driver. The fact that the economy was improving, even though it was still in bad shape, meant that the optimists could come back. Never underestimate the ability of people to be optimistic and believe that everything is going to be okay. Historically, what is important to the market is not whether growth is good or bad, but whether it is getting better or worse. Growth started getting less negative, and less negative is good news. Asia started going up. The Australian dollar started going up. The S&P was actually one of the last markets to turn higher in March 2009. By March to April, you were seeing a broad-based recovery in global markets.

What trades did you transition to?

Bullish strategies. Interest rates were pricing in another Great Depression. Once the market prices in a Great Depression, you think, "Well, maybe not." Ten-year yields were down near 2 percent. Things have to look really bad to justify that level. Once the outlook started to improve a little bit, yields could rise a lot from that level. So we went short long-term Treasuries, both outright and as a yield curve play. We went short the dollar, as a reversal of the prior flight-to-quality trade. We did a lot of different trades. Typically, in the portfolio, we will have 10 or 15 different trades on at any time. One reason why I am always hesitant to explain what trades we did is that if I get to the level of complexity of including all the trades, it can get very confusing. If I simplify it by saying that it's a bit like these two or three trades, then people say, "Oh, you did that; that's quite easy." Well, it isn't what we actually did, but you try to provide a simplification to make it understandable. Then people think that simplification is what you actually did. I think macro is most misunderstood when it is seen as storytelling. Storytelling is a nice way to talk about it, but it is only 10 percent of what is important.

And the other 90 percent?

Implementation and flexibility. You need to implement a trade in a way that limits your losses when you are wrong, and you also need to be able to recognize when a trade is wrong. George Soros has the least regret of anyone I have ever met. Even though he will sometimes play up to his public image as a guru who knows what is going on, it is in no sense what he does as a money manager. He has no emotional attachment to an idea. When a trade is wrong, he will just cut it, move on, and do something else. I remember one time he had this huge FX position. He made something like $250 million on it in one day. He was quoted in the financial press talking about the position. It sounded like a major strategic view he had. Then the market went the other way, and the position just disappeared. It was gone. He didn't like the price action, so he got out. He doesn't let his structural views on how he believes the market will play out get in the way of his trading. That is what strikes me about really good money managers—they don't get attached to their ideas. The danger in the narrative I have been giving you is that it may lead to the false impression that what you need to do to make lots of money is be really smart in economics and understand fundamentally what is going on. I don't really believe that is true.

What do you believe is true?

I actually subscribe to a lot of things in your books. You need a method that suits your personality. I don't believe that I am an amazing econ-omist who predicts the future. What I actually believe is that I recognize the world as I find it and that I am flexible enough to change my mind. In April 2009, I was really pessimistic. I thought the world was in terrible condition. But the market was telling me that I was wrong. So I thought, "Okay, I'm completely wrong. What is a different hypothesis of what is going on? Ah, here is a different hypothesis. I see what's going on. Let's do that instead." Then there is an explanatory story that comes out afterwards. But actually, the story came after my previous hypothesis had been proven wrong. It wasn't that I was smart and caught the turning point. I didn't. I just noticed that what I was doing was wrong and that I needed to do something else. To construct a portfolio, I need to build a set of hypotheses that I can test in the market.

So the empiricism comes first, then the macro theme to fit the observations, and finally the implementation of the trades.

Yes, but the point is that the macro theme has to be testable empirically in the market. It is not about starting out with any grand theme. The difference between what I'm doing and trend following is that there have to be logical fundamental linkages for the price movements. China is turning around, metal prices are turning higher, and the Australian dollar is moving up. What is that telling me? There is recovery some-where in the world. There is demand somewhere in the world. The S&P may still be going down, but there is divergence in the data. If the whole world is terrible, it doesn't fit anymore. So I can't stick with the-whole-world-is-terrible thesis. Something else is going on. What hypothesis would fit the actual developments? Asia actually looks all right now. A scenario that would fit is an Asia-led economic recovery.

If the new hypothesis is correct, then certain other things should happen in the future. In contrast to the trend follower, I am anticipating future trends, rather than waiting for the trends to develop and then jumping on. I may end up being in many of the same trades as a trend follower, but the timing is going to be very different.

Do you trade equity indexes or equities?

Equity indexes and baskets, yes, but not that much.

Why aren't you a fan of trading equities?

Interest rate markets or FX are usually better ways for me to express trades. The world is full of people who trade equities. I don't think another hedge fund that trades equities is particularly exciting. Also, a problem I have with equities is that equity stories make no sense to me. Equity people often make no sense to me. The reasons I think trades have worked are usually nothing like the reasons why equity people think they worked. In my entire life, I've personally only done one single-stock trade.

Out of curiosity, because it was the only one, what was it?

I bought Berkshire in 1999.

And that was because?

The price had halved because Buffett refused to be involved in the dot-com bubble. I thought that was the stupidest reason I had ever heard for a stock price to halve. Nasdaq is going through the roof. Warren Buffett, who is clearly one of the all-time legends of investing, is saying I don't understand this dot-com stuff; I'm staying away from it. And his stock price gets hammered because he's seen as a dinosaur that isn't part of the new paradigm. I thought that was idiotic.

Buffett being penalized for underperforming versus managers riding the long side of the dot-com bubble is a perfect illustration of a common investor mistake—failing to realize that often

the managers with the highest returns achieve those results because they're taking the most risk, not because they have the greatest skill. **How long did you hold the position?**

Until I started my hedge fund. I believed in myself more than I believed in Warren Buffett.

Let's go back to when you first started out at Citigroup the week the U.K. was forced out of the ERM. When did you begin trading?

My first trade ever was the year after. They gave new traders small limits they were allowed to trade. I remember doing a really good fundamental analysis about the U.K. economy and deciding that the rate hikes the market was pricing in were not going to happen. I proved to be perfectly correct. Three months later, they still hadn't hiked rates, and short sterling [U.K. short-term interest rates] rallied 100 basis points from where I had the trade idea. Well, I lost money.

How did you lose money when your forecast was exactly correct?

It's pretty straightforward. The implementation didn't match the hypothesis. The hypothesis was clearly a one-to-three-month horizon. So, I should have traded a one-to-three-month horizon. What did I do? I was constantly getting in and out because I was scared of losing money. The rational trade hypothesis was beautiful. The implementation was entirely emotional and stupid. I realized that you have to embrace uncertainty and risk. Over a three-month period, it is the trend that is important.

I guess the lesson is that the market is not going to let you make any money unless you're willing to take risk.

You have to embrace the logical consequences of your ideas, and that means that you have to have a stop loss that is wide enough.

So even though you were on the right side of the trend for three months, you lost money because you kept on getting stopped out.

Yes, because I had read trading books. It took me a while to realize that those trading books are counterproductive because the rules are generic and not specific. Most trading book rules are designed for people who have the error of excess optimism and are in emotional denial of their losses. Trading book rules are designed to protect traders who are gamblers. People who like trading because they like gambling are always going to be terrible at it. For these people, the trading books could be greatly shortened to the message: "Don't trade. You are really bad at this. So just don't do it." I don't actually have a gambler's mentality. I make different emotional mistakes. So, imposing trading book rules on me is a terrible misfit.

That is why your books are important. All the traders you write about have a method that is personal and fits them. You learn from everyone around you, but you have to do what makes sense for you, even if it's the opposite of what makes sense for other people.

So you don't use stops?

No. I do. I just set them wide enough. In those early days, I wasn't setting stops at levels that made sense based on the underlying hypothesis for the trade; I was setting stops based on my pain threshold, and the market doesn't care about your pain. I learned from that mistake. When I get out of a trade now, it is because I was wrong. I'm thinking, "Hmm, that shouldn't have happened. Prices are inconsistent with my hypothesis. I'm wrong. I need to get out and rethink the situation." In my first trade, prices were never inconsistent with my hypothesis.

What are some other mistakes you have learned from?

I don't have any great example of a mistake that cost me a material amount of money because I have very tight risk discipline on the downside. Stopping yourself from losing money is quite easy. I've never really had that problem. I'd say that most of my big errors have been opportunity errors. I sometimes believe in something so strongly that it acts as a constraint on doing trades that could be very profitable. For example, in late 2010, my underlying belief that the European sovereign debt crisis was a really big problem made it hard for me to participate in a sentiment and liquidity driven bull market. I failed to take part in the biggest macro theme of the year. From September on, equities were up a lot, and commodities were up a lot. It was a massive opportunity that I should have been in, and I wasn't. I missed the key point that no one else cared, and as long as no one cares, there is no crisis. It's the same reason I didn't make any money in the Nasdaq bubble. I thought, "I can't buy Pets.com."

But actually you can't make money in the Nasdaq bubble by definition.

You can.

How do you go long a bubble and protect yourself?

When it starts to go down, you sell it.

It turned out that the Nasdaq move up was relatively smooth, but a bubble could be very volatile.

That's when you don't get involved. Actually what I've learned is that bubbles last a long time, and that there's money to be made out of bubbles.

Without the benefit of hindsight, how could you play a Nasdaq-type move now?

The main thing about bubbles is that you need to be early. The worst thing you can do in a bubble is to be stubborn and then late to convert. I have avoided late conversions. But what I am trying to learn is to be an earlier convert to things that make no sense. I have an aversion to things that make no sense, and I should get over that.

I guess that sometimes the reason for a bull market is psychological rather than fundamental, and participating in the euphoria of a psychological move is itself the rationale for the trade.

Yes, and I don't mind that. What I have difficulty with is when the fundamentals are in conflict with the euphoria. I have tended to be premature in worrying about the conflicting fundamentals. I think in terms of the next 10 or 20 years I'd like to do a better job of monetizing other people's irrational euphoria.

So, one of your shortcomings has been in letting your rational assessment of a situation keep you from participating in a psychologically driven trade.

Yes, failing to participate in markets when the fundamentals are less important than the psychology.

But how do you recognize that type of situation?

Well, that's the key question, isn't it? [He laughs.] There are various gauges. A simple one is just price action. If it trades like a bull market, it's a bull market. Another indication is how passionately people defend things that make no sense. For example, some people believe that Barack Obama is not a U.S. citizen. The point is that beliefs that are completely invulnerable to evidence and passionately defended can be quite durable. It has nothing to do with the fundamental logic.

That's a political example. But what would be a tradable example?

Gold is special, magical, and great. It's not. But if people believe it, they buy it. And if they buy it, it goes up. That's why there's a bull market. You can't go to a meeting without someone saying, "What do you think about gold?"

What does that tell you?

It tells you that you should be long gold.

So, going back to the Nasdaq bubble, another example would be people saying that it doesn't matter if a company is losing money, all that matters is how many clicks they are getting on their website.

Yes, exactly. The utter irrationality of the fundamental justification doesn't matter. And if you try and point that out to somebody, they will just give you an even more ridiculous justification why the market should go up. You cannot shake them at all from their belief. Those are the characteristics of bubble markets. The reason why they have legs is because it takes such enormous evidence to make people change their minds.

How do you know when it does change?

You know the dot-com bubble is over when it starts going down. It will be the same thing with gold.

Right now as we talk, gold is somewhere just north of $1,500 and not far from its all-time high. So what you are saying is that the gold top could be now; it could be at $2,000; it could be at $2,500; it could be any number.

And that's okay. The thing about gold is that if you told me gold has a price of $100, that's fine. If you told me it's $10,000, that's fine as well. It can be any price. Gold is worth exactly what people think it's worth.

I am sure you know why that is true for gold.

What do you think?

This is one of those questions that can be answered unambiguously. Gold is the only commodity where the amount of supply is literally about 100 times as much as the amount physically used in any year. That is not true of any other commodity, such as wheat or copper, where total supply and annual consumption are much closer in balance, and true shortages can develop. There is never any shortage of gold. So gold's value is entirely dependent on psychology or those fundamentals that drive psychology. Many years ago, when I was a commodity research director, I would totally ignore gold production and consumption in analyzing the market. I would base any price expectation

entirely on such factors as inflation and the value of the dollar because those are the factors that drive psychology. I always found it ridiculous when other analysts would write lengthy reports on gold analyzing such things as annual production prospects and jewelry usage. Annual production and consumption of gold are always a tiny fraction of supply, maybe around 1 percent, so who cares how much they change. It has nothing to with the price.

Yes, that's exactly right.

It's one thing to say that a market in a bubble can go to any price, but quite another to determine when the bubble is over. You said just before that you know it's over when the price starts going down. But how do you differentiate between a correction and a reversal in the market?

That is a good question and quite a difficult one. There are several possible methods. The simplest method is to pretend you are a CTA.[4] A CTA will have a systematic way of defining when a trend has changed. Another way you can tell is if the market displays price action that is characteristic of the late stages of a bubble, such as an exponential price rise, similar to what we recently saw in silver [in May 2011].

Did you trade that market?

Yes, through options. The problem with markets like silver is that when they break, they can collapse rapidly, and there is gap risk. I think the natural way to trade a market that is in a bubble is from the long side, not the short side. You want to be long the exponential upmove without taking on the gap risk of a collapse. Therefore options provide a good way of doing this type of trade.

---

[4]Commodity Trading Advisor (CTA) is the official designation of regulated managers who trade the futures markets. The majority of these managers use trend-following systems to generate trades.

Since the silver price move exhibited characteristics of a bubble, why wouldn't you also consider trading the market from the short side?

Because tops are messy, and the reversals in bear markets are horrendous. It is very rare to find comfortable shorts in bear markets. If you consider Nasdaq as an example, it was quite an easy trade from the long side for a long time. It went from 1,500 in late 1998 to over 5,000 in early 2000 with hardly any meaningful corrections. From the short side, it was a really tough trade. After breaking down in very whippy fashion to under 3,100 in June 2000, the market then rallied back to near 4,300 in the next two months. This was a 40 percent rebound in a market that was clearly dead. Postbubble dead cat bounces can be vicious.

Sounds more like a dead tiger bounce.

I don't think you will find many people that have made the majority of their money shorting bubbles.

Does that imply that you didn't trade the Nasdaq from the short side even after you were sure the bull market was dead?

No, I didn't because the repercussions of the top were a lot easier to play than being short the Nasdaq itself. You had a broad bubble in assets. The U.S. economy had been built up by a massive mispricing of assets. Once the Nasdaq burst and everything unraveled, it was clear the economy would slow down. The economic downturn led to a big move in fixed income that provided a much calmer way to play that idea than a direct trade in equities.

So rather than consider the short side of the Nasdaq, you traded the long side of the bonds.

That's right.

Are there any current examples of markets that are in euphoria-driven states that are running counter to fundamentals?

I wouldn't say they are counter to the fundamentals, but rather that they are overpricing one particular outcome. For example, European sovereign debt may be fairly priced if you have a strong conviction that the outcome will be a federated Europe in which the German taxpayer will pick up the bills. If you anticipate a less optimistic scenario, then current prices may not make much sense. A few weeks ago, Spanish debt was trading at only 150 basis points over Germany.

So the market is pricing in a solution.

Yes, it's pricing a solution that may not happen; 150 basis points is not zero, but it is a lot closer to zero than the current 1,000-plus basis point premium on Greek debt. The relatively small premium for Spanish debt reflects a high degree of confidence in a particular outcome. I am not suggesting the more negative outcome is more likely, but simply that there is more uncertainty than implied by the current moderate premium.

In a situation like this where there is a binary outcome that is highly uncertain, but the probabilities are different from what the market seems to be pricing, do you participate in the market?

That is the main part of what I do. I look for deviations between the fundamental probability distribution I perceive and the probability distribution priced in by the market.

Being short Spanish debt is a trade where the downside is limited to the annual carry, but the upside can be very substantial. It seems that an inherent characteristic of most of your trades is that they have an asymmetric quality—the maximum loss is limited, but the profit potential is open-ended.

Yes, having a positive skew is very important. It is not about being right all the time. Most good macro traders will be right only about half the time or even less.

Is trading a skill that can be taught?

It can't be taught, but it can be learned.

What do you mean by that?

My natural trade time horizon is one to three months, but that doesn't mean it would be right for you. Since I don't know you, I can't tell you what your trading style should be. But if you are willing to put in the effort, you can learn what that style should be. If I try to teach you what I do, you will fail because you are not me. If you hang around me, you will observe what I do, and you may pick up some good habits. But there are a lot of things you will want to do differently. A good friend of mine, who sat next to me for several years, is now managing lots of money at another hedge fund and doing very well. But he is not the same as me. What he learned was not to become me. He became something else. He became him.

Are there traits that determine who will be a successful trader?

Perseverance and the emotional resilience to keep coming back are critical because as a trader you get beaten up horribly. Frankly, if you don't love it, there are much better things to do with your life. You can't trade because you think it is a way to make a lot of money. That won't cut it. No one who trades for the money is going to be any good. If successful traders were only motivated by the money, they would just stop after five years and enjoy the material things. They don't. They continue well beyond any financial need. They can be somewhat obsessive. Trading is simply what they do. Jack Nicklaus has plenty of money. Why did he keep playing competitive golf well into his sixties? Probably because he really liked playing golf. He probably had a compulsive need to do it.

Are there trading rules you adhere to?

I use risk guidelines, but I don't believe in rules in that way. Traders who are successful over the long run adapt. If they do use rules, and you meet them 10 years later, they will have broken those rules. Why? Because the world changed. Rules are only applicable to a market at a specific time. Traders who fail may have great rules that work, but then stop working. They stick to the rules because the rules used to work, and they are quite annoyed that they are losing even though they are still doing what they used to do. They don't realize that the world has moved on without them.

Besides failure to adapt, what other mistakes get traders into trouble?

People run large amounts of money with relatively unsophisticated risk management. Throughout 2008, I spoke to managers who said they had halved their risk. I would say, "Half, that's quite a lot." Then they would continue and say, "Yes, my leverage was four, and it is now two." I would answer, "Do you realize volatility has gone up five times?" In terms of volatility-adjusted leverage, their risk exposure had actually gone up.

I notice that you use VAR as a risk measurement. Aren't you concerned that it can sometimes be very misleading regarding portfolio risk?

Value at Risk (VAR) can be defined as the loss threshold that will not be exceeded within a specified time interval at some high confidence level (typically, 95 percent or 99 percent). The VAR can be stated in either dollar or percentage terms. For example, a 3.2 percent daily VAR at the 99 percent confidence level would imply that the daily loss is expected to exceed 3.2 percent on only 1 out of 100 days. To convert a VAR from daily to monthly, we multiply it by the square root of 22 (the approximate number of trading days in a month). Therefore the 3.2 percent daily VAR would also imply that the monthly loss is expected to exceed 15.0 percent (3.2 percent × 4.69) only once out of every 100 months. The convenient thing about VAR is that it provides a worst-case loss estimate for a portfolio of mixed investments and adapts to the specific holdings as the portfolio composition changes. There are several ways of calculating VAR, but they all depend on the volatility and correlations of the portfolio holdings during a past look-back period—and therein lies the rub. The VAR provides a worst-case loss estimate assuming future volatility and correlation levels look like the past.

The main reason the VAR gets a bad name is because people don't understand it. VAR does exactly what it says on the tin.

Which is?

It tells you how volatile your current portfolio was in the past. That is all. VAR is entirely backward looking. You have to recognize that the future will be different. If I think the world in the future will be highly volatile, then I will run a current VAR that is relatively low because I think the future will be more volatile than the past.

VAR gets a bad name because people manage risk by it, and the shortcoming is that volatilities and correlations can change very radically on an existing portfolio vis-à-vis what they were in the past.

But that is patently obvious.

If it is so obvious, how come so many people manage risk that way?

VAR doesn't blow up portfolios; people do.

Do you ever have a problem getting out of a losing trade?

I start by deciding where the market would have to go for me to be wrong. That's where I place my stop. That means that it's not difficult for me to get out of a position if the market goes there. The most common money management error I see is people setting stop losses that are really pain thresholds. When the market reaches their stop, they don't really want to get out because they still think they are right. They will get out because their stop is hit, and they are disciplined. But very soon afterwards, they will want to get back in because they don't think they were wrong. That's how day traders in Nasdaq in 2000 and 2001 lost a ton of money. They were disciplined, so they would close out their positions by the end of the day. But they kept on repeating the same trading mistake. They failed to recognize that they were completely wrong because we were in a bear market.

So the disciplined use of stops that are set too close could lead to the proverbial death by 1,000 cuts.

Yes, and that is why I think trading books that provide specific rules can be quite dangerous. They can lead to the illusion that you are in control and being disciplined. And it is true that you are restricting yourself from a single catastrophic loss, but it doesn't prevent repeated losses on the same idea.

Sometimes a close stop may be appropriate. If it is a short-term technical idea, and you don't like the trade anymore if the market breaks a level, then getting out on a close stop is fine. If, however, it is a fundamental idea that needs a long time to play out, then a short-term stop makes absolutely no sense. If your entry and exit strategy is out of sync with the reason you like the trade, then you don't have an internally consistent money management plan, which means it will fail.

So, you need to decide where you are wrong before you determine the stop point.

First, you decide where you are wrong. That determines where the stop level should be. Then you work out how much you are willing to lose on the idea. Last, you divide the amount you're willing to lose by the per-contract loss to the stop point, and that determines your position size. The most common error I see is that people do it backwards. They start with position size. Then they know their pain threshold, and that determines where they place their stop.

■ ■ ■

The popular perception of the successful global macro manager is a trader who has an ability to forecast major trends in world markets (FX, interest rates, equities, commodities) through skillful analysis and insight. O'Shea emphasizes that his edge is not forecasting what will happen, but rather recognizing what has happened. O'Shea believes that it is very difficult to pick a major turning point, such as where a market bubble will top, and that trying to do so is a losing strategy. Instead, he waits until events occur that confirm a trading hypothesis. For example, he thought that excessive risk-taking during 2005 to 2007 had inflated various markets beyond reasonable levels and left the financial markets vulnerable to a major selloff. Nevertheless, insofar as he sees his role as trading in response to the prevailing market facts, rather than forecasting turning points, he actually had bullish positions on during this time. He did not switch to a bearish posture until an event occurred that he saw as a confirmation that the markets were in the process of rolling over—the drying up of liquidity in the money markets in August 2007. He didn't need to forecast anything, but he did need to recognize the significance of an event that many ignored. Indeed, the S&P 500 went on to make new highs in the next two months.

O'Shea believes that how a trade is implemented is more important than the trade idea itself. He seeks to implement a trade in the way that provides the best return-to-risk and limits losses in the event the trade is wrong. For example, after liquidity dried up in the money markets in August 2007, O'Shea expected rates to be cut. Instead of expressing this trade idea only through long short-term interest rate instrument positions, O'Shea also implemented the trade as a yield curve spread: long short-term rate instruments/short long-term rate instruments. His reasoning was that the yield curve at the time was relatively flat, implying that a rate decline would most likely be concentrated on the short-term end of the yield curve. If, however, rates went up, the flat yield curve implied that long-term rates should go up at least as much as short-term rates and probably more. The yield curve spread provided most of the profit potential with only a fraction of the risk. In essence, it provided a much better return-to-risk ratio than a straight long position in short-term rates alone.

The Nasdaq peak provided another example of how O'Shea seeks the best return-to-risk strategy to implement a trade idea. After the break from the March 2000 peak, O'Shea felt fairly certain that the bubble had burst. Yet he did not consider short positions in Nasdaq, even though he believed the market had formed a major bubble top, because he recognized—correctly, as it turned out—that trading the short side was treacherous. Even though the market ultimately went sharply lower, in the summer of 2000, the index witnessed an approximate 40 percent rebound. A move of this magnitude would very likely have resulted in a short position being stopped out. O'Shea reasoned that a Nasdaq top implied that most assets would recede from inflated levels, which would lead to an economic slowdown and lower interest rates. A long bond position provided a much easier and more comfortable way to trade the same idea. Bonds subsequently witnessed a fairly smooth uptrend, in contrast to the highly erratic downtrend in Nasdaq.

Flexibility is an essential quality to successful trading. It is important not to get attached to an idea and to always be willing to get out of a trade if the price action is inconsistent with the trade hypothesis. O'Shea cites George Soros as a master of flexibility who has no attachment to his trades and shows the least regret about getting out of a position of anyone he has ever met. In April 2009, O'Shea was very pessimistic about the financial outlook, but the market behavior was telling him he was wrong. Since his bearish hypothesis was inconsistent with the market price action, he formulated an entirely different hypothesis that seemed to fit what was happening—that is, the markets were seeing the beginning of an Asia-led economic recovery. Staying with his original market expectation would have been disastrous, as both equity and commodity markets embarked on a multiyear rally. The flexibility to recognize that his premise was mistaken and to act on that awareness allowed O'Shea to experience a profitable year, even though his original market outlook was completely wrong.

O'Shea believes that the best way to trade a market bubble is to participate on the long side to profit from the excessive euphoria, not to try to pick a top, which is nearly impossible and an approach vulnerable to large losses if one is early. The bubble cycle is easier to trade from the long side because the uptrend in a bubble is often relatively smooth, while the downtrend after the bubble bursts tends to be highly erratic. There are two components necessary to successfully trade the long side of a bubble. First, it is important to initiate a trade early in the bubble phase. Second, since bubbles are prone to abrupt, sharp downside reversals, it is critical that the long-biased position is structured so that the worst-case loss is limited. For this reason, O'Shea would never be outright long in a bubble market, but instead would express a bullish posture through a position such as a long call, a trade in which the maximum risk is defined by the premium paid for the option. Low volatility bubble markets are especially well attuned to being traded via long calls.

Although macro trades are typically based on a fundamental market view, there does not always have to be a reason for the trade. Sometimes, the market price action itself can reveal that something important is going on, even if the fundamental reason is not apparent. O'Shea experienced this situation in the course of LTCM's demise, an event that strongly impacted most markets. Although O'Shea did not know the reason for the market action at the time, he reasoned that the magnitude of the move implied there was an important fundamental development, and he adjusted his positions accordingly. He quotes George Soros on this concept: Invest first; investigate later.

Many of the traders I have interviewed have emphasized the importance of a disciplined money management plan. O'Shea provides an insightful, more nuanced view. O'Shea explains that money management discipline could even be counterproductive if it is inconsistent with the underlying trade analysis. Many traders have the discipline to set stops and stick with them, but make the critical mistake of determining the stop points as pain thresholds rather than price levels that disprove their original trade premise. When they get stopped out, they still believe the original trade idea was correct. As a result, there will be a strong temptation to get back into the trade, leading to multiple losses on the same idea. The money management discipline may prevent a single large loss, but if the stop point is inconsistent with the trade analysis, it may not prevent a cumulative loss that is even larger. O'Shea's advice is first decide where you are wrong, and then set the stop. If the stop implies a larger loss than you are comfortable taking on a single trade, then size the position correspondingly smaller. Using this approach, if the market reaches the stop point, it will be consistent with your own beliefs that the original trade premise was wrong.

One common theme that seems to underlie almost all the trades that O'Shea discussed in this chapter is that they are structured to be right skewed—that is, the maximum loss is limited, but the upside is open-ended. Long options, long CDS protection, and long the TED spread are all examples of trades in which the maximum loss is constrained.[5]

---

[5]Maximum loss is limited to the premium paid for long options, the annual payments for long CDS protection, and zero for the TED spread (since it would be virtually impossible for the T-bill rate to be higher than the LIBOR rate).

Chapter 2

Ray Dalio

The Man Who Loves Mistakes

Ray Dalio is the founder, CIO, former CEO, and current *mentor* (the title he assumed in July 2011) of Bridgewater, the world's largest hedge fund. As of December 2011, Bridgewater had $120 billion in assets under management and more than 1,400 employees. Bridgewater is unique in many ways beyond its size:

- It has made more money for its investors than any other hedge fund in history—an estimated $50 billion over the past 20 years.
- Bridgewater's flagship fund has a near zero correlation to traditional markets.
- Bridgewater's flagship fund also has a very low correlation to other hedge funds.
- The flagship fund uses the relatively rare combination of a fundamentally based systematic approach. (Most hedge funds that are

fundamentally based use a discretionary approach, and most hedge
funds that use systematic approaches base them on technical input.)

- Bridgewater fosters an unusual corporate culture that encourages
criticism among employees, regardless of rank.
- Virtually all of Bridgewater's business is institutional (95 percent
institutional, 5 percent fund of funds).
- Bridgewater is among a small minority of funds with a 20-year track
record.
- Bridgewater was the first hedge fund to create separate alpha and
beta funds that could be combined in any mix desired by the client.

The track record for Bridgewater's flagship strategy encompasses
both managed accounts and funds, with each trading at multiple target
volatility levels and multiple currencies. The 18 percent volatility
strategy has achieved an average annual compounded net return of
14.8 percent (22.3 percent gross) over a near 20-year period, with an
annualized standard deviation of 14.6 percent (16.0 percent on gross
return data). The most impressive aspect of Bridgewater's performance
has been the firm's ability to generate strong returns on huge assets
under management. It is one thing for a hedge fund strategy to achieve
strong return/risk performance on $50 million, or $500 million, or even
$5 billion, but to do so on $50 billion is truly astounding. (Fifty billion
dollars is the approximate assets under management Bridgewater had in
its Pure Alpha strategy during 2010 when it recorded its highest annual
return ever.)

Ray Dalio is a big picture thinker. Question: What one word might
best describe Dalio's view of an economic model based on a thorough
analysis of the entire 67-year post–World War II U.S. economy?
Answer: Myopic. Dalio describes his approach as "timeless and universal." He believes an economic model should encompass multiple times
and countries. Bridgewater employs a fundamentally based computer
model that incorporates trading rules gleaned from both Dalio's
four decades of market observations as well as Bridgewater's analysis
of markets going back hundreds of years and spanning a broad range of
developed and emerging economies.

Dalio named his flagship fund *Pure Alpha* to differentiate it from the
majority of hedge funds he considers primarily beta vehicles. Dalio has

been critical of hedge funds that derive most of their return from beta, but charge the higher fees associated with hedge funds on their entire return, even though the beta-derived portion can be duplicated by passive long investments. Beta measures how much an investment varies given changes in a benchmark market (e.g., S&P 500). Essentially, beta-based returns are returns that are earned by assuming various risks, most commonly market direction risk.[1] In contrast, alpha refers to skill-based returns, which by definition are not correlated to any market or risk factor. The name of Bridgewater's flagship fund, Pure Alpha, leaves little doubt as to the type of return it seeks to capture. True to its name, Pure Alpha has had near zero correlation to equities and fixed income and very low correlation (0.10) to hedge funds.

Bridgewater also has a beta-based strategy, *All Weather*, which has an objective of delivering beta returns in a portfolio mix that is balanced so that it will do well in different market environments. In 2009, Bridgewater launched All Weather II, which is a constrained version of All Weather that limits "safe" environment investments when the firm's "depression gauge" indicator is activated.

The idea that the same fundamentals would have different implications under different circumstances and environments is an essential component of Dalio's analytical thinking. As a result, categorization is an important tool for both conceptualizing problems and finding solutions. One example of category-based thinking is what I would call *quadrant conceptualization*—two key factors and two states provide four possible conditions. Bridgewater's beta fund, the All Weather Fund, provides an example of this type of thinking. The fund combines two factors— growth and inflation—and two states—increasing and decreasing—and comes up with four conditions:

1. Growth increasing
2. Growth decreasing

---

[1]Market direction is only one type of beta risk. Other examples of beta risks include credit risk, liquidity risk, and short volatility risk. Beta returns are returns earned by assuming risk, and these returns can be duplicated by various combinations of passive long investments. Over the long term, beta returns will be positive because investors have to be compensated for assuming these risks.

3. Inflation increasing

4. Inflation decreasing

This four-part categorization reflects Dalio's view that changes in expected growth and expected inflation are the dominant reasons that some asset classes do well when others do poorly. The fund's strategy is to balance the portfolio with investments that do well in each of the above four environments. In contrast, most conventional portfolios substantially overweight assets that do well in the first category (i.e., growth-increasing environment), leading to unbalanced portfolios that can do poorly in other types of environments.

Another example of quadrant conceptualization is the way Dalio categorizes the economic outlook for different countries. Here he divides the world into two types of countries—creditors and debtors—and he defines two key distinguishing characteristics for each—countries that can exercise independent monetary policy and those that can't. So there are four classifications of countries:

1. Debtor countries with independent monetary policy (e.g., U.S., U.K.).

2. Debtor countries without independent monetary policy (e.g., Greece, Portugal).

3. Creditor countries with independent monetary policy (e.g., Brazil).

4. Creditor countries without independent monetary policy (e.g., China because it pegs its currency to the dollar, which impedes its ability to raise interest rates).

Dalio loves mistakes because he believes that mistakes provide learning experiences that are the catalyst for improvement. The concept that mistakes are the path to progress is one of the pillars of Dalio's life philosophy and the Bridgewater culture. Dalio is almost reverential in his comments about mistakes:

I learned that there is an incredible beauty to mistakes because embedded in each mistake is a puzzle and a gem that I could get if I solved it, i.e., a principle that I could use to reduce my mistakes in the future. I learned that each mistake was probably a reflection of something that I was (or others were) doing wrong, so if I could figure out what that was, I could learn how to be more effective. . . . While most others seem to believe that mistakes are bad things, I believe mistakes are good things because I believe that most learning comes via making mistakes and reflecting on them.

Dalio has set down his life philosophy and management concepts in *Principles*, a 111-page document that defines the Bridgewater culture and is required reading for employees. *Principles* is divided in two sections, the first, which Dalio calls "My Most Fundamental Principles," and the second, a resulting compendium of 277 management rules. Not surprisingly, many of the management rules focus on mistakes. A sampling:

- *Recognize that mistakes are good if they result in learning.*
- *Create a culture in which it is okay to fail but unacceptable not to identify, analyze, and learn from mistakes.*
- *We must bring mistakes into the open and analyze them objectively, so managers need to foster a culture that makes this normal and penalizes suppressing or covering up mistakes—highlighting them, diagnosing them, thinking about what should be done differently in the future and then adding that new knowledge to the procedures manual are all essential to our improvement.*
- *Recognize that you will certainly make mistakes and have weaknesses; so will those around you and those who work for you. What matters is how you deal with them. If you treat mistakes as learning opportunities that can yield rapid improvement if handled well, you will be excited by them.*
- *If you don't mind being wrong on the way to being right, you will learn a lot.*

If improvement through mistakes is one of the two core concepts in *Principles*, "radical transparency" is the other. Employees are encouraged to be extremely transparent, not tolerate dishonesty, criticize each other without reservation, or "let loyalty stand in the way of truth and openness." Managers are instructed not to talk about subordinates unless they are in the room. Virtually all meetings at Bridgewater are taped and made available to employees. Dalio leaves little doubt about his views on the topic of openness and honesty. For example, Management Rule #11 in *Principles* states: "Never say anything about a person you wouldn't say to him directly. If you do, you're a slimy weasel..."

Many of the rules in *Principles* actually are well aligned with the key characteristics required for trading success. As one example, the following admonition from *Principles* about the importance of accepting responsibility would fit equally well in a manual for successful trading:

> *People who blame bad outcomes on anyone or anything other than themselves are behaving in a way that is at variance with reality and subversive to their progress.*

I interviewed Dalio at his Bridgewater office, which is cantilevered over the Saugatuck River, with views of the surrounding woods, providing a bucolic work setting. Dalio tends to think in terms of interconnections rather than linearly, which can lead to rambling answers, as he readily acknowledges, "I see things in complex ways, and I have a problem communicating my way of seeing to others." As the allotted time for the interview approached its end, Dalio abruptly pronounced, "Okay, we're done."

■ ■ ■

As the world's largest hedge fund, you have come quite far. I wonder what your goals were as a young man?

I played around in the markets when I was a kid. I started when I was just 12. It was like a game, and I loved the game. The fact that I could make money playing the game was good, too, but it wasn't what motivated me. I never had any specific goals like making or managing some level of money.

It is amazing how many of the successful traders I have interviewed got started in the markets at a very young age—their teens and sometimes even younger.

That makes total sense to me because the way people think is very much influenced by what they do early in their lives. Internalized learning is easiest when we are young, which is why learning to play a sport or to speak a language well is easier at an early age. The type of thinking that is necessary to succeed in the markets is entirely different from the type of thinking that is required to succeed in school. I'm sure that my being involved in the markets from an early age profoundly affected my way of thinking.

How so?

Most school education is a matter of following instructions—remember this; give it back; did you get the right answer? It teaches you that mistakes are bad instead of teaching you the importance of learning from mistakes. It doesn't address how to deal with what you don't know. Anyone who has been involved in the markets knows that you can never be absolutely confident. There is never a trade that you know you are right on. If you approach trading that way, then you will always be looking at where you might be wrong. You don't have a false confidence. You value what you don't know. In order for me to form an opinion about anything involves a higher threshold than if I were involved in some profession other than trading. I'm so worried that I may be wrong that I work really hard at putting my ideas out in front of other people for them to shoot down and tell me where I may be wrong. That process helps me be right. You have to be both assertive and open-minded at the same time. The markets teach you that you have to be an independent thinker. And any time you are an independent thinker, there is a reasonable chance you are going to be wrong.

How did you get involved in the stock market as a child?

When I was a kid in the 1960s, just about everyone was talking about the stock market, more so than at any other time, even including during the tech bubble. I remember getting a haircut and discussing stocks with my barber. I earned some money caddying; I got paid $6 per bag, and I carried two bags at one time. I used that money to open an account. My father introduced me to his retail broker. He barely invested in stocks, but at the time, everyone had a retail broker.

Do you remember your first trade?

Yes, I bought Northeast Airlines, which flew between New York and Florida.

How did you pick that stock?

It was the only stock I had ever heard of that was also selling below $5 a share. So I could buy more shares. That was my whole analysis. It didn't make any sense, but I got lucky. The company was about to go bankrupt, but then it was acquired, and I tripled my money. So I figured this was easy. I don't remember anything more about any specific stocks I bought as a child. But what I do remember is that when I was about 18 years old, we had the first bear market in my experience, and I learned to go short. Then in college I got involved in trading commodities.

What attracted you to commodities?

I could trade them with low margin requirements. I figured that with low margin requirements, I could make more money.

Any early experiences in the markets stand out?

In 1971, after graduating college and before going to business school, I had a job as a clerk on the New York Stock Exchange. On August 15, Nixon took the U.S. off the gold standard, and the monetary system broke down. I remember the stock market then went up a lot, which is certainly not what I expected.

What did you learn from that experience?

I learned that currency depreciations and the printing of money are good for stocks. I also learned not to trust what policy makers say. I learned these lessons repeatedly over the years.

Any other early experiences stand out where the market behaved very differently from what you expected?

In 1982, we had worse economic conditions than we do right now. The unemployment rate was over 11 percent. It also seemed clear to me that

Latin America was going to default on its debt. Since I knew that the money center banks had large amounts of their capital in Latin American debt, I assumed that a default would be terrible for the stock market. Then boom—in August, Mexico defaulted. The market responded with a big rally. In fact, that was the exact bottom of the stock market and the beginning of an 18-year bull market. That is certainly not what I would have expected to happen. That rally occurred because the Fed eased massively. I learned not to fight the Fed unless I had very good reasons to believe that their moves wouldn't work. The Fed and other central banks have tremendous power. In both the abandonment of the gold standard in 1971 and in the Mexico default in 1982, I learned that a crisis development that leads to central banks easing and coming to the rescue can swamp the impact of the crisis itself.

Any other events stand out as learning experiences?

Every day provides tactile learning experiences. You are asking me to describe moments. I don't see it as moments, but rather as a string of tactile experiences. It is not so much a matter of cerebral memories as it is visceral feelings. You can read about what happened in the market after Mexico defaulted, but that is not the same as being in the market and actually experiencing it. I particularly remember my surprises, especially the painful ones, because those are the experiences that provide learning lessons.

I vividly remember being long pork bellies in my personal account in the early 1970s at a time when pork bellies were limit down every day.[2] I didn't know when my losses would end, and I was worried that

---

[2]Many futures markets have daily limits on the maximum permissible price move. If there was a large imbalance between buyers and sellers, such as might occur after the release of a surprisingly bullish or bearish government report, the market would open locked at the limit price because the equilibrium price would be outside the limit range. For example, if the price was 60 cents/lb., and the government released a report that made the market think prices should be at 50 cents, the decline would occur in daily steps of 2 cents because of price limits. On the first day, there would be lots of sellers, but virtually zero buyers, so the price would open and stay at 58 cents with no trading. Of course, when a market is locked in a sequence of limit moves, there is no way of knowing what the new equilibrium price will be—that is, where the market will trade freely.

I would be financially ruined. In those days, we had the big commodity boards, which clicked whenever prices changed. So each morning, on the opening, I would see and hear the market click down 200 points, the daily limit, stay unchanged at that price, and know that I had lost that much more, with the amount of potential additional losses still undefined. It was a very tactile experience.

What did you learn from that experience?

It taught me the importance of risk controls because I never wanted to experience that pain again. It enhanced my fear of being wrong and taught me to make sure that no single bet, or even multiple bets, could cause me to lose more than an acceptable amount. In trading you have to be defensive and aggressive at the same time. If you are not aggressive, you are not going to make money, and if you are not defensive, you are not going to keep money. I believe that anyone who has made money in trading has had to experience horrendous pain at some point. Trading is like working with electricity; you can get an electric shock. With that pork belly trade and other trades, I felt the electric shock and the fear that comes with it. That led to my attitude: *Let me show you what I think, and please knock the hell out of it*. I learned about the math of investing.

[Dalio walks over to the board and draws a diagram where the horizontal axis represents the number of investments and the vertical axis the standard deviation.]

This is a chart that I teach people in the firm, which I call *the Holy Grail of investing*.

[He then draws a curve that slopes down from left to right—that is, the greater the number of assets, the lower the standard deviation.]

This chart shows how the volatility of the portfolio changes as you add assets. If you add assets that have a 0.60 correlation to the other assets, the risk will go down by about 15 percent as you add more assets, but that's about it, even if you add a thousand assets. If you run a long-only equity portfolio, you can diversify to a thousand stocks and it will only reduce the risk by about 15 percent, since the average stock has about a 0.60 correlation to another stock. If, however, you're combining assets that have an average of zero correlation, then by the time you diversify to only 15 assets, you can cut the volatility by 80 percent. Therefore, by holding uncorrelated assets, I can improve my return/risk ratio by a factor of five through diversification.

What about the problem of markets becoming highly correlated? As we sit here today, if you tell me that the S&P is down 2 percent, I can tell you the direction of virtually every other market.

I don't think that's correct.

Really, you don't think that's true?

I think that's only true because of the way you are defining markets. For example, I can't tell you which way the Greek/Irish bond spread would move in response to the S&P being down. There are ways to structure your trades so that you can produce a whole bunch of uncorrelated bets. You have to start with your goal. My goal is that I want to trade more than 15 uncorrelated assets. You are just telling me your problem, and it's not an insurmountable problem. I strive for approximately 100 different return streams that are roughly uncorrelated to each other. There are cross-correlations that enter into it, so the number works out to be less than 100, but it is well over 15. Correlation doesn't exist the way most people think it exists.

What do you mean by that?

People think that a thing called *correlation* exists. That's wrong. What is really happening is that each market is behaving logically based on its own determinants, and as the nature of those determinants changes, what we call correlation changes. For example, when economic growth expectations are volatile, stocks and bonds will be negatively correlated because if growth slows, it will cause both stock prices and interest rates to decline. However, in an environment where inflation expectations are volatile, stocks and bonds will be positively correlated because interest rates will go up with higher inflation, which is detrimental to both bonds and stocks. So both relationships are totally logical, even though they are exact opposites of each other. If you try to represent the stock/bond relationship with one correlation statistic, it denies the causality of the correlation.

Correlation is just the word people use to take an average of how two prices have behaved together. When I am setting up my trading bets, I am not looking at correlation; I am looking at whether the drivers are different. I am choosing 15 or more assets that behave differently for logical reasons. I may talk about the return streams in the portfolio being uncorrelated, but be aware that I'm not using the term correlation the way most people do. I am talking about the causation, not the measure.

There has been some press recently about the culture at Bridgewater. How would you describe it?

The Bridgewater culture seeks truth by encouraging independent thinking and innovation in an environment of radical transparency. We recognize that there must be thoughtful disagreement and non-ego-impaired explorations of mistakes and weaknesses to achieve our goals. It is a culture in which people hold each other to very high standards and are completely honest with each other, while still being extremely considerate. It is a culture that values truth and transparency so much that we record almost all discussions so there can't be any spin.

I think that one of the greatest problems that plagues mankind is that people are always saying, "I think this, and I think that," when there is a high probability they are wrong. After all, to the extent that there is strong disagreement about an issue, a lot of the people must be wrong. Yet most of them are totally confident they are right. How is that possible? Imagine how much better almost all decision making would be if people who disagree were less confident and more open to trying to get at the truth through thoughtful discourse. Anyway, that's the approach that works well for us.

When there is a disagreement between you and Bridgewater employees whose opinion you respect, how is the difference of opinion resolved?

We reach resolutions by questioning each other, which leads to better understanding. *You say that. Why do you say that? What is the evidence?*

What do we need to look at? How can we resolve the difference? Who do we need to bring in to facilitate the conversation and help us move forward? And so on. That process produces discovery, and that's fantastic. If there is a disagreement about something that is to be built into our investment decision-making process, then the three chief investment officers would have to concur [Dalio, and co-CIOs Bob Prince and Greg Jensen]. By and large, we will almost always reach an agreement. If we didn't reach an agreement, we wouldn't make any change.

Does that imply that every time you take a position in the markets, all the key people have agreed on that position?

No. Our decision-making process is to determine the criteria by which we make decisions in the market. Those criteria—I call them principles—are systematized. These principles determine what we do under different circumstances. In other words, we make decisions about the criteria we use to make decisions. We don't make decisions about individual positions.

For any trading strategy, we can look back at when it won, when it lost, and under what circumstances. Each strategy develops a track record that we deeply understand and then combine in a portfolio of diversified strategies. If a strategy is not performing in real time as expected, we can reevaluate it, and if we agree it is desirable, we might modify our systems. We have been doing this for 36 years. Over the years, we develop new understandings, which we continually add to our existing understandings.

You have had only two drawdowns worse than 12 percent in 20 years with the worst being 20 percent. How have you managed to keep your drawdowns so controlled using a directional strategy?

There are two parts to the answer. First, as we discussed earlier, we balance risk across multiple independent drivers. We avoid having too much of the portfolio concentrated in any single driver. Second, we have stress-tested our strategies through multiple time frames and multiple scenarios.

I think many people experience drawdowns that are much larger than they expected because they never really understood how their strategy would have worked in different environments. There are managers who have been in the business for five years and think, *I have a great track record; this approach really works*. But they really don't have the perspective of how their strategy would have performed in different circumstances. Strategies that are based on a manager's recent experience will work until they inevitably don't work.

In contrast, we test our criteria to make sure that they are timeless and universal. Timeless means that we look at a strategy during all different times, and universal means that we look at how a strategy worked in all different countries. There is no reason why a strategy's effectiveness should change in different time periods or when you go from country to country. This broad analysis through time and geography gives us a unique perspective relative to most other managers. For example, to understand the current U.S. zero interest rate, deleveraging environment, we need to understand what happened a long time ago, such as the 1930s, and in other countries, such as Japan in the postbubble era. Deleveragings are very different from recessions. Aside from the ongoing deleveraging, there are no other deleveragings in the U.S. post–World War II period.

Are there risk limits in terms of individual positions?

There are limits in terms of position size, but not in terms of price. We don't use stops. We trade approximately 150 different markets, where I am using the term *market* to also mean spread positions, as well as individual markets. However, at any given time, we probably have only about 20 or so significant positions, which account for about 80 percent of the risk and are uncorrelated to each other.

When you are in a significant drawdown, do you do anything differently? Do you reduce your exposure?

I don't believe in reducing exposures when you have a losing position. I want to be clear about that. The only pertinent question is whether my being in a losing position is a statistically meaningful indicator of what the subsequent price movement will be. And it is not. For that reason, I don't alter positions because they are losing.

Is the implication that whether you are at a new high or you are down 15 percent, you will still size positions exactly the same way?

Yes, the positions taken and their size would be exactly the same.

If a position works poorly, does that cause you to reexamine your strategy?

Always. The best discoveries come from positions that don't work out. For example, in 1994, we were long a number of bond markets, and the bond markets sold off. We have multiple rules and systems that apply to the bond markets, and at the time, they indicated a net long position for each bond market. Afterward, we realized that if we took those same systems and traded them on a spread basis rather than an absolute basis, we could produce a much better return/risk outcome. That change took advantage of the universal truth that you can enhance the return/risk ratio by reducing correlation. If there is a research insight, we change our process.

That is an example of how a losing position caused you to change your process. But what about an individual position that is losing money? I understand that you do not get out or reduce a position simply because it is losing money, but what if you change your mind because you realize that you overlooked some factor or didn't give some factor enough weight?

No, it doesn't work that way. The way we change our minds is a function of how that information passes through our decision rules. Our decision rules determine the position direction and size under the circumstances.

So your trading process is fully systematized rather than dependent on discretionary decisions?

It is 99 percent systematized. These systems evolve, however, as the experience we gain might prompt us to change or add rules. But we don't make discretionary trading decisions on 99 percent of our individual positions.

What if there is some idiosyncratic event that is not incorporated in the system?

If it is something like the World Trade Center getting knocked down, then yes, we may exercise a discretionary override. In most cases, such discretion would be a matter of reducing risk exposure. I would say probably less than 1 percent of trades might be affected by discretion.

Is your process totally fundamentally driven, or does the system also include technical factors?

There are no technical inputs.

So in contrast to the majority of CTAs who use a systematic approach based only on technical factors, primarily or solely price, you also use a systematic approach, but one based on only fundamental factors.

That's right.

What is the origin of the Bridgewater system?

Beginning around 1980, I developed a discipline that whenever I put on a trade, I would write down the reasons on a pad. When I liquidated the trade, I would look at what actually happened and compare it with my reasoning and expectations when I put on the trade. Learning solely from actual experience, however, is inadequate because it takes too much time to get a representative sample to determine whether a decision rule works. I discovered that I could backtest the criteria that I wrote down to get a good perspective of how they would have performed and to refine them. The next step was to define decision rules based on the criteria. I required the decision rules to be logically based and was careful to avoid data mining. That's how the Bridgewater system began and developed in the early years. That same process continued and was improved with the help of many others over the years.

Are the individual rules in the compendium of rules that make up the Bridgewater system sometimes revised or do they remain static through time?

They are sometimes revised. For example, we used to look at how changes in the oil price affected countries. Between the first oil shock and the second oil shock in the 1970s, crude oil was discovered in the North Sea, and the U.K. went from being a net importer to a net exporter. That event prompted us to change how we configured the decision rule that related to oil prices so that when the mix of export and import items changed, the rule changed.

How are you able to manage such a large amount of money without substantially impeding your performance? In fact, in 2010, you managed to achieve your highest return ever, despite having your largest assets under management ever. Most hedge funds end up having size-related difficulties managing much smaller sums.

There are two major differences between us and most other hedge funds. Most hedge funds trade fewer markets, and they trade much more actively. We trade virtually every liquid market in the world, so the amount we have committed to any single market is small relative to our total equity. We also change our positions slowly. As you know, transaction costs are a function of the amount you have to move in a given time frame. Therefore, we have considerably more capacity than managers who trade fewer markets and turn their positions over more quickly.

What is your turnover rate per market, per year?

It depends what you mean by turnover rate. If you are defining turnover as moving from net long to net short rather than changes in magnitude, then the average time length is about 12 to 18 months.

So it is a very slow process.

Yes, on average.

What about a year like 2008 when markets are witnessing huge price swings in a matter of days?

In some years, the turnover rate might be significantly greater than in others, though in 2008, it wasn't much above the average. I believe you are thinking that we would be trading more during a volatile period, but that's not necessarily true. Our trades are driven directly by fundamentals and only indirectly by price to the extent that price changes make a market cheaper or more expensive.

I guess then that another reason why size may not be as much of an issue as might be surmised based on your huge assets under management is that you will have a tendency to be a seller when the market is heavily bid and a buyer when it is heavily offered.

While that is often the case, it wouldn't be true if the fundamentals were changing faster. We will trade in the opposite direction of the price movement if all the fundamentals remain unchanged. For example, if prices fall and the fundamentals didn't change, we would be buyers. But in practice, the fundamentals are also changing. So the direction of our trades will depend on both changes in fundamentals and changes in price.

But in a period like fall 2008 when markets were witnessing huge swings in a matter of days largely based on shifts in sentiment rather than changes in fundamentals, I assume you would be more likely to be going in the opposite direction of most traders. Whereas most traders would be selling to cut their exposure when a market was breaking sharply, you would more likely be a buyer and have lots of liquidity.

That's right, as long as there wasn't a bearish shift in the fundamentals as well.

Do you ever run into situations where size is an issue?

No, because we make sure that we do not run into the problem of size being an issue. We know our transaction costs very well, and we know how long it takes for us to get in and out of positions. We will limit our position size to assure that we can get out reasonably quickly and to keep our transaction costs small relative to the expected alpha of the trades in that market.

Is there a limitation as to how large you can allow the fund to grow?

Yes, we have been closed for several years.

But even if you are closed, in a year like 2010, your assets can grow dramatically just from profits.

We returned profits.

You did quite well in 2008, a difficult year for many hedge funds. What do you attribute your favorable 2008 performance to?

Our criteria for trading in a deleveraging had already been established because we had previously studied other leveragings and deleveragings. Our analysis included both inflationary deleveragings, such as Germany in the 1920s and Latin America in the 1980s, and deflationary delever-agings, such as the Great Depression of the 1930s and Japan in the 1990s. I had also directly experienced the deleveragings in Latin America and Japan. We felt that if these sort of big events had happened before, they could happen again. We also believed that fully comprehending these events was important to understanding how economies and markets worked.

Eight years before the deleveraging that began in 2008, we had developed and implemented what we call a *depression gauge*. It was designed to indicate when a depression-like environment was in effect based on a number of conditions coinciding, such as interest rates below a certain low level, contractions in private credit growth, a declining stock market, and widening credit spreads. We knew that when the depression gauge was on, we would have fewer reliable indicators, with some indicators being impacted more than others. For example, if interest rates are near zero, obviously, they can no longer be used as a viable indicator. We ran simulations of how our systems would have performed through both inflationary and deflationary deleveragings. If the depression gauge is triggered, our system rules and risk constraints are adjusted to fit the circumstances of a deleveraging period.

It was obvious in 2008 that investors were heavily leveraged in carry trade positions—that is, they had bought higher-yielding assets funded by shorting lower-yielding assets. These positions would have to be unwound when the credit bubble popped. We also could see that the banks had leveraged up rapidly and carelessly. We anticipated they would have large losses because, by reviewing their 10Ks, we knew the types of positions they held. By applying indicative pricings, we could mark their balance sheets to the market, which gave us insights into the negative implications for the economy and other markets. In short, by knowing how deleveragings occur, we could monitor the appropriate factors, and by understanding the cause-and-effect relationships in a deleveraging, it was not difficult to be well positioned in 2008.

Besides being well prepared to trade through a deleveraging, we also didn't have the same vulnerability to a year like 2008, as most hedge funds did, simply because the inherent structure of our Pure Alpha strategy avoids embedded betas. In contrast, most hedge funds mix betas and alpha. The truth about hedge funds is that much of what is packaged as alpha is really beta sold at alpha prices. The average hedge fund is about 70 percent correlated with stocks. Why are most hedge funds so skewed toward strategies that do well in good times? I think it is human nature for people to choose strategies that worked well during the recent past, which implies a long bias.

What is your big picture perspective of the current difficult economic situation facing the U.S.?

Currently, we have a situation where there is a broad global deleveraging, which is negative for growth. Debtor countries that can print money will behave differently from those that can't. Countries that can't print money will experience classic deflationary depressions. Those that can print money, such as the United States, can alleviate the deflation and depression pressures by printing money. However, the effectiveness of quantitative easing will be limited because the owners of the bonds that are purchased by the Fed will use the money to buy something similar; they are not going to use it to buy a house or a car. In addition, fiscal stimulus will be very limited because of the reality of the political situation. So it is unlikely that we will have effective monetary policy or effective fiscal policy. That means we will be dependent on income growth, and income growth will be slow—maybe about 2 percent per year—because income growth is usually dependent on debt growth to finance buying, and I don't expect any significant private credit growth. A growth rate of 2 percent is not sufficient to meaningfully lower the unemployment rate. There is a risk that if the economy deteriorates, we won't have any effective tools for reversing the situation. The current situation is analogous to being in a recession and not being able to lower interest rates.

If you had the power to enact policy, is there any policy that could ameliorate the current situation?

The best policy would be to spread out the problems over a long period of time so that nominal interest rates stay below nominal growth rates.

How do you do that?

You do it through a combination of monetary and fiscal policies that produce enough government spending to make up for the reduction in private sector spending to keep the economy from contracting. Avoiding an unmanaged contraction is essential in order to maintain social and political order. At the same time, there needs to be well thought-out debt restructurings because we can no longer allow our debts to rise faster than our incomes, and we need to gradually lower them.

If you do more fiscal spending, it would further increase the debt. We are dependent on foreign capital to buy our debt. Isn't there a risk that increasing the debt further through fiscal stimulus might scare away foreign buyers of U.S bonds?

There sure is. That is why it is very important that the fiscal spending is used for investments that generate returns that are greater than their costs. We can't afford to waste money.

Do you mean the spending should be focused on things such as infrastructure?

Yes, put idle people to work on useful projects. It is also socially good. I think it is very bad for society for people to be out of work for very long periods.

It is also a false saving. You are paying unemployed workers unemployment insurance and providing other safety net expenditures, and generating nothing in return. Whereas if you pay people to build bridges and repair roads, at least you're getting something out of it, and it has a multiplier effect.

That's right. I don't like the giving-money-away option because it will devalue the currency and cause investors to run away from U.S. assets. The government should try to make the expenditures a good investment.

Do you see a danger of the printing of money leading to inflation risk?

Not over the next couple of years. However, longer term, whenever a country has a balance of payments deficit and depends on foreign capital, there is a risk that foreign investors will pull back if they fear currency weaknesses as a result of the increased printing of money. The first sign of such a shift is a shortening of the duration of bonds bought by foreigners, which further tightens credit. Such a response occurred in 1931 to 1933 when interest rates went up, even though we were in a deflationary depression. Under these circumstances, the central bank will normally buy more bonds to make up for the difference, which is a monetization of the debt that causes the currency to weaken and a movement of money into real assets and other currencies to escape currency weakness. This phase usually takes a couple of years. Initially, there is a move from deflation to a low level of inflation. For example, when Roosevelt decided to print money and go off the gold standard in 1933, the move depreciated the dollar and just negated the deflation; it didn't bring about a high level of inflation. During such times, both gold and bonds can go up together, which is very different from a normal situation in which higher gold prices imply lower bond prices because of the inflation component. This pattern is exactly what has happened in the current cycle when we have had monetary easing and seen both gold and bonds go up.

When I read your description of long-term cycles, it sounded like the U.S. had gone through the fourth of the five phases—a country that still thinks it is rich, but isn't—and is now in the fifth stage: a country in decline. Is that an accurate interpretation of your views?

I believe so.

How long does this cycle typically last?

The entire cycle takes about 100 to 150 years; the fifth phase of a cycle (decline) lasts for about 20 years.

Assuming the U.S. entered its decline phase around 2008, your cyclical model implies the U.S. can remain in a general decline out to 2130. That is a pretty pessimistic outlook. Have there been any situations of countries in the decline phase of the long-term cycle where it hasn't been extremely painful?

The decline of the British Empire after World War II wasn't cataclysmic because the adjustment process was spread out over many years. So was Japan's deleveraging. Essentially a country's conditions can stay about the same for a very long period. It doesn't have to be terrible. But it can be terrible if it is badly managed.

At Bridgewater, criticism is encouraged, including subordinates criticizing superiors. Do any of your employees ever criticize you?

All the time.

Can you give me an example?

I was in a client meeting with a big European pension fund that was visiting managers in Connecticut. After the meeting, the salesperson criticized me for being inarticulate, running on too long, and adversely affecting the meeting. I asked others who had been at the meeting for their opinions. I was given a grade of "F" by one of our new analysts who was just one year out of school. I loved it because I knew they were helping me improve and that they understood that was what they were supposed to be doing.

What do you believe is the biggest mistake people make in investing?

The biggest mistake investors make is to believe that what happened in the recent past is likely to persist. They assume that something that was a good investment in the recent past is still a good investment. Typically, high past returns simply imply that an asset has become more expensive and is a poorer, not better, investment. The tendency of investors to buy after a price increase for no reasons other than the price increase itself causes prices to overshoot. When investors are making money because they're greedy and fearless, which is typically after a large price rise, doing the opposite is a good idea.

■ ■ ■

Dalio is a strong believer in diversification. In fact, he calls the potential improvement in return/risk through the addition of uncorrelated assets the "Holy Grail of investing." He states that return/risk can be improved by as much as a factor of 5 to 1 if the assets in the portfolio are truly independent.

Most people tend to focus on correlation as a primary tool for determining the relative dependence or independence of two assets. Dalio believes that correlation can be a misleading statistic and poorly suited as a tool for constructing a diversified portfolio. The crux of the problem is that correlations between assets are highly variable and critically dependent on prevailing circumstances. For example, typically, gold and bonds are inversely related because inflation (current or expected) will be bullish for gold and negative for bonds (because higher inflation normally implies higher interest rates). In the early phases of a deleveraging cycle, however, both gold and bonds can move higher together, as aggressive monetary easing will reduce interest rates (i.e., increase bond prices), while at the same time enhancing longer-term concerns over currency depreciation, which will increase gold prices. In this type of environment, gold and bonds can be positively correlated, which is exactly opposite their normal relationship.

Instead of using correlation as a measure of dependence between positions, Dalio focuses on the underlying drivers that are expected to affect those positions. Drivers are the cause; correlations are the consequence. In order to ensure a diversified portfolio, it is necessary to select assets that have different drivers. By determining the future drivers that are likely to impact each market, a forward-looking approach, Dalio can more accurately assess which positions are likely to move in the same direction or inversely—for example, anticipate when gold and bonds are likely to move in the same direction and when they are likely to move in opposite directions. In contrast, making decisions based on correlation, which is backward looking, can lead to faulty decisions in forming portfolios. Dalio constructs portfolios so that the different positions have different drivers rather than simply being uncorrelated.

Bridgewater makes heavy use of spread positions to create holdings that have different drivers. For example, even though different world bond markets may be exposed to similar drivers, various spread positions between those bonds can have different drivers. The use of spread positions is critical in mitigating the problem of highly synchronous behavior between positions in the portfolio in an investment environment that is characterized by shifts between "risk on" and "risk off" (a situation where a broad range of markets move in tandem in response to whether investors are risk-averse or risk-seeking).

Markets behave differently in different environments. The behavior of markets in deleveragings is very different from their responses in recessions. Any fundamental model that assumes static relationships between markets and economic variables will be flawed because those relationships can change dramatically in different market situations. For example, the same government actions that might lead to a sustained rebound in a recession might have little impact in a deleveraging. Dalio contends that any valid fundamental approach must be broad enough in scope—both temporal and geographical—to encompass all different environments. He believes such a "timeless and universal" approach is the only way to build a fundamental model that is sufficiently robust to represent the real world.

Investors are often baffled when markets respond to news events in counterintuitive fashion. Dalio vividly recalls these experiences when seemingly very bearish events, such as the United States coming off the gold standard in 1971 and the Mexican default in 1982, were to his great surprise followed by major market rallies. In part, this seemingly paradoxical market behavior can be explained by the fact that markets often anticipate the news. The other part of the explanation is that bearish events can trigger new events with bullish consequences. For example, developments that have very negative implications for the economy and investor sentiment can prompt central bank countermeasures that lead to rallies.

If there is a single essential lesson to learn from Dalio, it is that mistakes provide the path to improvement and ultimate success. Each mistake offers an opportunity to learn from the error and to modify one's approach based on this new information. Whenever you make a significant mistake in trading, write it down, both to reinforce the lesson and to serve as a future reminder. Then change your trading process based on this new experience. In this way, mistakes can become the essential ingredient for continual improvement as a trader, or for that matter any other endeavor.

Addendum: Ray Dalio's Big Picture View

Dalio's big picture perspective applies not only to temporal and geographic breadth, but also to viewing the markets and economies through the lens of long-term cycles and trends. Dalio's template for understanding economies consists of superimposing three forces that together explain the position and direction of any economy:

1. **Productivity growth**—Real per capita GDP in the United States has increased at an average rate of near 2 percent over the past 100 years as a result of productivity gains, but has fluctuated widely around this trend based on the prevailing long-term and business cycles.

2. **Long-term credit expansion/deleveraging cycle**—Initially, the availability of credit expands spending beyond income levels. As Dalio explains,

[This process] is self-reinforcing because rising spending generates rising incomes and rising net worths, which raise borrowers' capacity to borrow, which allows more buying and spending. . . . The up-wave in the cycle typically goes on for decades, with variations in it primarily due to central banks tightening and easing credit (which makes business cycles).

Although self-reinforcing, the credit expansion phase ultimately reaches a point where it can no longer be extended. Dalio describes this transition in the credit cycle as follows:

It can't go on forever. Eventually the debt service payments become equal to or larger than the amount we can borrow and the spending must decline. When promises to deliver money (debt) can't rise any more relative to the money and credit coming in, the process works in reverse and we have deleveragings. Since borrowing is simply a way of pulling spending forward, the person spending $110,000 per year and earning $100,000 per year has to cut his spending to $90,000 for as many years as he spent $110,000, all else being equal. . . . In deleveragings, rather than debts rising relative to money as they do in up-waves, the reverse is true. As the money coming in to debtors via incomes and borrowings is not enough to meet debtors' obligations, assets need to be sold and spending needs to be cut in order to raise cash. This leads asset values to fall, which reduces the value of collateral, and in turn reduces incomes. Because of both lower collateral values and lower incomes, borrowers' creditworthiness is reduced, so they justifiably get less credit, and so it continues in a self-reinforcing manner.

Dalio emphasizes that deleveragings are very different from recessions:

Unlike in recessions, when cutting interest rates and creating more money can rectify this imbalance, in deleveragings monetary policy is ineffective in creating credit. In other words, in recessions (when monetary policy is effective) the imbalance between the amount of money and the need for it to service debt can be rectified because interest rates can

be cut enough to (1) ease debt service burdens, (2) stimulate economic
activity because monthly debt service payments are high relative to
incomes, and (3) produce a positive wealth effect; however, in delever-
agings, this can't happen. In deflationary depressions/deleveragings,
monetary policy is typically ineffective in creating credit because interest
rates hit 0 percent and can't be lowered further, so other, less-effective
ways of increasing money are followed. Credit growth is difficult to
stimulate because borrowers remain overindebted, making sensible
lending impossible. In inflationary deleveragings, monetary policy is
ineffective in creating credit because increased money growth goes into
other currencies and inflation hedge assets because investors fear that their
lending will be paid back with money of depreciated value.

3. **Business cycle**—The business cycle refers to fluctuations in
   economic activity. Dalio explains that "In the 'business cycle,' the
   availability and cost of credit are driven by central bankers, while in
   the 'long wave cycle,' the availability and cost of credit are driven
   by factors that are largely beyond central banks' control." In the
   standard business cycle, the central bank can boost a lagging
   economy by lowering interest rates. In the deleveraging phase of the
   long wave cycle, central banks can't exert any influence by lowering
   rates because rates are already at or near zero.

It should now be clear why Dalio believes that any fundamental
market analysis based solely on the entire post–World War II period in
the United States is entirely inadequate. Although encompassing nearly
70 years, this period in the United States does not contain any
deleveragings other than the current one that began in 2008. And, as
explained, economies and markets behave very differently in deleveragings than in standard recessions. By focusing more broadly through
both time and geography, Dalio is able to draw upon past instances that
are comparable to the current situation (e.g., Great Depression, postbubble Japan, Latin American defaults).

In regard to the cycles that affect individual countries, Dalio takes an
even broader perspective, measured in centuries, which he calls, appropriately enough, "the really big picture." Dalio believes that all countries
move through a five-phase cycle:

Stage 1—Countries are poor and think that they are poor.

Stage 2—Countries are getting rich quickly, but still think they are poor.

Stage 3—Countries are rich and think of themselves as rich.

Stage 4—Countries become poorer and still think of themselves as rich.

Stage 5—Countries go through deleveraging and relative decline, which they are slow to accept.

This is how Dalio describes countries in Stage 4:

This is the leveraging up phase—i.e., debts rise relative to incomes until they can't anymore. . . . Because spending continues to be strong, they continue to appear rich, even though their balance sheets deteriorate. The reduced level of efficient investments in infrastructure, capital goods, and R&D slow their productivity gains. Their cities and infrastructures become older and less efficient than those in the two earlier stages. Their balance of payments positions deteriorate, reflecting their reduced competitiveness. They increasingly rely on their reputations rather than on their competitiveness to fund their deficits. They typically spend a lot of money on the military at this stage, sometimes very large amounts because of wars, in order to protect their global interests. Often, though not always, at the advanced stages of this phase, countries run "twin deficits"—i.e., both balance of payments and government deficits.

In the last few years of this stage, frequently bubbles occur. . . . These bubbles emerge because investors, businessmen, financial intermediaries, individuals, and policy makers tend to assume that the future will be like the past so they bet heavily on the trends continuing. They mistakenly believe that investments that have gone up a lot are good rather than expensive so they borrow money to buy them, which drives up their prices more and reinforces this bubble process. . . . Bubbles burst when the income growth and investment returns inevitably fall short of the levels required to service these debts. . . . The financial losses that result from the bubble bursting contribute to the country's economic decline. Whether due to wars or bubbles or both, what typifies this stage is an accumulation of debt that can't be paid back in non-depreciated money, which leads to the next stage.

And Stage 5:

After bubbles burst and when deleveragings occur, private debt growth, private sector spending, asset values, and net worths decline in a self-reinforcing negative cycle. To compensate, government debt growth, government deficits, and central bank "printing" of money typically increase. In this way, their central banks and central governments cut real interest rates and increase nominal GDP growth so that it is comfortably above nominal interest rates in order to ease debt burdens. As a result of these low real interest rates, weak currencies, and poor economic conditions, their debt and equity assets are poor performing and increasingly these countries have to compete with less expensive countries that are in the earlier stages of development. Their currencies depreciate and they like it. As an extension of these economic and financial trends, countries in this stage see their power in the world decline.

The foregoing Stage 4 and Stage 5 profiles sound like uncomfortably close descriptions of the United States (Stage 5—current situation; Stage 4 preceding decades), don't they?

Chapter 3

Larry Benedict

Beyond Three Strikes

T he road to success is often paved with failure. Larry Benedict did two things consistently during his early career: lose money in trading and get fired—the two often, but not always, related. Despite a complete lack of evidence that he possessed any trading skill, Benedict persisted in his quest to become a successful trader, somehow managing to find another trading job after each failure. Luckily for Benedict, there is no three-strikes-and-you're-out rule in pursuing a career.

Ultimately, Benedict proved to be as consistent in success as he was in failure. Benedict's transition point came in 1989 when he was hired by Spear, Leeds & Kellogg (SLK) to be an option specialist in the XMI index on the American Stock Exchange. As a specialist, Benedict gained some much needed experience and developed a feel for the markets. When volume in the XMI started to dry up three years later, Benedict became an off-the-floor index derivatives trader for SLK. In 1993,

Benedict's success as a trader led to his being named the Special Limited Partner for SLK's newly created proprietary trading department. After Goldman Sachs purchased SLK in 2000, Benedict left to start his own trading firm, Banyan Equity Management.

A trading friend describes Benedict's skill in the market as follows: "He has 'it.' It's hard to describe it. Why does Ichiro Suzuki repeatedly hit 350? I don't know. Benedict is like Rain Man in that office, but get him out of the office, and he can't even find his keys. In the office, he is like a friggen Maestro."

Benedict is a very active short-term trader. He averages about 100 to 200 trades a day. Several years ago, the pace was even more frenetic: closer to 500 trades per day. His core market is the S&P 500. He also trades foreign equity indexes, such as the DAX, Hang Seng, and Nikkei, domestic and foreign interest rate markets, major currencies, and key commodity markets, such as crude oil and gold. The S&P 500 is the hub, and Benedict pays a lot of attention to how the other major markets are correlating (either directly or inversely) with the S&P 500. Benedict is essentially a mean reversion trader—that is, he will be a seller into short-term upswings and a buyer into short-term declines. The entry level of his trades will be determined by the prevailing volatility of the market, his directional bias, if any, and changes in correlations between the markets he trades. Benedict will also trade longs in one market versus shorts in a positively correlated market (or longs in an inversely correlated market) if he thinks the short-term price relationship is overextended. Benedict maintains the risk balance of a constantly changing portfolio, containing both directly and inversely correlated positions, in his head. A former intern commented, "The things Benedict does mentally other people need computers to do."

Risk management dominates Benedict's approach. To say he is cautious is an understatement. If his losses in any month approach 2.5 percent, Benedict will liquidate the entire portfolio and start with a clean slate the next day, trading at a reduced position size. Typically, after a 2.0 percent to 2.5 percent decline, he will cut his unit size to one-half or less the normal level. Benedict will continue to trade at a smaller size until he starts making money again. The rapidity with which Benedict cuts his exposure explains why he has never had a large monthly loss. His worst month in 13 years of trading (seven years in his fund and six years previously in a managed account and proprietary account) was a moderate 3.5 percent loss.

David Horowitz, a former trader, and the chief operating officer for Banyan, describes Benedict as follows: "Larry is essentially a risk manager. It's not about making a lot of money. Of course, it's important to have return, but for Larry it's more important not to lose money. He knows that if he can manage the risk, he will make money. He understands when he is wrong, and he knows when he has to get out. Fundamental managers say, 'I'm going to buy this stock for the next six months because I think this will happen.' Technical managers say, 'If the stock goes here I will buy, and if it goes here I will sell.' Larry doesn't fit into either group. Larry has spent so much time in front of the screens watching these markets trade versus each other that he has a sense of when to buy and sell. Larry lets the market dictate to him what he should do, which is very different from how most managers approach trading."

After joining Spear Leeds in 1990, Benedict was net profitable for 20 consecutive years. The streak, however, ended in 2011—just barely—when his fund lost 0.6 percent. Since its inception in 2004, Benedict's fund has realized an average annualized compounded net return of 11.5 percent (19.3 percent gross). If this return does not sound sufficiently impressive, keep in mind that it was achieved with an extremely low annualized volatility of 5.8 percent and, even more impressive, a maximum drawdown of less than 5 percent. Benedict's return/risk numbers are exemplary. His Sharpe ratio is very high at 1.5. The Sharpe ratio, however, understates Benedict's performance because this statistic does not distinguish between upside and downside volatility, and in Benedict's case, most of the limited volatility is on the upside. Benedict's Gain to Pain ratio is an extremely high 3.4. (See Appendix A for an explanation of the Gain to Pain ratio.)

Benedict won't allow family or friends to invest in his fund, as one of his friends since childhood told me. "Larry will never take any investor money from friends or family. I tried to convince him to take money from me, but he wouldn't do it. When I was managing a multistrategy fund of funds, he wouldn't even let the firm invest because I was the one directing the investment. He doesn't want to bear the responsibility. After 2008, when his parents had lost a lot of money in their conventional investments, just like most other investors, while his fund was up 14 percent, I asked him, 'Larry, don't you now regret that you didn't let your parents and friends invest with you?' He answered, 'No, that doesn't change anything. It would just add another layer of distraction. I would rather write my parents a check if they needed the money than ever have them in the fund.'"

I visited Benedict at his offices in Boca Raton, Florida. Although there is ample space in their office complex, Benedict and his entire team are crowded together in a single room. Because of the confined quarters, and to avoid continuous distractions, we conducted the interview in an overly spacious, but entirely unassuming, conference room. Assistants would periodically come in to advise Benedict of market price moves and to get his trading instructions. I thought it odd that the conference room was about five times larger than might ever be needed, whereas the trading room was cramped. John Apperson, a managing director at Centennial Partners and an investor in Banyan who had brought Benedict to my attention, explained this oddity in a phone conversation several months later. "A number of years ago when Banyan expanded their operation a bit with the growth of assets, they were all jammed together in that little room you saw. They decided to build out a new trading room in a larger space. The first day after they had relocated, Larry had a bad trading day. He said, 'That's it. Rip it out. We are moving back.' What would appear to most of us as a much less comfortable work environment is not that way for Larry. Maybe he is more comfortable there because he can reach all his employees."

Benedict is a happily transplanted New Yorker who lives in Florida with his wife, Lisa, and three sons. He loves the casual Florida lifestyle and dresses the part. Even though Benedict had institutional investors visiting his offices the day I interviewed him, he was wearing shorts and a T-shirt (maybe they were his dress shorts). Although the room was surprisingly chilly (and I'm someone who likes air conditioning set to cold temperatures), Benedict, who was more appropriately dressed for a heat wave, seemed perfectly comfortable.

Benedict was downright jovial in our conversation, but he was surprisingly candid about making me aware of the darker side of his temperament. In the course of our interview, Benedict enlisted several witnesses, both in person and by phone, to testify to his predilection to anger outbursts—a character trait I would not have guessed he had without his assistance. I later learned that his staff stocks ample inventories of phones, cell phones, and especially keyboards—items that are particularly vulnerable targets of Benedict's periodic temper flares.

■ ■ ■

How would you describe your trading approach?

I am probably different from any of the other traders you'll interview. If you come into my office, you'll see that I don't look at charts at all during the trading day. I am just tape reading.

And you don't use fundamentals either?

I understand the fundamentals, but they don't come into play in my short duration trading.

You certainly are different. I have interviewed fundamental traders who don't look at charts, but you are definitely the first discretionary technical trader that I've interviewed who doesn't use charts. So right away, we can say you are in a category of one.

I sort of have the chart in my head. I look at prices and markets versus other markets. Our trade durations are very short, anywhere from a few seconds to a day or two.

What markets are you trading?

My main market is S&P futures, which I trade both on its own and versus other highly liquid futures markets, such as the euro, yen, T-notes, gold, and crude oil.

How did you get started in trading?

When I was a senior at Syracuse University, I had absolutely no idea what I wanted to do. I was dating a girl whose father was a soybean trader on the Chicago Board of Trade. On one of my vacations, he took me to the trading floor. That was my first exposure to the futures markets.

Did you know anything about futures?

Zero. I didn't know anybody who traded or who was even in the business.

What was your impression when you went on the floor?

It was the most awesome thing I ever saw. I thought, "This is what I got to do." I loved that it was aggressive and competitive. When I was growing up, I played a lot of sports, and I was ultracompetitive.

Did you try to get a job on the floor after you graduated?

A friend of my aunt's family was a market maker on the floor of the CBOE and helped me get a job as a clerk. At the time, I thought $5,000 was a lot of money. The guy I was working for had $15 million in his account, and on my first day on the job I remember walking a $1 million check over to Goldman Sachs. The clerk that I was replacing trained me for a day. He told me, "Listen, you're going to get fired every day. Just come back the next day." I'm 21 years old, in a new city where I don't know anyone, and I am being told that I will be fired every day. It was a bit unsettling.

On the first day, I was thrown into the fire. I knew absolutely nothing. My boss was hand signaling me from the pit. I didn't know the hand signals yet; I had to learn them from a sheet they handed you. We go back to the office after the first day of work, and he says, "My account is off by 20 lots. Get the hell out of my office, and don't come back. You're fired."

What did you do?

I came in to the office the next morning, tail between my legs, and sat down at the desk. He didn't say anything and acted as if everything was normal. And then two days later he says, "You don't know what you're doing. You're fired."

During those first few days, did you think that maybe you didn't want to do this? It sounds like a miserable job.

[He laughs hard.] It was miserable.

Did things get any better?

No, it was definitely a bad period of time. He really needed an experienced clerk. After six months we reached a mutual decision that I should leave. I took an easier job as a runner on the floor.

After working for about a year as a runner, I got a trading position for a firm run by Steve Fossett, the famous world adventurer. The deal was that you would put up $10,000 of your own money, and the firm supplemented it with $15,000. You kept all the profits on your own portion of the funds and 60 percent of the profits on the firm's capital. The firm supplied you with an exchange seat for which you paid a monthly rental fee.

What had you learned that made you think you could make money as a trader?

Not much. To be frank, I didn't have a handle on what to do. I was just making bets. I just thought I could do it. What's funny is that I remember calling my mom and saying, "My friend Andy is making a fortune, and I can't seem to make a dime." She said, "Oh, then just do what he does."

What exchange were you trading on?

I was originally on the CBOE trading options on stocks, such as Chrysler and Revlon. Then they moved me over to the New York Stock Exchange to trade the index, the NYA, which is where I was at the time of the 1987 crash. In 1988, I went to the Amex to trade the XMI, the major market index, which is an index based on 20 blue-chip stocks.

Did you trade on the day of the crash?

Yes, I came in short . . .

Wow, that's great.

No, I came in short straddles.[1] I was short 20 calls and 20 puts.

Oh my God, that drastically changes the picture.

What was ironic about that day is that not only did the puts skyrocket as the market crashed, but the calls also went up because volatility exploded. So I was losing money on both sides of the trade. The account went from somewhere around $25,000 to a deficit in a matter of hours. I was frozen. I called Steve Fossett to ask him what I should do. He said, "Stay on the bid; you'll get it." The market just kept falling, and I panicked and bought back my puts. I kept the calls. It didn't make sense to me that the calls should be way up when the Dow was down 500 points. I covered the calls a couple of days later.

Where was the account when you covered the puts?

It was probably in deficit around $10,000. This was not a big amount, but if you lose all your money, it doesn't make a difference if it's $20,000 or $1 million. I thought I was done. After I got out of my puts, I left the floor. I remember walking around Wall Street in a daze. There was a reporter from one of the local TV stations who asked me, "Can you give us a comment?" All I could say was, "This is unbelievable." That quote actually made it onto TV.

Yes, I remember that day well. Even 2008 paled by comparison because in 1987 virtually the entire move happened in one day.

One of my most important experiences was being on the floor on the day of the 1987 crash. Seeing that day taught me that anything can happen.

---

[1]A short straddle is a combined short call and short put position. A short straddle will make money (all or part of the premium received for selling the options) if the market trades within a moderate price range. It is, effectively, a bet that the market will not be volatile. If the market, however, witnesses a sharp swing in either direction, the short straddle position can be subject to large losses. The maximum profit on a short straddle position is limited to the premium received. The maximum loss, however, is not merely unlimited, but accelerates exponentially if there is a large price move in either direction.

How did it feel when you got out of the position?

It felt good [he laughs].

I assume you would have lost more if you stayed with the position?

A lot more. The put options went up so much by the end of the day that I probably would have been down several hundred thousand dollars if I stayed with the position. They crushed the market on the close, and the volatility went insane. The puts that I covered at 20 probably went as high as 200.

Since you had taken the account into a deficit, you obviously couldn't trade. What happened next?

The firm had a standard policy of replenishing traders' accounts with $25,000 if you blew through the first $25,000. You would become a prop trader for the firm.

It seems like an odd structure. What was the logic of the firm giving traders additional money after they lost the initial stake?

They felt that there was a good probability you would chew through the initial capital, which was partly your own money, because of the learning curve. They figured you would have a better chance once you had the experience. Also, they were earning commissions off your trades, so if you just broke even, they would do quite well. It was in their interest to try to keep you trading.

How did you do with the second $25,000?

I floundered and had gone through part of that capital as well when a friend of mine, who was a market maker, approached me with an offer to trade a $50,000 prop account for him and another guy. The deal was that they would allow me to lose $30,000 before pulling the plug on the account. I wasn't doing well with the Fossett account, so I made the switch.

Since you hadn't made any money, on what basis was he offering you the account?

He saw me trade in the pit, and I guess he thought I could make money. I don't know why he thought that, but he did. I also think he wanted to give me a shot. What happened was that after I had been trading the account for about one month, I lost $16,000. I called him that night to let him know about the loss I had taken. It was the most difficult call I ever had to make because he was a friend of mine, and he had given me an opportunity. He told me to take some time off to clear my head. After I came back, though, he told me they had decided to terminate the account.

I have to ask you this. You got fired from your first job. Then you got a trading job and blew through the money. They gave you more money, and you blew through most of that. Then a friend gave you a stake, and you lost money so quickly that he pulled the plug before you reached your cutoff point. [As I am reciting this litany, Benedict's laughter builds steadily.] Didn't you at some point say to yourself, "Maybe I'm not cut out to be a trader"?

No. I never gave up.

I know you never gave up, but not to be cruel, on what basis did you have any confidence?

I just wanted to learn how to do it and win. I saw all these other guys making money, and I thought if they could do it, I could do it. But up to this point, I had no strategy and no discipline. I was, however, gaining experience. All the mistakes I was making along the way—and there were many—were providing experience, which was critical. The lessons I learned from those early failures helped me become successful.

What did you do next?

The pit was like a fraternity. One of the other traders in the pit who worked for Spear Leeds offered me a job as a specialist. I was the specialist for the XMI calls. I owe a lot of my success to Spear Leeds. They gave me stability. Larry Lovecchio, who I worked for at Spear Leeds, taught me discipline. I watched how he traded—the risk he took and how he protected the capital.

Were you just making the market in the XMI calls or were you also trading a proprietary account?

Both. As the specialist you provide liquidity. You also have an inherent advantage in trading because you see the order book.

When you fill an order, how do you lay off the risk?

If I was a seller of calls, I would buy futures against it. I would keep the book close to delta neutral.

So you were essentially making the bid/ask spread and laying off the risk.

Yes, but as a specialist, you also have to anticipate. If the market is strong, and you know you will have call buyers all day, you buy futures ahead of that. In other words, you anticipate your hedge needs and adjust your delta. That process was part of developing a feel for the market, which I never had in all those years of just knocking around.

How did you develop that feel?

I started paying attention to the intermarket price relationships. For example, if the S&P was moving in an inverse lockstep to the bonds, and bonds were down for the day, but the S&P was not responding on the upside, it would tell me I should sell the S&P. It's funny, now, crude and the S&P are moving up and down together. That is something new. Before, we never even looked at crude.

[One of the firm's employees comes into the conference room to discuss a position with Benedict. Benedict gives him some instructions and then continues our conversation.]

Sorry about that. I traded so badly today.

What did you do wrong today?

I trade a lot of mean reversion. One of the things I do is three days up, three days down. If the market is up three days in a row, I want to start getting short, and if it's down three days in a row, I want to start getting long. The euro sold off during the past few days, and I started going long. The position will probably be okay, but it was down a number that was as much as I was willing to lose, so I covered most of it.

Do you know where you will get out before you get in?

It's based on the P&L. If I am down more than 2 percent month-to-date on any day, I will clear out everything. I wasn't near that point today, but the daily P&L was down more than I wanted to lose, so I liquidated.

How much was that?

$10 million.

In percentage terms?

A little less than 1 percent. I know that doesn't sound like much compared to most hedge funds, but I am a grinder.

But what did you actually do wrong today?

The stuff that I do just didn't work today.

But that's not doing something wrong. There's a big difference between losing on your trades and doing something wrong.

What I did wrong was this. I had a number in my mind for the year where I wanted to be. I wanted to get to about 14 percent gross for the year, which would get me above 10 percent net. I was close to there at the start of the month [November]. I kept pushing and pushing, and I just couldn't make any headway.

Was the mistake then pushing harder than justified by the trading opportunities?

Yes.

You run your risk control much tighter than most hedge fund managers. Where does that extreme risk-averseness come from?

I guess it comes from losing so many times early in my career when I didn't have any controls. I just don't want to lose again.

How did you go from trading the XMI to trading other markets?

The volume in the XMI was drying up. So I told Spear Leeds that I wanted to trade other markets, and they let me go ahead. That was when I began doing what I am doing today.

Your trading style is very short term. Do you have any longer-term market views?

I'm as opinionated as anyone else. I have a broad global macro view, but I express it in a day or a few days in duration.

Does it affect your trades?

I don't let it affect my trades. I have investors visit, and when they ask me my opinion on the market, I will tell them. I may tell them that I think the broad market looks negative, and then the next month the market is up 4 percent. They will call me and ask, "How could you be up last month when you were bearish and the market rallied? And the answer is that I let the market dictate to me how I should be trading, not my macro views of what I think the market will do.

You never let your macro views influence your trading?

Infrequently. In October 2008, I did something I normally don't do—I let a market assumption that I thought was right, but ultimately proved to be wrong, influence my trading. At the time, with the U.S. in a financial meltdown, I thought that Japan would dramatically out-perform the U.S. because it had already had its banking crisis. My mistake was that every hedge fund manager in the world was long Japan, Hong Kong, and China, and those markets went down more than the U.S. because they had to liquidate their positions. That trade cost me a lot.

Have the markets changed since your early days of trading?

The growing influence of high-frequency trading has changed the behavior of the market and has made it more difficult for someone like me who is a pure tape reader looking for clues in the market action. I am trying to adapt, as I always do, to changes in the market. On the other hand, the advent of electronic trading, which made high-frequency trading possible, has also been great for me.

Why is that?

Because now I don't have to talk to anyone. As you can see being up here, the phones don't ring. I can buy and sell anonymously. Before, when my orders were placed through the pit, the brokers would steal from me, and I still made money.

You probably have some anecdotes of times you got ripped off.

[Benedict laughs long and hard. He calls a broker on the speakerphone whom he has dealt with since the preelectronic trading days. They reminisce about some of the "rip-offs" Benedict experienced when orders were filled exclusively in the pits. The most egregious of these was Benedict getting a fill on a buy order at the low of the day, and then, later in the day, being told he no longer had a fill because the pit committee had invalidated the low of the day. For my benefit, Benedict next asked his broker friend to describe his demeanor in some of these situations.]

What was I like on the phone 10 years ago?

[Broker on speakerphone in a tone exaggerated to express obvious sarcasm] You were wonderful. You were always kind to me.

No, give me a straight answer.

[Broker] We considered making a tape called "Benny's Greatest Fits" [Benny being Larry Benedict's nickname].

I have someone here who is interviewing me, and I'm trying to explain the difference between executing orders now versus what it was like when orders went to the floor.

[Broker] You can't even compare the two.

I was explaining that I made money back at that time despite the disadvantage.

[Broker] It was the greatest disadvantage.

[Benedict thanks his friend and hangs up.]

The inherent disadvantage was that my order went into the pit, and they would yell, "86 for 400." You didn't have to be that smart to know that you could bid 86¼ because there were 400 bid at 86. It was a huge disadvantage. Now no one knows anything because the trade is on the computer.

What is the last time you lost your temper, and who were you angry with?

About four days ago. I was angry at myself. I ripped out the phone and threw it against the wall. I am the worst sore loser you ever met. I am brutal on myself. I can make money 9 days out of 10 and still be so angry about losing on the 10th day.

What happened four days ago?

I was getting hurt on a trade and released some aggression.

How often do you lose your temper?

Much less than I used to because the playing field has become level. Originally, my anger stemmed from my not being able to handle being ripped off and lied to. Before electronic trading, it used to be almost every day and sometimes even multiple times a day. When I was working for Spear Leeds, people could hear me on the other floor. That's how loud I was.

Who were you yelling at?

The brokers.

[An assistant brings in lunch, and Benedict addresses the question to him.] Do I have a bad temper?

[Assistant speaking] The evidence is over there. [He points to a broken phone on the floor.] We have stacks of broken phones.

Do you buy them in gross?

[Benedict speaking] At Spear Leeds, they actually charged my account for broken phones. They subtracted it from my P&L [he laughs]. I've gotten a lot better over the years, but I used to be very bad. [Benedict calls another friend on the speakerphone.] Do I have a bad temper?

[There is a 20-second laugh before the voice on the speakerphone replies.] You are a great guy, but you definitely have a dark side.

[Benedict] How dark?

[Friend] We don't want to go there. Put it this way, I wouldn't want to be on the other side of your wrath. Many phones have not survived you.

I understand that you worked for Marty Schwartz.[2] How did that come about?

I was at Spear Leeds at the time. I was trading the S&P 500 and getting a reputation of doing fairly well. Marty Schwartz was in the process of moving from New York to Florida and solicited me to come work for him. I knew of Marty from your book *Market Wizards* and thought it would be a privilege to work for him. I went to my boss, Peter Kellogg, and told him that I had an offer to work for Marty Schwartz in Florida.

---

[2]Marty Schwartz is a trader I interviewed in *Market Wizards* (New York: New York Institute of Finance, 1989).

Peter knew Marty and told me, "You can try it out, but no one can last very long with Marty. I'm going to do you a favor. I am going to keep you on the payroll."

Schwartz had a reputation for holding on to employees only briefly, either because he fired them or they quit. Benedict, who worked for Schwartz for several months, may have been one of his longest-term hires. Ironically, I visited Schwartz—the first time I had seen him since our original interview—on the same trip on which I interviewed Benedict. When I mentioned Benedict, he literally shuddered. His comments regarding Benedict, which I will not repeat here, were uniformly negative. Benedict's portrayal of Schwartz was equally unflattering, although he did credit Schwartz with paying for his relocation and acknowledged his phenomenal skill as a trader.

What did you learn from Schwartz?

Don't average losing trades. Be smaller than you need to be. Take profits.

What happened after your brief stint of working for Schwartz?

I went back to Spear Leeds. Peter Kellogg, who had warned me that I wouldn't last with Schwartz, liked me and gave me the opportunity to set up a Spear Leeds office in South Florida with another partner. We set up an operation with multiple managers trading different market groups. I directly traded a global macro portfolio and also oversaw the other traders.

Why did you leave Spear Leeds?

In 2000, Spear Leeds was bought out by Goldman Sachs. Goldman didn't want an operation in Florida and asked me to come back to New York. I loved it down here and had no desire to go back to a suit-and-tie world. Steven Schonfeld of Schonfeld Securities offered me an opportunity to run a managed account for him. That is when I set up Banyan.

What was your experience during 9/11?

9/11 was a major learning experience for me. That morning I got a call from the broker covering me at Goldman Sachs. He said, "There is a plane sticking out of the World Trade Center." I didn't know what was going on, but I figured it can't be good. My immediate response was to start selling futures.

Was the market selling off at the time?

Not at that point. I don't know if you remember, but the market was very strong going into 9/11. The crash hadn't hit the news yet. Then when the initial story came across the tape, it said that a small plane had hit the World Trade Center. The market actually went up. At the time, I had no idea what was really going on, but I thought it was ridiculous that the market was rallying, so I sold more.

The market went up after the news first came out?

Yes, go look at the chart. All of a sudden, the second plane hit the World Trade Center. The stock market hadn't opened yet, but the futures were trading. The market started dropping hard. I had the broker on the phone, and I told him, "I don't know what's going on, but I'm leaving and going to pick up my kids at school. Just sell me out of everything."

Why were you leaving?

I just wanted to get my kids. They were showing the planes hitting in New York and Washington.

But you were in Florida. What were they going to do—take out Palm Beach?

I agree. But what was going on was crazy, and I just wanted to be with my family.

Why did you liquidate your position before you left?

I didn't want to capitalize on people's misfortune. I felt weird having that short position. I still made a large profit on the day trade, but I left most of the money on the table relative to where the market traded when it reopened the following week. When the market reopened, I decided to be Mr. Patriotic. At the same time everyone else was selling, I was buying stocks and futures. Very quickly, I lost all the profit I had made on the 9/11 trades and then some.

You said that 9/11 was a major learning experience. In what way?

I learned that you can't be emotional in this business. It's a business and nothing else. Going long when the market reopened was a purely emotional trade.

Do you think that your going long when the market reopened was influenced by guilt at having made money on 9/11 by being short?

Maybe. I never thought about it that way. I don't want to make excuses.

Actually, you were cheering for one side, which is a lethal mistake for a trader. As you know, you have to be neutral in this game. Your story reminds me of Ed Seykota's provocative observation in the first *Market Wizards* book: "Everybody gets what they want out of the market." Putting it into context of your experience on 9/11, you wanted to not feel guilty about having made money being short on 9/11, and by losing it all by being long when the market reopened, that's exactly what you got.

You have seen a lot of traders both on the floor and off the floor. What are some common mistakes traders make?

One big mistake is averaging losing trades. Trading is very hard, but it is also easy if you maintain discipline. People blow up because they lose their discipline.

I originally met with Benedict in late 2010. I called him in July 2011 for a midyear update.

I've had a very bad year. We're down almost 3 percent, and I'm trading smaller.

Well, that's consistent with your risk discipline. I guess it's probably a good thing that you are trading smaller or else you would have been down more.

Absolutely, but one of the hard things about managing client money is that although I am very patient, the clients aren't very patient. One of my problems is that I want to make everyone happy.

I'll give you some advice: You always have to manage money for yourself, not your clients. Once you start adjusting your trading to fit what your investors want, you are in trouble. I've talked to a lot of managers who made that mistake.

After rereading the chapter, I felt that a key question had still not been satisfactorily answered. I called Benedict again in October 2011 with some follow-up questions.

One key question I still have is: What changed when you went from being a losing trader to a consistently winning one? Where was your edge coming from?

I learned to pay attention to how markets moved relative to each other. I became a correlation trader—the same thing I still do today.

Can you provide some examples to illustrate how you trade markets against each other?

My problem is that I could never teach my kids or friends what I do because it is so innate. I am constantly trading. It's not like there is one type of trade or even a few specific trades. I trade off of correlations, but I don't constantly trade the same way. I am sensitive to when the correlations are working and when they are not working. So a trade might work in one time frame, but not in another, and I am constantly adapting.

As soon as I put on a position, I immediately start looking for a trade that would be the best offsetting hedge. Say I go long the S&P, I would be looking at my 10 screens for the best hedge. It might be selling another index, or selling a deep-in-the-money call, or selling an out-of-the-money call, or buying bonds (when it is inversely correlated), or taking an inversely correlated position in the euro. And sometimes, I will not put on any offsetting trade, but just use a stop on the position.

But how do you decide which is the best hedge?

By watching the market movements. For example, right now the S&P is trading at 1227, and the bonds are coming off a bit, which tells me that the S&P should probably hold here and start to rally. If I buy it, and it doesn't rally, I would look to buy bonds against it.

Why would that be better than just getting out of the S&P?

This is where the correlation comes into play. The last time the S&P was trading at 1,227, the bonds were 25 bid, and now they are 20 bid. Usually, when the bonds go down, the S&P goes up. So the S&P should hold here, and if it doesn't, then the bonds should rally. I think I could buy the S&P here and buy the bonds and make money.

Do you have a current directional bias in the S&P?

I'm very bearish.

Why?

Because I don't think the European situation is going to end well [reference to the debt crisis of the weaker European countries], and they are bidding up the market expecting some grand solution that is probably not going to happen. But again, that is not what I do. I don't make major directional bets. I am a very opinionated guy, but for the first five years of the business, my opinion did nothing but lose me money. So I have to leave my opinions at the door. I think the market is going to eventually crash, but I have to stay in business, and I can't make that bet.

Did you have a position coming into the day?

I was modestly net long.

Why net long if you're bearish?

I came in long because today was option expiration day, and 85 percent of the time, they mark up the market on the morning of option expiration day. It has been going on for 25 years.

Can we go back to the S&P and bond example?

Okay, right now, the bonds are still at 20 bid and the S&P is bid $.75 higher. That move is equal to about 3/32 in the bonds, given that my bond position is about one-third the size of my S&P position. I could take profits on the S&P, put a stop in three ticks lower on the bonds, and if I'm not stopped out, take profits three ticks higher. The worst I would do is approximately break even, and if the bonds move up three ticks, I'll make money on both sides. It is that simple. I do lots of these trades every day. Sometimes my positions are big; sometimes they are small. Whether they are big or small depends primarily on how I am doing for the month and what our P&L is for the year to date.

Since you don't trade on your longer-term directional views, how do you decide whether you want to be long or short the S&P?

I try to look at anything the market thinks is important at the moment. Right now, I'm looking at financial stocks in the U.S. and Europe as well as European markets in general because those are the key factors that are driving the current market. I am sure a year from now, I will be looking at completely different things. A year ago, everything was China; now China is irrelevant. So that clue doesn't work anymore.

Why do you think you have been successful whereas so many other traders fail?

Since I started in the business, I have seen a number of traders who ended up committing suicide or being homeless. The one trait they all shared was that they had a gambler's mentality. When they were losing, they were always looking for that one trade that would make it all back. I learned early on that you can't do that. This is a business where you have to work. That is what I do. Every day I make hundreds of transactions. I grind out the returns. If you look at my daily returns, you will see there are very few big up days.

■ ■ ■

The essence of Benedict's approach is that he looks at markets in context of the price action in other markets, rather than in isolation. Markets are correlated, but these correlations come and go and can change radically over time. There are times when the S&P and T-bonds will move in the same direction, and times when they will move in opposite directions. There are times when the S&P 500 will follow crude oil prices, and times when the stock market ignores crude oil prices. Benedict is intently watching these intermarket relationships, not merely day by day, but minute by minute. At any given time, the price action in a market may be highly influenced (directly or inversely) by the price action of another market or several other markets.

Knowing the prevailing correlations is only the start. There is no rulebook as to what trades to do when a correlated market has a price move. Sometimes, the trade will be to anticipate a lagged response; sometimes the failure for a market to respond as expected may signal inherent market strength or weakness. Frequently, the implied trade may be to trade one correlated market versus another. For example, if two markets are positively correlated, Benedict may short the market that seems overextended, using a long in the correlated market as a hedge. The timing of such paired long and short positions will not necessarily be simultaneous, either on entry or exit, and will depend on the prevailing price levels of each market relative to its expected range.

In short, to say that Benedict uses market correlations as a key input is only the beginning. The selection and implementation of actual trades will be highly variable, depending on multiple considerations and past experience. The process is entirely discretionary, rather than formulaic.

The relevant lesson for traders is that the price action of other markets can contain useful information—Benedict's track record stands as a testament to this proposition. How this information can be used, however, must be discovered and developed by each individual trader based on personal observation and trading style. The message for traders is to be cognizant of how markets move relative to each other and to determine whether this source of observation can lead to useful trading ideas.

Benedict serves as a model for extreme risk management. There are two key aspects of Benedict's risk management approach. First, he limits portfolio risk to a small fixed amount (2.0 to 2.5 percent) before he responds with actions to mitigate further losses. Second, when this small drawdown threshold is approached, he reduces his position size and continues to trade smaller until he begins to be profitable again. A 2.5 percent portfolio risk level may be overly restrictive for many traders, but the key concept of setting a predefined loss point at which risk exposure is significantly reduced has widespread applicability. Also, reducing exposure when trading is not going well—an inherent component in Benedict's risk management approach—is generally a wise action for discretionary traders. (For systematic traders, however, reducing exposure after losses may lead to poor timing of position sizing.) The type of rigorous risk control practiced by Benedict may be as difficult for most traders to follow as the Ornish diet is for those trying to lose weight, but it can certainly be highly effective in avoiding significant losses.

Mark Rossano, who was given a small portfolio to manage while he was an intern at Banyan Capital, recalls Benedict's obsession with risk management, saying, "The biggest principle Larry pushes is that you are not a trader; you are a risk manager." He recounts Benedict's advice on risk control: "Never stay in a losing trade because you think it will come back. Minimize the loss. Accept the loss and walk away from it. The worst thing any trader can do is freeze. You need to know how you will respond in any situation. How are you going to not lose money while making money? How are you going to get out of your losers? How are you going to keep your winners from turning into losers?"

Trades should be motivated by opportunity. Traders should caution against trading out of a desire to make money. In late 2010, Benedict pushed to reach his target for a minimum annual return. By doing marginal trades he would not otherwise have taken, he only succeeded in falling further short of his target.

Chapter 4

Scott Ramsey

Low-Risk Futures Trader

I don't think I have ever been to a more unusual location for a hedge fund office—although the manager I had visited years ago located above a urology office in Brooklyn, New York, is probably a close second. To begin, Ramsey manages his fund from that hotbed of hedge fund activity—St. Croix, U.S. Virgin Islands. If I had been driven to Ramsey's office by a taxi, I would have sworn the driver had made a mistake or that I had incorrectly copied the address. But I had been picked up at my hotel by one of Ramsey's employees, so clearly I was in the right place. I stepped out of the car and gazed around the small shopping center. No building even remotely suggested the presence of office space. Ramsey's assistant led me into Gallows Bay Hardware and up the stairs. This was the location of Ramsey's trading firm, Denali Asset Management—an incongruous name for a firm located on a Caribbean island.

The location of his office is not the only unorthodox thing about Scott Ramsey. He dropped out of college with a near-perfect GPA and only nine credits short of a degree to pursue a career in futures trading. Although it is a decision that seems bafflingly irrational to me, give credit to Ramsey for knowing exactly what he wanted to do, and as he says, "It turned out okay."

Ramsey trades the highly liquid futures and foreign exchange (FX) markets. Although the majority of Commodity Trading Advisors (CTAs)[1] use a systematic approach, Ramsey is strictly a discretionary trader. He also differs from most CTAs by incorporating fundamentals into his decision-making process. Ramsey begins by establishing a broad fundamental macro view that determines his directional bias in each market. Once this bias is established, he will seek to go short the weakest market in a sector if he is bearish or long the strongest market if he is bullish, using technical analysis to time trade entry and position adjustments. Ramsey will score his best returns when he gets the fundamentals right, but even when he is wrong, his rigorous risk control keeps losses relatively small.

Ramsey's 11-year track record is better than that of many of the largest and best-known futures managers. He has never had a down year, and has been able to combine a solid 17.2 percent average annual compounded net return (25.7 percent gross) with relatively low volatility and moderate drawdowns. Return alone is a highly inadequate metric for a futures manager because it is so dependent on the exposure level chosen by the manager. Futures managers always use only a fraction of assets under management to meet margin requirements. Therefore, any futures manager can double returns by simply doubling exposure without any need for borrowing. High return could just as

---

[1]The term *Commodity Trading Advisor* is the official designation for managers registered with the Commodity Futures Trading Commission (CFTC) and members of the National Futures Association (NFA), and is a misnomer on at least two counts: (1) A CTA is a fund or account manager with direct investment responsibility and not an advisor as the name appears to suggest. (2) CTAs do not necessarily trade only commodities as the name implies. The vast majority of CTAs also trade futures contracts in one or more financial sectors including stock indexes, fixed-income, and FX. And, ironically, many CTAs do not trade any commodities at all, but trade only financial futures.

easily represent excessive risk-taking rather than manager skill. Consequently, in evaluating futures managers, the only meaningful metric is return/risk.[2] Ramsey achieved his returns with well below average risk statistics. The annualized standard deviation has been 11.7 percent, less than two-thirds of the net return level. The maximum drawdown has been less than 11 percent. Ramsey's Gain to Pain ratio is a very high 2.2. (See Appendix A for a detailed explanation of the Gain to Pain ratio.)

Ramsey is 53, but looks a decade younger. Clearly, if trading provides any stress, it certainly doesn't show. Ramsey was quite relaxed during our interview, as perhaps fitting for a manager domiciled on St. Croix. After the interview, we picked up my wife, Jo Ann, at the hotel, and Ramsey took us out to dinner at an incredibly good local restaurant (Bacchus— check it out if you are ever in Christiansted), which served the best sashimi dish I've ever had (presented on a block of salt) and had an extraordinary collection of Belgian beers.

■ ■ ■

When did you first become aware of markets?

I was a mechanical engineering student at the University of Missouri. My father had always pushed me to take some business classes. So, in my junior year, as an elective, I took an economics course. It changed my life. In engineering, there is always a right answer. All of a sudden, I am faced with economics where there are all these shades of gray. I was fascinated by it. Our economics professor suggested that we subscribe to the *Wall Street Journal*, which I did. Every day I would see these ads for precious metals and energy. This was in the late 1970s, when inflation was in double digits. At the time, my money was in a savings account earning the minimum interest rate, which was much less than the rate of inflation. I thought I should check into buying metals. So I responded to one of the ads in the *Wall Street Journal* and bought gold, silver, and copper.

---

[2]I would argue that return/risk is a more meaningful metric than return for other strategies as well, but for futures trading this contention is a statement of fact rather than opinion.

Were these futures you bought?

No, it was over-the-counter metals. I opened an account with First Commodity Corp of Boston (FCCB), which charged an exorbitant commission rate. I'm not proud of that decision, but I guess it shows I was a sucker for their marketing. I believe the CFTC shut them down for improper disclosures.

Why didn't you buy futures instead?

I was a novice. I didn't know about futures. This was my entrée into buying metals.

How did you know what the prices were since you weren't going through an organized market?

The prices were pegged off the futures market.

So you bought and sold at a futures linked price, but they charged you an exorbitant commission. I don't get it.

The way it worked was that FCCB charged you a flat fee of $1,200 per market, and then you could buy and sell as much as you wanted in that market for six months. But they would try to get you to trade in another market, so they could charge you another $1,200. If you were trading silver, they would try to talk you into doing a trade in copper.

But since the prices were pegged to futures, didn't you think of just going directly to futures?

That is what I eventually ended up doing. By the time I was a senior, I had a quote screen in my apartment. But, at this point, I had already paid the flat fee for trading for six months. I was trading the markets pretty actively. At one point, I was up over $10,000, which was an incredible amount to me. At the time, you could have bought two cars for that amount of money. I couldn't believe how easy it was to make money. You just bought something, and it went up. This was in 1979 when commodities were going ballistic.

On what basis were you making your trading decisions?

I really had no idea what I was doing. I would buy something, and when it went up, I would sell it. I was making money because I was buying in a rising market. I can actually say that I bought silver at $50, which is right near the all-time high. Then Volcker raised interest rates sharply to fight inflation and, on top of that, the exchange raised silver margins. Shortly afterwards, silver prices collapsed. The market went into a string of limit down days.[3] I couldn't do anything. I felt helpless, stupid, and powerless. Silver fell all the way down to $26 before it started trading. It was a gut-wrenching experience.

Did you get out as soon as it started trading?

The first day it traded, I got out. I lost all the money I had made plus some of the money I started with.

Did you stop trading after the big silver loss?

I took some time to reassess the situation. I read a lot of books on speculation. I had enough money left over to start trading futures. I hit it off well with a broker and opened an account with him. Much to my surprise as soon as I opened the account, I was assigned to another broker that actually traded the account. The broker I liked was just a marketing guy. Anyway, the next thing I knew I was long sugar, corn spreads, and other trades. He was a churn 'em and burn 'em broker. That account didn't last long.

Then I opened an account at the local Heinhold commodity branch in Columbia, Missouri. I think I only had a few thousand left. This time around, I was doing all the trading myself. A couple of friends gave me

---

[3]Commodity futures markets have a specified maximum amount the price can move on any given day—that is, the daily limit. In markets where the natural clearing price, or cash price, is below the daily limit, the market will open up limit down and not trade. Although there are lots of willing sellers, no one is willing to buy at a price that is above the cash market price. The market will remain "locked" limit down until the futures price reaches the cash market price. The episode Ramsey is referring to represents the longest string of consecutive limit down days that has ever occurred in any futures market.

some money, and I leased a quote terminal for my apartment. I spent many days watching every tick in certain markets and doing point and figure charts, in addition to my daily charts, instead of attending class. The results weren't so good. I made every rookie mistake in the books. Rather than taking the easy route and trading with the trend, I was trying to pick tops and bottoms, and I sat with losers and took small profits.

Losing money is what got me hooked. I had heard that allegedly 90 percent of the traders in the futures markets lost money, but I was determined to be in the 10 percent. I was an excellent student, easily in the top 10 percent, and I often set the curve on exams. Whenever I took a test, my attitude was that someone had to make the highest grade on the curve, and that it might as well be me. And it often was. So being in the 90 percent that lost money in trading was not acceptable. I didn't graduate college because I became so engrossed in futures trading that I had no interest in engineering anymore.

At what point did you drop out?

In my senior year. I had nine credits left to finish.

I find that hard to understand. It seems like it would have been such a trivial matter to finish college.

I am not saying I did the right thing, although in retrospect, it turned out okay.

Do you ever regret coming so close to graduating college and not finishing?

I never look back, although sometimes it can be embarrassing. Whenever prospective investors conduct their due diligence and ask where I graduated, I have to explain that I went to college for four years and had a high 3.9 GPA, but didn't graduate.

What was your plan?

My plan was to go to Chicago, start in the pits, and learn how this business worked from the bottom up. I initially got a job as a phone clerk at the

Chicago Mercantile Exchange. After a few months, it became apparent that there was no future on the floor unless you were in the pits. I got a job as a commodity broker.

Was sales something that you wanted to do?

No, it certainly wasn't my passion. I hated cold calling. What I wanted to do was trade. The broker job was a means to an end. It kept me involved in the markets. I remember my first month's check was $43. To this day, I wish I had framed that check, but at the time, I really needed the $43.

Were you giving your clients recommendations?

Yes. It was all based on technicals. At the time, I knew nothing about fundamentals.

What kind of technical analysis?

It was just the basic stuff: chart patterns and moving averages. The first book I had read on trading futures was John Murphy's book on technical analysis.[4]

How did your clients do?

They didn't make much money, but they didn't lose, either. I was able to keep them alive.

Well, that's actually better than most brokers, especially at the high commission levels of those days. How did you get them out of trades when you were wrong?

I used stops.

Did you always have stops in place?

I always had stops.

---

[4]John Murphy, *Technical Analysis of the Futures Markets* (New York: New York Institute of Finance, 1986).

How did you learn to do that?

One of the first books I read emphasized the importance of cutting your losses and letting your profits run.

Did any of your prior experience reinforce this basic concept?

During my senior year when I was trading futures from my apartment, I went long T-bills. The market was under steady pressure because Volcker was raising interest rates. At the time, I wasn't using stops. Every day, the position would go against me, but it would be by only about three ticks. I thought it was no big deal; three ticks is only $75 a contract. The next day the market would be down another two or three ticks. It was a small bit of pain, but not enough to get me out. After a few weeks, what should have been a 10-tick loss ended up being a 50-tick loss, and suddenly it was real money. I realized there was no reason for letting what should have been a small loss turn into a big loss.

I learned to trade first with my own money, which didn't work out that well, and then by advising clients as a commodity broker and doing okay. Then in 1982, I leased a seat on the IMM and went down to trade from the floor.

You gave up sales?

No. I teamed up with the broker in the office who had helped me get the job as a broker with the firm. We pooled our clients. I wanted to trade from the floor, and he stayed in the office.

How was your being on the floor going to be beneficial?

I thought that having information about who was doing what would be very helpful.

But in the office, you had the screens, which you didn't have on the floor. Wouldn't giving up the screens have been a disadvantage?

Good question. It turned out that it was. It was like putting blinders on. I learned to trade on a Quotron where I could see prices changing in all the markets. When I was in the pit, all I could see was what was going on in that one market. I couldn't feel what the other external influences were on that market. I had become used to seeing all the markets trade and observing the relationships between their price movements. In fact, the relationship between price movements in different markets is a core part of my current trading strategy. I also very quickly learned that standing on my feet all day screaming wasn't the way I wanted to make a living.

Did having the who-is-doing-what information provide any compensating benefits?

When a guy comes in and sells a 100-lot, you don't know what it means.

But you thought that it might be helpful before you went down to the floor?

I thought that the information you would get in the pit would be the Holy Grail. I just didn't think it through. The reality is that you get almost no useful information.

So being on the floor turned out to be a disadvantage rather than an advantage.

It was a big disadvantage.

How long was it before you realized you made a mistake?

I stayed on the floor for six months. I wanted to give it the old college try.

You felt more comfortable upstairs?

I felt more comfortable being able to see more markets.

By more markets, do you mean charts or just the prices?

At that time, the screens just gave you quotes, not charts. I received a printed chart book each week, and updated the charts every day. I think that was a great process. It made me pay attention to every market, every day. I did that for over 10 years. Even when we got CQG screens, which had graphics, I still continued to update my printed charts manually for a long time. It was a daily routine of looking at each chart and thinking about what the patterns were telling you. I would even turn the charts upside down to see whether the pattern looked different to me. Over time, it helped me develop a sense of pattern recognition.

Were you trading your own account when you were a broker?

I had been trading my own account all along.

How did you do?

I did fine. I made money virtually every year, but I didn't make a lot of money. One thing I did wrong was that I thought only technical factors were important and that fundamentals didn't matter. The other thing I did wrong was that every time I made money, I would pull it out. So instead of increasing my size over time, I stayed a one- and two-lot trader. I never really tried pushing myself. The evolution of a trader is when you start letting your money work for you and increasing your size.

What did you learn as a broker that allowed you to go from a string of early losses to making money almost every year?

Being a broker provided an excellent vantage point. By observing retail clients, I learned a lot about what not to do, like taking small profits and letting losses run—a lesson that I had also learned from my trading days in college. I learned about the psychology of the markets and how certain traders were surprisingly accurate at picking tops and bottoms— the wrong way—based on emotional decisions and market activity rather than technical or fundamental analysis. I learned the value of the classic "buy the rumor, sell the facts" kind of trading because it put you on the opposite side of retail buying. I also noted how the most obvious technical patterns were often the ones that didn't work. I still look for those trades today; the more obvious they are from a chart standpoint, and the more the opposite position makes sense from a fundamental standpoint, the more interested I am if the pattern fails. So, while I try to keep emotions out of my trading, which is the real challenge, I try to imagine how the guy who took the textbook trade and is losing money feels. Where will he finally capitulate? Is this the start of a big move the other way?

When did you go from being a broker to managing money?

The first step came in 1993 when one of my clients, who was a professional trader, asked me to manage $100,000 for him. I knew what it was like to trade my own money, but I didn't know what it was like to have power of attorney over someone else's money. I told him, "We're friends, and if I lose your money, I don't want it to affect our relationship." He said, "Scott, I give money to other people to manage; it's what I do. I think you have good ideas in the market. I want you to trade this account for me." I had decided that I would manage his money and my money for one year, and at the end of the year, if it worked out, I would register as a CTA and try to get other accounts.

And did you?

Yes, I started the CTA one year later.

How did you do?

I did okay, but not great. What was killing me in the process was that the brokerage firms who directed business to CTAs would set the commission rates. In my own account, I was trading at a $12 commission rate, which by today's standards is insanely expensive, but back then was a good rate. My customers were trading at a $50 commission rate, or even higher. So I had to trade my CTA accounts different from my own account because if I traded them at the same level, it would be churning. I might be up in my own account, while at the same time, the CTA accounts could be down. That disparity really bothered me and ultimately drove me to the decision that I had to manage money in a fund.

So your performance as a CTA prior to starting the fund was dragged down by high commissions. If you had been paying the lower commissions charged in the fund you subsequently started, would your performance in your early years as a CTA have been more in line with the fund performance levels?

No, because the performance difference was not only due to the disparity in commission rates. In order to avoid an excessive commission burden on the client managed accounts, I took only about one-quarter of the trades that I did in my own account. Ultimately, I decided to switch to a fund structure, not only to control costs, but also to assure that my investors' accounts were traded the exact same way as my own account. In 2000, I started the fund.

Did your methodology evolve over time?

It did. In my early years in the business, I was able to trade the markets technically and make money, while keeping my drawdowns very manageable. But I wasn't making the big money. I thought about what was holding me back. The lightbulb that clicked on for me was the realization that I had to also embrace fundamentals. That insight brought me back to my original interest in economics.

When did this transition occur?

In the 1990s, after I became a CTA. I remember one of my biggest trades. At the time, there was a general consensus that government borrowing was going to crowd out private borrowing, which it was expected would be very bearish for the bond market. I was reading all these bearish articles on the bond market, but I was looking at the market, and it wasn't going down. I thought, *Wait a minute. If everyone thinks this way, and it seems so logical, then if the market goes the other way, everyone is going to be wrong, and they will have to cover their shorts. That's your trade.* From that point on, it became a matter of not only looking at prices on a chart, but also thinking about why prices were where they were, how people were positioned, and the psychology of the market. You have to try to understand what people are thinking. I began to look at the market from the perspective of other traders. What would I be feeling if I were short bonds, thinking I had this great trade, and seeing the market go against me? That line of thinking led me to take the opposite position, long bonds, which turned out to be a huge winning trade.

Ironically, the way you incorporated fundamentals in that example was in a totally contrarian manner. You weren't using fundamentals to forecast a market direction. Instead, you were looking at the fundamentals that everyone else perceived and observing that the market was going the other way. Is that the standard way you use fundamentals?

The reality is that I'm not being paid to be right; I am being paid to make money. You have to have a degree of flexibility. Whenever I talk to investors, I make it clear to them that whatever I say today about the markets may or may not reflect the positions I have tomorrow or the next day. I recently reviewed a presentation I gave about six months ago, and I realized that everything I had predicted didn't happen—and yet, I made money in almost every month since then.

Can you give me some specific examples of how incorporating fundamentals improved your trading?

The major trade was long bonds, which coincided with the start of the fund in 2000. At the time, we had seen a long period of stock speculation. I thought that economic conditions couldn't get any better.[5] Anyone who had a pulse had a job, equity markets were at their highs, and yet we were not generating any inflation. If we were not generating inflation under those conditions, then what would happen if we started to slow at the margins? I was so focused on the long fixed-income trade that for the first three or four years of the fund, probably two-thirds of the trades were in fixed-income.

Was it the topping of the equity market in early 2000 that got you long in fixed-income?

The break in equities was definitely the catalyst for the fixed-income trade, but the trade was going to happen anyway. I use the fundamentals

---

[5]Strong economic conditions are bearish for bonds because they lead to higher interest rates.

to have a directional bias, and I use the technicals to confirm that bias. Once I had the catalyst, I could say that yields should never again see their previous high. I could then decide what I was willing to risk, and let the market work. I was long for years, but I traded around the position. Nothing goes in a straight line. I added on weakness and lightened up on strength.

What is a recent example of fundamentals influencing a trade?

Just last week, we had the European Central Bank bailing out Ireland, and boom, the next day, the DAX [German stock index] is at a new high, the TSE [Canadian stock index] is at a new high, and the S&P and Nasdaq are at new highs.

And what does that tell you?

It tells me that it is risk on for now. Otherwise, all these markets wouldn't be making new highs a few days after a crisis. They might rebound, but they wouldn't go to new highs. Think of taking a volleyball and pushing it underwater—that is your crisis event. Then you let go—the event dissipates—and the ball goes popping out of the water. That is exactly what we just experienced in the markets. Today, we had a terrible unemployment report, and yet the equity markets closed higher. The equity market's repeated resilience in the face of negative news items tells me that it wants to go higher. Chaos creates opportunity. We learn so much about the markets when we have crisis events.

We learn from how the markets respond?

Yes. There are simple things you can do. You can calculate in percentage terms how much each market responds to a crisis event. You can then rank the markets from strongest to weakest.

Is that what you do?

Absolutely. Just a simple exercise of measuring which markets were the strongest during a crisis can tell you which markets are likely to be the leaders when the pressure is off—the markets that will be the ball popping out of the water. For example, crude made a low early in the month, and on the crisis in Ireland, it didn't even retest that low. Then, as soon as the pressure was off, crude was $5 higher. Conversely, the markets that were weakest should be the markets that rally the least and the first ones to roll over on a general continued decline.

Is that how you pick your longs and shorts?

I always want to buy the strongest and sell the weakest. Always.

If you believe that all the markets in a sector are going higher, will you only be long the market you expect to be the strongest in that sector?

Yes, I want to be long only the market that is acting the best. The market that gets dragged up by a related market may even be a good short. Sometimes I will place a sell stop in a market that gets dragged up so that if it rolls over and starts going down, it will trigger a short position. Frequently, that market will continue to go down and go back to where it should be, while the leading market hardly corrects.

How long have the markets been in this highly correlated state?

We have been in an extremely correlated state since the 2008 financial crisis. I believe that the dog is stocks and the tail is everything else.

In general, or just recently?

Stocks rule, especially in the last few years. You better know which direction equities are going and watch how that influences other markets. Let's say in one week, equities go up and commodities go up. That makes sense and is what you would expect. But then assume that in the following week, equities continue to rise, but commodities stall. Then, all else being equal, you better be very suspect of your long commodity positions.

As an engineering student, you would seem a natural for developing a systemized approach; yet, you developed into a strictly discretionary trader. Why do you think that is?

It just fit my personality. I enjoyed the observation part of it. I am the guy who sits in front of the screen every trading day of the year and watches all the markets change. That is just what works for me. You're seeing things, and the wheels of your subconscious are spinning. Whether you recognize it right away or not, your mind is working out these patterns for you. Trading gets so ingrained in your psyche that it becomes second nature like driving a car. Sometimes you look at a chart and just know what to do without thinking about it.

How much do you risk on a single trade?

Typically, about 10 basis points of assets under management, but I may get out even more quickly. Some people can put on a trade, risk some specified percentage loss, and then give it months to work. I can't do that. If I put on a trade today, and it's not working by the end of the day, I'm out. I don't want to take any more risk. I might get back into it tomorrow at a worse price, but that is a premium I'm willing to pay to see the market acting the way I think it should be.

Do you literally mean to imply that if you are behind on a trade the first day, you get out?

Yes, 90 percent of the time. That's my personality. I am a chicken when it comes to taking risks.

If you get out if you are behind on the first day, presumably, you would also get out if you were behind on the trade on any subsequent day. Using such a tight exit condition, it sounds like you would be stopped out of a large percentage of your trades.

I might lose 10 times on an idea, until the 11th time when it works. If I then get the move I thought I was going to get, it will then more than make up for all the little losses. To me, the most important thing is to control the downside. Rigorous risk control is not only important in keeping losses small, but it also impacts profit potential. You have to put yourself in the position to be able to take advantage of opportunities. The only way you can do that is to have a clear mind. If you have trades that are not working, and your mental energy is going toward damage control, you can't think clearly about opportunities in the market.

What was your worst month?

I lost 10 percent in October 2003.

How is that possible given that you are only risking 10 basis points on each trade?

For me to be down 10 percent from a standing start would be a death by 1,000 cuts. But the drawdown on a trade can be much larger than the original risk if there is a large open profit. The 10 percent loss month followed a 10 percent gain in the previous month. I was long fixed income big-time, and the unemployment report was extremely positive. It led to a giant reversal. But I had made 200 percent over the course of the prior few years trading this one theme. That reversal turned out to be the end of the theme. If I look back, would I be willing to do the same thing again? Sure I would; I would be happy to have a huge run and give back 10 percent. I had a lot of risk on because I was being paid to take risk. I can get hit when I have been getting paid, but it is hard for me to get hit from a standing start. That is the key.

If you don't have any positions with large open profits, what would be a really bad month for you?

A 2 percent or 3 percent loss.

Besides looking at charts and chart patterns, do you use any technical indicators?

I use the Relative Strength Index (RSI), but not as an overbought/oversold indicator; instead, I look for divergences between the RSI and price. I look at the 200-day moving average and Fibonacci retracements. If the market sells off to the 200-day moving average and I'm short, I may be inclined to take the money off the table and watch how the market reacts. I particularly like to get combined signals, such as the price approaching the 200-day moving average and a 50 percent retracement. I'll pay a lot of attention to that type of indicator combination.

What personal characteristics do you think were instrumental to your being successful as a trader?

Discipline.

Have you had any lapses in discipline?

In the early days, sure, but I haven't taken a real hit for a very long time. I am very disciplined with my stops. If there is one principle that you cannot violate, it is: Know what you can lose.

Are there mistakes you have made that were learning experiences in terms of avoiding similar losses in the future?

I got involved in trading over-the-counter fixed-income. Call it style drift; call it whatever. When 2008 hit, the dealers wouldn't make a market on these things. I would have been up 26 percent for the year instead of 19 percent if it weren't for these trades. I will never again trade a market where liquidity is at the whim of a dealer.

Why with so many interest rate futures markets would you have a need to go to the over-the-counter market?

Good question, thank you. I thought the trade made sense.

But couldn't you express the same trade in futures?

It was a convergence trade involving Muni bonds, so I couldn't actually replicate it in futures. What I found was that there are such great benefits to trading in exchange-traded markets or the interbank market that giving up those benefits is just not worth it. Lower liquidity doesn't work with my style. I need to be able to stop myself out in 10 basis points if I want to.

Did you ever think you were wrong on a trade, but still had trouble liquidating it?

My failsafe is that I always have a stop in the market. Sometimes, though, my intuition tells me that I should get out right away, but

I don't do anything, hoping my stop won't be hit. Then sure enough, I end up getting stopped out. My misplaced hope and my desire to still be right sometimes cause my losses to be greater than they need to be. Hope is the worst four-letter word for a trader.

Do you think intuition is important to trading?

It is very important. I think intuition is a subconscious skill you develop over time.

How do you handle a losing streak?

I believe that you should always be swinging the bat. The question is when do you choke up on the bat. When I am in a drawdown, I will choke up on the bat—I reduce my position size. When I am more attuned to the market and playing with market money, I will increase my position size. But I never stop trading. In 30 years of trading, I bet you could count on one hand the times I have been completely flat.

How do you manage that and still take vacations?

I always time my travel for when the markets are closed. I still follow the markets when I am on vacation. I might trade in the morning and ski in the afternoon. Although this is not necessarily a good thing, I even get up several times every night to check the markets.

Do you set your clock or do you wake up naturally?

I wake up naturally. Sometimes I see something and realize that I have to respond immediately, and I have to get out of bed. Sometimes, however, waking up to look at the markets works with my subconscious. Some of my best trades have come from looking at the quotes on my iPhone when I wake up at night and thinking, *This doesn't look right*, and then going back to sleep. Then I wake up the next morning, and I realize that I shouldn't be in a certain trade. For example, I might think, *U.S. equities were strong, and the yen was down. The Nikkei should have been higher last night, and it didn't go up. Something is wrong; I should be short.*

What do you think is the biggest mistake people make in the markets?

Looking to outside sources for guidance in their positions. The belief that you can watch CNBC and get useful advice is very misguided. You really have to formulate your own opinion and not rely on so-called experts.

Do you ever have friends ask you for advice on trading?

Yes, once in a while.

Well, what advice do you give them?

I tell them that it's not about being right; it's about making money. Taking a loss is part of the process. You will have some percentage of losses; you just need to make sure that your losses are smaller than your wins.

At one time, I experimented with hiring traders to work for me. I had a trader who when he got stopped out of some positions in the morning would say, "My whole day is ruined." I would reply, "What do you mean your day is ruined? You have all this opportunity sitting in front of you. The market doesn't care if you lost money on a trade. It doesn't matter. Think about your next trade. You have to get past the idea that just because you lost money on a trade, it means you failed. Every trading decision you make is subject to some randomness. It doesn't matter whether you win or lose on any individual trade, as long as you get the process correct."

What other advice do you give to friends who are aspiring traders?

You need incredible dedication. Trading is not a hobby. Treat trading like a business. Keep a journal of your trades. If you make a mistake in the markets, write it down.

About nine months later, I contacted Ramsey with a few follow-up questions.

Can you give me an actual example that illustrates your trade selection process?

The starting point is always some fundamental premise. Many investors viewed QE2 as "money printing"—a widespread perception that encouraged a shift of dollars into alternative assets including other currencies, gold, and equities.[6] I actually didn't share this view; I thought QE2 was nothing more than the Fed swapping a noninterest-bearing asset (cash) for an interest-bearing asset (a note or a bond) with the private sector. But my own views were irrelevant; it was the market perception that mattered. My expectation was that once QE2 ended, the shift of assets out of the dollar would also stop, and the dollar would recover.

Okay, so I thought the dollar should rally after QE2, but against what? I monitor at least 20 currencies against the dollar. I wanted to sell the first currency that weakened. If you think about it, under this condition of alleged "money printing," anything that can't rally against the dollar is really a bearish currency! The weak link turned out to be the Turkish lira, which was breaking out to a two-year low against the hated dollar.[7] If it couldn't rally versus the dollar when the Fed was "printing money" like crazy, what was it going to take?

Although I had a directional bias based on my view of the macro environment, I didn't take the trade until the lira broke out of its two-year trading range. The market had to prove itself before the trade was entered. If there had not been a breakout, there would not have been a trade.

But what about the tendency for markets to have false breakouts?

The key distinction here is that I had a fundamental reason to expect the breakout. The breakout approximately coincided with the end of QE2.

---

[6]QE2 was the Fed's second round of quantitative easing (buying longer-duration treasuries and other securities to lower longer-term rates) that began in November 2010 and ended in June 2011.

[7]In a Turkish lira/dollar chart, a new *low* in the lira would show up as a new *high*—that is, it would take more lira to buy each dollar.

Also I used a protective stop below a recent relative low[8]—a point I thought should not be reached if my trade premise was correct—to limit my losses if I was wrong.

Can you give me another example of a trade that illustrates your approach?

In 2011, gold managed to rally over $500/oz., while platinum was barely able to gain $100/oz. Therefore as a trader, if my directional bias is long, I want to buy gold, and if my bias is short, then platinum stands out as the best vehicle for the trade. Novice speculators, however, would tend to do the exact opposite: They would buy platinum as a proxy for gold because "it hasn't yet made the move." Whatever the reason, the point is that many traders buy platinum because they are bullish gold. Buying a laggard as a proxy for a leader is a bad idea, and as a trader, I am keen to take the other side of such a trade when I see a potential setup.

In mid-August [2011] gold surged to over $1,900, a new all-time high. Platinum only managed to retest the high end of its trading range. Both markets were seriously overbought, sentiment was extreme, and there were price divergences. All of these considerations suggested that the precious metals markets were vulnerable to a steep correction. And sure enough, over the course of three days, gold corrected over $200, and platinum fell hard as well. That was the test. In the aftermath, you find out what the markets are really made of. Gold subsequently recovered quickly, and over the next couple of weeks soared $220 to a new all-time high of $1,924. Platinum, however, rebounded by only about half this amount. Platinum seemed to be a train wreck waiting to happen. I felt that platinum should lead on the downside because it was the weakest link in the precious metals complex. My strategy was to sell platinum on a downside penetration of the reaction low that had formed following the break from the 2011 high and to add on a downside breakout of an extended trading range. The beauty of selling the weak link is that this market has already shown its reluctance to make new

---

[8]Ramsey is referring to the chart. So a relative low would represent a point of relative lira strength—that is a point at which it took less lira to buy one dollar than in prior or succeeding days.

highs. Therefore, I think the risk is the lowest, and sometimes the reward is also the highest.

These examples are very helpful. Can you give me one more?

My challenge is to pick up on the subtle nuances of the various markets and to anticipate changes or accelerations in trends. I've found that by observing how the markets relate to one another, you can often detect when patterns of behavior change. A change in behavior is usually a failure of one or more related markets to confirm an existing move and serves as a warning sign.

Since the 2008 financial crisis, market correlations have been extremely high. So high, in fact, that the media now simply refers to trading days as either "risk on" or "risk off." In my opinion, the driver is usually the equity market. The typical stimulus-response pattern is:

$$\text{Equities Up} = \text{Commodities Up} = \text{Dollar Down}$$

The opposite price movements occur on "risk off" days. Furthermore, if commodities are up, then commodity currencies are up. These patterns have been unmistakable and consistent.

In mid-September [2011], however, this market behavior abruptly changed. Although stocks were closing at month-to-date highs, commodities were weaker, with the commodity index approaching year-to-date lows, and the dollar was stronger for the month. This counter-to-anticipated price action was huge! Copper, in particular, which is typically a leading indicator for the economy and commodity prices, was leading the way down, trading just above year-to-date lows, and clearly unable to benefit from the equity strength.

My strategy was simply to sell commodities and commodity currencies if they violated key technical levels—I used reaction lows and new month-to-date or year-to-date lows as the entry levels—and to risk recent reaction highs if filled. The beauty of this strategy is that if your trade entry point gets hit, you are selling the weakest markets first. They are showing that they are unable to rally in the current environment. Never sell the strongest markets until they fail.

■ ■ ■

An important lesson Ramsey provides is that even technically oriented traders—as Ramsey himself was in the early years of his career—can benefit greatly by incorporating a fundamental perspective. It is not a matter of performing any complex fundamental analysis to derive price projections, but rather a question of trying to understand the key fundamental drivers that are likely to determine the direction of the market. For example, by understanding that fundamentals were as negative as they could be for bonds at the start of 2000, Ramsey correctly assumed that bonds had very limited scope on the downside and that any weakening in the strong economy or the prevailing speculative fervor could set in motion a major bull market. As another example, Ramsey expected the end of QE2 to lead to a reversal from dollar weakness to dollar strength.

Once he has established a firm fundamental opinion, Ramsey utilizes technical analysis to confirm his anticipated scenario. Combining his technical methodology for entering and exiting trades with a strong fundamental directional bias provides Ramsey with a more effective trading approach than would be possible using technical analysis alone. The idea is to identify the big picture fundamental factors that are likely to drive the market in one direction and then to use technical analysis to trade in that direction.

Fundamentals can also be useful as a contrarian indicator. Ramsey will look for situations where there appears to be a predominant market perception that is being contradicted by the market action. Ramsey cites the example of a bond market where there was a lot of concern about government borrowing crowding out private borrowing, but interest rates failed to rise. In this context, a bearish fundamental factor had bullish price implications because of its failure to impact prices.

Ramsey will always buy the strongest market in a sector for long positions and sell the weakest market in a sector for short positions. Many novice traders make the error of doing the exact opposite. They will buy the laggards in a sector on the typically mistaken assumption that those markets haven't yet made their move and therefore provide more potential and less risk. When Ramsey is looking for a reversal in a sector, he will focus on establishing a position in the market that lagged most on the prior price move. For example, when Ramsey anticipated the dollar would reverse to the upside at the end of QE2, he sought to sell currencies, such as the Turkish lira, that had been weak despite the prior dollar weakness.

Ramsey pays a lot of attention to price movements in related markets. The failure of a market to respond as expected to a price move in a correlated market can reveal inherent strength or weakness. For example, after years of moving together, in early September 2011, equity prices rallied, but commodity prices weakened. Ramsey read the failure of commodity prices to respond to equity market strength as a signal of impending weakness. During the second half of September, commodity prices and commodity currencies (e.g., Australian, New Zealand, and Canadian dollars) plunged.

Perhaps the hallmark of Ramsey's trading approach is his rigorous control of risk. Ramsey will typically risk a mere 0.1 percent on each trade from point of entry. Once he is ahead on a trade, he will allow for more risk latitude. This approach all but assures that losses on new trades are likely to be quite moderate. The only time Ramsey is vulnerable to a significant monthly loss is when there are large open profits from winning trades. Although the use of a 0.1 percent stop point from entry is probably too extreme (or perhaps even inadvisable) for most traders to adopt, the general concept of using a relatively close stop on new trades and allowing a wider stop after a profit margin has been created is an effective risk management approach that could work well for many traders.

Success in trading requires dedication. Ramsey continues to trade and monitor his positions even when he is on vacation. He also awakens himself multiple times each night to check on his positions. This type of all-encompassing commitment to trading it is not necessarily recommended as a lifestyle, but rather is offered as an observation of one of the characteristics of trading success. For Ramsey, however, I suspect such commitment is not a burden, as trading is a passion, not a chore.

Chapter 5

Jaffray Woodriff

The Third Way

J affray Woodriff knew three things: He wanted to be a trader; he wanted to use a computerized approach; he wanted to do it differently from anyone else. The majority of futures traders, called CTAs, use trend-following methodologies.[1] These programs seek to identify trends and then take a position in the direction of the trend until a trade liquidation or reversal signal is received. A smaller number of systematic CTAs will use countertrend (also called *mean reversion*) methodologies. As the name implies, these types of systems will seek to take positions opposite to an ongoing trend when system algorithms signal that

---

[1]Commodity Trading Advisors (CTAs) are managers who trade futures and are registered with the Commodity Futures Trading Commission (CFTC). This official nomenclature is poorly chosen on at least two grounds: Commodity Trading Advisors are managers, not advisors, and a large majority of the trading they engage in is in financial markets (e.g., stock indexes, interest rates, and currencies) rather than commodities.

the trend is overextended. There is a third category of systematic approaches whose signals do not seek to profit from either continuations or reversals of trend. These types of systems are designed to identify patterns that suggest a greater probability for either higher or lower prices over the near term. Woodriff is among the small minority of CTAs who employ such pattern-recognition approaches, and he does so using his own unique methodology. He is one of the most successful practitioners of systematic trading of any kind.

Woodriff grew up on a working farm near Charlottesville, Virginia. Woodriff's perceptions of work were colored by his childhood experiences. When he was in high school, Woodriff thought it was sad that most people loved Fridays and hated Mondays. "I was going to make sure that wasn't me," he says. "I really wanted to find a way to make Mondays as exciting as Fridays."

Another childhood experience taught Woodriff a lesson about work incentives. One summer, he and his sister were hired by their uncle to harvest grapes in his vineyard. Initially, they worked alongside local workers. Even though they were getting paid by the quantity harvested, Woodriff was amazed that the other employees still worked slowly and wasted time. Spurred by the incentive that was directly linked to the amount of work completed, Woodriff and his sister were earning two to three times as much per hour as the other workers. Upset about the slowness at which the harvesting was progressing, his uncle eventually fired the local workers and hired migrant workers. Woodriff discovered that the migrant laborers worked so diligently and efficiently that they were earning more than twice as much as he and his sister were. Clearly, they understood incentives. Woodriff's high regard for the fairness and efficacy of incentive-based payment is reflected in his firm's highly unusual incentive-only fee structure (0 percent management and 30 percent incentive versus the more typical 1 percent to 2 percent management and 20 percent to 25 percent incentive).[2]

---

[2]Management fees are collected on assets under management. Incentive fees are collected as a percent of profits earned above a *high-water mark*—the highest NAV level at which incentive fees were previously collected. Almost all CTAs and hedge funds charge both types of fees; Woodriff charges a higher-than-normal incentive fee, but no management fee.

Woodriff attended the University of Virginia, which was only 20 miles from his family's farm. He knew he wanted to be a trader before he graduated from college. Much to his mother's consternation, after graduating in 1991, Woodriff never sought a job, but instead continued to apply himself to developing futures trading systems. A CTA he formed in partnership with a classmate shortly before his college graduation lasted only a few months. His partner's family had put up the seed money for their venture, which was the reason his partner owned 65 percent of the CTA. Woodriff was amenable to the minority share, but what he had not counted on was that his partner thought he was Woodriff's boss, an unacceptable arrangement prompting Woodriff's quick departure.

Several months later Woodriff formed another CTA partnership, Blue Ridge Trading. Woodriff was responsible for trading, and his partner, Robert Jordan, ran the business and did the marketing. Woodriff was hardly an immediate success. Trading began in October 1991. For the first three months and the subsequent two full years, Blue Ridge ended up slightly below breakeven for the period as a whole. But then in the third year, 1994, Woodriff's systems generated an 80 percent plus return for the first six months. Woodriff and Jordan had never bothered to sign a partnership agreement. Up to that point, they had split the firm's small net earnings. With his systems beginning to generate significant profits, Woodriff thought it was time to formalize their business relationship with a written agreement. This decision would probably not have been problematic in itself, but the terms that Woodriff proposed so angered Jordan that he broke off the partnership and filed a lawsuit against Woodriff. Woodriff's relationship with Blue Ridge ended shortly thereafter, and the firm was closed down a few months later.

Woodriff then established his own CTA, Woodriff Trading. He began trading in August 1994 with less than $50,000 raised from family members. In the final five months of 1994, Woodriff lost 16 percent. He then lost an additional 12 percent in 1995. But this very inauspicious beginning was followed by a spectacular 180 percent gain in 1996. The performance streak continued into 1997, as Woodriff was up another 64 percent for the first four months of the year. But in the following five months, Woodriff surrendered more than half his year-to-date profits. At the peak, assets under management had reached only $3 million.

After his drawdown from the 1997 high point, losses and withdrawals had reduced assets to only about $1.5 million. Woodriff was frustrated by his inability to raise substantial assets, the 20 percent drawdown from the 1997 high, and most of all by the fact that running the CTA business in addition to trading left him with no time to pursue his true career passion: predictive modeling. Woodriff decided he might do better seeking a proprietary trading job in New York. He returned the remaining assets to his investors, closed Woodriff Trading, and moved to New York to search for a job.

A friend of Woodriff had an uncle who was a highly prominent hedge fund manager. On her own volition, she arranged for Woodriff to interview with the president of the firm. Woodriff vividly recalls this interview, which took place in what he describes as "an amazing space." Woodriff spent about five minutes telling his story and explaining what he did. The firm's president then spent 10 minutes telling Woodriff that they had already tried every possible combination of what he was talking about, and it didn't work. He informed Woodriff that they didn't have a job for him because he was not "the type of person they hire." Woodriff laughed when he recalled his interviewer's advice, "You are wasting your time. This is a complete dead-end for you. You really need to be thinking about jobs outside of finance. I'm so glad we had a chance to meet today and talk this through."

A friend of a friend had arranged for Woodriff to interview at Société Générale in New York. The trader who interviewed him was setting up a desk of proprietary traders and felt that Woodriff's approach would be completely uncorrelated to any of the other traders and therefore a good fit. Woodriff very successfully traded a proprietary account for Société Générale from 1998 until March 2000. He found that not having to deal with the business side was a great advantage in that it allowed him the time to continue his research. It was during his time at Société Générale that Woodriff first applied and began using his systematic style of trading for a long/short equity account, which was the precursor to his firm's equity trading program.

Woodriff left Société Générale because his boss, Jonathan, was leaving to start a multimanager hedge fund operation and had invited Woodriff to join him. Jonathan had told Woodriff that three other portfolio managers would be part of the group. One of these managers had worked for George Soros and Paul Tudor Jones and was a familiar name to Woodriff. Woodriff was excited about being part of an elite trading group. In preparation for the new venture, several months earlier, Woodriff had asked Michael Geismar, a former roommate who had also worked for him at Blue Ridge, to come to New York to work as his right-hand man. Geismar prepared a trading operation. Shortly after Woodriff left Société Générale, Woodriff began trading a proprietary equity account using his system, while waiting for the hedge fund operation to launch.

Woodriff attended a meeting to discuss setting up the new multi-manager fund and was surprised that he was the only one to show up besides Jonathan. When he told Geismar about the meeting, Geismar said, "You've got to meet these other managers."

At the next meeting, Woodriff again found that he was the only other manager there. "Jonathan, where is everyone else?" he asked.

Jonathan replied, "Well, I have been working really hard to get everyone, but I'm afraid that it is just you and me."

Woodriff, who had anticipated this possibility, answered, "I'm sorry Jonathan, it's just you."

Woodriff had gotten off to an extremely good start with his proprietary equity account, and after the hedge fund plan fell through, his intention was to just continue trading this account and live off the profits. Since Woodriff had started the account with only $300,000, and he also had to pay Geismar's salary, I was rather incredulous when he told me this. "You weren't planning to start a new CTA and manage client money? You were planning to just live off the profits?"

"Oh, absolutely!" he answered. His reply and his actions at the time reflected the degree of confidence he had in his system. And although it sounded like a preposterous plan to me, his confidence was not misplaced. Aided by a highly volatile equity market that was particularly favorable for his approach, in return terms, his account compounded twentyfold in the first 25 months.[3]

---

[3]The actual account compounded by a lesser amount because Woodriff was withdrawing money from the account to cover his living expenses and pay Geismar.

In April 2001, Woodriff and Geismar moved back to Charlottesville. As his account grew, Woodriff thought it made sense to diversify by starting another proprietary account to trade his system on the futures markets, as he had originally done. In addition, because at the time the equity account traded only on the opening, he felt that only futures would give him sufficient capacity to build a truly scalable management business if he chose to do so. The plan was to trade the futures account for two years, establish a track record and smoothly running operation, and then *consider* opening the program to outside investors. Woodriff emphasized the word *consider* because he says that, at the time, he was not at all sure he wanted to undergo the work and complications implicit in shifting from just managing his own money to establishing a money management operation. At the end of 2002, the third co-founder, Greyson Williams, joined the budding firm, and Quantitative Investment Management (QIM) as a company was officially established in May 2003. As it turned out, Woodriff never got to the two-year decision point. In late 2003, a broker recommended QIM to a client, and Woodriff, along with Geismar and Williams, decided they were ready to manage other people's money.

QIM trades a futures program and an equity program, and both have exhibited strong return/risk performance. The futures trading program accounts for about 85 percent of the near $5 billion of assets under management. From the October 2003 start date for the first client account through 2011, the futures trading program achieved an average annual compounded return of 12.5 percent, with an annualized standard deviation of 10.5 percent, and a strong Gain to Pain ratio (GPR) of 1.43. (See Appendix A for an explanation of the GPR.) A proprietary account trading the futures program, which has a longer track record (inception: December 2001) and trades at much greater leverage than the client accounts, has realized an average annual compounded return of 118 percent, with an annualized standard deviation of 81 percent and a GPR of 1.94. (Besides the difference in start dates, the higher GPR is a consequence of the absence of performance fee charges on the proprietary account.) The track record for QIM's equity program consists of nonoverlapping proprietary and client accounts. The proprietary account, which traded between April 2000 and September 2005, had an average annual compounded return of 115 percent, with a 69 percent annualized standard deviation and a very high GPR of 2.69. Since its inception in May 2008, the equity program for client accounts had an average annual compounded return of 34 percent, with an annualized standard deviation of 20 percent and a very high GPR of 2.38.

Woodriff emphasizes that co-founders Michael Geismar and Greyson Williams have been critical to QIM's success. He is also extremely proud of the fact that QIM has had zero turnover in staff since its inception. (There are currently 31 employees.)

I interviewed Woodriff at his firm, QIM, located in Charlottesville, Virginia, a pretty college town. We talked in Woodriff's office, which was noteworthy for the number of books scattered everywhere, with several stacks on the low table between us. Many of these books were still new. Woodriff is clearly a voracious reader. My impression was that he buys any book that catches his interest and leaves it in plain sight so he will eventually get to it. Woodriff is 42, but looks much younger. If I didn't know him in context of being the founder of QIM, I would sooner have guessed that he was in his late twenties than in his early forties. Woodriff had looked forward to our meeting and was extremely disappointed that he had come down with a bad cold a day earlier. He repeatedly apologized for what he considered his foggy thinking and imprecise recollections. "God, I wish I weren't sick. I'm not thinking clearly," he said.[4]

■ ■ ■

How did you get interested in developing computerized trading systems?

When I was about 9 or 10 years old, I became interested in odds and probability. I would obsessively roll a pair of dice to see seven win, and six and eight duke it out. It just fascinated me to see the results come out over time—to see the randomness, but also the certainty with which seven would always beat six and eight.

---

[4]Woodriff was the first interview I conducted for this book and also the last chapter I completed. A little more than a year later, I sent Woodriff the completed chapter to check for accuracy. His e-mail back finished on the following ironic note: "If you can believe it, coming full circle for this chapter, I am coming down with another bad cold right now and my head is fogging up!"

When I was 12, I read about computers. It was an article about the new Commodore, a $300 computer, which in today's terms would be several thousand dollars. I convinced my parents to buy the computer for me, but because it was so expensive, they agreed only on the condition that I return it in time for the 30-day money back guarantee. It was that or no computer at all for me. This Commodore was the type of computer where you saved your files on a cassette tape, which I thought was really neat technology. The thing I wanted to program was rolling dice, so I could roll dice faster. It felt a little weird having a computer decide what was random and not seeing the dice, but it was fun writing the program. To get more time on the computer before I had to return it, I even skipped school for a couple of days by pretending to be sick, using the old thermometer-near-the-lightbulb trick.

How did you teach yourself programming?

I think there was some sort of manual. Also, it was such a simple program except for the random number generation, which was a function already programmed on the computer. Even though I begged my parents to keep the computer, they sent it back. But I am really glad I got to do 30 days of programming back then. I think it was a really good thing for my evolving brain to experience. I did very little programming again until college.

Were any other childhood experiences influential in your becoming a trading system developer?

Absolutely! A year earlier, I had gotten really interested in baseball statistics after my grandfather, who lives in Pennsylvania, took me to see the Philadelphia Phillies, my favorite baseball team. I calculated and recorded full-page statistics on the Phillies from the box scores in the newspaper after every game. This early experience shows how diligent I was with numbers very early on if I became excited about something. Beginning when I was 12, I read Bill James's *Baseball Abstract* cover to cover each year. He was creating and quantifying new and interesting statistics. I don't remember the details now, but James created statistics that gave you more information and were more predictive. For example, if you had a 21-year-old hit .311, that was more interesting than a 26-year-old with the same batting average. In retrospect, Bill James's style of quantitative analysis was a very important influence in how I eventually ended up thinking about the process of building trading systems to predict the markets. After having been dismissed for several decades, over the past 10 years, Bill James's analytical style has been recognized and deployed by the baseball establishment.

What is the connection between what Bill James did for baseball statistics and your approach to trading systems?

James was creative in coming up with better measures. For example, the first batter in the rotation, who batted after the worst hitters, would have fewer opportunities for RBIs than the batter in the fourth position. James would do normalizations for those types of disparities. He would find leadoff batters who would have had a lot of RBIs once you adjusted for their batting slot and who therefore should have been batting third or fourth. I loved the logic of normalizing data.

When did you first get involved in the markets?

When I was born, my family put money for me in a managed trust. When I was 18, I started checking the prices of the stocks in my trust account in the daily paper. I checked it for a few days, and it bored me because the prices didn't change much from day to day. But I noticed that the option prices moved much more, that is, in percentage terms. At that time, the most liquid options were the OEX, which were options on the S&P 100 index. I talked my dad into opening an account for me with $2,500. My broker recommended a trade to me, in typical broker fashion. "It's a layup," he assured me. It lost money, and I never followed another broker's recommendation in my entire life. Boom. Done. One trade; I will never do it again.

What was the trade he recommended?

I don't even remember if it was a stock or an option. All that I remember is that he was so sure of it, and it didn't work. Then I started looking at how I might be able to predict the direction of the market.

What did you trade?

I basically traded the OEX options. I only did one stock trade that I can recall. I was away on the day of the October 19, 1987, crash. When I got back the following morning, the market was down even more. I had been watching a tech company that a family friend had recommended, which had run up from $20 to $40. I had wanted to buy it much lower, but never did because it just kept going up. On the morning of the 20th, the price had fallen all the way back into the low teens. I called the 800 number for Schwab at least 50 times to try to place my order, and I kept getting a busy signal. Finally I got through. I gave my account number to the woman who answered and said, "I want to buy 100 shares of CHPS."

She said, "Okay, account number so and so you are selling 100 shares of CHPS."

I excitedly answered back, "No, no, buy!"

She said, "You must mean sell. No one is buying!"

And I again said, "No, I want to buy, B–U–Y."

She said in a surprised voice, "Really? Everyone's selling."

I answered, "I'm buying." So she placed the order, and it was filled at $14.50, after which it rallied sharply. I think what is significant about that trade is that it shows I was willing to be a contrarian even at the very beginning.

On what basis were you doing your option trades?

There, too, I was a contrarian. I used the put/call ratio as my primary indicator. I really liked the logic of it. I also watched the ARMS Index.

Is there something about your personality that is contrarian?

I just can't stand being part of the herd and simply accepting the consensus. I want to evaluate everything on my own.

How did you do in your trading?

It's funny. I was looking through my old brokerage statements this morning before you came in, and I was surprised to discover that the memory of my first trades had become distorted. I had been under the impression that my first 10 option trades all made money. However, what I found out in checking the brokerage statements was that it was actually my first 10 put trades that made money. But I had also been buying calls, and most of those trades lost money. I had conveniently forgotten that it was the long put positions that made money, not all the trades. Of course, we were in a down market at the time, so it wasn't surprising that the long put positions consistently made money. I now feel I need to go back to anyone I ever told that my first 10 trades were profitable and set the record straight. Up to that point, on balance, I had still done very well, because the put trades had made a lot of money. My starting $2,500 account had more than quadrupled to over $10,000. Then, on my 11th put trade, I lost more money than I made on the first 10 put trades combined.

What happened on the 11th put trade?

The market rallied sharply, so the puts expired worthless.

Since you were a buyer of puts, why would you have lost so much on one trade?

Because I kept on increasing my trade size as I made money.

So you blew it all on one trade?

Yeah.

Did that trade end your trading at the time?

No, I continued to trade, but I didn't do that well. That summer I tried daytrading. I got a whole real-time quote setup. My plan was to spend the summer staring at the trading screen. After about the third day of doing that, I realized, *This isn't me. This just doesn't work for me.*

Did you have any idea what you wanted to do when you were in college?

I wanted to trade. When I was a junior in college I competed in the AT&T investment challenge, which was a real-time trading contest for college students. There was a $50 entry fee. I entered under my own name, and I also entered under my roommate's name. I wanted to get my roommate, Will, to enter the contest as well, but he had no interest in trading. So I did a second entry under his name. I traded the two accounts differently to increase my odds of winning. There were 10 winning slots, and I came in sixth, but it was on Will's entry. The sixth place prize was $3,000. In addition to the cash prizes, the top 10 winners also won a weeklong trip to the Bahamas for themselves and a companion. I told Will, "You have to accept the prize. It's under your name."

Was there an official prize ceremony?

Oh, yeah.

Who went up to get the prize?

Will did. The prize check they gave Will was about this big.

[Woodriff draws a large rectangular shape in the air with his hands.]

The next morning, we went to the local bank to try to cash it. The check wouldn't fit through the teller window.

I don't get it. They gave you an oversized check?

It was a mock check, but we didn't realize it because it looked official. We were hung over, and we were idiots. It just didn't occur to either one of us that the check was just a prop. We received the real check in the mail later.

I felt really guilty that I had played two hands to win the trading contest. On the fifth day, there was a picnic, and I went up to one of the two guys running the event and confessed to him that I had entered twice. "Are you kidding me?" he said. "We wish everyone would enter 10 times. We want people to do multiple accounts and try different strategies. You didn't have to enter under your friend's name."

Did you have any game plan of how you wanted to get into trading?

I quickly figured out that I didn't want to be a broker working for commissions or a money manager working just for management fees.

The incentive fee structure appealed to me. I liked the idea of having your pay directly linked to how well you did.

Besides knowing your preferred fee structure, did you have any idea of how you planned to trade the markets?

I knew there was a very good chance I might not be able to figure out how to beat the markets, but I also knew there were some people who were beating the markets, thanks to your first *Market Wizards* book and other sources. As soon as I learned about the efficient market hypothesis, I was on a mission to prove it wrong.

Right around that time, I took a course in economics. I was horrified by some of the conclusions academics had come to, such as the efficient market hypothesis. I refused to learn the material because I thought a lot of it was wrong. The professor had given multiple-choice tests throughout the course. I pleaded with him to use essay questions instead of multiple-choice questions for the final exam. A week before the exam, he announced that it would be multiple choice. I was so frustrated that I decided to take the final exam with a box of crayons on my desk, and I made sure to sit up front, so everyone could see it. I wrote a note on the exam explaining that I was answering the questions with what I thought were the right answers, but that for those questions where I thought he was looking for a different answer, I would explain why I thought he was wrong and write that answer in a separate column. I also wrote that I would fail the exam if he went straight down the line and didn't pay attention to the alternative answers I provided. He ignored everything I wrote and just went straight down the line. He gave me a failing grade of 51. I don't really care that much about getting a 51—in fact I'm glad I did—because I know how wrong some of the "correct" answers were.

Did you have any mentors?

People ask me all the time if I had any mentors. The truth is that I am self-taught. I have thought through this so many ways, and there is no other way to put it. But if you ask me what manager I set out to emulate, it's clearly Paul Tudor Jones. It has nothing to do with his trading style, because I learned pretty early on that I had no interest in being a discretionary trader. Right around the time I read *Market*

Wizards, he came to give a talk at Darden, University of Virginia's graduate business school. He wasn't that famous then.

Do you remember anything specific about his talk that had an influence?

I remember his confidence, his charisma, and that I liked him, but that is about it. I loved the fact that he was a University of Virginia graduate.

How did you originally develop your trading system?

After I graduated from the University of Virginia, I didn't have my own computer, so I used the computers at the engineering school. The computer lab was this huge room with extremely high ceilings—I don't know what it had been used for before—filled with over 100 computers. I started looking at trend-following models, which was kind of interesting, but I thought there were already lots of successful trend followers out there, and I didn't want to compete with them. I wanted to do something different.

Just from our conversation so far, it is clear to me that there was another reason why you wouldn't have pursued a trend-following approach. It would have been totally out of character for you. A trading approach that, by definition, requires staying with the herd would have been exactly opposite your natural instincts. Even if it worked, you would have had trouble following it.

That's true. My contrarian nature was opposed to doing what other people were doing. I also believed that if everyone thought trend following worked, it would start to work less well. I was never going to be a trend follower. That was clear. Mean reversion was more interesting. But I didn't like mean reversion either.

Why didn't you like mean reversion?

Because I found something that worked much better. *Right then. Right in that computer lab.* [Woodriff speaks these words very emphatically, conveying this was a pivotal moment in his life.]

What did you find?

I had the realization that I could build a whole third class of models that were trend neutral on average—that is, trading models that were neither trend following nor countertrend. I built a couple of these models and did some preliminary tests. I came to the conclusion that there was a lot of edge in this type of approach.

Out of my sheer excitement in discovering this style of model—an approach that still remains at the core of what I do today—I couldn't wait to do more extensive testing. To speed things up, I was working on two computers. But then the lab got crowded, and I had to give up one. I started thinking, *This place is going to empty out sometime tonight.* I decided to get all my data prepared so that I could simultaneously use many of the lab's computers that night. I was very excited about the idea. People started to leave, and then I had two computers, then four, and eventually I was jumping between 20 computers running my backtests.

Were you testing your system on one market on each computer?

That is exactly what I was doing. I was so excited about the results I was getting that I worked all night and continued through the next day. It was going so well that I pulled a second all-nighter. I worked for nearly 40 hours straight, keeping myself awake with the caffeine from drinking a Pepsi every hour. I was still living on the farm at the time. It was dangerous driving home on the second morning. I remember almost falling asleep at the wheel a couple of times. I got home, took about 3 minutes to tell my father what I had accomplished, and then went to bed. I slept for 24 hours straight. When I woke up, I felt completely refreshed. I remember sometime later reading that you can't catch up on your sleep and thinking, *Not true!*

What did you do next?

I went back to the computer lab and continued cranking, although I didn't pull any more all-nighters.

Did you make any further discoveries?

I discovered that it was much better to use multiple models than a single best model.

Sometime after that week with the two consecutive all-nighters when I had that feeling, "Whoa, I think I've got it," I told my mom, "I know you are really frustrated that I didn't interview for jobs after graduating college, and that instead, I am trying to do this trading thing, which I realize you think is crazy. But I want you to know that if I am successful in what I am working on right now, I will do very well with it. I don't want you to think that I'm doing this just to make money. The really great thing about what I'm doing now is that if I am that good at applying predictive modeling, I will be able to generalize the same approach into science. So I won't just be a trader, even if I am very successful at it. And the more successful I am at it, the better the chance it will generalize to science."

Did you ever apply it to science?

I have set up a foundation called the Quantitative Foundation. The long-term plan is to improve statistical prediction methodologies and software. I prefer the terms *statistical prediction* or *statistical learning* to *data mining*, which has deservedly earned a negative connotation through its misuse.[5] We haven't done much so far, but we didn't plan on doing anything yet, since we are still in the phase of making money from our edge in these techniques, as opposed to going out and building software for scientists. We want to build the software so that it is not a gift to our competitors.

How do you get around the problem that if you supplied the software for scientific applications, other people could use it as a

---

[5]Data mining refers to the process of using computers to analyze large amounts of data to discover patterns in the data. Although data mining techniques can uncover patterns in data that would be impossible for humans to find empirically or by prior hypotheses, it can also identify meaningless patterns that are nothing more than chance occurrences or the product of flaws in the analytical process. When searching very large numbers of combinations of past price data for patterns, it is easy to come up with many patterns that worked well in the past simply by chance, but have no predictive value. This common pitfall of applying data mining to price data is the reason why the term often has derogatory connotations in reference to trading systems.

predictive tool in the financial markets, which would presumably reduce the edge you are currently profiting from?

It is going to take a number of years to develop the generalized software from the time we fully engage in this endeavor—possibly as long as five years or more. Maybe by that time, QIM will be closed for some reason. If QIM were to go through a long stretch of poor performance, and we decided to close it down, it wouldn't invalidate the predictive modeling techniques I have come up with. In some ways, it would actually validate them by showing that it was possible to have an edge for many years, and finally other people caught up and found the same things we did and knocked those inefficiencies out of the market. That would probably be a good time to offer predictive software for more general use. But it is not a question I have to grapple with now because I am nowhere near the goal of having generalized predictive modeling software to provide to scientists in a wide variety of disciplines and domains. We are building a war chest to do that eventually. We started the foundation with $50 million, and there is about $100 million now.

So what is your foundation doing now?

As a foundation, we still have to give away a specified percentage of money every year.

Where does the money go to?

So far the money has been given to schools and local charities.

So the main project of the foundation is something that you would focus on in the post-QIM portion of your life.

That's the general concept, although there are interesting scenarios in which the predictive modeling project could operate in parallel with QIM.

When you first started managing money under Blue Ridge, for the three months in your inception year and the subsequent two full years, you were actually down slightly on balance. Then in the first six months of the following year, you were up over 80

percent. That is such a stark contrast in performance that it seems that something significant must have changed in your trading approach during those early years. Was there some major change to your methodology during this period, and if so what was it?

I started out using market-specific models. I ended up realizing that these models were far more vulnerable to breaking down in actual trading because they were more prone to being overfitted to the past data. In 1993, I started to figure out that the more data I used to train the models, the better the performance. I found that using the same models across multiple markets provided a far more robust approach. So the big change that occurred during this period was moving from separate models for each market to common models applied across all markets. The second change that occurred was increased diversification. I started out trading only two markets and then for some time traded only three markets. But as assets under management increased, and I realized it was best to use the same models across all markets, I added substantially more markets to the portfolio. The transition to greater diversification also helped improve performance. By 1994, I was trading about 20 markets, and I was no longer using market-specific models. Those changes made a big difference.

When you were only trading two or three markets, how did you decide which markets to trade?

That was part of the problem. I was cherry-picking the markets that looked best in backtesting.

It sounds like you were still making some rookie curve-fitting mistakes at that time.

Absolutely. I was still making some very bad data mining errors in those initial years.

Was the system you were using at Blue Ridge after you switched to using the same models on all markets an early version of what you ended up doing at QIM?

It was similar, but much less sophisticated—fewer models generated with far less computing power.

But it was conceptually similar?

Oh, absolutely. It was the same thing. It was just a very early version of it.

How did you come up with the idea for systems that seem to work well and that were neither trend following nor mean reversion?

[Woodriff looks for one of the many books stacked throughout his office, and finding it, begins to talk about it. Ironically, it is a book that he has not yet read.]

Before you go there, I asked you the question about how...

Oh, yeah, I was trying to avoid that question.

I know. [Woodriff laughs.] But I am not supposed to let you do that. Part of your breakthrough was your idea of trying to find common systems that work stably across markets. Another important concept was to trade multiple systems instead of a single system. But neither of those two ideas is unique. Probably the majority of CTAs trade multiple systems, and a substantial percentage of CTAs also use the same systems across different markets. Those two elements are no doubt critical, but they are not by themselves the key. They don't differentiate you from a large segment of CTAs. Whatever your special sauce is would lie in the system concepts you came up with.

I wanted to set up a structure that would allow me to try out a huge number of combinations. When I first started out, I could only try out thousands of combinations, but as computing power dramatically increased over the years, I was eventually able to try out trillions of combinations. But it was critical to do that without overfitting the systems to the data.

I finally found a way. There are books about the predictive modeling process that specifically caution against "burning the data"—that is, you have to greatly limit the number of combinations you ever try. And I found that advice markedly stupid because I knew I could find a way to try any number of combinations and not overfit the data. You get new out-of-sample data every day. If you are rigorous about acknowledging what that new data is telling you, you can really get somewhere. It may take a while. If you are trading the system, and it is not performing in line with expectations over some reasonable time frame, look for overfit and hindsight errors. If you are expecting a Sharpe ratio above 1, and you are getting a Sharpe ratio under 0.3, it means that you have made one or more important hindsight errors, or badly misjudged trading costs. I was using the data up to a year before the current date as the training data set, the final year data as the validation data set, and the ongoing real-time data as the test. Effectively, the track record became the test data set.

I understand why you would look for a method that was not trend following, given your aversion to following the herd, but why would you inherently avoid a mean reversion approach?

For the same reason I didn't pursue trend following—namely, other people were doing the same type of thing. Mean reversion may have been a better fit for me than trend following, but I wanted my own style. I wanted an approach that fit my personality, which is a very important point that I got out of one of your first two *Market Wizards* books. Mean reversion partially fit my personality, but because people knew about it, it didn't fully fit my personality. So I looked for other ways to crunch the numbers that would be neither trend following nor mean reversion.

Without giving away trade secrets, what is the essence of that third approach?

I was trying different combinations of secondary variables that I generate from the daily price data.

Can you give me an example of what you mean by secondary variables?

An example would be a volatility measure, which is a data series that is derived from price, but has no direct relationship to price direction. I got the idea for secondary variables from Bill James.

What is the connection between what Bill James did with baseball statistics and what you call secondary variables?

James was taking the basic data and formulating different types of statistics that were more informative, and I was taking the price data and defining different quantifications derived from that data, that is, secondary variables, that could be combined to provide useful market signals.

Are all your secondary variables derived just from daily open, high, low, and close price data?

Absolutely. That is all I am using.

You don't throw in any other statistics, such as GNP or any other economic variables?

If I could, I would. I actually tried that, but I couldn't get it to work.

How would generating these secondary variables give you a trading system?

I combined different secondary variables into trend-neutral models.

What do you mean by a trend-neutral model?

They were neither trying to project a continuation of the trend or a reversal of the trend. They were only trying to predict the probable market direction over the next 24 hours.

How many models are there in your system?

There are over a thousand.

Since there are so many, could you give me an example of just one trend-neutral model to provide a better idea of what you mean? I assume giving away just one out of a thousand models wouldn't reveal a meaningful amount of the system.

The issue is that the models share common characteristics. It is hard to give you an example without jeopardizing our intellectual property.

Is your system discovery process a matter of seeing patterns in the market and then testing whether they worked, or is it a matter of coming up with theoretical hypotheses and then testing them to see if they worked?

I know what to grab.

[He gets up again in search of another book—this time it is one of mine, *Stock Market Wizards*. He flips through pages and then finds the spot he is looking for.]

This is really key. I wouldn't spend the time to do this unless it was really important.

[Woodriff begins reading my interview with David Shaw. He flips through a few excerpts and then reads the following response by Shaw to my question of how he can tell whether a market pattern represents something real as opposed to a chance occurrence.]

> *The more variables you have, the greater the number of statistical artifacts that you're likely to find, and the more difficult it will generally be to tell whether a pattern you uncover actually has any predictive value. We take great care to avoid methodological pitfalls associated with "overfitting the data." . . . Rather than blindly searching through the data for patterns—an approach whose methodological dangers are widely appreciated within, for example, the natural science and medical research communities—we typically start by formulating a hypothesis based on some sort of structural theory or qualitative understanding of the market, and then test that hypothesis to see whether it is supported by the data.*

[Woodriff speaking emphatically] *I don't do that.* I read all of that just to get to the point that I do what I am not supposed to do, which is a really interesting observation because I am supposed to fail. According to almost everyone, you have to approach systematic trading (and predictive modeling in general) from the framework of "Here is a valid hypothesis that makes sense within the context of the markets." Instead, I blindly search through the data.

It's nice that people want hypotheses that make sense. But I thought that was very limiting. I want to be able to search the rest of the stuff. I want to automate that process. If you set the problem up really well with cross validation, then overfitting is a problem that can be overcome. I hypothesized that there are patterns that work, and I would rather have the computer test trillions of patterns than just a few hundred that I had thought of.

There is one aspect of the process, though, that is manual. The secondary variables that are used to construct price-forecasting models have to make sense. For example, it makes sense that price-derived data series, such as volatility or price acceleration, might provide important information. The list of secondary variables derived from price is the part I built manually. Then I have a framework for combining the secondary variables in all sorts of combinations to see what works.

I wanted to hand that work off to the computer, but I knew how important it was to have the hindsight bias and overfit problem figured out. As an aside, I am still trying to reverse engineer some of the models that we have come up with that are so interesting and amazing. What do these patterns say about the psychology of the marketplace? Frankly, I'm not sure yet.

You are constructing models by selecting combinations of secondary variables formed from a list of hundreds of possible secondary variables. Depending on the specific selection constraints you use, there would be millions if not billions of possible combinations. Superficially, selecting 1,000 models from such a large list of possibilities sounds very much like a data mining process.

Data mining can be a very positive process. It is just that most people who do data mining are terrible at it. There are various things that you can do to make the data mining process work. It doesn't work on every data set. For some data sets, there is simply no edge available. Luckily for me, my intuition that there was an edge available in a nontrend following, noncountertrend type of model was correct. My intuition was that there should be other emergent patterns in the price data that are more complex than trend following.

What are some of the things you can do to avoid the pitfalls of data mining?

The first thing you need to do is to get some idea of how much of the apparent edge is completely spurious.

How do you do that?

Let's say instead of training with the target variable, which is the price change over the subsequent 24 hours, I generate random numbers that have the same distribution characteristics. I know that any models that I find that score well training on this data are 100 percent curve-fitted because they are based on intentionally bogus data. The performance of the best model on the fictitious data provides a baseline. Then, you need to come up with models that do much better than this baseline when you are training on the real data. It is only the performance *difference* between the models using real data and the baseline that is indicative of expected performance, not the full performance of the models in training.

What are some of the worst errors people make in data mining?

A lot of people think they are okay because they use in-sample data for training and out-of-sample data for testing.[6] Then they sort the models based on how they performed on the in-sample data and choose the best ones to test on the out-of-sample data. The human tendency is to take the models that continue to do well in the out-of-sample data and choose those models for trading. That type of process simply turns the out-of-sample data into part of the training data because it cherry-picks the models that did best in the out-of-sample period. It is one of the most common errors people make and one of the reasons why data mining as it is typically applied yields terrible results.

---

[6]To avoid hindsight bias error in developing trading systems, the available past data is segmented into seen data (i.e., "in-sample") that is used for system development and unseen data (i.e., "out-of-sample") that is used for system testing. Any results on the in-sample data are ignored because they are hindsight-biased. Although segmenting the data to reserve unseen data for testing is a necessary condition to avoid misleading results, it is not a sufficient condition as Woodriff goes on to explain.

What should you be doing instead?

You can look for patterns where, on average, all the models out-of-sample continue to do well. You know you are doing well if the average for the out-of-sample models is a significant percentage of the in-sample score. Generally speaking, you are really getting somewhere if the out-of-sample results are more than 50 percent of the in-sample. QIM's business model would never have worked if SAS and IBM were building great predictive modeling software.

Because if they did, lots of people could use this software for financial modeling?

And lots of people do, but they have a very tough time modeling properly with the software, and they end up doing data mining of the bad kind.

Why do you think you as a single individual have been able to come up with data mining procedures that are much more effective in financial markets than the software produced by these large corporations with tons of PhDs?

Because the commercial software is focused more on the problem of allowing users to handle large quantities of data than on providing users with very strict protocols to make sure they don't curve-fit the data. People are so excited about building and using software that allows them to handle so much more data than ever before that they are missing the point of doing the process properly. Not only does the software fail to guide the user in doing data mining correctly, it actually leads users in the wrong direction because it allows them to generate bogus evidence to support their pet theories.

Do you give the same weight to data from the 1980s as data from the 2000s?

Sometimes we give a little more weight to more recent data, but it is amazing how valuable older data still is. The stationarity of the patterns we have uncovered is amazing to me, as I would have expected predictive patterns in markets to change more over the longer term.

Is the implication then that models don't get dropped even if they perform poorly?

It takes a tremendous amount of deterioration to drop a model. We don't react to the short-term results of a model because the current year performance of any single model is simply not at all predictive of the next year's performance. What is predictive is how the model performed over the entire 31 years. The extra 3 percent of data provided by the most recent year doesn't make much difference in how a model has performed over the entire training period.

Your assets under management in the futures program alone have been as high as $5 billion. Is capacity a problem? Do you have to make changes to accommodate larger assets under management?

One of the changes we have made from the early years, which has greatly expanded capacity, is to execute trades throughout the trading session as opposed to only on the opening. Another change that has increased our capacity is that we have shifted the allocation process to give greater weight to more liquid markets. We trade a larger percentage in stock indexes and interest rates than we used to and a smaller percentage in nonfinancial futures contracts. Although this change has reduced our diversification, we were quite willing to make it because there is a strong pattern for our edge to be greater in more liquid markets. So besides increasing capacity, the shift to allocating a greater percentage to more liquid markets has also improved performance.

Are you then sizing your positions in each market based on relative liquidity?

We started shifting our weightings to the more liquid markets in 2006 and about six months ago we switched our risk weightings to be exclusively based on liquidity, with the one exception being the S&P, which has very substantial excess capacity.

The other important point that needs to be made about capacity is that it is not static; it moves around a lot with changes in volume and volatility in the underlying markets. We estimate our current capacity at

$6 billion to $9 billion. But we always add the caveat that if volatilities decline by 50 percent on average across the markets, our capacity would be reduced by a similar amount.

How do you control risk?

The core of the risk management is evaluating the risk of each market based on an exponentially weighted moving average of the daily dollar range per contract. This risk management metric has kept our volatility relatively stable near the target level, even through periods of wide gyrations in the markets. One of the things I'm particularly proud of in terms of risk management is that through the chaos of 2008 and 2009 our volatility remained very near our target level of 12 percent annualized.

I assume then that you were trading a much smaller number of contracts in each market per million dollars in 2008 than you normally do?

Absolutely. As volatility increased, the number of contracts we were trading dropped precipitously.

What other risk management procedures do you use besides adjusting the trading size for changes in the volatility of the underlying markets?

The volatility adjustment has worked extremely well for the entire history of the program. The part of our risk management process that has worked poorly during the past two years is our leverage reduction policy. In its initial formulation, whenever there was an intramonth drawdown of 6 percent from a monthly equity peak, we cut our exposure to 75 percent of normal.[7] On an 8 percent drawdown, the

---

[7]In 2011, QIM changed the exact calculation it used to reduce leverage during periods of poor performance, but the new formulation was similar in both conceptual and practical terms. It is, therefore, simpler to talk about their leverage reduction as one process.

exposure was cut to 50 percent, and on a 10 percent drawdown, it was cut to 25 percent. Then there were analogous rules for increasing exposure back up as the drawdown was reduced. From 2003 through 2009, the leverage reduction rule very slightly lowered our return/risk, but it made it much easier to sleep because whenever we were in a significant drawdown, our trading size would be smaller. However, in 2010 and 2011, our leverage-reduction policy really hurt us badly because the periods when our models were really on fire occurred when our exposure was lowest. To borrow a term from trend following, we were *whipsawed* by our own risk overlay.

That is the dilemma, isn't it? If you believe that mean reversion applies to the performance of trading systems, then if a system doesn't work well for a period of time, there is probably a greater-than-normal probability that it will do well in the subsequent period. Yet, if you are reducing your risk after a drawdown, that would be the exact time when you would have your smallest exposure. On the other hand, there is the argument that by reducing exposure on drawdowns, you reduce the risk of ruin. Ironically, I think that both perspectives are true—reducing exposure after losses will mitigate the chances of a catastrophic loss, but it will do so at the cost of adversely impacting performance.

What misconceptions do people have about markets?

The worst misconception is about what should constitute the "free market." In the name of free markets, the over-the-counter (OTC) market continues to grow without bounds as a massive profit center for Wall Street banks. Allowing the OTC markets to be unregulated and opaque makes as much sense as leaving 50 eight-year-olds unsupervised for a month. The OTC markets are very often used to take advantage of clients who are "sophisticated" in the legal definition, but are naive in practice. The OTC markets have been built to maximize asymmetries of information and are an example of how markets should not operate. Markets should be fair and transparent, as the futures and equities markets have mostly evolved to be.

What are the worst mistakes the public makes in markets?

Overtrading and listening to tips.

Do losing periods cause any emotional strain? How do you handle it?

Yes, periods of poor performance are difficult. I generally handle it by focusing very hard on improving the trading system.

How would you summarize the trading rules you live by?

Look where others don't. Adjust position sizes to overall risk to target a particular volatility. Pay careful attention to transaction costs.

Any final words?

When I was in my teens, my highly insightful father was somehow able to instill in me the discipline of objectively evaluating your own progress. That lesson, more than anything else, has been critical to my success.

■ ■ ■

Woodriff's views, confirmed by his long-term success, provide four important insights about trading systems:

1. It is possible to find systems that are neither trend following nor countertrend that work better than either of those more common approaches (judging by the comparison of Woodriff's return/risk to the return/risk of the universe of systematic traders).
2. It is possible to apply data mining techniques to search huge quantities of data to find useful patterns without necessarily falling victim to curve fitting. (Although, as an important caveat, most people trying to do so will misuse the approach and end up finding patterns that worked very well in the past, but fail in actual trading.)
3. Old price data (e.g., data 30 years old) can be nearly as meaningful as recent data.

4. Systems that work well across many markets are more likely to continue to work in actual trading than systems that do well in specific markets. The lesson is: Design systems that work broadly rather than market-specific systems.

Woodriff's core risk management technique—adjusting position sizes in line with changing overall volatility—has applicability to a wide range of traders, even those who don't use a systematic approach. As markets become more volatile, Woodriff will trade a smaller number of contracts for the same asset size. Woodriff uses the average dollar range in contract value for each market traded as the metric for adjusting portfolio exposure. Using this approach, Woodriff has been able to maintain his portfolio volatility close to the desired target level, despite widely fluctuating volatility over the past 20 years.

As I have found to be true of virtually all successful traders, Woodriff developed a methodology that suited his personality. He felt a deep inner need to develop an approach that was different from what anyone else was doing, and that is what he did. He was also able to recognize from very early on when a methodology didn't suit him. After setting up a real-time quote system to manually day-trade the markets, he abandoned the process after only three days, as he quickly realized, *This isn't me. This just doesn't work for me.*

Part Two

MULTISTRATEGY PLAYERS

Part Two

Chapter 6

MULTISTRATEGY
PLAYERS

Chapter 6

Edward Thorp

The Innovator

C an the markets be beat? Not unless you are lucky, according to proponents of the efficient market hypothesis (EMH), which assumes that the markets discount all known information and immediately reflect all new information. What about traders who have achieved exceptional track records including some of those profiled in this book? EMH believers have a ready response, which is a variant of the popular Shakespearean monkey argument—that is, if you have enough monkeys randomly striking keyboard keys (they have recently traded in their typewriters for PCs), one of them will eventually type *Hamlet.* By analogy, the implication is that if you have enough traders, some of them will do exceptionally well simply by chance. While the Shakespearean monkey argument is perfectly valid, the question that is always left unaddressed is: How many monkeys would you need to get a randomly generated copy of *Hamlet*? Answer: A lot of monkeys. Unimaginably more monkeys than could be squeezed into the visible universe. The relevant question then is: If trading results are based on chance, how many traders would you need to get one or more with a track record as good as one of the best actually achieved? (If EMH is correct, then all trading results are a matter of chance.) Thorp's track record provides a useful proxy to answer this question.

Thorp's original fund, Princeton Newport Partners, ran for 19 years (November 1969 to December 1988) and had an average annualized compounded gross return of 19.1 percent (15.1 percent after fees). It is not return, but rather the extraordinary consistency of return, that sets Thorp apart. Princeton Newport Partners compiled a track record of 227 winning months and only 3 losing months (all under 1 percent)—an extraordinary 98.7 percent winning percentage. To calculate the probability of this achievement if markets were efficient, we make the simplifying assumption that the average win and average loss were equal. (This is a very conservative assumption since, in fact, Thorp's average win was significantly higher, which implies that the probability of Thorp achieving his win percentage by chance will be even lower than the estimate we derive.) Given the assumption that the average win and loss are about equal, the probability of any single trader achieving 227 winning months (or better) out of 230 is equivalent to the probability of getting 227 or more heads in 230 coin tosses, which is approximately equal to an infinitesimally small 1 out of 10^{63}. Even if we assume 1 billion traders, which is a deliberate exaggeration, the odds of getting at least one track record equivalent to or better than Thorp's would still be less than 1 out of 10^{62}. To put this probability in context, the odds of randomly selecting a specific atom in the earth would be about a trillion times better.[1]

There are two ways of looking at these results:

1. Boy, Thorp was unbelievably lucky!
2. The efficient market hypothesis is wrong.

Track records such as Thorp's prove conclusively that it is possible to beat the market and that the large group of economists who insist

---

[1] The estimated number of atoms in the earth is 10^{50} (source: www.wolframalpha.com).

otherwise are choosing to believe theory over evidence.[2] The contention that it is possible to beat the markets, however, does not say anything about the difficulty of the task. In fact, it is the difficulty in beating the market (the vast majority of market participants fail to do so) that helps create the illusion that markets are efficient.

Thorp's career encompasses an extraordinary number of first achievements:

- He co-developed (along with Claude Shannon) the first wearable computer that could be used to win at roulette.
- He developed the first blackjack betting strategy that provided a positive edge to the player, which he divulged in his global best seller, *Beat the Dealer*. The book changed the way casinos operate.
- Thorp along with Sheen Kassouf developed the first known systematic approach to trading warrants and other convertible securities (e.g., options, convertible bonds, convertible preferred stocks) by hedging them with offsetting stock positions, an approach they detailed in their book, *Beat the Market*.[3]
- He was the first to formulate an option-pricing model that was equivalent to the Black-Scholes model. Thorp had actually used an equivalent form of the formula to very profitably trade warrants and options for years before the publication of the Black-Scholes model.
- He was the founder of the first market neutral fund.
- He established the first successful quant hedge fund.
- He was the first to implement convertible arbitrage.
- He was the first to implement statistical arbitrage.
- He was likely the first person to uncover that Bernie Madoff was a fraud—he developed conclusive evidence of the fraud many years before Harry Markopolos did.[4]

---

[2]The empirical evidence provided by track records such as Thorp's is only one of many refutations of the efficient market hypothesis. For a detailed discussion of this subject, see the forthcoming book by the author, tentatively titled *How Markets Really Work (and How They Don't)*.

[3]Random House, New York, 1967.

[4]The fraud investigator who repeatedly provided evidence to the SEC that Madoff was a fraud, evidence that they failed to act on.

Thorp, a PhD mathematician, and near PhD physicist, came to the markets via gambling, but not gambling in the conventional sense. Normally, casino games of chance have a negative edge for the player, and the longer one plays, the greater the chance of financial ruin. This type of gambling is the antithesis of what Thorp was interested in. Thorp was, in fact, extremely risk averse, a by-product of his having grown up during the Depression. Thorp's goal was to remove the gambling from gambling. He sought to devise strategies that would place the edge in casino games in his favor—a task that had been assumed to be impossible. Amazingly, he was successful in devising strategies to gain a significant edge in multiple casino games including roulette, blackjack, baccarat, and Wheel of Fortune. Ironically, devising the strategies to win at what were always assumed to be unbeatable games proved to be easier than the execution. Winning from casinos presents practical problems. Winning players get noticed, and casinos have low tolerance for players who win by any means other than pure chance.

Thorp thought that the markets might provide a better alternative to apply his research. The markets were after all the largest game, and no one could kick him out if he figured out a consistent way to win. So he turned his research focus on the stock market. This research led to his discovery that warrants (long-term options) were mispriced. In working on the problem of how to price warrants and options, Thorp was introduced to Sheen Kassouf, who was also a professor at the University of California at Irvine (in economics) and who was working on the same project. Thorp and Kassouf collaborated for a while, and in 1967, they co-authored their findings in *Beat the Market*. As a continuation of this work, Thorp eventually developed a version of what would later become the famous Black-Scholes option-pricing model. This formula was considerably more powerful than the research published in *Beat the Market*, and Thorp kept the formula to himself. After several years of very successfully trading his own money and managing money for a number of colleagues, in 1969, Thorp partnered with an East Coast broker, James Regan, to launch the first quant hedge fund (also the first market neutral fund), Princeton Newport Partners.

Princeton Newport Partners (PNP), as implied by its name, was structured as a two-office operation: Thorp headed up the research, programming, and trade generation in Newport Beach, while his partner, James Regan, ran the order execution, business administration, compliance, and marketing from the Princeton office. Thorp had divided the firm so that he could focus on doing what he loved—research—and rid himself of the business side obligations. The firm's divided structure worked extremely well for 19 years, but also led to its demise.

In December 1987, 50 federal agents raided the Princeton office to gather files and tapes as evidence of securities violations. United States Attorney Rudolph Giuliani eventually brought racketeering charges against PNP, the first time the RICO statute had been invoked against a securities firm. In August 1988, Regan and four other members of the Princeton office were indicted on 64 counts. The charges essentially boiled down to two items: stock parking (leaving shares with another party to conceal true ownership) and stock manipulation related to a Drexel securities offering.[5]

Although the PNP employees were originally convicted, their convictions were subsequently overturned, and none served any time in jail. Journalists covering the case almost universally assumed that Giuliani's Draconian prosecution (e.g., invoking the RICO statute), which was widely seen as out of proportion relative to the charges, was really intended to compel Regan and the other PNP employees to provide testimony against Michael Milken and Drexel.

Thorp was completely unaware of the transgressions of the Princeton office and only found out that there was a problem at the time of the raid itself. The Princeton office defendants were not forthcoming with information, and Thorp learned more about the case from the press than from his partner. Thorp was never charged or for that matter even interviewed. However, his firm had been irreparably damaged. A few

---

[5]Thorp recalls the specifics of the stock parking charge as follows:

I was told that a trader at Drexel (Bruce Newberg, one of those charged in the PNP case) had a $25 million capital line from Drexel, which he fully used. But there were more opportunities so, to exploit them, he sold some of his positions to PNP with a guaranteed buyback "up" 20 percent annualized. Using the money so obtained, he could do more good trades. The problem from the regulatory standpoint is that the parking concealed who really owned the positions.

months after the indictments, Thorp decided to close down PNP. Delegating the transaction and business side of his firm had been a major convenience, but it allowed for actions to occur that destroyed his hedge fund, despite having arguably the single best return/risk track record in the industry.

Following the closure of PNP, Thorp maintained the Newport office, where he continued to trade his own account. During 1990 to 1992, he focused primarily on trading Japanese warrants, which he found to be broadly mispriced. He eventually was forced to abandon this strategy when the dealers dramatically widened their bid/ask spreads, wiping out about half the potential profit on each trade.

Thorp had successfully traded a statistical arbitrage strategy since the mid-1980s. In 1992, he was asked to run the strategy for a large institutional client. Two years later, he started his second hedge fund, Ridgeline Partners, to open the statistical arbitrage strategy to other investors. Ridgeline traded very actively, averaging about 6 million shares per day and accounting for about ½ percent of total NYSE volume. Thorp ran the strategy over 10 years. He averaged a 21 percent average annual compounded return with only a 7 percent annualized volatility—another remarkable track record.

After closing down Ridgeline in 2002 (for reasons discussed in the interview), Thorp devoted his time to managing his allocations to other hedge funds. He also developed a trend-following system, which he traded from late 2007 until early 2010.

I interviewed Thorp over a two-day period in his large, light-filled Newport Beach office, which had a 180-degree view with the Pacific Ocean to the west and the surrounding towns to the north. Thorp is 78, but his physical vigor and mental sharpness belie his age. A fitness enthusiast all his life, he continues a routine that includes running, walking, and working out with a physical trainer twice a week. His memory was remarkably precise, as he often cited not only the year of many past events, but the specific month as well. Thorp seemed proud of his many achievements, but in a manner of satisfaction with a life well lived and without a trace of arrogance.

■ ■ ■

When you were growing up, did you have any idea where you were headed in life?

No. My father was very hostile to business. We suffered through the Great Depression. He was a security guard because that was the only work he could find. He was a soldier in World War I. He enlisted in time to be part of the American expeditionary force. He suffered multiple shrapnel wounds. Although he got a Purple Heart, Silver Star, and Bronze Star, he came back with a great hostility toward war based on what he had seen. A lot of my father's attitudes rubbed off on me, including the pain and suffering of the Depression and an aversion to war, unless it is what you call a necessary war.

Was your father an educated man?

He was. He had about a year and a half of college, but unfortunately didn't have the money to continue. He was really smart, though. He had a natural math ability. So did my mother. He also was a very good writer. It didn't amount to much, but he won a writing contest in Chicago and got a typewriter in 1934. I wrote an elementary probability book on the same typewriter in 1965.

I got interested in science when I was eight or nine. I went to an academically deficient high school. I think we ranked 31 out of 32 in the LA school system. So I basically taught myself. I set up a laboratory behind the garage in a laundry room that I shared with my mother. I bought chemicals with the money I made delivering newspapers at 2 A.M. I was interested in physics, chemistry, astronomy, and electronics, and I had a grand time learning all these things. My intention was to go to college to become an academic scientist, most likely a chemist. I was averse to business because I bought into my father's point of view that it was full of thieves who didn't have the best interests of the world in mind and were after whatever they could get.

Do you believe that the Depression experience affected the way you later viewed markets and risk?

We had to be very careful with any possessions we had because it was all hard to come by. We had very little money and were just barely getting along. So nothing was wasted; everything was conserved. It was the same with my science experiments—I reused old parts over and over again in multifarious ways. As far as risk goes, it made me think very carefully about planning for the future and trying to make sure that I had the downside covered so that I wouldn't be caught in some awful economic circumstance where I wouldn't have enough to get by on. It didn't so much worry me, as it was something that I thought about. We got used to having very little money, but enough by being very careful and working hard.

I believed that if you worked hard, good things would come. I expected to become a science professor in a university. But there were some things that happened along the way that may have been harbingers of my future path. For instance, when I was eight, there were WPA workers out in front of the house—this was in the 1930s. It was a very hot summer day. They were perspiring heavily and were obviously very thirsty. I went to the store, bought a pack of Kool-Aid for a nickel, made six glasses out of it, and sold it to them for a penny apiece. A penny actually had considerable value in those days. In the winter, I shoveled snow. At first, I charged a nickel, but I found that there was so much demand that I raised the price to a dime, and then to 15 cents. The first year, when I was eight, I made several dollars, but the next year the other kids caught on, and the market changed.

A classic example of no barriers to entry.

Another thing happened that had a hint of the future. I had a cousin who was not a totally scrupulous guy and who discovered that you could jiggle the slot machines that were located in gas stations and make them pay out more than they should. This was a fairly astonishing fact that you could go around jiggling machines and get a lot of extra nickels out of them. I didn't make a career out of it, but I just noted that there was a gambling situation where you could extract extra money.

When I was in high school, I had a very talented English teacher who was influential in teaching me about writing. He really cared about the kids. I wouldn't say it was totally uncommon, but it certainly wasn't the norm. He had gone to Las Vegas on a trip. Afterward, I was over his house for dinner, and he mentioned that it was impossible to beat those guys.

That started me thinking about roulette. The ball seemed like a planet. I thought it might be possible to beat roulette by measuring the position and velocity of the ball and the rotor.

How old were you then?

I was 15.

So even at that age you apparently knew Newtonian physics.

When I was 16 they had a Southern California physics contest in which the best physics students competed. All the other students were 17 or 18 years old, but I placed first by a very wide margin.

You were self-taught in physics?

I taught myself in my own way. I was always an out-of-the-box thinker. I got hold of a college physics textbook and got through about two-thirds of it by the time of the physics contest, but that was apparently enough. I graduated when I was 16 and was able to attend college through a combination of scholarships and savings from my newspaper route. I graduated with a degree in physics from UCLA, and then I received a master's in physics. I had almost completed all the requirements for a PhD—I had done all the coursework, written exams, and orals—and was working on the last part of my thesis and ran into some math issues. It was a thesis on quantum mechanics.

I realized I needed to take more math courses. UCLA physics at the time was deficient in their math requirements. I basically had only the first two years of college math plus a few advanced math courses, but nothing close to what a math major would take. I had to jump into the graduate courses in math to get up to speed on the math I needed to finish the calculations in my thesis. Once I did that, I realized that considering the amount of math I had to learn, I could get out of math faster than I could get out of physics. So I ended up getting my PhD in math.

So you were literally almost a double PhD in math and physics.

Exactly.

You never finished your thesis to get a PhD in physics?

No, it wasn't worth my time anymore, although it wouldn't have taken much more time to get it.

Did you like math better than physics?

It was kind of odd. When I was in physics, the way they did things didn't make logical sense to me. They would discuss models of things, but they wouldn't explain the assumptions carefully. I liked the logic of math a lot better. Once I learned the logic of math, I could come back to physics and see quite clearly the assumptions they were making and why they were making them.

As a math professor, how did you get involved in developing blackjack betting systems?

In December 1958 when I was teaching at UCLA for one year before going on to teach at MIT, my wife and I were going to Las Vegas for a low-cost vacation. I knew better than to gamble because the odds are against you. One of the professors in the math department who heard I was going to Las Vegas told me, "There is a new article in the *Journal of the American Statistical Association* that tells you how to play at almost even in blackjack." I thought that if I could play at almost even, I could have some fun without it costing me much. Of course, I didn't think it through all the way because although it might not cost much on average, my experience was not going to be average. It was going to be some random fluctuation around the expected modest negative edge, which could be favorable or unfavorable. I read this article, and it said that I could play with a house edge of only 0.62 percent, which was far better than any other game in Vegas.

I made a blackjack strategy card, and when I got to the tables, I sat down with 10 silver dollars and began to play. People at the table were getting clobbered because the dealer had a really good run of luck. My little strategy card, which the other players had laughed at when I first sat down, was doing pretty well. I was holding my own.

What was the strategy that the article had recommended?

It was what is now known as the basic strategy in blackjack.[6] After about 20 minutes, I got a hand with an ace and seven, a soft 18, and the dealer had a nine showing. The strategy said hit. The other players groaned when I did, thinking I was a fool. The next card was a four, so I had 12. The other players thought I had gotten just what I deserved. I then got a string of aces and twos, which gave me six cards with a total of 16. The strategy said hit again, and I got a five, which gave me a seven card 21. Now the other players really got excited. They thought that the strategy card was magical rather than stupid. I played for a while longer, and eventually ended up losing 8 of my 10 dollars. When I went back to UCLA, I reread the article, and I realized that there was a potential for beating the game by keeping track of the cards played.

I guess the article assumed no knowledge of the cards played with all outcomes equally likely on every deal.

Exactly, the article assumed a full-deck strategy all the time. On average, that is the right assumption, but if you have more information, like what cards have been played, then you can improve on those odds.

I was convinced that it was very likely that there would be significant swings in the edge back and forth. The question was how to identify those swings. I wrote the authors of the blackjack article, and they sent me all their lab manuals with the calculations. I spent about five or six weeks mastering all the details of what they had done. My plan was to repeat their calculations with some cards removed from the deck. For example, take out the twos, take out the threes, and so on. I was using a desk calculator and making very slow progress. I decided to estimate how long my calculations would take. I found was that if I did everything I wanted to do, it would take me several thousand years. By

---

[6]The basic strategy is a set of rules of when to stand, hit, split, and double, depending on the player's card and the dealer's card. For example, the basic strategy indicates standing with 16 if the dealer's card is between two and six, and hitting otherwise. The basic strategy does not involve any card counting.

that time, I had taken a job at MIT. At the time, MIT had an IBM 704 computer, which was then the best available commercial computer.

What year was this?

1959.

Wow, that is very early. I remember being a senior in college 11 years later and trying to run an econometric model on the IBM 360. You would type the program on a stack of punch cards, and if there was one misplaced comma, the program would bomb, and you would have to submit the program all over again.

That was my experience as well. The IBM 704 was new and rare at the time, and it served 30 New England universities. As a faculty member, I was able to reserve some time on it. I did not know much about programming, but I ended up developing things that programmers already knew about, such as subroutines. I modularized the program and tested blocks separately to make sure they ran and got the results I thought they should get. Then I put the blocks together. I would take a block in for testing—the block might be something like calculating doubling down expectations. Similar to your experience, two and three days later, my cards would come back with a rubber band and piece of paper around them, indicating the grammatical mistakes I had made. Initially I was bogged down with grammatical errors, but then I got much more accurate in doing it, and things began to run much more smoothly.

By 1960, I started getting results back, and they were really exciting. When I ran the combination of four aces out, the edge went to −2.5 percent. That result implied that if there were four extra aces in the deck, the odds would go to +2.5 percent. You might ask, how can you have four extra aces? Of course, you can't, but if you are down to half a deck and none of the aces are out, the odds are the same as a full deck with eight aces.

Did you calculate the odds by varying one card at a time and holding everything else constant?

Yes, that tied into the image I had when I read the original paper back in UCLA. You can picture the blackjack probability problem as a 10-dimensional space, with the fraction of each card varying along a single axis. The fraction of each card is one-thirteenth, except for the cards with a 10 value, which pool and have a combined fraction of four-thirteenths. You can think of any deck—that is, any combination of cards—as being a point in that 10-dimensional space. The coordinates of each point are determined by the fraction of each card value remaining in the deck.

What was the strategy you eventually developed?

When I first wrote a paper on this for the proceedings of the National Academy of Sciences, I described a fives strategy, but that was because it was simple and everyone would get it. But it wasn't the strategy I planned to use or did use. In the fives strategy, if all the fives are out, you have a 3.3 percent edge. A simple application would be to bet with the basic strategy 90 percent of the time and make really big bets 10 percent of the time when all the fives are out. That was a good strategy in the sense that no one expected this feature of the game. Everyone thought that the aces and 10s were the important thing. The problem with the strategy was that decks with all the fives out occurred only about 10 percent of the time. The next strategy I developed was based on 10s. My reasoning was that since there are a lot of 10s in the deck, a 10s-based strategy would provide considerably more fluctuation in the odds.

Is the idea that even though the fives strategy provides a higher probability bet, the 10s strategy provides far more opportunities?

Exactly. Fives were actually the card that had the most influence. Aces were next, and then 10s and 6s.

Did you have trouble getting your paper published given the gambling subject matter?

Here is how I got it published. I knew I had to get into print fast because there were unscrupulous people around who would claim they had discovered the same information. I had been through several rounds in my career where people had stolen things that I had written in the math world and claimed it was theirs. I decided I wanted to get quick publication, and I wanted to get it into a prestigious journal. The best way to do that was to get it published in the National Academy of Sciences, but you had to find a member who would submit the paper for you or else they wouldn't take it. I researched the Cambridge area where I was located and found that there were two members. One member was an algebraist at Harvard who wouldn't have any idea what I was talking about and probably wouldn't have cared if he did. The other member was Claude Shannon at MIT. Shannon was a joint professor of mathematics and engineering, and one of only two Distinguished Professors at MIT. I went to his secretary and asked if I could get an appointment. She said, "He might see you for five minutes, but he doesn't talk to people if he is not interested. So don't expect more than a very brief interview."

Did you know anything about his reputation when you went to see him?[7]

No, I didn't know anything other than that he was a member of the National Academy of Sciences and a distinguished professor at MIT.

I went over to Shannon's office on a gloomy winter afternoon, just after lunch, and found this elfish-looking man, about 5'7", salt-and-pepper hair, very trim, with a twinkle in his eye and very ready intelligence. I told him what it was I wanted. He read my abstract and said,

---

[7]The opening paragraph in the Wikipedia entry for Claude Shannon provides the following synopsis:

Claude Elwood Shannon (April 30, 1916–February 24, 2001) was an American mathematician, electronics engineer, and cryptographer known as "the father of information theory." Shannon is famous for having founded information theory with one landmark paper published in 1948. But he is also credited with founding both digital computer and digital circuit design theory in 1937, when, as a 21-year-old master's student at MIT, he wrote a thesis demonstrating that electrical application of Boolean algebra could construct and resolve any logical, numerical relationship. It has been claimed that this was the most important master's thesis of all time. Shannon contributed to the field of cryptanalysis during World War II and afterwards, including basic work on code breaking.

"Well, instead of calling it 'A Winning Strategy for Blackjack,' we better call it 'A Favorable Strategy for Twenty One,' which sounds a little more academic and dignified." He cross-examined me for about 10 or 15 minutes and said, "It looks like you have found all the really big ideas here." He indicated that we needed to condense the paper, which is why many of the discoveries that were in my book were not in the paper; they were edited out for size. Then Shannon asked, "What else are you working on?"

At this point, I need to go back to 1955 and pick up the roulette story. I had just gotten my master's in physics, and I was sitting in the dining room of the University Cooperative Housing Association (UCHA), an independent low-cost student living group near the UCLA campus, where I resided. People would gather there to take study breaks and to argue about everything. Someone brought up roulette and was explaining why you couldn't possibly win. I said, "I don't think that is true." I made my case. Some of the people were interested in working on it. I started a little group, which faded away fairly rapidly, but I pursued it on my own.

A fellow I was tutoring bought me a half-size roulette wheel in appreciation for my help—he knew I wanted one—and I bought a stopwatch that ticked in hundredths of a second, which was a fairly large expenditure for me. I did field experiments, setting up a movie camera on a tripod and using the stopwatch to measure time. I did observations to determine how repeatable the ball motion was. If it wasn't repeatable, it would mean there was too much randomness for the process to work. I plotted charts of where the ball was at various points in time. The results looked pretty good; the process did seem repeatable.

I also created an analog experiment by letting a roulette ball slide down an inclined track across the floor. The idea was that I could translate the rotary motion of the wheel into a linear equivalent. I could take the potential energy at the height at which I launched the ball as the amount of kinetic energy the ball was going to get when it rolled down. I wanted to see if the same amount of potential energy converted to kinetic energy would send the ball to approximately the same place on the floor each time. It did. It wasn't proof, but it told me that I couldn't rule out the possibility that predicting roulette might work. One night, my wife had invited my in-laws over to dinner, and I was so engrossed in my experiments that I lost track of what was going on around me. They wondered where I was because I didn't show up at the dinner table. They came looking for me and found me rolling balls down the track. I'm sure that, at that moment, they must have thought that their daughter had made a very serious mistake.

Or that you had lost your marbles. How does this tie back to Shannon?

When Shannon asked what else I was working on, I started telling him about my roulette experiments. Shannon was the ultimate gadgeteer. He got very excited because this idea was right up his alley. The few minutes I had been allocated stretched into several hours. We decided to continue the project together. We ordered a reconditioned wheel from Vegas. I remember it cost $1,500. There was great excitement when it arrived at Shannon's house in a huge packing case. We set it up in Shannon's basement on a slate pool table, which was rock solid. We got strobe equipment from MIT so that when you spun the ball, you could flash the strobe, which would light up briefly, making the ball look stationary. The effect was like a strobe light in a disco. We also had a large clock with a second hand that made one revolution per second, with the dial divided into hundredths of a second. We were able to hit the strobe and stop the clock at the same time, so that we could see where the ball was at an exact time. This setup allowed us to make a lot of measurements. After several months of work, we determined that we could get a huge 44 percent edge in roulette by predicting the most likely octant in which the ball would land. So we built the first wearable computer, which is now in the MIT Museum.

How big was it?

It was about the size of a pack of cigarettes. The plan was the same one I had formulated sitting around the MIT co-op dining room one Sunday afternoon. One person would wear the computer and do timing with switches in the toes of his shoe. The other person would wear a radio receiver and make the bets.

I understand conceptually that Newtonian physics could be applied to predict a most probable landing area for the ball in roulette, but what I've never understood is how could you physically time a moving ball's location accurately enough for a computer to yield a usable answer.

That's a good question. The way it worked was we would use the hotel insignia on the outside stationary border of the wheel as a reference point, and each time the double zero passed this point, we would hit the switch to mark that time.

But how could you time that accurately enough?

That is where the strobe came in. We practiced in Shannon's basement with very subdued light, and the strobe would light up to show us where the ball actually was compared to where we thought it was. It took some training. We learned to anticipate just the right amount. With practice, we were able to get the standard error to within the ball's diameter.

I assume you have to wait for the ball to spin around a few times, so the velocity slows, before you make your estimate.

Yes, you basically want the ball to be going as slowly as possible when you place your bet, because the nearer you time it to the end, the more accurate your prediction.

But you have two moving objects: the wheel and the ball. You mentioned the wheel, what about the ball?

The way it worked was that you would hit the toe switch when double zero passed the mark, and you would hit the switch again the next time it passed the mark. So now, the computer knows how fast the rotor is going. The ball is spun after the rotor measurements.

Oh, I see, there is no need for simultaneous measurements. First you measure the speed of the wheel, and then you measure the speed of the ball, each time taking two points.

Exactly, there are four clicks: the first two tell you the velocity of the rotor, and the second two tell you the velocity of the ball. My idea was for the computer signal to be the tones in the octave—each tone corresponding to an octant of the wheel. Shannon came up with the beautiful idea to design the program so that it cycled through the tones, providing the best estimate at each moment. When you clicked the fourth time, the tones would stop. The last tone you heard was the octant to bet on. What was nice about that approach was there was no compute time. The computer was continuously calculating the best estimate, and when you clicked the last time, the computation was over.

So as time is going by, the estimate is constantly changing.

Exactly, each tone tells you what the current estimation is. The program was designed to give you the estimate, assuming the last click occurred at that exact moment. Once we heard the last tone, we would bet on all five numbers in that octant.

When did you actually apply your roulette betting system in a casino?

Shannon and I and our wives went on a trip to Vegas in August 1961. We had to wire ourselves up.

Who wore the computer and who wore radio receiver?

Shannon was better at estimating the ball position than I was, so he was the timer and wore the computer. He stood next to the wheel and wrote down numbers just like any silly system player.

As a diversion.

Exactly. The casinos won't bother you if you are doing that. I wore the receiver and sat at the far end of the table, where I couldn't even see the wheel.

So you heard the tones.

Yes, I heard the tones. I had a little speaker . . . [A loud timer tone goes off on Thorp's desk—I swear I am not making the timing of this up.]

Whoops, that's the lunch warning. [Thorp had made lunch reservations and set the timer as a reminder.] The speaker was small enough to push into your ear canal. Initially, we had tried copper wires that were as thin as hairs, but they had almost no tensile strength and would break far too easily. We found steel wires that we used, which had a moderate amount of tensile strength, but still not enough, and they also broke periodically. Inevitably, one of the wires would break, and then we would have to leave the roulette table and do a lot of soldering.

How many bets could you get off before the wires broke?

About 12 to 15, and then something would go wrong.

How would Shannon know that something was wrong?

I would just get up and leave the table. One time I was sitting next to the wheel, and there was a lady sitting next to me. Suddenly, she looked at me, and her eyes popped wide open. She was just horror stricken. I knew something was wrong. So I left immediately and went to the men's room. There was a big, black thing, which looked like an insect, coming out of my ear—it was the speaker with wires. The wires were painted with flesh colored nail polish, so they couldn't be seen.

How did that week turn out?

We turned single dimes into piles of dimes.

With a 44 percent edge, why did you use such a conservative bet size?

We wanted to prove that our strategy worked. Also, we were having a lot of trouble with the equipment.

What did your actual edge turn out to be?

It seemed to be consistent with our calculation.

Did you do follow-up trips where you wagered more meaningful amounts?

No, and there were multiple reasons why I didn't. First, blackjack was rolling full blast and occupying a good chunk of my time. Second, not long afterward, I accepted a position at New Mexico State University, which made continued collaboration with Shannon difficult. Third, I questioned whether I wanted to pursue a venture where I had to disguise myself. Fourth, everyone else was really scared.

They were afraid of . . .

Casino violence.

Yes, I would imagine. It was one of the questions I was going to ask you about. You say everyone else; what about yourself?

For some reason I never was scared.

Why?

I just don't scare. I am aware, and I avoid taking foolish risks. When I was playing blackjack in Las Vegas, I always made sure I was around people and lights.

But that wouldn't have helped if the casino caught you.

That's true. If they caught you, they would drag you into the back room and beat you. But at this point, I felt I had a shield of publicity from my blackjack exposure in the press. If they had done anything to me, I could really have made them look bad. I think they probably knew that. Many years later, I learned that they did discuss whether to do me in. In 1964, there was a huge meeting of the Nevada Resort Hotel Association in Las Vegas after *Life* magazine published an article titled *The Professor Who Breaks the Bank*, which created a lot of publicity for blackjack betting systems. The article caused a huge uproar among the casino owners, and they had a meeting to discuss what to do about it. Thirty years later, a fellow by the name of Vic Vickrey who was at the meeting wrote an article about it. Apparently, they discussed various alternatives including getting rid of me and breaking knees. Fortunately for me, they settled on the right option, which was changing the rules.

But at that point, the ideas were already out there, so "taking care of you," wouldn't have done anything for them anyway.

It would have been useless, and they realized that.

Some years ago, I read a book called *Eudaemonic Pie* about a group of physics students who also developed a shoe computer using Newtonian physics to predict the most likely outcome for roulette spins. Was there any connection between you and them?

Here is the connection. In the second edition of *Beat the Dealer*, I mentioned there was a way to win at roulette. In 1969, I got a call from a mathematician named Ralph Abraham inquiring about a roulette system. At that time, I thought that I would never use it myself again, so I might as well let the information out. Within a few years, some physics graduate students did the same thing. They had the next generation of electronics and arrived at the same 44 percent edge.

Let's go back to blackjack. Was your article published in a scientific journal?

It was published in 1961 in the *Proceedings of the National Academy of Sciences*.

What was the response?

There wasn't so much a response to that article as there was to a talk I gave at the same time at the annual meeting of the American Mathematical Society. I submitted an abstract of the talk called *Fortune's Formula: A Winning Strategy for Blackjack*. The abstract committee reviewed my proposal, and unbeknownst to me at the time, they were going to reject it as the work of another crank. They get a lot of submissions from people purporting to prove the mathematically impossible, such as proofs for trisecting an angle with a compass and straight edge alone, or gambling systems for games that are impossible to beat.

Did they read your paper?

The paper wasn't out yet. All they had was the abstract. Fortunately, one of the members on the abstract committee was a number theorist,

John Selfridge, whom I had worked with at UCLA. He told the committee, "I know this guy, and if he says it's true, it is almost undoubtedly true." I only found out about this a few years later when, by pure chance, we were both on the same plane, and he told me what had happened. When I arrived for my talk, I was expecting maybe 40 or 50 people to show up for a fairly sedate presentation. Instead, the room was overflowing with about 300 people.

I guess it shows that mathematicians are more interested in blackjack than people think.

Actually, a good part of the audience didn't look like mathematicians. They had sunglasses on and pinky rings. So I gave my talk. At the end of the talk, I had about 50 copies of my paper to hand out. As soon as I was finished, the audience just surged for the papers. I dropped them on the podium and took off out the back. There were a lot of reporters who were very interested in my talk. One of the reporters was Tom Wolfe.

The Tom Wolfe?

Yes, white suit and all. He interviewed me and was very excited about it. He wrote a story for the AP wire, which set off a furor. Twenty thousand letters rained into the MIT math department. I had all six secretaries answering letters. I didn't estimate how long it would take to answer all the letters, just like, at first, I didn't estimate how long it would take to do the calculations for my original blackjack betting system using a desk calculator. After the secretaries had soldiered through answering several thousand letters, I was finally told, much to my relief, "You're tying up the entire math department. We can't do this anymore."

I also had people calling who wanted to bankroll me. One particularly persistent caller was a fellow from New York named Emanuel Kimmel who claimed he knew his way around the gambling world. He wanted to bankroll me with $100,000. I decided to meet with him. One evening in February, on a typical terrible Boston weather night, a midnight blue Cadillac pulled up, and two attractive, young, blonde women wearing fur coats got out. They were followed by Kimmel who appeared to be about 65 years old, on the short side, with a shock of white hair, and wearing a large cashmere coat. He came into the house and introduced the young ladies as his nieces. My wife, Vivian, looked at them suspiciously.

I guess she wasn't buying the niece story.

Vivian was much more perceptive, but I was willing to accept it at face value. Kimmel asked me a lot of questions about blackjack and then asked me to demonstrate the system. After a couple of hours, he decided to go ahead.

After your book *Beat the Dealer*, which revealed your blackjack system to the public, was published and became a best seller, were the casinos beginning to lose money as a result?

What happened was this: There were a number of really good players, maybe a thousand or so, who extracted money from the casinos. Then there was a much larger number of players who used the basic strategy, so they could play much longer without losing as much. And finally, there was a much larger number of people who heard that you could beat the game, but were poor players. As a result of an influx of new players, blackjack became the most popular casino game. The casinos might have had a thousand or so blackjack players who made $100,000 or $200,000 a year and maybe 10,000 players who weren't losing as much. But, on other hand, they might have had 1 million players who thought they could win when they couldn't and were losing more because they were playing longer. The upshot was that the casinos really had a good thing, but they thought it was a bad thing. They started a war with the card counters. They tried to ban them. They beat up some of them.

Do you know people who were beat up?

Oh, yeah, Ken Uston was a well-known blackjack team player who was taken into the back room and had his cheek broken. He wrote a book about his experiences. There were also books by other people. The casino brutality was pretty well documented. Did you ever see a movie called *Casino*?

Sure. Was the depiction of Las Vegas in that movie accurate?

Yes, very much so. That's the way it was in the 1970s. In the 1960s, when I was playing, it was worse.

And yet you had no fear?

Well, I didn't know a lot of this stuff then.

Given the use of multiple decks and reshuffling, it is still possible for a skilled player to get an edge in blackjack?

It was still possible through the 1990s. The movie *21* is an example of that. The MIT players on whom that movie was based actually just used my system.

The 10s–count system?

They used the complete point count, which counts high cards as −1, low cards as +1, and divides by the total number of unseen cards.

Is that the best approach you came up with?

Yes. It is provable that the complete-point-count system is approximately the best possible system at an equivalent level of simplicity.[8] The 10s-count system used to be about as good, but as the casinos went to multiple decks and reshuffling, the advantage of the complete point system began to grow. The rule of thumb is if they shuffle the deck halfway through, you can still win, but it is too much work, for too little money. If they shuffle two-thirds of the way through, that is just fine.

---

[8]An equivalent level of simplicity means using only a single nonzero integer size for point-count values (e.g., −1, 0, +1). There are other systems that have a greater variety of values that may provide modest improvements in either strategy or bet sizing.

What was the first time you tried your blackjack system in a casino?

The first time was during spring vacation at MIT in 1961. I went with Kimmel, who was Mr. X in the book, and his friend Eddie Hand, who was Mr. Y in the book.

Did you know about their mob associations at the time?

No, Hand seemed like a rough type, but I thought that was just his gruff manner. Both of them were very wealthy. When I was in Kimmel's Manhattan apartment practicing before we went on our gambling trip to Reno and Tahoe, he complained that he lost $1.5 million whenever it snowed in New York because he owned 64 parking lots in Manhattan. Hand owned a trucking business, which years later he sold to Ryder industries, and I know his warrants alone were worth $47 million because I was following the warrant market at the time.

What was your experience on the first trip with them?

They wanted to put up $100,000. I had a high degree of confidence in the theory, but I had never played for real money. I didn't know what surprises the casinos might have in store for me. I wanted to first prove that the system worked in practice rather than try to make an enormous amount of money. So I talked them down to starting with $10,000. I started out by betting $1 on the bad hands and a maximum of $10 on the good hands. It drove them crazy because they were looking to make some big money. I discipline myself and paced myself. It was a lesson about managing money that stuck with me forever after.

Which was?

Don't bet more than you are comfortable with. Just take your time until you're ready. After about eight hours of betting $1 to $10, I got comfortable. I then went to $2 to $20 for about two hours, and that felt comfortable. Next I went to $10 to $50 for about one hour until that felt comfortable. Then I upped it to $25 to $300 and got used to that after an hour or two. Finally, I increased it to $50 to $500—you couldn't bet any higher than $500. I played for a total of about 20 hours at the two higher levels and predicted that my $10,000 bankroll should about double during that time. We actually made $11,000, which was extremely close to the prediction.

How did you make the transition from roulette and blackjack to looking for edges in the market?

Knowing that people were wrong about casino games being unbeatable made me stop and think. If you can beat roulette and you can beat blackjack, what else is there? The next game I looked at was baccarat. I could prove that the main game was not beatable, but the side bets were. At that time, I had moved from MIT to Mexico State University. I took a trip with the head of the math department, the university comptroller, and our wives to test out this baccarat system in the casinos.

I tried to be inconspicuous, but on our first night at the baccarat table, I was recognized by one of the readers of my book, who said, "Hey, that's the guy who wrote the book." The casino people overheard this, and one of them ran over to the phone to call upstairs for instructions. He came back to the table laughing and told the pit boss, "Let them play. This idiot thinks that just because he can win at blackjack, he can win at baccarat. We'll show him a thing or two."

I set the bet size so that we would win about $100 an hour because I knew they wouldn't stand for much more than that. I just wanted to prove that we could do it. I won about $100 an hour for six hours. The casino was fine with that, and they thought it was just luck. We came back the second night and again won about $100 an hour until closing time. Now they were getting less friendly. They put shills on either side of me to watch my every move. Then they got the idea that I was marking the cards. The pit boss and some other people scrutinized the cards, but they couldn't find anything because there was nothing to find.

On the third night, they were friendly again, and asked if I wanted a coffee, which I accepted. I drank the coffee, and then I noticed that I couldn't follow the count. My head felt really funny, and I got up and left, letting my colleagues to do the playing. My colleague's wife was a nurse, and she told me that my pupils were dilated like those of a drug addict. They plied me with coffee and walked me for hours to get me back into shape. The next night we went back, and they offered me coffee again.

Why did you keep going back to the same place?

There were only two places with baccarat in town. I declined the coffee and asked for just a glass of water instead.

Why did you ask for anything? Why didn't you just say you weren't thirsty?

I figured whatever they were using, they would put in the water, and I would be able to tell what it was. I put a drop of water on my tongue, and it tasted like someone had emptied a box of baking soda into it. That drop was enough to put me out again. I left, and they told my colleagues that they didn't want them or me playing there anymore. We had one day left, before heading back, so we went to the other casino. Since it was our last day, I said, "We might as well take the gloves off and play for $1,000 an hour." We played for two and half hours and made $2,500.

The owner walked up with one of the largest security guards I have ever seen and said, "We don't want you playing here anymore."

I asked, "Why not?"

He said, "No reason; we just don't want you here."

So we left.

The next day, on our drive home, the accelerator locked in the down position on a mountain road, and the car couldn't be stopped. The car sped up to 80 on this curvy mountain road.

It sounds like straight out of a movie.

It does [he laughs]. I had the presence of mind to downshift as much as I could, turn off the key, step on the brake and pull out the emergency brake. I was able to bring the car to a stop. We had a flag on the car, and a Good Samaritan who knew about cars stopped to help us. He looked under the hood and said, "I have never seen anything like this accelerator rod." Something had fallen off to make the accelerator rod lock down. He was able to temporarily fix it so that we could drive home.

I guess the other passengers in the car must have been quite panicked.

Well, we could have been killed.

Why would the casino have tampered with your car after they had already banned you from the premises?

I can't tell you it was tampered with; all I can tell you is what happened.

We got off on a tangent. I had asked you about how you made the transition from casino games to markets.

After my successful casino games—I also developed a system for beating Wheel of Fortune—I got to thinking about games in general and thought, *The biggest game in the world is Wall Street. Why don't I look at and learn about that?*

I knew almost nothing about the market. In 1964, I decided to spend the summer learning about the stock market. I read everything from Barron's to books such as the *Random Character of Stock Prices*. After a summer of reading, I had a lot of thoughts about what to do and what to analyze.

Were any books particularly helpful?

Most of them were helpful in the negative. For example, *Technical Analysis* by Edwards and McGee was very helpful in the negative.

What do you mean by "helpful in the negative?"

I didn't believe it. The book convinced me that technical analysis was a road not to go down. In that sense, it saved me a lot of time.

But one could come up with a rational explanation of why chart analysis might work—namely that the charts reflect the net impact of all the fundamentals and the psychology of all the market participants.

You can't prove a negative. I can't prove it doesn't work. All I can say is that I did not see enough substance there to pursue it. I didn't want to take time to try things unless I thought they were pretty good.

So after your summer of reading and research what avenues did seem worthy of exploration?

I didn't come with much after that first summer, and everything was on hold for the academic year. The next summer, I continued my research into the stock market. One hot and sunny June day, I was sitting under the shade of a tree in my backyard, and in my first hour reading, I came across a periodical called *RMH Warrants and Low Price Stock Survey* by Sydney Fried. I think the publication still exists; his son runs it now. I realized that the pricing of warrants should be mathematizable.

The huge amount of variables that might apply to trying to forecast stock prices were almost all eliminated if you focused on warrants instead. I wrote down a short list of the factors that I thought should determine the warrant price. These included the price of the underlying stock, the strike price, the volatility, the time to expiration, and the interest rate level. There were all the same factors that everyone today agrees determine option prices. I started thinking about what formula might define the warrant price. That fall, I transferred to the University of California at Irvine (UCI). On my first day on campus, I was telling the head of the School of Information and Computer Science about my efforts to derive a warrant pricing model, and he told me that there was someone else at the university doing the same thing. That person turned out to be Sheen Kassouf, who had already written a thesis that contained a theoretical model for determining warrant prices. It wasn't a very good model, but it wasn't bad. It was certainly much better than not having any model. Kassouf had already been trading warrants and making fairly steady money by hedging his warrant positions. We started working together, a joint endeavor that ultimately led to our co-authoring *Beat the Market*.

Did *Beat the Market* have an option pricing formula in it?

It had Kassouf's empirically based formula.

How close was that to the formula you eventually developed?

It was entirely different.

Why would you write a book telling people how to price warrants and find mispriced trade opportunities when that information was not yet out there?

We actually answer that question in the book. We thought it was only a matter of time before other people came up with similar discoveries. We reasoned that if we were the first to write about it, prospective investors would read the book and come to us, and we would be able to manage money.

Do you think that was the right decision? Don't you think you and Kassouf might have been better off exploiting the warrant trading on your own instead of publishing the ideas?

I don't think so because historically ideas don't just appear in one place; they tend to appear in several places at almost the same time.

Like Newton and Leibniz.

Exactly, or Darwin and Wallace.

When did you start managing money?

It sort of happened on its own while I was at UCI. Both Kassouf and I were managing our own accounts. Word got out on campus, and people started asking us to manage their money. People who invested were making over 20 percent per year, and they told their friends. Before long, I had a dozen accounts, and a lot of happy people on campus.

What was the strategy you were using at that time?

The theme in *Beat the Market* was that warrants with less than two years to run typically traded at premiums that were too high. The typical trade we did was to short the warrant and hedge it by buying the stock.

Delta hedging?

We started out with a static hedge and then decided that dynamic delta hedging was better.[9]

Did you and Kassouf manage money together?

No, because we had different ideas of how we believed the strategy should be implemented. Kassouf thought he could tell something about the direction of stock prices and would sometimes take a fundamental view on a stock, whereas I was afraid to do that because I didn't believe I had any forecasting power. I thought we should always hedge to be delta neutral.[10] So we went our separate ways. He and his brothers started a managed money business, while I managed my individual accounts for a while.

When did you develop your own option-pricing model?

In 1967, I took some of the ideas about how to price warrants in the *Random Character of Stock Prices* by Paul Cootner and thought I could derive a formula if I made the simplifying assumption that all investments grew at the risk-free rate. Since the purchase or sale of warrants combined with delta neutral hedging led to a portfolio with very little risk, it seemed very plausible to me that the risk-free assumption would lead to the correct formula. The result was an equation that was equivalent to the future Black-Scholes formula. I started using this formula in 1967.

---

[9]In a static hedge, the warrant position is counterbalanced by an equal delta opposite position in the stock at time of trade implementation, resulting in a delta neutral combined position. (*Delta neutral* means that the value of the combined position will remain approximately unchanged for small changes in price.) In a dynamic delta hedge, the offsetting stock position is continually adjusted to maintain an approximately delta neutral total position.

[10]*Delta neutral hedging* means that purchases and sales of the underlying stock are used to keep the combined position balanced so that it is approximately unaffected by small price changes in either direction.

Did you apply your formula (that is, the future Black-Scholes formula) to identify overpriced warrants and then delta hedge those positions?

I didn't have enough money to have a diversified warrant portfolio and to also place the hedge, since each side of a hedged position required separate margin. I used the formula to identify the most extremely overpriced warrants. I found warrants that were selling at two or three times what my formula said they should be priced at. So I just went naked short warrants.

Selling warrants without a hedge seems to be in total contradiction to your desire to minimize risk. What if the market had a large rally?

That is exactly what happened. In 1967 to 1968 there was a large bull market. Small cap stocks were up 84 percent in 1967 and 36 percent in 1968. It was a terrible time to have net short exposure. However, the formula was good enough and the warrants were so overpriced that I still broke even on the naked short positions. The formula really proved itself under the most adverse circumstances. As far as I know, the short warrant positions I implemented during 1967 to 1968 were the first actual application of the Black-Scholes formula in the markets.

When did Black-Scholes publish their formula?

I believe they discovered it in 1969 and published it 1972 or 1973.

Did you consider publishing your formula?

The option-pricing formula seemed to me to be a big edge on everybody else. So I was happy just to use it. By 1969, I had started my first hedge fund, Princeton Newport Partners, and I thought that if I published the formula, I would lose the edge that was helping my investors. I thought the best thing would be to keep quiet and just keep using it. It was like having a card counting system, but not writing a book about it. Once Black and Scholes published their formula, it was too late. I don't have any regrets.

I believe that convertible bond arbitrage was probably the core strategy used by Princeton Newport Partners. Did you come up with innovations to the strategy that you can talk about now?

A convertible bond is a corporate bond that holders can convert into a fixed number of shares at a specified price. In effect, a convertible bond is a combination of a corporate bond and a call option. Because the embedded option has monetary value, convertible bonds will pay lower interest rates than corporate bonds. Convertible arbitrage funds will typically buy convertible bonds and hedge by shorting sufficient stock to neutralize the long exposure implied by the embedded call option (an activity called delta hedging*). Originally, the embedded optionality in convertible bonds tended to be underpriced, and convertible arbitrage funds could earn substantial profits by buying underpriced convertible bonds and hedging the market risk with short stock positions. While the core strategy remained unchanged, increased competition drove down mispricings and made the sophistication of the convertible bond pricing model more important.*

In the simple convertible bond-pricing model, a convertible bond is treated like a corporate bond with a warrant attached. The corporate bond is assumed to provide a floor to how low the convertible price can go. So if you have a 5 percent B grade convertible bond, the assumption is that the price will never be less than a 5 percent nonconvertible B grade bond. We learned that if the stock price fell sufficiently far, then the grade of the bond would also fall, and consequently, the assumed price floor was not a floor. We were able to build that characteristic into the model and get a much more accurate convertible bond-pricing model as a result. Our model also analyzed the entire family of related instruments to the underlying stock, which included convertible bonds, options, warrants, and convertible preferreds, to find optimal hedge combinations across all these related instruments.

After Princeton Newport Partners closed, I called up Fisher Black because I thought we had a better convertible bond model than anyone else and wanted to see if I could sell it to Goldman Sachs. Fisher Black flew out and spent three days reviewing our model. He agreed that it looked very good, but the problem was that the coding of the model was tailored to the Digital Equipment computers we used, which meant they would have had to recode the program to run on their equipment. So he ended up not buying it. The following two or three years, he built his own convertible bond model. I don't know whether he used any of our ideas, but it really doesn't matter.

How important was determining the optimal bet size in your trading success? How and why did you decide to use the Kelly criterion as the method for determining bet size?

The Kelly criterion is the fraction of capital to wager to maximize compounded growth of capital. Even when there is an edge, beyond some threshold, larger bets will result in lower compounded return because of the adverse impact of volatility. The Kelly criterion defines this threshold. The Kelly criterion indicates that the fraction that should be wagered to maximize compounded return over the long run equals:

$$F = P_W - (P_L/W)$$

where

$F = $ *Kelly criterion fraction of capital to bet*
$W = $ *Dollars won per dollar wagered (i.e., win size divided by loss size)*
$P_W = $ *Probability of winning*
$P_L = $ *Probability of losing*

When win size and loss size are equal, the formula reduces to:

$$F = P_W - P_L$$

For example, if a trader loses $1,000 on losing trades and gains $1,000 on winning trades, and 60 percent of all trades are winning trades, the Kelly criterion indicates an optimal trade size equal to 20 percent (0.60 − 0.40 = 0.20).

As another example, if a trader wins $2,000 on winning trades and loses $1,000 on losing trades, and the probability of winning and losing are both equal to 50 percent, the Kelly criterion indicates an optimal trade size equal to 25 percent of capital: 0.50 − (0.50/2) = 0.25).

Proportional overbetting is more harmful than underbetting. For example, betting half the Kelly criterion will reduce compounded return by 25 percent, while betting double the Kelly criterion will eliminate 100 percent of the gain. Betting more than double the Kelly criterion will result in an expected negative compounded return, regardless of the edge on any individual bet.

The Kelly criterion implicitly assumes that there is no minimum bet size. This assumption prevents the possibility of total loss. If there is a minimum trade size, as is the case in most practical investment and trading situations, then ruin is possible if the amount falls below the minimum possible bet size.

I learned about the Kelly criterion from Claude Shannon back at MIT. Shannon had worked with Kelly at Bell Labs. I guess Shannon was the leading light at Bell Labs and Kelly was perhaps the second most significant scientist there. When Kelly wrote his paper in 1956, Shannon refereed it. When I told Shannon about my blackjack betting system, he told me to look at Kelly's paper in deciding how much to bet because in favorable situations, you will want to bet more than in unfavorable situations. I read the Kelly paper, and it made a lot of sense to me.

The Kelly criterion of what fraction of your capital to bet seemed like the best strategy over the long run. When I say long run, a week playing blackjack in Vegas might not sound very long. But long run refers to the number of bets that are placed, and I would be placing thousands of bets in a week. I would get to the long run pretty fast in a casino. In the stock market, it's not the same thing. A year of placing trades in the stock market will not be a long run. But there are situations in the stock market where you get to the long run pretty fast—for example, statistical arbitrage. In statistical arbitrage, you would place tens or hundreds of thousands of trades in a year. The Kelly criterion is the bet size that will produce the greatest expected growth rate in the long term. If you can calculate the probability of winning on each bet or trade and the ratio of the average win to average loss, then the Kelly criterion will give you the optimal fraction to bet so that your long-term growth rate is maximized.

The Kelly criterion will give you a long-term growth trend. The percentage deviations around that trend will decline as the number of bets increases. It's like the law of large numbers. For example, if you flip a coin 10 times, the deviation from the expected value of five will by definition be small—it can't be more than five—but in percentage terms, the deviations can be huge. If you flip a coin 1 million times, the deviation in absolute terms will be much larger, but in percentage terms, it will be very small. The same thing happens with the Kelly criterion: in percentage terms, the results tend to converge on the long-term growth trend. If you use any other criterion to determine bet size, the long-term growth rate will be smaller than for the Kelly criterion. For betting in casinos, I chose the Kelly criterion because I wanted the highest long-term growth rate. There are, however, safer paths that have smaller drawdowns and a lower probability of ruin.

I understand that if you know your edge and it is precisely defined—which of course is not true in the markets—then the Kelly criterion is the amount you should bet to maximize the compounded return and that betting either a smaller or larger fraction will give you a smaller return. But what I don't understand is that the Kelly criterion seems to give all the weight to the return side. The only way the Kelly criterion reflects volatility is through its impact on return. Besides the fact that people are uncomfortable with high volatility, there is the very practical consideration that your down-and-out point is not zero as the Kelly criterion implicitly assumes, but rather your maximum tolerable drawdown. It seems to me that the criterion should be what maximizes growth subject to the constraint of minimizing the risk of reaching your cutout point.

Suppose you have a bankroll of $1 million and your maximum tolerable drawdown is $200,000. Then from the Kelly criterion perspective, you don't have $1 million in capital, you have $200,000.

So, in your example, you still apply the Kelly criterion, but you apply it to $200,000. When you played blackjack, did you apply the Kelly criterion straightforward?

Yes, assuming I was sure the dealer was not cheating, because my objective was to make the most money, in the least time.

What about when you managed the fund?

When I managed the fund, I wasn't forced to make a Kelly criterion decision. If you use hedges to theoretically neutralize your risk, then the Kelly criterion might well imply using leverage. In Princeton Newport Partners where all positions were hedged, I found that I couldn't leverage up my portfolio as much as the Kelly criterion said I should.

Because?

Because the brokerage firms wouldn't give me that much borrowing power.

Does that imply that you would have traded the Kelly criterion if it was feasible in a practical sense?

I probably wouldn't have because if you bet half the Kelly amount, you get about three-quarters of the return with half the volatility. So it is much more comfortable to trade. I believe that betting half Kelly is psychologically much better.

I think there is a more core reason why betting less than the Kelly amount would always be the rational decision in the case of trading. There is an important distinction between trading and playing a game such as blackjack. In blackjack, theoretically, you can know the precise probabilities, but in trading, the probability of winning is always an estimate—and often a very rough one. Moreover, the amount of extra gain forgone by betting less than the Kelly criterion is much smaller than the amount that would be lost by betting more than the Kelly criterion by the same percentage. Given the uncertainty of the probability of winning in trading combined with the inherent asymmetry in returns around the Kelly fraction, it would seem that the rational choice is to always bet less than the Kelly criterion, even if you can handle the volatility. In addition, there is the argument that for virtually any investor, the marginal utility of an extra gain is smaller than the marginal utility of an equal percentage loss.

That's true. Say I am playing casino blackjack, and I know what the odds are. Do I bet full Kelly? Probably not quite. Why? Because sometimes the dealer will cheat me. So the probabilities are a little different from what I calculated because there may be something else going on in the game that is outside my calculations. Now go to Wall Street. We are not able to calculate exact probabilities in the first place. In addition, there are things that are going on that are not part of one's knowledge at the time that affect the probabilities. So you need to scale back to a certain extent because overbetting is really punishing—you get both a lower growth rate and much higher variability. Therefore, something like half Kelly is probably a prudent starting point. Then you might increase from there if you are more certain about the probabilities and decrease if you are less sure about the probabilities.

In practice, did you end up gravitating to half Kelly?

I was never forced to make that decision because there were so many trade opportunities that I usually couldn't put on more than a moderate fraction of Kelly on any single trade. Once in a while, there would be an exceptional situation, and I would hit it pretty hard. One good example was ATT and the Baby Bells. Old AT&T stock was going to be exchanged for the new stock plus stock in the seven Baby Bells. You could buy the old AT&T and short the new AT&T when issued and lock in a price spread of about 3/4 percent.

How large did you put on that trade?

Five million shares, which was equal to $330 million. It was the largest trade done on the New York Stock Exchange up until that point in time.

What was your capital base at the time?

Around $70 million.

How did you determine what size to put on?

That was all we could get.

I assume you did the trade that large because it was the proverbial risk-free trade.

That's the way it looked, but to be clear, there are no zero-risk trades.

Do you want to expound?

There was some remote possibility that we overlooked something. There is always the possibility that there is some unknown factor.

How did you first get involved in statistical arbitrage?

In 1979, we launched a research effort that I called the *indicators project*. We looked for indicators that might have some forecasting power— items such as earnings surprises, dividend payout rates, and book to price. We had a list of about 30 or 40 of these indicators that we investigated. As part of this project, one of the researchers looked at stocks that were most up and stocks that were most down during the recent past. He found that the stocks that were most up tended to underperform the market in the next period, while the stocks that were most down tended to outperform the market. That finding led to a strategy of buying a diversified portfolio of the most down stocks and selling a diversified portfolio of the most up stocks. We called that strategy MUD for most up, most down. My friend UCI mathematician William F. Donoghue used to joke, little realizing how close he was to a deep truth, "Thorp, my advice is to buy low and sell high."

We found that this market neutral strategy had about a 20 percent annual return before costs. It had fairly high risk because the two sides did not track as closely as we would have liked. There were two issues: One was to get the risk down, and the other was to get the transaction costs down. We felt we could get the cost down and that the risk wouldn't be a problem because the strategy would be part of a much larger portfolio. So it seemed like a viable strategy.

You settled on using the most up and most down stocks as the most effective indicators, but I'm curious as to whether any of the other indicators you tested also showed efficacy.

They did. For that period of time, we found a very marked pattern for stocks depending on whether or not they paid dividends. Stocks that paid no dividends seemed to have above-normal returns. Stocks that paid low dividends had below-normal returns, but as the dividend payout went up, the total return tended to increase as well. There was effectively a U-shape curve that favored buying stocks with no dividends and high dividends and selling stocks with low dividends. Earnings surprises also seemed to have an impact for a considerable period of time—weeks and even months—suggesting the market was slow to assimilate this type of information. These were not all original discoveries. We combed the literature and tried to stay current in the network of people conducting this type of research. Combining the research available from other sources with our own original ideas gave us a fairly long list of indicators that seemed to have an edge. But Princeton Newport was doing so well on a risk-adjusted basis with the strategies it had already that we put the statistical arbitrage strategy aside. It wasn't clear that the marginal improvement that could have been obtained by adding statistical arbitrage to the existing strategies warranted diverting the resources that would have been needed for its implementation.

When did you turn back to it again?

In 1985, we placed an ad in the *Wall Street Journal* looking for people who had reliable ideas that would produce provable excess returns. One of the calls we received in response to that ad was from Gerry Bamberger, who turned out to be the person who had discovered statistical arbitrage at Morgan Stanley. My recollection is that he developed the strategy around 1982 and was eventually shouldered aside by Nunzio Tartaglia who was his immediate superior. Tartaglia had come in some time later and took over the strategy. So Bamberger was disaffected and left Morgan Stanley. He saw our ad and came out to Newport Beach for an interview. He was very secretive at first, but as soon as he started talking about his strategy, I realized it was the same statistical arbitrage approach we had come up with, except that he had added a dimension that significantly reduced the risk. The innovation that Bamberger had added vis-à-vis our own strategy was that he grouped the stocks by industry and set up long/short portfolios within each industry. By adding industry neutrality, he significantly reduced the risk of the strategy.

When Bamberger explained his industry neutral approach, was your immediate thought "That's obvious; why didn't we think of that?"

When Bamberger explained his portfolio structure, I said, "Yes that's obvious." But I didn't say, "Why didn't we think of that?" probably because we had put the project aside. I believe that if we had decided to include statistical arbitrage in our portfolio, we probably would have migrated to the sector neutral approach rather quickly.

After Bamberger told you what he was doing, where did it go from there?

We created a joint venture that Bamberger ran from New York. We funded it, and he programmed it.

I'm curious. You already essentially knew what Bamberger was telling you, and his innovation was one that you could have easily implemented and would likely have done on your own had you not put the statistical arbitrage project aside. So you really didn't need Bamberger. Given that, what was your motivation for entering into a profit-sharing agreement with him?

It was almost like a franchise operation. He was very smart and very efficient. He got his own people together, and ran his own shop. It was well worth paying him to do all this. We probably would have incurred similar costs doing it in-house.

So it wasn't a matter of paying Bamberger for the idea, but rather the execution of the idea. Essentially, you felt here was somebody who clearly understood the concept and could implement an idea that you weren't using anyway.

Exactly. There were almost no administrative costs in working with him. He was also someone who was very honest and principled.

In a series of articles Thorp wrote about his experiences with statistical arbitrage,
he provided the following character sketch of Bamberger:

> *Gerry Bamberger was a tall trim Orthodox Jew with a very high I.Q.,*
> *an original way of looking at problems in finance, and a wry sense of*
> *humor. He spent several weeks working with us in Newport Beach.*
> *After a few days I noticed that Gerry always brought a brown bag for*
> *lunch and always ate a tuna salad sandwich. I finally had to ask, "How*
> *often do you have a tuna salad sandwich for lunch?" Gerry said, "Every*
> *day for the last six years." He was a heavy smoker and I'm extremely*
> *sensitive to tobacco smoke—we did not hire smokers nor allow smoking*
> *in our office—so part of our negotiation was about how to handle this.*
> *We respected each other and worked out a compromise that met each of*
> *our needs. Whenever Gerry needed a cigarette he would step outside our*
> *ground floor garden office.*[11]

How did the fund work out?

It ran for a couple of years and did quite well, and then the return started
to decline. By that time, Bamberger had made a fair amount of money
from the joint venture, and he decided to retire. At that point, I refo-
cused on the strategy and decided there was a better way to do it, which
could get the return back up again. My thought was to make the strategy
factor neutral. We did a principal components analysis of the portfolio
and tried to neutralize the principal factors.

What specific factors did you end up neutralizing the portfolio against?

In factor analysis, there are two different approaches. One is what I
would call an economic factors analysis in which you actually know
what the factors are, such as equity index prices, oil prices, etc. The other
approach is abstract factor analysis where all you have are the returns for
each security, and you process it with mathematical models and end up

---

[11]http://edwardothorp.com/id9.html.

with a collection of abstract factors that don't necessarily coincide with economic factors. The abstract factors best describe the actual historical data you are using.

What is this type of approach called where the factors aren't specific items but rather mathematical constructs?

I call it abstract factor analysis, and principal component analysis is another version of this approach. If you have a huge collection of data points, you can find these things called principal components, which are vectors in the data space that are perpendicular to each other, and they best describe the data.

Is the perpendicularity the reason why multicollinearity is not a problem[12]?

Yes. In abstract factor analysis, you don't have that issue, but with economic factors, you can have factors that are closely related to each other.

That sounds like it is a big advantage for using abstract factors over economic factors.

Yes, I think it's the way to go. The abstract factors can often get identified with specific economic factors or linear combinations of those factors. For example, it always turns out that the biggest abstract factor, or equivalently the biggest principal component, is the stock market.

But you actually don't need that information; it is only an interesting aside. You could be completely ignorant of the real world and still apply abstract factor analysis.

That's right. We applied the factor neutrality approach, and the returns went up, and risk went way down.

---

[12]If this question is intelligible, no explanation is necessary; if it isn't, any adequate explanation would be far too lengthy and tangential.

What year did you make the change?

We started researching this idea in 1986 because we saw the returns of Bamberger's approach beginning to decline.

So you began working on this approach while Bamberger was still there?

Yes, he left in 1987.

Did you completely lose touch with Bamberger after he retired?

Actually, in the mid–1990s, his wife contacted me and asked if I would write a recommendation for him for a law school application. I was happy to do it. As I understand, he did go to law school and get his degree, but I don't know what happened to him afterward.

You took statistical arbitrage to the next level by applying factor analysis. Where did it go from there?

There was a hiatus in running statistical arbitrage between the time Bamberger left and the factor analysis approach was implemented. The October 1987 crash occurred during that gap in trading, which is too bad because that was the single best period for the strategy up to that point. So we missed out on some really great returns, but we still had returns in the high 20s pretty consistently until 1989 when Princeton Newport was wound down after the Princeton office ran into its well-chronicled legal troubles with Giuliani.

Can we talk about that episode? How did your partnership with Regan, who ran the Princeton office, come about?

In 1969 when I met him, Regan was a stockbroker who was looking to do something better than just being a broker. It occurred to him that hedging might be a good way to go and that he should start a partnership to do it. He made a list of four candidates who might be potential partners in such a venture, and I was on that list. He conducted the search shortly after I co-authored *Beat the Market* with Kassouf, which received a fair amount of publicity. I was looking for someone to do the business and administrative side, so it seemed like a pretty good fit. He was doing the things I didn't want to do, and I was doing the things that he couldn't do.

When did you first find out that the Princeton office was being investigated?

I first heard about it when someone in our office got a call from a trader in the Princeton office, saying that federal agents were spilling off the elevators and grabbing all the records. I found out later that Regan and others in the Princeton office knew something was going on as much as a year earlier because of information requests.

So effectively you found out the day before the story ran in the newspapers?

Yes.

What was your reaction?

I had no idea what the motivation for the raid was or what the government was trying to find.

Regan never gave you any inkling of what was going on?

Not a peep.

Were you are wrong about your assessment of Regan?

I think he evolved over time, and in later years, he wasn't the same person I knew when we first formed our partnership. I think success slowly transformed him.

What was your response when you found out?

I negotiated with Regan and the other defendants of the Princeton office to contribute $2.5 million toward their defense, but to cap the partnership's liability to that amount. Their argument was that the partnership should pay the total defense bill, but my attitude was that if they were guilty, then the partnership shouldn't pay anything. So we settled on the $2.5 million number. That ended up being much less than the actual legal bill, which totaled over $12 million.

So you and Regan were in adversarial roles regarding this matter?

Yes, especially since I wasn't getting any information from those guys. They had circled the wagons.

How did the Princeton office operate under the circumstances?

It was difficult because they were distracted by all the legal stuff, but it was still limping along. Several months after the indictment, I met with Regan and told him, "I don't know what is going to happen here. I am willing to run the whole operation until this is all over. If you and the other defendants are willing to step down now, assuming you are acquitted, I will be happy to reinstate all of you at the same terms, and I will put that in writing if you like."

But there was absolutely no response. It was like I was talking to a deaf man. I decided this was not the type of relationship I wanted to continue in. The partnership closed shortly afterward except for winding down the existing positions.

Did you think of restarting the fund on your own?

I didn't want to do all the stuff that was involved in running a hedge fund; that was why I got a partner to run the business side in the first place. I also wanted a little bit of time out.

What happened after Princeton Newport Partners shut down?

I kept a small staff in the Newport Beach office. During 1990 and 1991, we primarily traded Japanese warrants, which was very profitable until the dealers began dramatically widening the spreads on us. The trades might have had a 30 percent profit potential, but the bid/ask spreads became so wide that the transaction costs were 15 percent. So we had to give it up as a strategy.

Then I heard that statistical arbitrage was doing well, and one of my largest previous investors wanted me to resurrect it as an investable strategy. In 1992, we restarted the strategy. It only made about 5 percent or 6 percent in that first year, but we were encouraged because it seemed that there was no reason other than random fluctuation for the below-normal return that year.

How did the strategy perform in the intervening years after the closing of Princeton Newport Partners when you weren't trading it?

The period between 1989, when we closed Princeton Newport Partners, and August 1992, when we restarted statistical arbitrage, would have been good. We happened to restart trading in a low spot for the strategy, but we stayed with it, and the performance got better and better. For the approximate 10 years we ran the program, returns before fees and leverage averaged 21 percent annualized with a standard deviation of only 7 percent.

Why did you shut the program down in 2002 when it had such a strong return/risk track record?

There were a couple of reasons. First, returns seemed to be declining. I had no idea whether this trend was temporary or permanent, but I suspected it would continue because there was much more money chasing the same strategy than ever before. We could have attempted to continue innovating to stay ahead of the trend and keep returns up, but that would have meant a lot of thinking and effort on my part. At that point, I said to myself, *Life is getting shorter; it is time to do some other things.* Another reason for shutting down the fund was that I had a couple of key employees who wanted a much larger share of the pie—an unreasonably large amount, I thought—so I said, "That is too much, good-bye."

Did you ever again look at how the program was performing?

We did look at it a few years ago. It was running at about 8 percent annualized, which is not too bad in a 2 percent world, but not good enough to make me want to go back and do it.

What was your involvement with David Shaw, who was another relatively early practitioner of statistical arbitrage?

In 1988, David Shaw had left Solomon and was looking for someone to fund him in a statistical arbitrage startup. I didn't know exactly what he wanted when he came out here, but we talked for about six hours, and it seemed that his strategy was redundant with ours. So we parted on friendly terms.

So it was basically a matter of you both realizing that you were working on the same thing, and there really wasn't a match.

That is exactly right.

What did you do after you shut down the statistical arbitrage fund in 2002?

I managed my investments in other people's hedge funds.

Do you have any recommendations on investing in hedge funds?

I don't have any recommendations now because I have run low on hedge fund candidates.

Why is that?

Twenty years ago I understood the details of the hedge fund world very well because I was running one myself, and I knew a lot of the players and methodologies. I had a pretty good idea of which hedge funds had an edge and which ones were just asset gatherers. Since then, there has been an explosion in the number of hedge funds and assets under management, trends that have been accompanied by the entry of many more mediocre players. The increase in assets under management also tended to lower the return per dollar invested, as more money chased similar strategies. Finding the good hedge funds also became more difficult as there were much larger numbers of managers to wade through. Over the years, hedge funds began to shift from having edges to being asset gatherers. At the same time, the fees hedge funds charged increased.

There was a time when a flat 20 percent profit incentive fee would do it. Then it became 20 percent incentive plus 1 percent management fee, and then 2 percent management fee. All of these trends made it more difficult for the investor to extract good returns from hedge funds.

Do you feel the hedge fund industry is following the path of the mutual fund industry, which became equivalent to the market, or actually worse than the market once you take into account transaction costs?

I believe the overall returns make hedge funds a less compelling investment than they once were.

Where do you see the steady-state equilibrium for the hedge fund industry?

It seems to me that the steady state would be when there is no excess risk-adjusted return in the hedge funds.

Wouldn't you expect there to be some excess return simply because hedge fund investors have to be compensated for accepting greater illiquidity?

I agree with that.

Where do you think we are now? Do hedge funds still have some premium in risk-adjusted returns versus other investments?

My instincts are that they still have an edge, but not by very much.

Do you still invest in hedge funds?

I haven't found new good ones to invest in for a while. If I did, though, I would happily invest.

So you are still invested in ones from earlier days?

Yes, but the number is diminishing, as I decide some of these funds aren't as good as I thought they were, or their returns have declined.

When you were actively searching for new hedge funds to invest in, with the number of hedge funds having grown so much, how did you decide which ones to look at?

I screened out funds that had an annualized standard deviation greater than 15 percent or had an annualized return less than 12 percent or had a bad year.

Were there any managers you met who were good at the markets through an intuitive sense rather than any explicit analytics?

I spent a day with Bruce Kovner many years ago, and I thought he had a good qualitative grasp of all kinds of interconnections in the markets.[13] If you were a person who was able to think like Bruce Kovner, you could follow that path and be successful. I co-invested with Bruce on one of his ideas. Bruce bought an oil tanker and allowed a number of people he knew to invest alongside with him. I think I owned 20 feet of this tanker. It was called the Empress Des Mers, and at the time, it was the largest oil tanker in the world. The tanker could be bought for a little above scrap value because there was a surplus of tankers at that time, and the older tankers were in mothballs. I think this tanker had a scrap value of about $4 million, and Bruce bought it for $6 million. We just sat on it. It was sort of like an option on the oil market. When activity picked up in the oil market, there was a huge demand for tankers, so our tanker got used over and over and made a lot of money. It was in service until only a few years ago when it became so obsolescent that it was sold off for scrap.

How did you meet Warren Buffett?

When I started managing accounts trading warrants when I was at UCI, I got a reputation around school. One of the people who heard about me was Ralph Gerard, who was dean of the graduate school. He happened to be an investor with Buffett Partners Limited, which was being closed down because Buffett felt that stocks were at crazy heights in

---

[13]Bruce Kovner is the founder of Caxton Associates, a highly successful global macro fund, and was profiled in my book *Market Wizards* (New York: Institute of Finance, 1989).

1968, and he didn't feel there was much more he could do. Gerard needed to find an alternative investment to place the money that he was getting back from Buffett. He introduced me to Buffet, and we all played bridge at Gerard's house a few times. I knew Buffet was a really smart person when I met him in 1968. I remember telling my wife that given his ability to analyze companies, his rate of compounding, and the scalability of the approach, I thought he would be the richest person in the U.S. someday. He was for a period a few decades later, and from time to time thereafter. I lost track of Buffett, and then one day in 1982, I learned that Berkshire Hathaway, the company whose stock he had been distributing in 1968, had been turned into his own private mutual fund. I immediately realized what that meant. So I went out and bought Berkshire Hathaway shares. They had been selling for $12 a share in 1964, and here I was buying them at $985 a share.

Do you have thoughts on futures trend following as a strategy?

I believe there are versions of it that have a Sharpe ratio of about 1.0 or more, but that is low enough so that there is still a significant risk of getting shaken out of the strategy.

I take it then that you believe there are trends inherent in the markets.

Yes. Ten years ago, I wouldn't have believed it. But a few years ago, I spent a fair amount of time looking at the strategy. My conclusion was that it works, but that it was risky enough so that it was hard to stay with it.

Did you ever use trend following as a strategy?

I did.

When did you trade futures?

We began the research project in 2006, and launched the trading program in late 2007. It was promising, and we were thinking of bringing it up in large scale with institutional money. But in early 2010 my wife was diagnosed with brain cancer, and my heart wasn't in it. Life is too short. I didn't want to launch another major activity, so we gradually wound down the program.

So the program had worked well while you're using it.

Reasonably well. It wasn't as compelling as the Princeton Newport strategies or statistical arbitrage, but it would have been a good product, and it seemed to be better than most of the other trend-following programs out there that were managing a lot of money.

What kind of Sharpe ratio was your program running?

It was a little better than 1.0 annualized.

Since you are no longer using the strategy, can you talk about what modifications you made to improve a plain-vanilla trend-following approach? Was there something about your program that made it different from other trend-following approaches and that might explain why it did somewhat better?

We combined technical and fundamental information.

What kind of fundamental information?

The fundamental factors we took into account varied with the market sector. In metal and agricultural markets, the spread structure—whether a market is in backwardation or contango—can be important, as can the amount in storage relative to storage capacity. In markets like currencies, however, those types of factors are irrelevant.

Would it be accurate to describe your approach as combining technical trend-following rules with market specific fundamental filters that define favorable and unfavorable environments?

Yes.

Were there other enhancements you made to the standard trend-following approach?

We had some risk-reducing approaches built into the system. We tracked a correlation matrix that was used to reduce exposures in correlated markets. If two markets were highly correlated, and the technical system went long one and short the other, that was great. But if it wanted to go long both or short both, we would take a smaller position in each.

Since correlations between markets change so radically over time, even changing sign, how long of a lookback period did you use?

We found that 60 days was about best. If you use too short of a window, you get a lot of noise; if you use too long of window, you get a lot of old information that isn't relevant.

What other risk-reducing strategies did you incorporate into the system?

We also had a risk management process that worked a bit like the old portfolio insurance strategy. If we lost 5 percent, we would shrink our positions. If we lost another few percent, we would shrink our positions more. The program would therefore gradually shut itself down, as we got deeper in the hole, and then it had to earn its way out. We would wait for a threshold point between a 5 percent and 10 percent drawdown before beginning to reduce our positions, and then we would incrementally reduce our position with each additional 1 percent drawdown.

At what drawdown point would your position be reduced to zero?

Twenty percent.

How far down did you get?

Our maximum drawdown was about 14 percent to 15 percent, by which point we were trading only about one-third of our normal base position size.

How would you get restarted if the drawdown reached 20 percent?

You wouldn't. You have to decide ahead of time how much of a drawdown would imply that the system is not as good as you thought it was, and therefore shouldn't be traded.

In hindsight, do you think reducing your exposure on drawdowns was a good idea?

It all depends on how confident you are about your edge. If you have a really strong conviction about your edge, then the best thing to do is sit there and take your lumps. If, however, you believe there is a reasonable chance that you might not have an edge, then you better have a safety mechanism that constrains your losses on drawdowns. My view on trend following was that I could never be sure that I had an edge, so I wanted a safety mechanism. Whereas for a strategy like convertible arbitrage, I had a high degree of confidence as to the payoff probabilities, so reducing exposure on drawdowns was unnecessary.

In a strategy like trend following where you couldn't accurately assess the probabilities, as you could in a strategy such as convertible arbitrage, what percent of the Kelly criterion was your bet size?

We didn't use the Kelly criterion at all in trend following because the bet size was such a small fraction of Kelly that it didn't make any difference. I would guess that we were probably using something equivalent to 1/10 or 1/20 of Kelly.

I understand that you looked at Madoff at an early point in his career. Can you tell me about that experience?

Back in 1991, one of the major institutional investors in the Princeton Newport fund asked me to review their allocation process for their pension fund. I spent several days at their offices reviewing their hedge fund managers. One of these managers was remarkable in that he printed positive returns of about 1 percent to 2 percent virtually every month.

They had been invested with this manager for a few years. I asked them to show me the statements. I looked at the statements and very quickly determined that the manager was a fraud.

How did you reach that conclusion?

The first step was to look at what the manager said he did. His purported strategy was to buy a stock, buy a put a little below the stock price, and sell a call a little bit above the stock price. The premium he received for the call approximately balanced the premium he paid for the put. Buying the put protected him from losing much in any given month, but it certainly didn't mean that he would win every month. Suppose you have a month with a strong upmarket. He will do well because he will make the difference between the strike price of the call and the price at which he bought the stock. On the other hand, suppose you have a significant down month. Then he will lose because the puts he bought will get exercised at lower prices than where he bought the stock. Since he was doing the same strategy in all the stocks, he shouldn't be getting much diversification in months where most stocks were up or down. So he should have some very good months, but he should also have some very bad months. But those results were not showing up. His returns were not consistent with the market, given the strategy he claimed to employ. So the immediate question I had was: Why not?

When I looked at the record, I noticed that miraculous trades would be put on periodically that would get rid of the potential losing months and make them winners and get rid of the big winning months and make them moderate winners. And those miraculous trades were long or short S&P futures positions that just happened to come in the right month and the right amount to smooth everything out.

After this initial review, I asked my client, "When do you receive your trade confirmation statements?"

"Well," he answered, "they come in bundles every few weeks."

"Who is the accountant?" I asked.

"He is a friend of Madoff," they said. "He runs a one-man shop and has been Madoff's accountant since the 1960s."

I held my nose and asked, "Who is in charge of information technology?"

"Oh, his brother, Peter Madoff," they answered.

I told him that I wanted to go over and check out the operation. They called up to arrange for my visit. Bernie was away in Europe, raising more money as it turned out. His brother Peter said, "There is no way I will let him in the front door." I asked them to ask why, but Peter wouldn't give a reason. To me, the whole thing smelled. I told my institutional client that I wanted to take their daily confirmations and monthly statements and analyze them in more detail. "Fine," they said, "do the analysis and report back to us."

I brought boxes of the confirmations and statements back with me to California and went over the information carefully. We looked at the individual trade confirmations and determined that most of the trades could never have been made. We chose to focus on the option trades because the stock trades were too difficult to prove false. Half the option trades were for options that didn't even trade on the transaction date. Zero volume. About a quarter of the rest couldn't have traded at the prices quoted. For the remaining quarter, we couldn't tell if the trades occurred. I took 10 of these trades to a high-placed brokerage friend and asked him if he could find out who the counterparties were on those trades. He checked and found out that Madoff's organization didn't appear as counterparty on any of the trades.

I told my institutional client, "He is printing fake trades. He is making it all up. What you should do is get out as soon as you can and as quietly as you can. This is a huge Ponzi scheme that will get bigger and bigger, and one day it is going to self-destruct."

Did they get out?

They did.

Did you take it any further?

I thought of trying to expose it, but I had already had a belly full of government with Giuliani and Princeton Newport Partners. I also had previously found some small frauds and was told by a lawyer friend of mine who spent eight years working for the SEC that it would be a waste of time reporting it.

Why is that?

Because they didn't care about stuff like that.

What are your thoughts on the efficient market hypothesis?

Based on our daily success in Princeton Newport Partners, the question wasn't "Is the market efficient?" but rather the appropriate questions were "How inefficient is the market?" and "How can we exploit the inefficiencies?"

The claim of market efficiency, which implies that no market edge is possible, is a hollow statement because you can't prove a negative. But you can disprove market efficiency if there are people who have a demonstrable edge. There is a market inefficiency if there is a participant who can generate excess risk-adjusted returns that can be logically explained in a way that is difficult to rebut. Convertible arbitrage is a good example. You can lay out exactly how it works, why it works, and approximately how much return you expect to get.

How would you summarize your philosophy of the markets after all these years?

I think inefficiencies are there for the finding, but they are fairly hard to find.

Do you think it has gotten harder to find inefficiencies, given the increased competition?

It has gotten harder for me, but that may only be because I am older and less interested, and have more money, which makes me less motivated.

Do you have any advice for someone who wanted to pursue the markets as a challenge?

The approach that worked for me was the title of a book written much later by my ex-sister-in-law, *Do What You Love and the Money Will Follow*.

Anything else?

Try to figure out what your skill set is and apply that to the markets. If you are really good at accounting, you might be good as a value investor. If you are strong in computers and math, you might do best with a quantitative approach.

■ ■ ■

Gambling and investing may not sound like they have much in common, but to Thorp they were quite similar—they were both probability-based games for which the problem of finding an edge could be solved analytically, even though such a solution was widely assumed not to exist for either. Thorp defied the standard preconceptions in both gambling and investing and applied the same type of scientific thinking and mathematical reasoning to each of these endeavors. It is therefore not surprising that the same principles and risk management he employed in gambling are as pertinent to providing trading lessons as those he used in the markets.

Beating roulette was once considered a mathematical impossibility. By approaching the problem in a completely different way—focusing on predicting the most likely termination zone for the ball—Thorp was able to create a giant 44 percent edge. The broad lesson is that sometimes what seems impossible is entirely possible if approached from a completely different perspective. A similar condition might apply to trading. Even if one grants that the markets can't be beat with conventional approaches, it by no means implies that unconventional approaches would have the same limitation.

Thorp's insight in how to improve the odds in blackjack betting vis-à-vis the "basic system" (that is, correct probabilistic decisions on when to hit, hold, split, or double down) was to vary the bet size. By betting more on high-probability hands than on low-probability hands, Thorp was able to transform a losing game—even one played with perfect decisions (other than bet size)—into a game with a significant positive edge. There is an important analogy here that applies to traders: Varying the position size can be as important as the entry methodology. Trading smaller, or not at all, for lower probability trades and larger for higher probability trades can transform a losing strategy into a winning one. (Thorp had to bet something on even low-probability blackjack hands, but the trader can forgo lower probability trades altogether.)

Although, in trading, probabilities cannot be accurately assessed, as they can in blackjack, traders can often still differentiate between higher and lower probability opportunities. For the quantitative trader, such an assessment might be based on a statistical analysis of past results for different strategies. As for discretionary traders, many of them have strong differences in confidence level for different trades. If a trader does better on high-confidence trades, then the degree of confidence can serve as proxy for probability of winning. The implication then becomes to trade larger on high-confidence trades and smaller, or not at all, on low-confidence trades.

The degree of confidence in a trade is relevant not only in determining the trade size, but also in deciding on the appropriate risk management approach. When Thorp did arbitrage trades where the maximum theoretical risk could be approximately estimated, he did not consider reducing exposure if the position went against him. In contrast, when Thorp employed a trend-following strategy, in which the trades were directional and the edge far more uncertain than the edge in the various arbitrage strategies he had previously used, he made exposure reduction on drawdowns part of the methodology.

A lesson that Thorp learned in gambling was: "Don't bet more than you are comfortable with. Just take your time until you're ready." He drove his original blackjack backers crazy by starting out betting $1 on the bad hands and a maximum of $10 on the good hands—ridiculously small wagers given his edge and the objectives of his backers. Thorp's perspective on risk and comfort level provides sound advice for traders as well. Emotions are deadly for trading, and the surest way to guarantee that emotions will impact trading decisions is by trading beyond one's comfort level.

Many traders mistakenly believe that there is some single solution to defining market behavior. If only they could find that solution, trading would become like operating a money machine. Many traders are continually searching for this Holy Grail of trading methods. The reality is that there is no single solution to the markets, and any solutions that do exist are continually changing. Successful traders adapt to changing market conditions. Even when they find patterns or methods that provide a market edge, they will change their approach as dictated by the market. Finding success in the markets is a dynamic rather than static process.

Thorp's approach to statistical arbitrage is a case study in adapting to markets. The initial concept was to balance long positions in stocks that had gone down the most with short positions in stocks that had gone up the most so that the portfolio net exposure was near zero. When the return/risk of this strategy started to deteriorate, Thorp switched to a variation of the strategy that added sector neutrality to market neutrality. Then when even sector neutral statistical arbitrage started to lose its edge, Thorp switched to a strategy variation that neutralized the portfolio to the various factors. By the time the third iteration was adapted, the original system version had significantly degraded. By adapting and changing the strategy, Thorp was able to consistently maintain extremely strong return/risk performance, whereas staying with the original system because it had worked so well at one time would have fared poorly.

What is the optimal size for any trade? Theoretically, this question has a precise answer: the Kelly criterion, which it can be mathematically demonstrated will yield a higher cumulative return over the long run than any other strategy for determining trading size. There is a rub, however. The Kelly criterion assumes that the probability of winning and the ratio of the amount won to the amount lost per wager are precisely known. Although this assumption is typically true for games of chance, in trading, the probability of winning is unknown and, at best, can only be estimated—often with a wide degree of error. If the Kelly criterion is used to determine the trade size, there is a steep penalty for overestimating the probability of winning (or the ratio of the average win to average loss). In fact, the negative impact of overestimating the correct trade size is twice as large as the negative impact of underestimating the correct trade size by the same amount. Therefore, if the precise probabilities of winning are not known—as is usually the case for trading applications—then the bet size should be significantly smaller than the full Kelly amount.

Also, even assuming the correct Kelly trade size was precisely known, the resulting equity stream would be far too volatile for most people's comfort level. The high volatility implicit in the Kelly criterion is not merely an aesthetic issue, but has important practical implications as well. The greater the volatility of the equity stream, the greater the chance a trader will abandon the approach on one of the drawdowns. Thorp recommends that using half Kelly is a better alternative (than full Kelly) for most people, even if the probability of winning (and the average win/average loss ratio) can be reasonably estimated. If the estimate for the probability of winning is subject to wide error, then only a very small fraction of Kelly should be risked on any trade. When Thorp was faced with such a situation (that is, when he traded a trend-following system), he estimates that his trade size was probably less than one-tenth of Kelly—such a small fraction of Kelly that he didn't even use the Kelly criterion to size trades.

Where does this all leave us in regard to using the Kelly criterion for trade sizing? It depends. If you believe you can roughly estimate your probability of winning and the average win/average loss ratio, then the Kelly criterion can be very useful in defining the appropriate trade size. Even in this instance, however, half Kelly will be a better choice than full Kelly for most people. If, however, the probability of winning is subject to wide error, then even half Kelly is probably much too large, and the Kelly criterion would be of limited use.

Chapter 7

Jamie Mai

Seeking Asymmetry

I became aware of Jamie Mai through Michael Lewis's book, *The Big Short*, which manages the neat feat of creating an entertaining narrative about the complex, esoteric world of mortgage-backed securities (MBS) that lay at the heart of the 2008 financial crisis. Ironically, based on the trades Lewis described, I drew a very different impression about the balance between luck and skill in driving the success of Cornwall Capital (Mai's firm) than Lewis himself did.

Lewis's colorful narrative of Cornwall as a hedge fund started in a shed on a shoestring budget, trading a small brokerage account, gave no hint of the firm's institutional context. The reality is a bit duller. Cornwall was originally founded as a family office to diversify the capital of Mai's father, who ran AEA Investors, a prominent, long-standing private equity firm that was recently rated one of the 10 most consistent performing buyout fund managers in the world.

Shortly after he started Cornwall, Mai was joined by Charlie Ledley, a former colleague from a private equity firm at which they had both worked. A third key principal, Ben Hockett, joined Cornwall in 2005 as head trader. The three collaborated closely in developing Cornwall's investment program, which combined the bottom-up fundamental value approach in which Mai and Ledley had been trained with Hockett's capital markets experience and expertise in derivatives and fixed income trading. Ledley left Cornwall (on good terms) in 2009 to join a large Boston-based hedge fund. Hockett remains at Cornwall and is the firm's chief risk officer and head trader.

Cornwall's strategies range from thematic fundamental trades to trades that seek to profit from esoteric market inefficiencies. The one unifying characteristic virtually all of Cornwall's strategies share is that they are structured and implemented as highly asymmetric, positive skew trades—that is, trades in which the upside potential far exceeds the downside risk. One of these trades, a short bet on subprime mortgages, led to Mai, Ledley, and Hockett becoming key characters in Lewis's book. Although this particular trade was unusually profitable—Cornwall ultimately made about 80 times the initial premium they paid out for subprime default protection—it was entirely representative of the types of trades Cornwall seeks out.

Beginning in May 2011, Cornwall switched to a new fund structure open to outside investors. Through the years, Mai had encountered several outstanding trade opportunities that could easily accommodate far more capital than his family office could invest. In a few of those instances, he explored the possibility of raising outside investor money to participate in the trade idea, but decided the lag involved was too long. The catalyst that finally convinced Mai to restructure the fund to accommodate investors was born of the frustration of being unable to participate in a rare pure arbitrage opportunity in 2008 because he lacked sufficient assets.[1] Mai decided to open the fund to only a handful

---

[1]The background behind this trade was the collapse in crude oil prices that accompanied the 2008 financial meltdown and resulted in a highly unusual spread structure for crude oil futures. Nearby oil prices were trading at enormous discounts to more forward futures. It was possible to take delivery of oil, hedge it by selling a much higher-priced forward futures contract, store the oil on a tanker, and then redeliver it against the forward contract at

of like-minded, sophisticated investors with whom he could be reasonably transparent and share ideas, rather than seeking to maximize assets under management.

For the near nine-year period since its inception, Cornwall Capital has realized an average annual compounded net return of 40 percent (52 percent gross).[2] The annualized standard deviation has been relatively high at 32 percent (37 percent gross). Cornwall's Sharpe ratio of 1.12 (1.23 gross) represents very good performance based on this widely used return/risk measure, but greatly understates the true return/risk performance of the fund. Cornwall is the poster child for the inadequacy of the Sharpe ratio if applied to managers with non-normal return distributions. The crux of the problem is that the Sharpe ratio uses volatility as the proxy for risk. Because of the asymmetric design of its trades, Cornwall's volatility consists mostly of upside volatility. In other words, Cornwall's volatility is high because they have many instances of very large gains. However, I have yet to meet an investor who finds large gains to be a problem. The risk measure of the Sharpe ratio, the standard deviation, will penalize exceptionally large gains. Using a return/risk measure such as the Gain to Pain ratio (see Appendix A for description), which employs a loss-based rather than volatility-based risk measure, the superior quality of Cornwall's performance is readily evident. Cornwall's Gain to Pain ratio is exceptionally high at 4.2 (5.2 based on gross returns).

I interviewed Mai in the conference room of Cornwall's office in three sessions spaced over a period of six months. We met after trading hours, with the longest interview conducted over a take-out dinner. Mai was friendly and open in discussing his trading strategies.

---

expiration. The price difference between the two contracts far exceeded the costs of operating the tanker for the interim period. It was a classic locked-in arbitrage trade. The only hitch was that you needed a tanker, and you can't buy part of a tanker. Cornwall was simply too small to accomplish this transaction with its own funds, and it would have taken too long to raise money from investors.

[2]Statistics are for the January 2003 to December 2011 period and are based on the original fund through April 2011 and the new fund open to outside investors beginning May 2011. To calculate net return, the fees charged on the new fund were deducted from the returns of the original fund, which managed proprietary funds and did not charge any fees.

Note: Readers unfamiliar with options may find it useful to first read Appendix B, which provides a short primer on options, in order to better understand the trading related references in this chapter.

■ ■ ■

Did you have any reservations about participating as a subject in Michael Lewis's book *The Big Short*?

For sure. In fact, we originally had no interest in being profiled. When Michael approached us in 2009, Charlie and I were probably spending half our time on noninvestment work, trying to impact financial reform policy. We thought it was incredibly scary that nobody was talking about the fundamental structural flaws in credit derivatives that made the financial crisis so hard to resolve.

We were also talking to print and broadcast journalists to assist in their efforts to understand and communicate the forces responsible for the crisis. For example, when Michael first approached us, Charlie had recently provided extensive background information to NPR's *Planet Money* program. The episode they subsequently produced, called "The Giant Pool of Money," was a near-verbatim rendition of the story Charlie and I were telling to anyone who would listen.[3] And at that time, not many people would.

So when Lewis came along, we talked to him openly. In his case, we provided a more technical narrative that focused on why subprime mortgage securitizations got so out of hand. While he asked to include us in the book, we never considered it seriously, particularly since he told us that he wanted to focus on my relationship with my father.

---

[3] *The Giant Pool of Money* was an hour-long, award-winning program that originally aired on *This American Life*, a weekly hour-long radio broadcast, hosted by Ira Glass and distributed by Public Radio International (PRI). The program provided a remarkably lucid and entertaining exposition of the intricacies of the mortgage crisis. *The Giant Pool of Money's* success gave rise to NPR's *Planet Money* radio show, hosted by Adam Davidson and Alex Blumberg, the team that had produced the program. *Planet Money* is a highly creative, entertaining, and insightful financial program. I have listened to every podcast since the program's inception, and I highly recommend it.

Pretty far along into the project, Michael came back to ask us again. He said, "Hey, guys, I haven't been able to find any other investors who shorted subprime mezzanine CDOs, and I really need you to participate so I have a narrative device to walk through the mechanics of CDOs."[4] Understanding the basics about CDOs is central to understanding how the credit crisis happened. We explored the possibility of shielding our identities through pseudonyms or fictionalizations. We couldn't come up with a good alternative, so after a bit of arm-twisting by Michael, we reluctantly agreed.

Were you satisfied with the way the book turned out?

Yes, I was. It laid bare the role of subprime mortgage securitizations in causing the credit crisis in a way that was accessible to a reader without a background in finance. I think it's had a positive impact on the public dialogue. I wish the narrative had extended to include more about the aftermath, particularly the government policy of forbearance and the inextricable interrelationship between systemic risk and credit derivatives. But I suppose that those extensions were beyond the book's purview.

How do you feel about the way you and your partners were portrayed?

Although, broadly speaking, I am fine with how Lewis portrayed us, his depiction reflected at least a touch of artistic license. I suppose it could have been a lot worse. He nicely captured some of the aspects of our methodology, but I think his portrayal might lead readers to draw inaccurate inferences about our investment approach.

Specifically, how did you feel you were portrayed inaccurately?

I think a reader can walk away with the feeling that we were just cowboys taking reckless risks, when in fact the opposite is true.

---

[4]If this comment is unintelligible to you, don't worry. A primer on mortgage-backed securities and their role in the financial crises is provided later in this chapter before our conversation related to Cornwall's short trade in collaterized debt obligations (CDOs).

Yes, he made you sound like lucky gunslingers. I remember when I read the book, my impression was that your portrayal came across as something along the lines of "never was there a long-shot investment venture less likely to succeed." The sequence of trades sounded like a series of 10 to 1 bets that all paid off in a giant profit pyramid. Yet when I read the descriptions of each of the trades, my impression was: That's not luck; that's actually a great asymmetric trade, which makes all the sense in the world. As I read it, you were finding greatly underpriced options, or investments with option-like characteristics, and taking advantage of the opportunity for a reasonable possibility of very large gains with well-defined, limited risk.

I didn't think that came across in the book.

Well, I think it was mostly between the lines. I assume the average reader probably wouldn't have come away with that impression. But the facts were there, so you could draw your own conclusions.

I'm glad you drew the ones you did.

While I can understand how some of your trades could make literally multiples of the investment, I was puzzled by the magnitude of the gains indicated by Lewis. Based on the numbers in the book, it sounded like you multiplied your initial $110,000 stake more than a thousandfold, which sounds a bit incredulous.

It is, though in fairness to Michael he had one major constraint in telling our story, which was that he had to leave my family out of it. My father has run one of the oldest leveraged buyout firms in the United States for over 20 years, and before that he ran the investment bank for Lehman Brothers. Cornwall Capital is a family office he and I formed together in 2002. The whole conceit of three dropouts lacking in direction and operating on a shoestring budget made good copy while preserving my family's privacy, but it didn't accurately reflect the fact that we had capital and a clear idea of how we wanted to evolve our investment approach. We did our first trade in my small Schwab account because we hadn't finalized the structure of the family's comingled investment vehicle. So, the $110,000 figure was accurate, in a narrow sense; it just was not representative because there was a lot more capital behind it, and we had a clear plan for the extension of the strategy.

I noticed that you were a history major in college. That hardly sounds like the background of someone looking to get into trading. Were your career objectives different earlier on?

Well, I couldn't tell you what my career ambitions were as an undergraduate, but I didn't necessarily think I was taking the option of a finance career off the table by majoring in history. I'm very lucky to have the father I do. He always encouraged me to follow my own path. He is a great role model. He's one of those rare people who can be wildly successful in his career and remain very down to earth. He is the most clear-headed thinker I know, and if I've inherited one trait from him that has helped me as an investor, it's an ability to see things in straightforward, practical terms. You might say we are both good at identifying the obvious. As for my career path, when I decided I was ready to buckle down, my father nudged me toward accounting as a backdoor way to get into private equity. It's a better background for private equity than the traditional career paths of investment banking or management consulting. There is truth in the adage that accounting is the language of business.

Did you go back to school for an accounting degree?

Yes. At the time, NYU had a special master's of accounting program that was sponsored by the "Big Six" accounting firms who wanted to diversify their staff pool to include undergrads with liberal arts degrees. In fact, one of the prerequisites to be hired into the program was that you hadn't taken any prior accounting courses. There was a summer crash course to cover four years of accounting classes, and then you were thrown into the financial audit group as a first year staff accountant. I was hired by Ernst & Young, LLP and worked primarily on audits of large investment banks.

Did you go into private equity after you finished your degree?

Yes. I went to work for Golub Capital, which was then a small private equity firm—Charlie Ledley was its first ever investment analyst, and I was the second—but has now grown its assets under management from less than $100 million to several billion dollars.

What did you learn there that was useful to you later on?

I think my experiences in private equity provided me with a solid foundation in fundamental value analysis. The due diligence process on an acquisition candidate requires dissecting the company's data at the most granular level. It's very easy to get lost in the weeds analyzing narrow issues whose complexity increases the deeper you dig. But you need to drill down because that's often where you find the information that leads to the questions that cause the investment thesis to unravel.

A necessary skill in private equity is the ability to kill bad deals quickly, since the resource-intensity of an analytical "deep dive" creates such high opportunity costs. One skill I learned from another former boss and mentor of mine, Will Thorndike at Housatonic Partners, was that finding answers is much easier when you know in advance what the questions are. Understanding what the right questions are can be deceptively difficult, but once you do, the rest is straightforward deductive analysis to determine whether the hypothesis is right. Usually it isn't, in which case you throw it into the waste bin with the 98 percent of other hypotheses that never amount to anything.

How did your private equity experience translate forward when you got involved in the investment side?

I was drawn first to special situations, as they seemed to be a natural fit for the hypothesis-driven and rigorous analytical approach I'd been taught. My definition of a special situation is one where a price dislocation has occurred, either at a single company or across an industry, because the market has identified a particular idiosyncratic risk and assigned an uncertainty discount to it. It's easy to frame the questions in special situations because the market has already identified the problem and applied the discount. We love classic bull versus bear battlegrounds, as they are dynamic, often complex, and involve events that can be probabilistically estimated. Although markets are generally good at estimating the magnitude of a contingent liability, they are often poor at evaluating outcomes probabilistically. Examples include litigations, regulatory actions, or other events that create the perception of going concern risk.

A specific example?

One of our first special situations involved the cigarette maker Altria. In 2003, Altria's market cap had declined close to 50 percent in response to a spate of rating agency downgrades, reflecting negative developments in a few of the larger class action litigations underway at the time. Obviously, the contingent liability for the tobacco companies was massive. So it wasn't unreasonable that a few individual cases should have the, potential to introduce meaningful uncertainty risk. Each case embedded the potential for 9- or even 10-figure settlements, not to mention the risk of setting a precedent favorable to future plaintiffs. It wasn't hard to create a story that ended in insolvency for the tobacco companies.

At the same time, we heard a couple of smart investors argue that the ratings agencies had gotten it wrong. In their view, structural realignments were likely to protect the tobacco companies from dismemberment. Specifically, they cited a global settlement with all 50 state attorney generals and the fact that U.S. taxpayers had already gained a controlling economic interest in the tobacco companies, with the majority of revenues from cigarette sales going to various federal, state, and local government agencies.

We liked the bullish argument and decided to take a closer look. Commercial litigations tend to throw off lots of publicly available information. We learned everything we could about each of the major cases winding its way through the courts at the time. We also found lots of smart litigators who were not involved in these cases, but were following them closely. The information they provided enabled us to assign at least rough probabilities to various outcomes. We spent two months gaming out the scenarios from the tobacco litigation and concluded the discount was seriously overdone.

As a general observation, markets tend to overdiscount the uncertainty related to identified risks. Conversely, markets tend to underdiscount risks that have not yet been expressly identified. Whenever the market is pointing at something and saying this is a risk to be concerned about, in my experience, most of the time, the risk ends up being not as bad as the market anticipated.

How do you estimate what discount the market is building into the price?

It was fairly easy in this case, given the obvious correlation between the rating downgrades and the stock price. Although we couldn't be sure that the correlation reflected causality, it seemed likely. As a complementary approach, you could also calculate the breakup value of the company—how much the nontobacco-related businesses, such as Kraft, were worth on their own. Then by subtracting this value from the stock price, you could back into an estimate of the value the market was assigning to the tobacco business. The difference between this value and the value of the tobacco business absent any litigation uncertainty provided an estimate of the litigation discount implicit in the market price.

What was the trade that you actually did?

It seemed quite clear to us that substantial new information was likely to come out relatively soon that would either validate the rating agencies' concerns about the litigation, in which case, the stock price would sell off substantially, or the reverse, in which case, the stock would appreciate substantially. Thus there was an above-average probability of a large price move in one direction or the other. We had already seen cases where the option market assigned normal probability distributions to situations that clearly had bimodal outcomes. So the first thing we checked was whether the Altria options still assumed a normal probability distribution, despite the presence of a bimodal event. Sure enough, the Altria option prices still implied a normal distribution, which meant the out-of-the-money options were way too cheap. Since our work suggested a greater likelihood for a bullish outcome, we bought the out-of-the-money calls. The calls appreciated sharply when one of the key cases supporting the rating downgrades was thrown out on appeal shortly after we initiated our investment. We made about 2.5 times our money on the trade. Although we made a large return for a short holding period, in hindsight, we sold far too soon.

Any other examples of a trade opportunity that was created by mispriced options related to a corporate event?

In 2002, Capital One dropped from $50 to $30 in one day after the company announced it had reached an agreement with regulators to sharply increase its reserves against its subprime-laden loan portfolio and to improve its credit risk assessment procedures. The previous storyline had been that Capital One's long string of strong earnings was driven by its superior quantitative models for assessing subprime credit risk. Now, there was a serious question as to whether the company's impressive financials were more a product of fraudulent accounting than better risk modeling. A full-blown bull/bear battle ensued with some analysts claiming the company was a fraud and other analysts saying that the management team was totally above board and topnotch. The odds that the stock would still be near $30 in two years seemed vanishingly small. Either the company would be vindicated or it would go under.

So either the stock is a zero or it is going much higher. Did you have a bias as to which scenario was more likely?

We did a ton of research. We did background checks on management. We spoke to people who had gone to college with the CEO because the essential question related to the ethical character of management. Although we were not a large investor, we were tenacious about getting access to the management team. We spoke to the chief risk officer, who not a lot of other people wanted to speak to, but for us, he was gold. We were particularly concerned that the biggest driver in their P&L was this one line item that was amalgamated as "securitization income." There was no visibility at all as to what went into this figure. We thought that if there was anything wrong with the company that was where it would be. Over time, the risk officer became quite comfortable talking to us. He spoke to us openly and did not seem at all like someone trying to spin a story.

What was the trade that you put on?

We thought buying the out-of-the-money calls provided the best way to express the trade because the potential bimodal outcome made a large price move much likelier than usual for the stock. Under these circumstances, the out-of-the-money calls were most mispriced and they had more embedded leverage. We were looking at buying the January 2005 $40 calls, which were trading near $5. Then there was some marginal bearish news, and the stock traded down to about $27. The calls we were looking to buy went down from $5 to $3.50. That was a big percentage move, which made the juice in the trade look that much greater, and we bought the calls.

How long did you stay in the trade?

We held the options for over a year, during which time, Capital One stock fully recovered. We ended up making about six times our money on the calls.

The Altria and Capital One trades provided examples of situations where the normal probability distribution assumption implicit in option pricing models was inconsistent with market realities. What other inconsistencies do you believe exist in the way options are priced?

Options are priced lowest when recent volatility has been very low. In my experience, however, the single best predictor of future increases of volatility is low historical volatility. When volatility gets very low in a market, we consider that a very interesting time to start looking for ways to get long volatility, both because volatility is very cheap in an absolute sense and because the market certainty and complacency reflected by low volatility often implies an above-average probability of increased future volatility.

Do you favor long-dated options?

Often, the longer the duration of the option, the lower the implied volatility, which makes absolutely no sense. We recently bought far out-of-the-money 10-year call options on the Dow as an inflation hedge. Implied volatility on the index is very low. The Dow companies would be in the best position to pass along higher prices. There is also an interest rate bet implicit in buying long-term options that can be quite interesting when interest rates are very low, as they are now. By being long 10-year call options, we are taking exposure on the risk-free rate implicit in the option pricing models. If interest rates go up, the value of the options can go up dramatically.

Are there other option-pricing inconsistencies you look for?

Option models generally assume that forward prices are predictive of the future movements in the spot price. Academic research and common sense suggest that this relationship is often invalid. Forward option-pricing models can break down, particularly in interest rate markets with steep term structures and low volatility levels.

A simple example of this anomaly would be a rates trade we did in 2010. At the time, the current Brazilian interest rate was around 8 percent and the 6-month forward rate was over 12 percent. The 6-month forward option prices were distributed around the forward rate of over 12 percent. In other words, the option prices implicitly assumed the 6-month forward rate as the expected level. The implied volatility at the time was around 100 basis points normalized, which meant the market was assigning the odds of nothing happening for the next six months or so—that is, rates staying near 8 percent—as over a four-standard-deviation event.[5]

We did not have conviction about the future direction of Brazilian interest rates, much less the actual levels. But we thought the assumption that a spot rate in six months near the current spot rate was a greater

---

[5]Mai explained that the typical quoting convention for implied volatility in interest rate markets, known as "normalized volatility," is the number of absolute basis points reflecting a one-standard-deviation event, as opposed to the standard convention of quoting implied volatility in other asset classes in terms of percentage changes in the underlying security. Normalized volatility of 100 basis points equals a much smaller volatility, as measured in "traditional" percentage terms, when rates are high than when they are low—a characteristic that may have been an additional factor amplifying the anomaly.

than four-standard-deviation event—an assumption that was embedded in the option price—represented a mispricing. We structured a trade that had a strike price around 10 percent, which was cheap because it was well out-of-the-money based on the forward interest rate (above 12 percent), but it was actually well in-the-money based on the current interest rate (8 percent). Rates could have gone up by an amount equal to half the difference between the forward and spot rates, and we still would have made money.

Why was the market expecting such a sharp increase in Brazilian interest rates?

There were several factors. Commodity exports are a major driver in the Brazilian economy. At the time, rising commodity prices and strong growth in China (a major importer) were resulting in increased domestic inflation. There was a high conviction that the Brazilian central bank was about to initiate an extended series of very substantial rate hikes. While we certainly understood why the market saw rate hikes as likely, we thought the plus 400-basis point increase implied by the forward rate was probably exaggerated. Another contributing factor to expectations for higher rates was that interest rates are a mean reverting asset, and, historically, rates had been closer to 12 percent than 8 percent.

Okay, that was an example of a wide differential between spot and forward rates leading to an anomaly in option prices. What other types of anomalies do you look for?

Forward-looking assumptions based on backward-looking statistical correlations are another source of some interesting opportunities. In the aftermath of the 2008 financial crisis, a clear risk-on/risk-off paradigm emerged in the markets, and particularly the foreign exchange (FX) markets. If it was a risk-on environment, everybody piled into currencies with exposure to emerging markets and commodities, such as the Australian dollar. When it was a risk-off environment, everyone fled currencies like the Australian dollar and piled into safe-haven currencies, such as the Swiss franc. Before the 2008 financial crisis, the correlation between the Australian dollar and Swiss franc had ranged between modestly positive to modestly negative for many years—in other words, there was no strong relationship between the two. After the financial crisis, however, the Australian dollar and Swiss franc exhibited extreme inverse correlation because of the risk-on/risk-off psychology that dominated the markets. It got to the point where, if the Swiss franc was up sharply, you could be relatively sure that the Australian dollar would be down sharply and vice versa.

At the time, we happened to be looking for an efficient way of getting short the euro. Implied volatility on the euro puts was expensive. We cheapened the premium substantially by taking our exposure through a *worst of* option, which is an exotic option that is priced based on a correlation input in addition to the standard inputs for a vanilla option.

That's a new one for me. What is a *worst of* option?

In a *worst of* option, you pay a single premium for a basket of options. In the trade we did, there were puts on two crosses in the basket: euro versus Australian dollar (EUR/AUD) and euro versus Swiss franc (EUR/CHF). *Worst of* option structures are cheaper because the payout is determined by whichever option performs more poorly from the buyer's perspective. As long as one of the options expires out-of-the-money, the option buyer will lose the entire premium. The expected correlation between the different options comprising a *worst of* basket is therefore a relevant price input, in addition to the standard inputs that determine option prices.

The *worst of* option we purchased was very cheap because a strong negative correlation had emerged between EUR/AUD versus EUR/CHF; if one cross went down, the recent correlation suggested that the other cross was likely to go up, which should in theory protect the option seller. Our view, though, was that we wanted exposure to the euro crashing, and we felt that if the euro tanked, it would crash against both the Australian dollar and the Swiss franc, swamping the recent risk-on/risk-off inverse correlation effect. If we had taken a bearish bet on the euro using plain vanilla puts in the EUR/AUD or EUR/CHF crosses, we would have had to pay a premium of about 4½ percent of notional. But we could do the *worst of* basket trade, which we thought the market was mispricing because of a correlation effect that we believed was vulnerable, for less than one-tenth that amount.

I guess the market was pricing the premium at a level that assumed that the current correlation was the most likely future correlation without taking into account that there was a potential event—a debt fear induced selloff in the euro—that could radically alter the existing correlation.

Yes, and if the correlation was −0.60, the dealers would sell us the option priced at a correlation assumption of −0.50 and high-five each other because they had just ripped our faces off.

What happened in this particular trade?

The euro did break down against both the Australian dollar and Swiss franc in mid-2009, and we ended up netting over six times our invested capital on the trade.

It seems like the common denominator in all your trades is taking advantage of the fact that markets always price securities on the implicit assumption that changes from prevailing levels are equally likely in either direction, where in reality, idiosyncratic fundamental factors can make a move in one direction much more likely. For example, in this particular instance, the event-related potential for a sharp selloff in the euro made the possibility that the inverse correlation between the Australian dollar and Swiss franc would diminish, or even reverse, much greater than the possibility that the correlation would become more negative. The market always assumes symmetry, and you look for potential asymmetry.

Exactly. Our trades range widely in probability of payoff, but they all share the characteristic of being priced cheaply relative to the perceived probability and magnitude of a win. We have a trade on now that I really like.

I don't know if you read Jeremy Grantham of GMO. He is a widely respected value investor who looks across all asset classes and writes commentaries and editorials about what he is seeing. For some time now, he has been arguing that high-quality, consumer oriented franchises, particularly those that have great international brands, are cheap relative to the rest of the S&P based on both dividend yield and enterprise value to cash flow. In my view, he has laid out a fairly compelling argument that places relative valuations in the context of a cycle, wherein the low-quality names tend to outperform early in the cycle, and the high-quality names tend to outperform toward the end of the cycle. There is an index called the XLP, which is an index of U.S. consumer staple companies such as Procter & Gamble, Coca-Cola, and Johnson & Johnson. If Grantham is right, at some point we should see a revaluation of the stocks in this index.

I assume that in the current cycle since the 2009 low, the XLP has gone up less than the S&P?

It has gone up a lot less. Initially, we considered buying options on the XLP, which were relatively inexpensive. But Ben came up with a much better way to structure the same trade idea based on the XLP's low beta of 0.5 versus the S&P500.

Beta is the expected change of a security relative to the change in the benchmark (e.g., S&P 500) for a small change in price. A beta of 0.5 indicates that the XLP is expected to change by 0.5 percent if the S&P 500 changes by 1 percent.

One observation that we found particularly striking was that despite the XLP's low beta, since the start of the index at the end of 1998, the net percentage changes in the XLP and the S&P over the entire period were almost identical. The XLP was up less in the bull markets and down less in the bear markets, but for the period as a whole, the net change was about the same. Seeing that both indexes had approximately the same net change over a long period—a period that included both the Internet boom and bust and the credit boom and bust—makes the notion that the XLP has a beta of 0.5 versus the S&P seem counterintuitive if applied to longer periods. In addition, we thought that cash flow and dividend valuations implied the potential for a 25 percent revaluation of the XLP versus the S&P. We went to an exotic option dealer and asked them to price an outperformance option that would be based on the performance of the XLP versus the S&P. What is the single measure that the dealer is going to use to price the odds that the XLP will outperform the S&P?

The beta.

Right. So with the beta equal to only 0.5, the model price for an outperformance option was very cheap. Translated into English, those inputs are saying that the XLP and S&P are likely to move in the same direction; however, the XLP will move only half as much as the S&P.

But if we had a down market, then the lower beta would imply a higher probability of outperforming—namely, it would imply that the XLP would go down less than the S&P.

That's a great point, and it is the reason why, to get the option cheaply, we had to strike the option at the current spot price. So there was a dual condition for the option to pay off: The XLP had to outperform the S&P and the S&P had to be unchanged to higher. This was essentially a conditional long beta position. It was conditional on the XLP out-performing the S&P, and it was long beta because it could only pay off in an up market.

What made you think the timing for the trade was right?

We didn't have any conviction that the market was going higher. We almost always want to have some long beta exposure, however, and by making the option conditional on the XLP outperforming the S&P, we were able to get beta exposure to the market extremely cheaply. When you own options, you're always fighting against the time decay. Figuring out how to make the option premium cheaper is one way of mitigating that decay.

So the basic premise is that beta is measured based on daily relative price changes, which can be a very poor indicator of long-term relative price changes.

Right, a fact that is obvious if you look at a long-term chart comparison of the XLP versus the S&P. Volatility is a terrible proxy for measuring potential price change over longer intervals of time. For example, if an asset price changes by a constant percentage each day, its volatility will be zero. One of our strategies is called *cheap sigma* and is predicated on the idea that markets sometimes trend and that volatility will dramatically understate the potential price move of markets that trend. For example, in 2007, Charlie noticed that the Canadian dollar was trending very smoothly as it broke the dollar mark for the first time in decades. Spot went from about 1.10 [Canadian dollars per U.S. dollar] to about 0.92—a very large price move. The market volatility, however, was very low. Based on the volatility, a nonsensically improbable event had just occurred.

That's past tense. How does that relate to a trade you did?

If the three-month implied volatility says that the price move that has just occurred was a three and a half standard deviation event, we are going to like the odds of buying deep out-of-the-money options for a price move back in the opposite direction.

So the basic concept is that option prices will tend to be priced too low in smoothly trending markets.

Yes, and this is another type of option mispricing. The broader principle is that the explicit and implicit assumptions that go into option pricing models often diverge from the underlying reality. Looking for those divergences can be a very profitable exercise because you can wait and do nothing until you see a probability that is wildly mispriced. Option math works a lot better over short intervals. Once you extend the time horizon, all sorts of exogenous variables are introduced that can throw a wrench into the option-pricing model.

Another example of a distortion that is introduced when the time interval is extended relates to the fact that the option-pricing models assume that volatility increases with the square root of time. This assumption may provide reasonable approximations for shorter time intervals, say one year or under, but if you have a very low standard deviation, and you extend it for a very long time, it doesn't scale properly. For example, if a one-year standard deviation is 5 percent, assuming that the nine-year standard deviation will only be 15 percent is probably an underestimate.

I guess the reason is that the longer the time period, the greater the potential for a trend, and hence the greater the chance that a longer-term price move will exceed the standard deviation implied probability, which increases only by the square root of time.

Yes.

Wouldn't that in turn imply that any long-term option is likely to be priced too low?

We love long-term options.

All the trades we have discussed seem to share two common denominators: a mispricing that arises because standard market pricing assumptions are inappropriate for a given situation and an asymmetric return/risk profile—that is, open-ended return and curtailed risk. Are there any other common denominators in your trades?

For any trade idea we come up with, we always go in hoping that our work will lead us to table-pounding confidence about a directional view. When we find it, nothing is better. Unfortunately those situations happen only very rarely. Almost invariably, at some point along the way, we end up disproving one of the predicates to our hypothesis, or decide that the risk we are evaluating really is inscrutable, or that we overlooked some important factor, and the situation was never interesting to begin with. The reality is that we have a business model in which we dig 50 dry wells for every idea we explore that leads to a trade in which we find conviction.

To varying degrees, all of the trades we've discussed so far have reflected situations where we did not have a high level of conviction ourselves about the outcome we were seeking to make money on. Instead, we had conviction that the odds were substantially mispriced, providing us positive expected value, even though we might not have had a strong view about the direction of the underlying market.[6]

Whereas the classic value investor achieves capital preservation by taking risks only when he is confident that he won't lose a meaningful amount of money, we think about risk more probabilistically. We are just as fanatical about capital preservation, but instead of achieving a margin of safety by knowing that a company has assets or cash flow that are not valued properly by the market, we achieve our margin of safety by having a high expected value. We are comfortable losing 100 percent of our premium four times in a row, as long as we believe that a 25-times payout is likely to occur if we make the same bet 10 times consecutively.

High conviction on an event path priced like a low-probability event is our Holy Grail. The subprime credit default swap (CDS) trade was the poster child for a high-conviction trade priced as an improbable event. We got to the trade late, which is typical for us because we like situations where there is a compelling reason why a trade should be working, and the only counterargument is that everyone says it should work, but it hasn't. Over the course of a couple of months, we went from having a probabilistic view that the markets were too confident that home price appreciation would continue indefinitely to having a very high level of conviction that a liquidity bubble existed that would inevitably provide the catalyst for its own demise.

■ ■ ■

Some background explanation is required to understand the following portion of this interview, which deals with Mai's trade in shorting mortgage-backed securitizations.

---

[6]The expected value is the sum of the probability of each outcome multiplied by its value. If we simplify by assuming there are only two outcomes—winning trade and losing trade—and estimate the average amount for each of these outcomes, then the expected value could be defined as the probability of a win times the average win size minus the probability of a loss times the average loss size. For example, if you estimate the probability of a win at 20 percent, and a winning outcome is expected to be $10,000 and a losing outcome $1,000, then the expected gain for the trade is +$1,200 (derived as follows: 0.2 * $10,000 − 0.8 * $1,000 = $1,200).

A subprime mortgage bond is a type of asset-backed security (ABS) that combines multiple individual subprime mortgages into a security that pays investors interest income based on the proceeds from mortgage payments. These bonds typically employ a structure in which multiple tranches (or classes) are created from the same pool of mortgages. The highest rated class, AAA, gets paid off in full, then the next highest rated class (AA), and so on. The higher the class, the lower the risk, and hence the lower the interest rate it receives. The "equity tranche," which is not rated, absorbs the first few percentage points of losses (typically 3 to 5 percent), and is wiped out if this loss level is reached. Next, the lowest rated debt tranche (often called the "mezzanine" tranche) absorbs additional losses, a greater credit risk for which investors are paid a higher rate of interest. For example, if the equity tranche was 3 percent of the issue and the mezzanine tranche 4 percent, the mezzanine tranche would begin to be impaired if losses due to defaulted repayments exceeded 3 percent, and investors would lose all their money if losses reached 7 percent. Each higher tranche would be protected in full until losses surpassed the upper threshold of the next lower tranche.

During the housing bubble of the mid-2000s, the risks associated with the low-rated BBB tranches of subprime bonds, which were high to start, increased dramatically. There was a significant deterioration in the quality of loans, as loan originators were able to pass on the risk by selling their mortgages for use in bond securitizations. Effectively, mortgage originators were freed from any concern whether the mortgages they issued would actually be repaid. Instead, they were incentivized to issue as many mortgages as possible, which is exactly what they did. The lower they set the bar for borrowers, the more mortgages they could create. Ultimately, in fact, there was no bar at all, as subprime mortgages were being issued with the following characteristics:

- No down payment.
- No income, job, or asset verification.
- Adjustable rate mortgage (ARM) structures in which low teaser rates adjusted to much higher levels after a year or two.

There was no historical precedent for such low-quality mortgages. It is easy to see how the BBB tranche of a bond formed from these low-quality mortgages would be extremely vulnerable to a complete loss.

The story, however, does not end there. The BBB tranches were difficult to sell. Wall Street alchemists came up with a solution that magically transformed the BBB tranches into AAA. They created a new securitization called a *collateralized debt obligation* (CDO) that consisted entirely of the BBB tranches of many mortgage bonds.[7] CDOs also employed a tranche structure. Typically 75 percent to 80 percent of a CDO was rated AAA, even though it consisted of 100 percent BBB tranches.

Although the CDO tranche structure was similar to that employed by subprime mortgage bonds consisting of individual mortgages, there was an important difference. In a pool of mortgages, there was at least some reason to assume there would be limited correlation between individual mortgages. Different individuals would not necessarily come under financial stress at the same time, and different geographic areas could witness divergent economic conditions. In contrast, all the individual elements of the CDOs were clones—they all represented the lowest tier of a pool of subprime mortgages. If economic conditions were sufficiently unfavorable for the BBB tranche of one mortgage bond pool to be wiped out, the odds were very high that BBB tranches in other pools would also be wiped out, or at least severely impaired.[8] The AAA tranche needed approximately a 20 to 25 percent loss to begin being impaired, which sounds like a safe number, until one considers that all the holdings are highly correlated. The BBB tranches were like a group of people in close quarters contaminated by a highly contagious flu. If one person is infected, the odds that many would be infected would increase dramatically. In this context, the 20 percent cushion of the AAA class sounds more like a tissue paper layer.

How could bonds consisting of only BBB tranches be rated AAA? There are three interconnected explanations.

---

[7]CDOs were a general type of securitization that were also built from many other types of instruments, but these other constructions are not germane to this discussion.

[8]Although correlations for individual mortgages could also be significant during severe economic downturns, the degree of correlation would still not be nearly as extreme as the correlations between different BBB tranches.

1. Pricing models used historical data on mortgage defaults. Historical mortgages in which the lender actually cared whether repayments were made and required down payments and verification bore no resemblance to the more recently minted no-down-payment, no-verification loans. Therefore, historical mortgage default data would grossly understate the risk of more recent mortgages defaulting.

2. The correlation assumptions were unrealistically low. They failed to adequately account for the sharply increased probability of BBB tranches failing if other BBB tranches failed.

3. The credit rating agencies had a clear conflict of interest: They were paid by the CDO manufacturers. If they were too "harsh" (read: realistic) in their ratings, they would lose the business. They were effectively incentivized to be as lax as possible in their ratings. Is this to say the credit rating agencies deliberately mismarked bonds? No, the mismarkings might have been subconscious. Although the AAA ratings for tranches of individual mortgages could be defended to some extent, it is difficult to make the same claim for the AAA ratings of CDO tranches consisting of only the BBB tranches of mortgage bonds. In regard to the CDO ratings, the credit rating agencies were either conflicted or incompetent.

Cornwall Capital's primary strategy for shorting the housing bubble was buying credit default swaps (CDS) on the AA tranches of CDOs. The buyer of CDS makes ongoing premium payments (equivalent to the bond interest rate payments) to the seller for protection against the risk of default in the underlying security.

■ ■ ■

How did you get involved in trading the subprime mortgage market?

I first became aware of the opportunity in October 2006 when a friend sent us a write-up of a presentation made by Paul Singer of Elliot Associates. Singer walked through the sleight-of-hand that banks used to amalgamate the riskiest tranches of subprime mortgage-backed securitizations (MBS)—the BBB tranches that investors were starting to shy away from—into a new collateralized debt obligation

(CDO), the majority of which was rated AA or higher.[9] Singer demonstrated that housing prices didn't have to fall for the AA tranches of these CDOs to fail; they simply had to stop rising. The assertion that institutional investors were willing to accept the paltry returns associated with AA or higher rated securities for that kind of risk didn't even seem plausible. If it hadn't been someone with Singer's reputation making these assertions, I would never have believed him.

It turned out that Ben had come across a variation on the same idea a couple of weeks earlier when he received a presentation from Deutsche Bank that pitched buying protection on the mezzanine tranches of MBS. These were largely the BBB tranches of the mortgage securitization pools that were going into the CDOs Paul Singer had talked about. So he and Charlie had already started to do some work at the MBS level when we became aware of the CDO angle.[10]

In the past, one important argument that was given to support the value of CDOs was that they provided portfolio diversification—that is, the collateral that went into CDOs was sourced from different asset classes. One could argue that there was a diversification benefit to having credit card receivables, aircraft leases, and various forms of real estate debt in a single structure. By late 2006, however, CDOs were composed almost entirely of the lowest-rated tranches of subprime mortgage securitizations. This homogeneous composition of the CDOs meant that the argument justifying a lower correlation assumption went out the window. The upshot was that the CDOs provided us with the opportunity to buy protection [equivalent to going short] on the worst

---

[9]Mortgage-backed securitizations (MBS) are a subset of asset-backed securitizations (ABS).

[10]As explained above, the CDO combined many BBB tranches and created AAA and AA tranches consisting of nothing but these low-rated MBS tranches. The justification for this transformation was that the BBB tranches of different securitizations were uncorrelated. This assumption, however, made no sense at all because if the BBB tranche of one subprime mortgage securitization became impaired, it was highly likely that the BBB tranches of other subprime securitizations would also become impaired. The higher rating of the top CDO tranches meant that CDS protection could be bought far cheaper, making the CDOs a more attractive vehicle than MBS for establishing short subprime mortgage positions.

quality bonds at premium levels that were in line with high–grade corporate bonds.[11]

What did you do next?

Since we did not have the domain expertise necessary to do bottom–up fundamental analysis in the MBS space, we hired a highly regarded research analyst who had recently left BlackRock to create his own hedge fund. He was able to evaluate the quality of the collateral underlying all the MBS issuances we were interested in analyzing based on such metrics as loan–to–values, FICO scores, and seasoning of non-performing loans. He then came up with a list of the worst ABS issuances, based on his fundamental analysis. We then went out and looked for CDOs that had the most overlap with his list. We were pleasantly surprised to find CDOs that had a large overlap.

It wasn't until much later that we realized that the security-selection acumen we thought we'd demonstrated in picking some of the worst-performing CDOs was in fact a reflection of much deeper work that had been done by other investors, such as Michael Burry of Scion Capital, who knew the market much better than we did. It turned out that the reason we were able to find CDOs whose collateral happened to be the absolute worst-performing subprime MBS was because Burry had gone to dealers months earlier and convinced them to create synthetic securitizations for the specific names he wanted to buy protection on [i.e., short].

By arriving relatively late at the scene toward the end of 2006, we unwittingly put ourselves in a position to reap even greater rewards from the dealers' avarice. In selling CDS to guys like Burry, they were synthetically replicating the bonds he wanted to short. It didn't take long for credit derivative dealers to have the thought that if synthetic MBS made

---

[11]The higher ratings assigned to the upper-tier tranches of CDOs implied (incorrectly) that these bonds had a low chance of default. Therefore, Cornwall could buy protection that paid off if these bonds defaulted for only the small premium associated with bonds with AAA and AA ratings. Since the premium paid for the default protection is the maximum risk in the short position, the CDOs provided a way to short the worst quality subprime bonds with minimal risk exposure.

sense, then so did synthetic CDOs.[12] In the same way they had sold a handful of value investors like Burry synthetic protection on their hand-picked selection of junk-rated mortgage bonds, they repackaged those same securities and sold them to us in the form of a synthetic CDO. As far as I know, we were among the first investors to go short CDOs. Due to the zero correlation assumption implicit in the CDO construction, we were able to buy protection on the AA tranche, which consisted entirely of the worst quality subprime MBS, for only LIBOR + 50 basis points. It was, without a doubt, complete and utter insanity.

When did you put on your short positions [i.e., buying CDS protection on CDO tranches]?

We started in October 2006, and the last of our positions was put on in May 2007. The market collapse began on February 1, 2007. Most people think the financial crisis started when Bear Stearns failed, but in our view, it started more than a year earlier on February 1, 2007 when the ABX started tanking. [The ABX is an index referencing 20 subprime mortgage bonds with a separate index listed for each of five tranches, ranging from AAA to BBB–.] Since the bonds in the CDOs we had shorted were of even poorer quality than the bonds referenced by the ABX index, the selloff in the ABX implied sharply lower values for our CDOs.

Did you get fully positioned?

No, we would have kept shorting.

Why didn't you put on your entire intended position at one time?

We were developing our conviction on the trade, and our conviction level spiked up when the ABX tanked and CDO prices didn't move.

---

[12]The buyer of CDS protection on a bond (i.e., the short seller) pays premiums equivalent to the bond interest rate payments, in effect, creating a synthetic bond. These synthetic bonds can be bundled into a synthetic CDO, which has the same income stream as a CDO consisting of the same physical bonds. Since savvy traders, such as Burry, bought protection on the bonds with the worst quality mortgages (i.e., went short those bonds), the resulting synthetic CDOs were composed of securitizations ideal for shorting.

How come the CDO prices didn't decline if an index based on bonds similar to those in the CDOs was falling sharply?

The dealers had bought massive amounts of MBS to hold in inventory in anticipation of turning them into CDOs. So they were stuck with a huge amount of inventory of the crappiest MBS at the time when the ABX index based on those securities was falling sharply. They went into overdrive to turn as much of the inventory as possible into CDOs. If the proper mark-to-market prices were allowed on the existing CDOs, it would have killed the CDO market, and the dealers would have been stuck with huge inventories of MBS before they could turn them into CDOs.

So the dealers were deliberately mispricing the CDOs?

Oh, yes. You have to remember that the buyers of the CDOs were not the most sophisticated investors. People are hesitant to use the "F" word [fraud], but extreme naïveté would be the only other explanation, if you could believe that's plausible. We saw a research report by Lehman on a CDO issued at a yield of 70 basis points. We called the secondary desk at Lehman and asked if we could buy protection on that CDO at 70 basis points. They laughed at us. We asked whether we could buy protection at 300 basis points. They said they couldn't offer that to us, either. So we asked, "How could you issue a CDO at 70 basis points that you are unwilling to assume the risk on at 300?" They said they would have to get back to us. Of course, they never did. In the meantime, our counterparty, Bear Stearns, is marking our CDO positions at cost. The ABX fell 30 percent, and our CDOs were still being marked at cost.

Were you arguing with them about the marks?

Not so much. We were more concerned about the integrity of the financial system. We bought a ton of puts and CDS on Bear Stearns because we thought they would go bankrupt.

Was there collusion among the dealers to keep CDO prices unchanged, even in the face of collapsing prices of the MBS that made up the CDOs?

It's hard to see how there wasn't. The real malfeasance occurred in February when the ABX fell off a cliff, but the CDO machine kept grinding away. We went to the SEC to try to make them aware that there was a profound, systemic failure occurring in the integrity of capital markets.

What was the specific advice you gave them?

We told them they needed to look at the CDOs and the assumptions the rating agencies were using to rate the CDOs because transactions were occurring at prices that were completely out of line with the value of the securities being sold. Ultimately, it was all about the rating agencies. The rating agencies rated thousands of securities with the same grade as U.S. Treasuries when they weren't worth more than the paper they were printed on the day they rolled off the press. And yet, despite this horrific record, the market still jumps when the rating agencies opine about the creditworthiness of a sovereign bond. I can't believe they have any credibility left at all. It is difficult to come up with a more extreme case of failure to do a purported job. Until recently, the rating agencies have shielded themselves from any responsibility, not on the substance of their argument, but rather by deflecting any claims under the shield of free speech in the First Amendment.

I'm afraid I know the answer, but what happened after the SEC meeting?

They seemed thoughtful and interested in what we had to say, but it's not clear to us if they ever followed up.

What caused the dealers to finally mark down the CDOs?

It was precipitated by the launch of the TABX, which was an index that created synthetic CDO tranches based on the mezzanine tranches of the ABX index. When the TABX was created in early 2007, mezzanine tranches of the ABX index were already trading at prices that reflected substantial impairment. By implication, the lower tranches of a CDO constructed from these bonds would be worthless. Thus, the TABX provided the first observable data indicating that the mezzanine tranches, up to the "A" tranches, and perhaps even the "AA" tranches of an index replicating CDOs had already lost total value. Yet the banks, who were desperately trying to get their MBS inventory off their books, were still issuing similar CDOs at par. The TABX made it impossible for the banks to continue this charade. I don't recall what precipitated the tsunami, but at the beginning of August, there was a wave of risk reduction, and everyone wanted to own the CDS protection that we held.[13] When we liquidated in August 2007, we had positions that were marked at $50,000 on Friday's close and that we sold for $4.5 million on Monday.

What other types of trades haven't we discussed?

We love trades that appear to be approaching limits—trades that are so close to their absolute limit that they have tremendous asymmetry. Some examples are CDS protection on European banks in 2007 for three basis points and CDS on the ABX index for nine basis points. The CDO trade also had the characteristic of being near a loss limit, but was special because of our high conviction for a large profit potential.

Any others?

We also look for trades where the market price level itself implies asymmetry. A good example is the Korean stock market in 2005, a situation in which we did a ton of work and ended up having conviction that the entire market was mispriced.

Sometime in 2003 or 2004, it came to our attention that listed companies in South Korea looked very underpriced based on the fundamentals. Whereas all the other Asian markets that had tanked in 1997 during the currency crisis had subsequently recovered, South Korea continued to languish. It was not clear why this should be the case, especially since it appeared that South Korea had done a better job than any of its neighbors in adopting all the fiscal and market reforms imposed after the crisis. Specifically, South Korea had complied with all the terms of the emergency IMF loan, including austerity measures, and had overhauled securities laws and regulation to a level that was on par with the U.S. South Korea already had a deep cultural respect for the rule of law, with lots of precedent for enforcing private property rights.

---

[13]The precipitating event in August 2007 was the drying up of liquidity in money markets. This episode is discussed in the Colm O'Shea interview (Chapter 1).

Despite all of these positive characteristics, Korean equities traded at an increasing discount to the rest of Asia. So we spent a lot of time trying to figure out whether there was a good explanation for this apparent anomaly. Our model is to always find experts in the domain, river guides so to speak. We developed a close relationship with a scion of the family controlling one of Korea's largest consumer electronics companies. He is an American, but was nevertheless very much an insider who gave us great access. We got our fingernails dirty. I probably traveled to Korea 10 times in the space of 18 months. We met lots of people on the buy side, the sell side, and in industry. We hired an undergrad from Berkeley who had recently emigrated from Korea. He did a lot of Korean-to-English translations of financial statements.

After all this research, we became convinced that the logic for why Korea was cheap was circular. Korea was cheap because it had consistently been cheap. For several years, Korean companies that generated steady and impressive cash flows kept getting cheaper. Investors who had bought Korea earlier as a value trade had gotten burned, even though it seemed like their thesis was sound. By the time we arrived at the scene, there were lots of companies trading at substantial negative enterprise values. [A negative enterprise value implies that the market is assigning a negative value to the company, excluding its cash assets and debts.] There were companies with market caps of $300 million, no debt, and $550 million cash on the balance sheet, which was expected to increase to $650 million in the following year. In this case, there was tremendous asymmetry simply because these companies had nowhere to go but up.

What got the market to realize value eventually?

The passage of time. The inexorable accumulation of profits can only be ignored for so long until it acts as a catalyst for higher prices.

You talked earlier about how most of your trade ideas don't work out once you do the deep research. Can you give me an example of how research disproved what you thought was a great idea at the outset?

A perfect recent example was related to our hypothesis that the nonlinear impact of increasing coal imports by China could create a trading opportunity. China is by far the world's largest consumer and producer of thermal coal, accounting for about 50 percent of global activity. The market has grown at roughly 10 percent per year for decades now, which is in line with long-term GDP growth. Unlike most other commodities, which it must import, China has abundant physical reserves of coal. Demand growth has been consistently supplied by increased domestic production, with a small residual surplus that was exported. So, despite being the world's largest market by far, at roughly 3 billion tons per year, China's coal market operated essentially as a closed system.

We noticed, however, that there was a strong trend in the export/import balance. China had gone from being a net exporter to a net importer, and the pace of this trend shift was accelerating. It had taken nearly a decade for net exports to drop from roughly 100 million tons, to zero at the end of 2008. Yet it took only a year to cover the same ground in the other direction. By 2010, net imports were 150 million tons. Evidence that China was having major difficulties in expanding coal production at anywhere near the rate of its annual consumption increase reinforced the trend we were seeing in imports. If China needed to source 10 percent of its demand from international markets, total seaborne coal volume would have to jump over 50 percent. Our initial hypothesis was that China's thermal coal imports were likely to provide a secular tailwind to international thermal coal markets.

Our next step was to look at ways to express the trade. We settled on dry bulk freight as the most levered way to take exposure to increasing seaborne coal volume. The early indicators were promising, given that the shipping companies we looked at seemed to be trading at depressed multiples of cash flows, despite a healthy rebound in freight volumes and dry bulk rates since the advent of the global recession in 2008. We expected to see rapidly growing dry bulk demand outstripping growth in supply, which we speculated had dropped off significantly due to the global recession. The picture that came into focus, however, made it clear that our intuition had been completely wrong. It turned out that the supply pinch we expected to see had actually occurred several years earlier in connection with rising emerging market imports of commodities, such as iron ore. High freight rates had sparked a shipbuilding boom in the three to four years preceding the financial crisis. In 2010, new capesize freighters hitting the water equaled almost 20 percent of the global installed base. Fleet capacity is on track to increase by a similar amount in 2011. We concluded that, even if China had to source 100 percent of its marginal growth through seaborne freight markets, there was no way demand could come close to absorbing the dry bulk capacity coming on line.

So, ironically, you were looking at the dry bulk shippers as a potential buy, but once you dug into the fundamentals, you concluded they were actually a sell.

Yes, and not only a sell, but our highest conviction short trade in 2011.

Did you then go short the dry bulk shippers?

It is hard to see any circumstances in which we would go outright short a stock—your gain is limited, your loss is unlimited, and your exposure grows as you are wrong. Instead, we bought out-of-the-money puts on some of the dry bulk ship operators. When rising implied volatilities made those premiums prohibitively expensive, we shifted toward in-the-money puts to reduce the time value decay.

■ ■ ■

There are five main pillars to Mai's investment strategy:

1. **Find mispricings in a theoretically priced world**. Mai seeks to identify trade opportunities that arise because prices, particularly for derivatives, are based on one of a number of standard pricing assumptions that may be entirely inappropriate based on the specific circumstances applicable to the given market. When these assumptions are unwarranted, they create mispricings and trading opportunities.
2. **Select trades in which the probabilities appear to be significantly skewed to a positive outcome**. As a general rule of thumb, Cornwall requires that the estimated gain if the trade succeeds multiplied by the probability of a positive outcome must be at least twice as large as the estimated loss if the trade fails

multiplied by the probability of a negative outcome. Of course, these gain-and-loss amounts and their respective probabilities must be based on subjective estimates. Nonetheless, the key point is that the probability-weighted gain must be lopsided relative to the probability-weighted loss.

The rigorous standard for qualifying trades will lead to a concentrated portfolio. Typically, Mai will have only 15 to 20 independent risks (consisting of one or more separate trades) at any one time. This concentrated portfolio approach should not be confused with the proverbial "put all your eggs in one basket, but watch that basket very closely." The important distinction is that although Mai's portfolio is very concentrated, the asymmetric construction of his trades assures that the downside is always severely constrained if he is wrong.

3. **Implement trades asymmetrically**. Mai structures trades so that the downside is severely limited, while the upside is open-ended. One common way of achieving this type of return/risk profile is by being a buyer of options (of course, only at those times when a mispricing is identified).

4. **Wait for high-conviction trades**. Mai is perfectly content to stay on the sidelines and do absolutely nothing until there is a trade opportunity that meets his guidelines. Having the patience to wait for high expected value trades greatly enhances the return/risk of individual trades.

5. **Use cash to target portfolio risk**. Because most of the trades in the portfolio are derivatives, which require much smaller cash outlays than outright positions, Mai will hold a large cash component in the portfolio (typically, 50 to 80 percent). By increasing or decreasing this cash component, Mai can target his desired portfolio risk level.

Prices for derivatives, such as options, are determined by pricing models that embed certain assumptions. These models are used because they generally provide reasonably good approximations. The assumptions these models are based on, however, are sometimes inappropriate for a market given the specific prevailing fundamentals. The acceptance of these assumptions as being universally applicable when, in reality, they are not, leads to trading opportunities. Mai identified five generally accepted assumptions that sometimes are invalid.

1. **Prices are normally distributed**—Options are priced based on the assumption of a normal distribution, which effectively implies that future prices near the current level are most probable and that probabilities drop steeply for prices further removed from current levels. In some instances, however, large price moves are much more likely than implied by the normal distribution. Consider, for example, Mai's comments regarding Capital One: "The odds that the stock would still be near $30 in two years seemed vanishingly small. Either the company would be vindicated or it would go under." In such circumstances, options priced in line with option-pricing models will be severely mispriced; specifically, out-of-the-money options will be priced far too cheaply. These mispricings can create profit opportunities. If the probability of a large price move is much greater than normal, as was the case with Capital One, then out-of-the-money options can provide a significant probability of gain, while being priced consistent with long-shot probabilities.

   Another implication of the normal distribution assumption is that it is always equally likely for prices to go up X percent as down X percent. Although this assumption may often be a reasonable approximation, there are times when it is far more likely for a market to go up by a given percentage than down by the same amount or vice versa. A good example of such an asymmetric price outlook was the Korean stock market when Mai implemented his long position. At the time, the market was not only severely undervalued relative to other Asian markets, but prices were so low that many companies had market capitalizations that were less than their net cash balances—that is, the companies were effectively being valued at less than zero. In such circumstances, the odds of a large price advance are significantly greater than the odds of an equivalent price decline.

   There is an important corollary here: The contention by many academics that the market price is always right is inconsistent with the empirical evidence. There are times when the market price is clearly wrong, and these situations provide major trade opportunities.

2. **The forward price is a perfect predictor of the future mean**— This assumption implies that options will be priced with probabilities centered at the corresponding forward price. Sometimes, however, when the forward price is well removed from the current price, it may not be reasonable to assume that a price change equal to the difference between the forward and spot price is the most likely market outcome. Frequently, there may be good reason to assume that some price between the forward and spot price is more likely than the forward price. If this is true, out-of-the-money options (puts if the forward price is higher and calls if it is lower) may be underpriced. The Brazilian interest rate trade Mai described provided a good example of such an opportunity.

3. **Volatility scales with the square root of time**—This assumption, which is embedded in option pricing, may be reasonable for shorter time intervals. For longer time periods, however, this volatility assumption may understate potential volatility, particularly if current volatility is low, for two reasons. First, the longer the time period, the more likely volatility will revert to the mean from current low levels. Second, longer periods allow for more opportunity for trends to result in larger price moves than implied by the volatility assumption.

4. **The trend can be ignored in the volatility calculation**— Option pricing models gauge the probability of price moves of a given magnitude based on volatility and time. Trend is not part of the calculation. The implicit assumption is that the direction of daily price changes is random. Consequently, a trending market can result in price moves that would be deemed improbable by the pricing model. If there is a reason to expect a trend, then out-of-the-money options are likely to be underpriced. Mai's Canadian dollar option trade was based on this premise.

5. **Current correlations are good predictors of future correlations**—Some market correlations tend to be fairly consistent (e.g., gold and platinum tend to be positively correlated over the broad spectrum of time), while other market pairs may exhibit variable correlation patterns (e.g., the Australian dollar and Swiss franc that were part of Mai's *worst of* basket trade). Correlation-based trades will tend to assume future correlation equal to the correlation

in the past lookback period. Such an assumption may often be invalid for markets that have variable correlation patterns.

One of the great misconceptions of the investing public is equating risk with volatility, which is wrongheaded on multiple grounds. First, frequently, the most important risks don't show up in the track record and hence are not reflected by volatility. For example, a portfolio of illiquid positions held during a risk-on period may have low volatility, but large risk if market sentiment shifts to risk-off. The other side of the coin is that sometimes volatility can be high because of abrupt, large gains, but the theoretical risk of the investment is limited. Mai's strategy provides a good example of an investment approach that has high volatility and constrained risk. Mai's track record shows a lot of volatility because of a predilection to large gains—not a characteristic most investors would associate with risk or consider undesirable. Although the volatility is very high, the risk is tightly controlled because trades are structured to be asymmetric—the maximum possible loss on each trade is well defined and far smaller than the potential gain. Mai's investment approach demonstrates the principle that high volatility does not necessarily imply high risk.

Flexibility is one of the hallmarks of Market Wizards. Mai routinely changes his view as dictated by the research. His trade in dry bulk shippers provides a perfect example. He started off with the idea that these companies were a buy, but ended up taking the exact opposite exposure when his research indicated that his initial premise had been entirely erroneous. Good traders get out of a position when they realize they have made a mistake. Great traders are capable of taking the opposite position when they realize their original concept was dead wrong.

Chapter 8

Michael Platt

The Art and Science of Risk Control

Michael Platt achieved career clarity at an early age. "I have had a very easy life," he says, "because I never had to think about what I wanted to do. I wanted to be a trader from when I was 12, and I started when I was 13." Platt continued to successfully trade stocks through high school and university with one major exception: His stock account lost half its value in a single day—the crash of October 19, 1987. This episode was the first and last time Platt experienced a large percentage loss.

After graduating from the London School of Economics in 1991, Platt joined JP Morgan where he had an extremely profitable eight-year career, trading a wide range of fixed income derivatives. His success at the firm led to repeated promotions, culminating with his appointment as managing director in London with the responsibility of heading up proprietary relative value trading. Platt left JP Morgan in 2000, along with William Reeves, to co-found BlueCrest. The firm has been extremely successful, growing to close to $29 billion in assets under management and nearly 400 staff by early 2012. The majority of assets are in two programs: a discretionary strategy headed by Michael Platt, and a systematic trend-following strategy headed by Leda Braga, who joined the firm in 2001.

The discretionary trading strategy has achieved an average annual compounded net return of just under 14 percent.[1] The hallmark of BlueCrest's performance is not its return, but rather its extraordinary risk control. In 11 years of operation, the discretionary strategy's largest peak-to-trough equity drawdown has been under 5 percent. Keep in mind, this track record includes the 2008 financial meltdown in which many hedge funds witnessed single days with larger drawdowns. The return/risk of the discretionary strategy headed by Platt is off the charts with a Gain to Pain ratio of 5.6. (The Gain to Pain ratio is a loss-based, as opposed to volatility-based, return/risk measure; see Appendix A for a more detailed explanation of this metric.)

The consistent and extended low-risk numbers achieved by Blue-Crest's discretionary strategy are not a matter of chance. Platt is obsessive about risk control. It permeates his own trading and the design of every aspect of the strategy. The discretionary strategy has kept losses remarkably low through a three-tiered process of combining broad diversification—seven teams trading different strategies and sectors—extreme tight reins on the losses of individual traders, and oversight by a seven-person risk management team. Platt is really serious about risk control.

I met Platt at the firm's Geneva office. We talked in a conference room that was memorable for its unusual color: orange. When discussing trading strategies, Platt speaks at a speed that is somewhere between a rushed New Yorker and the fast-talking executive in the famous Fed Ex commercial. When the topic of conversation is a four-legged fixed income trade, keeping up with Platt can be a challenge.

■ ■ ■

---

[1]BlueCrest did not provide performance data statistics due to certain jurisdictions' private placement rules. Performance statistics were obtained from other reliable sources.

How did you get interested in markets?

I have always liked puzzles. When I was 10 years old, my dad gave me a Rubik's cube, and 36 hours later, I could do it from any position in under one minute. I always regarded financial markets as the ultimate puzzle because everyone is trying to solve it, and infinite wealth lies at the end of solving it. When you are solving any puzzle, you have to start off from the perspective "What do I know for sure?" Do I have any bedrock to start off my analysis? It's shocking how little you know for certain in financial markets. One of the only things I could say with certainty was that markets trend because I can observe trends in any financial market, in any time era. You could go back 150 years in cotton futures, and there are trends everywhere. The same is true for equities, bonds, short-term rates, everything.

It seems illogical that markets trend. Markets should discount all information and then be static waiting for the next piece of information before changing price level. But that is not what they do. And the reason they trend is because our minds just don't work properly. We make an estimation of the future based on all the knowledge we have of the past at the current moment. We remember the past in bullet point form. We'll never remember this conversation verbatim; we'll remember bullet points. All the things that are happening currently, we have a high level of detail on because they are instantaneous and all around us. It turns out that when you recall the past, you have lots of gaps because you only retain an edited summary of it. You fill in those gaps the same way you fill in a wall with plaster. The material with which you fill in the gaps in your past recollections is called *today*. So how you feel today, whatever you are thinking today, whatever is going on today is what you're going to use to fill in the gaps in the past.

It is well known that people misremember the past. There is a famous experiment in which about 200 people watch a slide sequence of a car going to the end of a street, turning right, and then hitting a pedestrian. Half the group see slides with a stop sign at the end of the street, and the other half see a similar set of slides with a yield sign. The subjects are then asked some questions about what they saw. Within each group, half the subjects are asked one question that refers to a stop sign, while the other half are asked the same question with a reference to a yield sign. All the participants are then shown two nearly identical slides and asked to pick the slide they saw. The only difference between the two slides is that one has a stop sign and the other a yield sign. A large majority of the people who were asked a question that contradicted what they saw (a reference to a stop sign when they saw a yield sign or vice versa) misidentified the slide they actually saw. The point is that once they are presented with contradictory information, the majority of people misremember something that they watched only a few moments ago because they use the more recent information to fill in what they can't remember exactly, or at least are not 100 percent sure of. They are filling in the gaps in their bullet point memory of the past with information from the current moment.

If the market is going up today, your forecast is going to be that it will continue going up because it is how you feel at the moment that is the most important thing. Today becomes how you felt in the past because you misremember. So everything is about today. If it is going up today, it will go up tomorrow. In this sense, financial markets become self-referential.

I would have a different explanation of why markets trend. I believe markets trend because there is some important underlying change in fundamentals that has not been adequately discounted, or sometimes markets trend because they anticipate such a fundamental change. But any major trend has some fundamental catalyst.

Markets may initially trend for fundamental reasons, but prices overshoot by ludicrous amounts. At some point, prices go up today simply because they went up yesterday.

Okay, you know that markets trend. What else do you know for certain?

You also know that diversification works. That is what the systematic trend-following strategy is built on: markets trend and diversification works. It doesn't have any economic information.

But that leaves open two questions: How do you accurately identify trends without being overly subject to whipsaws, and how have you managed to keep risks so constrained?

First, the systematic trend-following strategy trades over 150 markets. Second, the systematic team looks at past correlations in weighting those markets. Currently, because of the whole risk-on/risk-off culture that has developed, diversification is quite hard to get. When I first started trading about 20 years ago, U.S. and European bond markets weren't really that correlated. Now, these markets move together tick by tick.

So how do you get diversification when you have such extreme correlation?

You have problems getting it. Recently, everything works or everything doesn't work. For example, we have had periods where everything worked for the systematic trend-following strategy and we made $1 billion. It's all really one trade, isn't it?

Well, that's exactly my point. How then do you control the risk? How do you protect yourself against a market reversal where everything then goes against you at the same time?

There are lots of ways the program deals with this problem, but the main method is using a response curve, which means that when a trend gets really overextended, our system will liquidate the position, and when the market reverses, it will reinstate it. That part is not really secret. We share that information with our investors. But how we do it—how we determine when a market is overextended and how we execute trading out of and back into positions—that is a matter of an insane amount of mathematical research, and, of course, is proprietary. The systematic team is continually researching the correlation between markets, modeling markets versus other markets, and pursuing virtually every angle of analysis you can think of. The program has literally millions of lines of code. It's the best you can do with a bunch of markets that are reasonably correlated now. The biggest protection we have is liquidating out of overextended trends. If the trend goes further still, too bad. More often than not, it is a good decision. It saves your bacon on the big reversals.

The real Achilles' heel in systematic trend following is if you get whipsaw markets.[2] How has your systematic trend-following strategy avoided getting hit by more significant drawdowns during these types of markets?

Our system will tend to keep the position small if the trend is perceived as being weak.

Is your systematic trend-following strategy fully defined or is it changed over time?

The strategy is always changing. It is a research war. Leda has built a phenomenal, talented team that is constantly seeking to improve our strategy.

Is the implication that if you stay with a static system, eventually, it will degrade?

Yes, I hear that [Platt names a well-known CTA with a long track record] original system is now insanely volatile and unprofitable.

On a recent plane trip, I read the *Complete Turtle Trader* by Michael Covel, a book about the group of traders originally trained by Richard Dennis and Bill Eckhardt using a variation of a simple breakout system originally developed by Richard Donchian. In the book, Covel details the actual rules of the once secret system. Now, I am pretty familiar with breakout systems, and I knew from computer testing that they don't work all that well. They make moderate returns with lots of volatility. I, therefore, was quite curious to see what modifications the turtle system made to transform what I knew to be a mediocre system into an effective

---

[2]A whipsaw market is one that swings back and forth repeatedly and abruptly in a wide trading range. These markets tend to trigger trend signals shortly before reversing direction, causing many trend-following systems to experience a succession of losses.

one. So, as I read the book, I jotted down any rules that were modifications of a basic breakout system. When I looked at these modifications, none of them seemed to be all that significant, and I couldn't understand how they could make such a big difference. At the end of the book, Covel provided an appendix containing the track records for many of the turtle traders. Throughout the book, he had mentioned one of these traders as being the best of the group. I checked the track record for this trader, which went back to the mid-1980s, and saw lots of huge returns in the earlier years. Then I looked at just the last eight years and mentally estimated that the average annual return during that period was maybe only 2 percent higher than the T-bill rate, but with substantial volatility.[3] The whole great track record was really pre-late-1990s, and since then, the performance had degraded into mediocrity. I'm sure most investors don't look past the impressive total track record statistics and fail to realize that all the outperformance occurred well in the past and that the more recent period statistics are radically different.

We went off on a bit of a tangent. I asked you about how you got interested in the markets, and you told me about your interest in puzzles. But we never talked about how you actually first became involved in markets.

My grandmother traded equities. I got involved in stock trading through her. She was a long-term investor and did very well at it. She was a very strong woman. She wasn't interested in baking a cake for me; she was interested in what stock I wanted to buy or sell. I told my grandmother about a trust savings bank whose shares were going to be floated. "It's going to open at a premium," I told her, "because they are going to sell it cheap so everyone buys the shares."

She said, "Okay, then let's get involved." She asked me, "How much do you want to buy?"

---

[3]Since margins on futures represent only a small fraction of their assets under management, CTAs will typically earn interest income close to the T-bill rate. Therefore, only the returns in excess of the T-bill rate represent the alpha provided by the CTA.

"As much as I can," I told her.

She said, "Okay, I'll lend you the money." She lent me the cash, and I filled out the application forms, which were clearly in her name. We bought £500 or £1,000 of stock—I don't remember the exact amount—at £.50, and it opened at £.99.

How did you get the idea to buy the stock?

I read about it. When I was 12 or 13 years old, I got a copy of this magazine called *Investors Chronicle*, which had interesting articles about the market, trading options, and lots of company analyses. I read it every week after that. By the time I was 14, I knew every single stat on every single company. At the time, the U.K. was going through a privatization phase, and I was just buying all of the stocks when they went public and flipping them. I must have made £20,000 to £30,000.

This is all while you were still in high school?

Yes. When I was at university, I continued trading my own account. I got hammered in the stock market crash of 1987.

Tell me about that experience.

I woke up that Monday morning and glanced out the window. It looked like there was some sort of hurricane going on in London. Trees had been knocked down. The place looked like a bombsite. I thought to myself, "What a terrible morning." I turned on the radio and that's when I heard the stock market was crashing.

How much of your money did you have invested at the time?

Oh, all of it. I had no understanding of proper diversification and money management at the time. By the time I got to check on prices, my account was down 50 percent. My broker was telling me, "Don't sell. Don't sell."

So what did you do?

I sold it all. I just took the loss.

In that particular case, getting out turned out to be the wrong thing to do.

I thought to myself, I had £30,000, and now I have £15,000. I can still have a good time at university with that amount in the next few years.

That was it for how long?

Not very long. Very soon after I bought shares in a stock that had gotten crushed, which rebounded a lot. So I made some money back on that.

So far, we have only talked about the trend-following system. How much of BlueCrest's trading is systematic?

We run approximately $29 billion [updated as of end of 2011], which is about evenly divided between systematic and discretionary approaches. Interestingly, for the prior three calendar years [2008 to 2010[4]], we made almost identical returns in both systematic and discretionary strategies, but with a better Sharpe ratio on the human side.

Which markets are traded in the discretionary strategy?

The big three are fixed income, credit, and emerging markets.

What about equities?

We don't trade equities except for one small program.

Why not?

It's too qualitative; I prefer quantitative approaches.

Can't equities be quantitative?

We do have a small program, which is a systematic program trading single stocks. It is basically an intelligent market maker. It models the price of every stock, using all of the other stock prices as the input. It looks for divergence. If, for example, Fidelity decides to liquidate a given

---

[4]This interview was conducted in May 2011.

stock, their selling will probably push the stock out of line with the basket of stocks. We will buy the stock and sell the basket, and we will do the same thing with other stocks.

So it is basically a statistical arbitrage approach.

Yes it is. We have done a phenomenal amount of work on quantitatively selecting single stocks.

The implication of that is that there have been a lot of dead ends.

Yes, there have been.

I recall that you did have another equity strategy at one time. What happened to it?

Yes, we did. It was a market neutral strategy for investors who wanted the relative value approach in equities. It made money, but it wasn't top quartile. I want our products to be in the top two percentile, not in the bottom half. In August 2007, we had about $9 billion in gross exposure in this strategy. I am sitting there, and I see LIBOR suddenly jump 10 points. This had never happened in my trading career. I thought, this just feels very bad and scary.[5]

Ten basis points doesn't sound like that much.

Yes, but it was for no reason at all. I looked at some bank balance sheet leverage statistics. One U.K. bank was 60 times leveraged. Its balance sheet was 7 percent of world GDP and over 150 percent of U.K. GDP. Banks wouldn't lend to each other because they had too much exposure. It didn't feel right.

A couple of weeks later, I went to give a talk at an investor conference in Lugano. Whenever I give a talk on global markets, I never write anything down. I just speak off the cuff. As I am presenting this speech, I find myself giving this huge rant about how I believed there

---

[5]Colm O'Shea (Chapter 1) was another trader who cited this same event as being particularly critical.

was going to be a global credit crunch. I said, "Asking people in the credit market how they feel is like asking someone who has jumped out of the 50th floor window how he feels as he passes floor 10. He is currently all right, but he is not going to be soon." I heard myself coming out with this stream of consciousness.

You didn't plan this talk?

I never plan talks. I went on and on about how the credit markets are ready to implode. There are about 200 people in the room. When I finished, there was dead silence. They really thought I had gone off the deep end.

What did you predict was going to happen?

I said there was going to be a total credit crunch, an equity market meltdown, and a flight to quality bonds.

Had you adjusted your portfolio to reflect these expectations?

No, it just dawned on me as I was giving the speech. I went back to the office and thought, *$9 billion of stocks going into a credit crunch; I don't want any of this crap.* I got the fund manager into my office and said, "Look, August was not that great." The strategy was down about 5 percent in August. I continued, "Honestly, I don't believe in this anymore. There's going to be a credit crunch, and the stuff you've got is going to be absolutely toxic. Let's shut the strategy down."

Even though it was market neutral?

Yes, because I was afraid of a lack of liquidity.

Actually, August 2007 was the month when many statistical arbitrage and some market neutral funds got killed. A 5 percent loss for a market neutral fund that month is not really that extreme.

I have no appetite for losses. Our discretionary strategy's worst peak-to-trough drawdown in over 10 years was less than 5 percent, and this strategy lost approximately 5 percent in one month. One thing that brings my blood to a boiling point is when an absolute return guy starts talking about his return relative to anything. My response was, "You are not relative to anything, my friend. You can't be in the relative game just when it suits you and in the absolute game just when it suits you. You are in the absolute return game, and the fact that you use the word relative means that I don't want you anymore."

What made you so convinced of an impending credit crunch?

It was just the huge excess leverage in the system everywhere you looked, and when LIBOR jumped by 10 basis points, it was like seeing the first crack.

What happened to LIBOR liquidity after that point?

It went straight down. The LIBOR–OIS spread started to widen.

What is the OIS?

The OIS is the overnight index swap, which is a weighted average of overnight lending rates. The LIBOR-OIS spread reflects the illiquidity premium. If you lend money for 90 days, you demand a premium because you can't get it right back. If I lend you cash for 90 days, I want to be paid more than if I lend it to you overnight. I could lend you money overnight for 90 days, but I have the option to break it at any time. If I give up my option to break the loan, I want to be compensated. The market price for the option to break—that is the LIBOR-OIS spread—used to be almost nothing because people were so confident. Then suddenly, when liquidity dried up, the option to break was worth 200 basis points, and then more than 300 basis points. In fact, you couldn't even get 90-day money at the end.

Anyway, when this crack appeared in the market, I knew I didn't want to have equity exposure. So during the next six weeks, we liquidated the entire $9 billion of exposure. The strategy was shut, and the money was sent back to investors. We watched the markets very carefully, and in early 2008, I transferred a vast proportion of the firm's money into two-year treasury notes. I got rid of all the money market funds. I put all the traders into a wind down of counterparty exposure.

We dumped outright exposure to every bank possible and went maximum long fixed income. The systematic trend-following strategy was consistently moving into a similar position. It started reversing from long to short in equities and commodities and going hugely long in fixed income. Again, it was all the same trade, wasn't it?

So when the market meltdown hit later in 2008, you were positioned perfectly.

In 2008, BlueCrest made the most amount of money for its investors in its history up to that point. Even though we were making loads of money, many of our investors redeemed simply because they couldn't get their cash from anyone else. We were making about $500 million a month and in numerous months paying out about $1 billion. It was a bit depressing.

It hardly sounds depressing. The main thing is that you were making money when everyone else was losing. You didn't have to worry about the money; the money would always come back if you have the performance.

It did. Also, it helped a great deal that we didn't gate.[6] When investors started returning to hedge funds, we got an unusually large share of the net investments. According to Deutsche Bank research, in 2010, net inflows into hedge funds totaled $55 billion. We got one dollar in nine out of those inflows.

---

[6]A gate is a common provision in hedge fund prospectuses that allows the fund to curtail total investor redemptions beyond some specified amount (e.g., 10 percent of assets under management per quarter). If investor redemptions exceed the gate threshold, and the gate provision is enforced, then the hedge fund would only meet investor redemptions pro rata up to the specified maximum redemption level for that redemption period. The unmet portion of redemption requests would be filled pro rata in subsequent redemption periods within the same gate provisions, until redemptions were totally fulfilled. When a gate is enacted, it can sometimes take investors one or more years to receive all their money back. During the financial meltdown of late 2008 to early 2009, an unusually large number of hedge funds enforced gate provisions, as there were widespread investor redemptions due to the liquidity crunch and general market panic.

You not only did very well in 2008, but you also did well in 2009 when markets rebounded strongly. What were the trades that accounted for the 2009 gains?

We faded a lot of the very big call and put skews in the market. The out-of-the-money strikes were insanely expensive. So we shorted a lot of out-of-the-money options and protected ourselves with offsetting long positions in the at-the-money options. The tails were enormously fat because of what had happened in 2008. The breakeven points on the shorts in the out-of-the-money strikes were so crazy that you needed to have another major crisis to come anywhere near losing money on the position. And I didn't think we were going to have another crisis six months after the 2008 crisis.

Generals fight the last war. Speculators trade the last market. How have you managed to keep your risk so incredibly restrained through all types of markets?

I talk about macro themes a lot because they are fun to talk about, but it is the risk management that is the most important thing. The risk control is all bottom-up. I structured the business right from the get-go so that we would have lots of diversification. For example, on the fixed-income side, I hire specialists. I have a specialist in Scandinavian rates, a specialist in the short end, a specialist in volatility surface arbitrage, a specialist in euro long-dated trading, an inflation specialist, and so on. They all get a capital allocation. Typically, I will hand out about $1.5 billion for every $1 billion we manage because people don't use their entire risk allocation all the time. I assume, on average, they will use about two thirds. The deal is that if a trader loses 3 percent, he has to give me back half of his trading line. If he loses another 3 percent of the remaining half, that's it. His book is auctioned. All the traders are shown his book and take what they want into their own books, and anything that is left is liquidated.

What happens to the trader at that point? Is he out on the street?

It depends on how he reached his limit. I'm not a hard-nosed person. I don't say, you lost money, get out. It's possible someone gets caught in a storm. A trader might have some very reasonable Japanese positions on, and then there is a nuclear accident, and he loses a lot of money. We might recapitalize him, but it depends. It is also a matter of gut feel. How do I feel about the guy?

Is the 3 percent loss measured from the allocation starting level?

Yes, it is definitely not a trailing stop. We want people to scale down if they are getting it wrong and scale up if they are getting it right. If a guy has a $100 million allocation and makes $20 million, he then has $23 million to his stop point.

Do you move that stop up at any point?

No, it rebases annually.

So every January 1, traders start off with the same 3 percent stop point?

Yes, unless they carry over some of their P&L. One year, one of my guys made about $500 million of profits. He was going to get a huge incentive check. I said to him, "Do you really want to be paid out on the entire $500 million? How about I pay you on $400 million, and you carry over $100 million, so you still have a big line." He said, "Yeah, that's cool. I'll do that." So he would have to lose that $100 million plus 3 percent of the new allocation before the first stop would kick in.

Your structure of cutting a trader's book on successive 3 percent losses builds asymmetry into the performance. The downside is limited, but the upside is unlimited. In fact, you are structuring traders like they are options.

Yes, completely.

In addition to the broad diversification and the tight 3 percent/3 percent two-tiered risk constraint on each trader, are there any other elements to the risk management strategy?

We have a seven-person risk management team.

What are they looking for?

The key thing they are monitoring for is a breakdown in correlation.

Wouldn't it be the other way around? Wouldn't higher correlation increase risk?

No, because most of our positions are spreads. So lower correlations would increase the risk of the position. The most dangerous risks are spread risks. If I assume that IBM and Dell have a 0.95 correlation, I can put on a large spread position with relatively small risk. But if the correlation drops to 0.50, I could be wiped out in 10 minutes. It is when the spread risks blow up that you find out that you have much more risk than you thought. Controlling correlations is the key to managing risk. We look at risk in a whole range of different ways.

What else does the risk management team look for?

They stress test the positions for all sorts of historical scenarios. They also scan portfolios to search for any vulnerabilities in positions that could impact performance. They literally ask the traders, "If you were going to drop $10 million, where would it come from?" And the traders will know. A trader will often have some position in his book that is a bit spicy, and he will know what it is. So you just ask him to tell you. Most of what we get in the vulnerabilities in positions reports, we already know anyway. We would hope that our risk monitoring systems would have caught 95 percent of it. It is just a last check.

Anything else on the risk side?

Being long volatility is great protection against all scenarios. Typically, we are neutral to long volatility, and I hate shorting out-of-the-money strikes. We made an exception in 2009 because, as we discussed earlier, the out-of-the-money options were very overpriced, and we hedged them with long in-the-money positions. I expected the out-of-the-money positions to roll off valueless, and they did.

You have picked a lot of traders in your career. What do you look for when you hire a trader?

I want market makers, people who know that anything can happen. The type of guy I don't want is an analyst who has never traded—the type of person who does a calculation on a computer, figures out where a market should be, puts on a big trade, gets caught up in it, and doesn't stop out. And the market is always wrong; he's not. Market makers know that the market is always right. You are wrong if you are losing money for any reason at all. Market makers have that drilled into their head. They know value is irrelevant in times of market stress; it's all about positions. They understand that markets will trade against positions. They get it. It is built into their books. It colors the way they think. I look for the type of guy in London who gets up at seven o'clock on Sunday morning when his kids are still in bed, and logs onto a poker site so that he can pick off the U.S. drunks coming home on Saturday night. I hired a guy like that. He usually clears 5 or 10 grand every Sunday morning before breakfast taking out the drunks playing poker because they're not very good at it, but their confidence has gone up a lot. That's the type of guy you want—someone who understands an edge. Analysts, on the other hand, don't think about anything else other than how smart they are.

But, of course, on the systematic trend side, you would want analysts.

That's a completely different world. I am talking about the human discretionary trading. I am talking about a different type of analyst— market macro analysts who do their research and come up with a theory.

I can give a great example to illustrate your point.

I mention a particular hedge fund manager I know who I think is brilliant and who was early and right in calling major macro themes, yet did poorly trading off his correct ideas.

There are a lot of people like that. There are a lot of people that if you listen to their ideas, you can make more money off their thinking than they can. I troll around. It's a treasure hunt for information. I talk to lots of people. Every now and then, someone says something, and I know I'm going to make much more money off of it than they will. There's a big difference between shooting wine glasses at 20 yards and shooting a wine glass pointing a gun back at you.

I want guys who when they put on a good trade immediately start thinking about what they could put on against it. They just have the paranoia. Market makers get derailed in crises far less often than analysts. I hired an analyst one time who was a very smart guy. I probably made 50 times more money on his ideas than he did. I hired an economist once, which was the biggest mistake ever. He lasted only a few months. He was very dogmatic. He thought he was always right. The problem always comes down to ego. You find that analysts and economists have big egos, which just gets in the way of making money because they can never admit that they are wrong.

What percent of the people you give money to work out?

A very high percentage. Market makers are just reliable. One trader who didn't work out was the fixed-income analyst I mentioned before—the only analyst I hired. I really liked him, and I made a lot of money on his ideas, but he couldn't keep his car on the road.

Maybe you should have kept him on just for his ideas.

I would actually have been happy to have him stay, but he just got too disillusioned. He decided he just wanted to be a schoolteacher and get some sense of accomplishment by doing social good.

So what was his failing? Did he get the trends right, but couldn't trade?

He was very good at identifying relative value opportunities and mispricings, but he had no idea about macro. You can be as smart as you like about analyzing instruments, but there is no hedge against being wrong. If you think rates are going up when they're going down, I don't care what trade you've done, you're going to lose money. You might lose less if you've been particularly clever about how you implemented the trade, but you're still going to lose.

What other traders didn't work out?

There were three market makers we hired that didn't work out. One flatlined—he just became gun shy—and left. The other two lost money.

Was there anything different about the traders who didn't work out versus the majority who did?

Both the ex-market makers who blew up became way too invested in their positions. Their ego got in the way. They just didn't want to be wrong, and they stayed in their positions.

What about the firm's risk monitoring?

Well, they just hit their stops. I don't interfere with traders. A trader is either a stand-alone producer or gone. If I start micromanaging a trader's position, it then becomes my position. Why then am I paying him such a large percentage of the incentive fee?

In your own trading book, what is the breakdown between directional and relative value trades?

It completely depends. Sometimes I have no directional trades on, and sometimes directional trades dominate my book. Basically, I like buying stuff cheap and selling it at fair value. How you implement a trade is critical. I develop a macro view about something, but then there are 20 different ways I can play it. The key question is: Which way gives me the best risk/return ratio? My final trade is rarely going to be a straight long or short position.

How would you characterize yourself as a trader?

I don't have any tolerance for trading losses. I hate losing money more than anything. Losing money is what kills you. It is not the actual loss. It's the fact that it messes up your psychology. You lose the bullets in your gun. What happens is you put on a stupid trade, lose $20 million in 10 minutes, and take the trade off. You feel like an idiot, and you're not in the mood to put on anything else. Then the elephant walks past you while your gun's not loaded. It's amazing how annoyingly often that happens. In this game, you want to be there when the great trade comes along. It's the 80/20 rule of life. In trading, 80 percent of your profits come from 20 percent of your ideas.

How do you avoid or minimize losses?

I don't trade unless I have done all the work and really have a view. If I enter a trade, and the minute I put it on, I feel uncomfortable, I will just turn around and get right out. Also, I look at each trade in my book every day and ask myself the question, "Would I enter this trade today at this price?" If the answer is "no," then the trade is gone. Most of the trades that I do stop myself out of, I stop out because of time rather than because of a loss. If I really love the trade and get strongly positioned, and then a month later, it still hasn't moved, alarm bells start ringing in my head. I think to myself, *That is a really great idea you have, but the market is just not playing ball.*

What do you look for to make a trade?

There are three things you need to make money in a market. You need a decent fundamental story, a good trend that looks like it will carry on, and the market handling news the way you think it should. Bull markets ignore any bad news, and any good news is a reason for a further rally.

Can you think of an example where the market response to the news was counter to what you expected and impacted your trade?

In 2009, I was long 2-year notes/short 10-year notes one-year forward, looking for the yield curve to widen, and a lot of news came out that I thought would hurt me. One news item after another, I saw the screen and thought, *I am going to get screwed in this position.* But I didn't. After a number of these instances, I thought, *the yield curve just can't get any flatter no matter what comes out.* So I quadrupled my position. It was a great trade. The spread went from 25 basis points to 210, although I got out at 110.

Any other examples where the market action was the catalyst for a trade?

When the whole debt fiasco in Europe started to unfold, the euro plunged from 1.45 to 1.19. Everyone was bearish, and so was I. I thought, *I am in this trade. I have made a lot of money. It is going down to*

1.00. I should increase my position. I had drunk the Kool-Aid along with everyone else. As I'm looking at the screen, the euro suddenly trades back up to 1.21. That should not have happened. The ex-market maker part of my brain starts thinking, *Everyone has the trade on. Everyone believes. Everyone who was long euro is now out. There is still a trade surplus. Wouldn't it just be a disaster for everyone if the euro suddenly went back up again?*

Was there any news that triggered the rebound in the euro?

No, it was just the price action combined with the consensus—that was enough to get me out. I like to know what the consensus view is because you really do make the most money when the consensus shifts.

How do you get the consensus?

It is not easy to get. If you ask people their position, they're not exactly going to tell you, are they? My favorite question to ask people is, "What is your opinion?" The minute you ask people for their opinion, they feel important. If I ask a hedge fund manager for his opinion on where the 30-year bond will be trading in three months' time, and he starts talking about factors that will push interest rates up, I know that he is short bonds because the correlation between his three-month forecast and his current position is going to be 100 percent. There is no doubt about that. If he was long, he would have picked some plausible story about why rates should go down. It's amazing how much information you can get about people's positions by simply asking them about their opinions.

Have there been any situations where the market abruptly reversed direction and you were positioned the wrong way in meaningful size? If so, how did you handle it?

I once went on a trip with ARK, which is a charity I sponsor, to help design a feeding program for children, which has turned out to be a great success, reaching 60,000 children. At the time, I had a massive long position in European interest rate futures. While I was on the flight to South Africa, the European Central Bank (ECB) hiked rates very unexpectedly. It was a massive hit. It was probably the only time I got an ECB call wrong. As soon as I landed, I got a phone call from an assistant telling me the ECB had just hiked rates and asking me what I wanted to do.

"How much are we down?" I asked.

"About $70 million to $80 million," he answered.

I said, "If they started hiking, they won't stop at 25 basis points. I can see this trade turning into a $250 million loss by week's end. Dump everything aggressively. Take the price to a place where it trades."

When I am wrong, the only instinct I have is to get out. If I was thinking one way, and now I can see that it was a real mistake, then I am probably not the only person in shock, so I better be the first one to sell. I don't care what the price is. In this game, you have an option to keep 20 percent of your P&L this year, but you also want to own the serial option of being able to do that every year. You can't be blowing up.

What mistakes do you think traders make—not necessarily the traders working with you—that get them into trouble?

I think the two biggest mistakes traders make is that they don't do enough homework, and they are a bit too casual about risk.

■ ■ ■

Yes, I know you have heard it a thousand times, but risk control really is critical to trading success. According to Platt, it is "the most important thing." And Platt is a master of risk control. "I hate losing money more than anything," he says, and that aversion strongly colors his trading approach.

The principle of minimizing losses permeates Platt's trading habits. Risk management begins with trade implementation. Platt will express a trading theme, say an expectation that interest rates will decrease, by implementing the trade in a way that minimizes risk relative to the same return potential. Thus Platt will rarely implement directional trade ideas as outright long or short positions. He will be much more likely to use long options or complex spread structures that will provide equivalent return potential, but with theoretically constrained risk. Of course, Platt will strictly limit the maximum loss on any individual position, but he does not stop there. If he feels uncomfortable in a trade after he enters it, he will get right out. Most of the trades that Platt stops himself out of never get to their stop-loss points. If a trade does not work within a reasonable amount of time, Platt will just liquidate rather than give it room to his original stop point. Platt also reevaluates each of his positions daily and asks himself whether he would still place the same trade today. If not, he will liquidate it.

Perhaps the most potent risk control Platt employs in BlueCrest's discretionary strategy is maintaining an extremely tight rein on what a trader can lose before capital is withdrawn. A mere 3 percent loss is enough to trigger a 50 percent reduction in a trader's allocation, and the same small additional percentage loss is all it takes to remove a trader's entire allocation. These rigid rules seek to prevent any trader from losing more than 5 percent of his initial stake. (The combination of two successive 3 percent losses is less than a 5 percent loss because the second 3 percent loss is incurred on only 50 percent of the starting stake.) In his own trading book, Platt is subject to the same rules as his traders, but he has never approached the 3 percent loss point.

You would think that with such extreme loss limitations, it would be very difficult for individual traders, and in turn the strategy, to make much money. It seems that with only 3 percent leeway before their capital allocation is slashed that traders would be risking too little on their trades to make much of a return. How then has the discretionary strategy managed to average nearly a 14 percent per year net return? The key is that the 3 percent/3 percent risk rule applies to a trader's starting stake. So certainly, the rule encourages traders to be very cautious at the onset, being highly selective in their trades and tightly limiting the loss on any trade. But as traders get ahead, their cushion widens, as trading gains augment the small initial 3 percent loss allowance. Once they are comfortably in the black, traders can take much more risk, thereby creating the potential to achieve large returns, despite the highly restrictive initial loss limitation. Essentially, the trader allocation risk control strategy assures capital preservation, while at the same time keeping upside potential open-ended by allowing greater risk-taking with profits. It is, effectively, an asymmetric risk management strategy.

Risk control is important for many obvious reasons, which include avoiding account-incapacitating losses, minimizing emotional pain, and constraining the adverse impact of compounding—large percentage losses require increasingly greater percentage gains to get back to even. Platt, however, points out a far less obvious reason for avoiding losses: Losing trades mentally impede the trader and often result in missed winning trade opportunities. As Platt colorfully describes the trader's mindset after incurring a foolish loss, "You feel like an idiot, and you're not in the mood to put anything else on. Then the elephant walks past you while your gun's not loaded." Platt says that trading follows the 80/20 rule—80 percent of a trader's profits come from 20 percent of the trades. If the psychological fallout from a trading loss causes a trader to miss a trade in the 20 percent, it can be a big deal.

Platt pays a lot of attention to how the market responds to news. He cites the interesting observation of a trade in which there was a continuing stream of news items adverse to his position, and yet the market did not move against him. Platt read the inability of the market to respond to the news as confirmation of his trade idea, and he quadrupled his position, turning it into one of his biggest winners ever.

Although BlueCrest's systematic trend-following strategy is not in the same return/risk league as the discretionary strategy, it is nonetheless one of the best-performing trend-following strategies, achieving an average annual compounded net return of 16 percent with a maximum drawdown of under 13 percent. When queried about how the systematic trend-following strategy achieved its superior performance vis-à-vis other trend-following strategies, Platt mentioned two key factors. First, their system will liquidate positions when trends get overextended without waiting for trend reversal signals. Second, there is continuous ongoing research and implementation of changes to improve the system. System trading is a dynamic rather than static process. Platt believes that systems that don't change will eventually degrade. In Platt's words, system trading "is a research war."

Part Three

EQUITY TRADERS

Chapter 9

Steve Clark

*Do More of What Works
and Less of What Doesn't*

Steve Clark's fund, the Omni Global Fund, has achieved remarkable performance consistency. The strategy has been profitable in every year since its inception 10½ years ago (2001).[1] The worst year was a 0.7 percent gain in 2011. Omni's 19.4 percent average annual compounded return is impressive, but what truly sets Omni apart is that it achieved these strong returns while containing the worst peak-to-valley equity drawdown to a modest 7 percent. The fund's Sharpe ratio is an extremely high 1.50. The Sharpe ratio, however, which makes no distinction between upside and downside volatility, understates the fund's performance because volatility has been

---

[1]The strategy was rebranded as the Omni Global Fund in February 2007. Prior to that time, the strategy was called the Hartford Growth Fund and was not open to outside investors.

heavily skewed to the upside—there have been many months with gains above 4 percent, and some much higher, but only two months with losses above this level (both less than 5 percent). As a result of the combination of strong gains and moderate losses, the fund has an extremely high Gain to Pain ratio of 4.1. (See Appendix A for an explanation of the Gain to Pain ratio.) In 2008, an absolutely disastrous year for event-driven hedge funds—the Hedge Fund Research (HFR) index for this sector was down 22 percent for the year—Omni was actually up 15 percent. Warren Buffett has said that, "It's only when the tide goes out that you discover who's been swimming naked." 2008 made clear that Omni was swimming fully clothed in multiple layers.

Steve Clark was brutally honest—probably more so than any other trader I have ever interviewed. He seemed to hold nothing back, whether it was about his past experiences or his feelings. His emotions at times were palpable. His directness made this an unexpectedly compelling interview for me. Clark began our conversation by telling his story from the time he finished school at the age of 17.

■ ■ ■

I did my A levels a year early, and left school at the age of 17. I knew nothing about university. No one in my family had been to university.

You came from a working-class background?

I was the third generation, all living in the same council house—government housing is what I guess you would call in the U.S.—on the outskirts of London. I didn't know my father; he didn't hang around. I lived with my mother, brother, and grandparents. My mother was always working, so I was sort of half-raised by my grandparents.

One day, I got a call from Grant, a school friend who now works here—a call for which I am eternally grateful. He was considered one of the posh kids at school because his parents actually owned their own house. "You should come and work in the city,"[2] Grant said. "There

---

[2]"The city" is a small historic section in central London that is the heart of the financial district.

are 25-year-olds earning £50,000." I didn't know what I wanted to do, but I thought I would go there, and earn some money until I decided what I wanted to be when I grew up. I'm still waiting. I naively thought, *Okay, I will go work in the city then and be a trader*. I didn't even know what a trader was.

Was Grant working as a trader?

He was working as a trading assistant. I had no concept what that meant, either.

What were you doing at the time?

I was working for a hi-fi installation company. I was designing the layout of home stereo system installations, lifting things, and driving a van.

Did you try to get a job in the city?

I wrote lots and lots of places and always got the same answer, "no degree, no interview," or "no experience, no interview."

That is exactly what I would have expected.

I did get one interview for a backoffice job at Manufacturers Hanover. I had a terrible interview. I talked about how I wanted to be a trader, with absolutely no thought given to the fact that the fellow interviewing me wanted somebody to work in the backoffice. Needless to say, I didn't get the job. But I learned from that interview process. I realized that the sensible thing to do was to get some experience. At the time—this was 1986—there was a shortage of backoffice people. I got a job as a temporary filing clerk and then moved to different temporary jobs, each time embroidering my CV. Anytime I was offered a position and asked if I could do it, I said that I could. I figured that I could learn how to do it once I was at the job. I did that for several months, and then I got two permanent job offers: one was from Merrill Lynch to run part of the backoffice, which paid £30,000, and the other was from Warburg Securities to be a blue button.

What is a blue button?

On the stock exchange floor, you had badges with your firm written on it and a number. The color of your badge indicated your role. Blue buttons were boys who were trainees, but who in reality were treated as slaves. The blue button job paid £7,000. So it was £30,000 on the left hand versus £7,000 on the right hand, but the £7,000 job got you on the trading floor. I thought that was clearly the place I needed to be. I still remember my interview for the job. The guy asked me about what relevant experience I had. I certainly knew nothing. I didn't read the *Financial Times*, and I didn't pretend to read the *Financial Times*. The only clever answer I gave was when he asked me whether I ever gambled.

I asked, "Do you mean like gambling on the horses?"

He answered, "Yes, exactly."

I replied, "I would never bet on anything where the odds were against me. Why would you do that?"

I didn't know whether that was the right answer or the wrong answer, but it was my instinctive answer. I got the job.

I started on South African gold shares, and literally my job was to get tea, coffee, and sandwiches, book trades, and answer the phone. I really had a miserable time on the first desk I was on. I couldn't understand what was going on, and no one was willing to answer a question or teach me anything. It was a very poor experience. But I was a very good blue button. I was very good at doing the P&Ls. I got transferred to the European desk where the people had a completely different attitude. They were very happy to talk to me and to teach me.

At what point were you allowed to trade?

After I was there for about one year, I was given the Scandinavian market-making book. I was going to run the book for one week because the trader was on holiday. This first week that I was given a book to run on my own was the week of the October 1987 crash.

So, literally, October 19, 1987, was the first day you were allowed to trade?

Yes.

That has to be the most interesting trading start date I have ever heard, or I am sure that I will ever hear. At least you had no positions coming in.

Oh, no, I took over the book.

And your boss was incommunicado?

He was on holiday. The previous week we had been told that we would be receiving a large institutional buy order for a basket of stocks. The trader I worked for had bought those stocks in anticipation of buying support. So I came in Monday morning long only.

The most vivid memory I have of the day is making a price in a stock called Electrolux. I get a call asking for a price on Electrolux. I say they are 43 bid/44 offered. He offers 10,000 shares at 43. I buy 2,500 shares and put the phone down. I then change my price to 42½ bid/ 43½ offered. The phone rings again, and I give the caller my new quote. He offers 10,000 shares, and I buy 2,500 at 42½. I reason that if I drop my price by a full $1 to 41½/42½, and I get hit on the offer, I would be selling my shares at a loss. This is how I was thinking on the morning of the crash. So I set the price at 42/43. The phone rings, and once again I get hit with an offer, so I bought another 2,500 shares at 42.

At this point, I turn around to the German trader, who unlike me had lots of experience, and show him my trades and say, "I've done these trades; what price should I make now?" He looks at me like I am a complete imbecile. Meanwhile, the phone is ringing. He picks up the phone. I was going to make the next price 41½/42½. He makes the price 36/37 and still gets hit with an offer at 36. So I had been making the totally wrong prices. I had no clue to what was going on. But I learned a very valuable lesson from that experience: The price is where anyone is prepared to deal, and it can be anything. I had one year of experience and had seen only a limited amount of volatility. In my mind, I couldn't comprehend changing the price by more than $1, let alone $6, which is nearly a 15 percent change. I had never witnessed that before. Actually, not many people had ever seen anything similar before.

Where was the market price? You weren't determining the market price, were you?

Oh, I was determining the price. All the systems were down. So I was getting calls from people asking me the price.

Weren't other people making a market in the stock?

There were other market makers, but you couldn't see their prices.

So the German trader understood the market was falling out of bed.

After he looked at my trades he told me, "Your position is growing. You cannot afford to let your next trade be a purchase. Whatever you have to do, you need to make sure that your next trade is a sell." He quoted the price down by $6 and still ended up buying.

What about the long inventory you came in with at the start of the day?

You couldn't do anything that day. You just had to ride the whole thing down.

What about people who called wanting to sell? As a market maker, did you have to facilitate the trade?

You just quoted the prices down to a point where you didn't buy any more.

So after those initial trades at the wrong price, you didn't do much at all. I guess you just quoted prices down far enough to make sure you wouldn't get any more sell orders.

That is exactly right. My book—the book I had taken over for the week—lost several million pounds that day. The German trader was short everything, so he made several million pounds.

He sounds like a smart fellow.

He was a smart guy. Years later I employed him. Actually, years later, I also employed the trader who ran the Scandinavian book, who was my boss.

From that point on, I began to trade other books in the European area when people were on holiday. I eventually became the most profitable trader in the group.

How? What were you doing that made you so profitable?

I was very proactive in orientating the book. If I was in something that was wrong, I would cut it. I wouldn't defend it. I wouldn't average down. I would just cut it, cut it, cut it.

What does being proactive mean for a market maker?

I was very active in positioning myself. I would trade around news, trying to orientate myself on the right side of the market. I would develop my own views on stocks and be happy to run with those views. Also, I was so inexperienced that I didn't have the fear—the fear that cripples people who have been in the business too long. I have seen that so many times. Very few people maintain their ability to take risk throughout their career. Most don't. Most can't. They have had too many bad things happen to them, too many fat tails, and it damages people.

Not having fear and cutting positions when they are going against you speak to a willingness to take risk and an ability to control risk. But to make money, you still have to be on the right side of the market, which raises the question: How were you calling the directional moves to have some sort of an edge?

You have to go back to the facts. What do you know? If you know there is a buyer for XYZ stock at some price below the market, you know one fact. You know there is a buyer there. What else do you know? Go back and see what happened the last time the market got to this level. You can look at the chart. I also used volume as a screen for what stocks I should be looking at. My thought process would be: *There is lots of volume. Something is going on. Can I develop a view from that?*

How important were charts to your trading?

Charts are simply a record of how things have traded in the past. That's it. I am not a big believer in chart analysis. It is extremely appealing to think that you can take a data set from the past and predict what will happen in the future. It is very attractive because as a human being you are always looking for certainty. You can use charts to give you a plus or minus toward your view, but you can never start with the chart. To say that you can predict the future from past data is patently untrue. You can talk about percentage probabilities of what might happen next, but you can't go any further than that. So I would combine the charts with other facts, such as what I knew about where the orders were and the market volume.

How long were you a market maker for Warburg Securities?

I stayed for two and half years. I left because I was only being paid £13,000 per year, and I was clearly the best trader they had in that area. Lehman Brothers offered me a job for £50,000 per year. I went back to Warburg and told him that I was leaving because I had a much better offer.

They said, "We can put you at £28,000."

I said, "Why £28,000? Why not £50,000?"

"Well," they said, "We have all these tiers, and you are a trainee."

I thought that was total bullshit. They could do whatever they wanted. So I went to Lehman Brothers.

Here is where it gets interesting. Warburg was number one rated. I came from a place where you were imbued with the feeling that you were the best. I went to Lehman Brothers, and I couldn't make a penny.

Why is that?

Because I had no idea how to make money outside of the Warburg environment, which was so rich in order flow information.

So going back to the question I originally asked you, was the edge then coming from knowledge of where the orders were?

The opportunity to make money was there because of the franchise, but the fact that I was making multiples of the people around me indicated that I was doing something better than they were.

You were using that order flow information better. But it must be very helpful to know there are a lot of buy orders below the market, and if you are long and wrong, the stock should run into buying support, and you shouldn't get hurt much.

Yes, it is a nice comfortable place to be.

But if you have no idea where the orders are, it's not quite so easy. Was that a revelation?

Oh, totally. I was so happy at Warburg. I loved going to work. I didn't want to leave, but I thought I had to. I've always been driven to be rational. £50,000 versus £28,000; I had to go. The decision was so clear. So I went to Lehman, and I couldn't make any money. It was a terrible shock to my ego. I began to doubt my ability. It was a very depressing time. It lasted for several months. I've seen this happen to many traders, and I have gone through it several times myself. When you find that you can't make any money, smaller and smaller losses take on greater and greater emotional significance, and you lose all perspective.

I can remember this incident very clearly. I was playing basketball one night, and I got a call from our New York office to tell me that there had been a big move in Novo, a Danish company, which was one of the European stocks I covered. It was up $2 from the European close. I asked if the stock was bid. He said there was 100,000 shares bid. As a gut reaction, I went short the entire amount. It was the biggest position I had taken by a mile.

But since you were so gun shy, why would you take on a position that large?

I reverted to my old Warburg mode when my brain would have calculated the risk and just done the trade.

Why did you think it was a good risk?

It was up $2 from the close, which was a big move for a stock that didn't move that much. It was just a gut reaction. I came in the next morning and bought the stock back for a $100,000 turn. From that moment on, I couldn't stop making money.

I guess because you got your confidence back. But you still had no order flow to work against, so where was your edge?

I developed very strong relationships with other brokers, so I used their order flow information. I was also trading news flow.

What would determine if you were a buyer or seller after a news item hit?

It was a matter of sampling views of brokers that I trusted. I've always thought that when you are trading over a short to medium term, your own views on the fundamentals of a story are totally irrelevant. What you have to do is gauge what the market thinks of the story. I would sample opinions, and if there were enough people saying that we were going to see buying on the back of the news item, I would go long. If I didn't see momentum develop, I would cut it, and if I did see upward momentum, I might increase the position size. I am a big believer in buying on the way up.

So you were speaking to people who you thought were more right than wrong.

Yes, and they had order flow. That was one element of my trading. I also started to screen for volume. I thought that my trading was good enough so that if I could find volume or a story, I could trade it.

I was trading successfully, and then I read your book [*Market Wizards*]. It was a seminal moment in my trading career. I was reading about people in your book and thinking, *That is what I do. That is one of my rules.* It was like these people had copied what I do. How could they know? It was an awakening because for the first time in my life I realized that I had a method. Up until that point, I thought I was playing a videogame, and I couldn't believe I was getting paid to do it. I enjoyed it so much that I would have done it for nothing. The one thing that I really took away from your book was that once you understand you have a method, you can tweak that method.

Time and time again, I give traders who work for me one piece of advice: Do more of what works and less of what doesn't. Young traders come to me and say, "Well, I have been running this book, and these things have been going really well, but I keep losing money on this." I tell them to just stop doing the things that are not working. Dissect your P&L and see what works for you and what doesn't. It is a very interesting process to analyze where your profits come from, and traders often don't know.

How did that advice apply to you at the time?

I decided to look at what I did as a trader. Where did I make money? That was the point at which I started to move to event-driven trading.

Where were you making money?

I had a series of trades where I had an edge. They were arbitrages. So I started looking for more arbitrage trades.

You were doing best in arbitrage trades, so you focused on arbitrage. Where were you not doing well?

I wasn't doing badly anywhere, but the arbitrage trades were by far the most consistent and profitable. There was really only one trade at the time where I took a big loss, and it was strictly hubris. The stock was 1912DS, a Danish shipping company, which traded at an extremely high share price of 140,000 Danish kroner. It traded in lots of one share or five shares. For some reason, I had become bullish on the stock and bought a lot of it. Then there was an article in the paper that said the company was a fraud. I had bought the stock at 140,000. It opened the next day at 100,000 offered and nothing bid. I remember the sick feeling in my stomach that morning. I worked out what the loss was at a price of 100,000 and thought, *That's too big; I can't show that today.* So what I did was write down the price of that stock a little bit every day for the next three months, while I traded as hard as I could to make money.

So the stock didn't trade?

There were literally no trades for a long time. There were no bids.

Wasn't there a settlement price anywhere?

No, this was the Wild West. Traders marked their own book. No one checked it. Smoothing losses was the status quo.

How much was the ultimate loss?

I don't remember exactly, but I sold it somewhere higher than 100,000.

So the company wasn't a fraud then?

No, the article turned out to be total nonsense. That trade taught me a very valuable lesson: Price is irrelevant; it is size that kills you. If you are too big in an illiquid stock, there is no way out. I wanted to cut the position, but I couldn't. The other lesson this trade taught me is to focus on what works. The trade was just a punt. I bought it because I thought the momentum would carry it up. After that trade, I became much more focused on just looking for arbitrage trades, which was where I was making most of my money.

How did you make a transition from a market maker role to a hedge fund manager?

After Lehman, I switched to NatWest. It was the same job, but a much bigger business. I was hired to run market making for international shares. After three years there, I got bored, and I also wanted to make more money. I told them that I was leaving to set up a hedge fund. I really had no concept of what setting up a hedge fund involved, but I figured whatever it was, I could do it. They told me if I left then, I wouldn't get my bonus. But I didn't care. I found a hedge fund manager who said he would seed me with $5 million. I then spent several months getting the hedge fund set up. By the time I was done and ready to go, he wouldn't return my phone calls. He had been annihilated by the bond market in 1994 and had lost most of his assets. He clearly wasn't going to speak to me. So I had a hedge fund with no assets.

Didn't you think about where you would raise the money before you decided to leave NatWest to start a hedge fund?

No.

You just figured you would open a hedge fund and money would come?

That absolutely was my attitude. When I decided to go "work in the city," I had no idea what that meant, but I resolved that I would just go and do it. How hard could it be? I figured it couldn't be that hard, and ultimately it wasn't that hard. It was the same with starting a hedge fund. I just figured I would do it. It never occurred to me that I wouldn't be able to raise any money. I didn't think I needed a lot of money because I had no concept of leverage. I knew I could get 10 times leverage. So if I wanted to trade a $50 million book, all I would need would be $5 million. It didn't occur to me that people wouldn't want you running money at 10 times leverage. I really was completely naive about the whole thing. I just did it. I set up a hedge fund with no money. I had $300,000 of my own cash in the fund, and that was it.

What was the name of your hedge fund?

It was LS asset management.

What did the LS stand for?

Now there is an interesting tale. We had a nickname at the time for people who threw money around: Lairy Shag.

Lairy Shag?

It was a market term for a bit of a player. Someone brash. Exactly the wrong image you would want to give investors if you're asking to manage their money. It worked well, though, because I could always tell people the LS stood for "long/short."

Sort of like someone who is a shooter.

Yes. We'll have a go at this; we'll have a go at that.

Were you able to start trading the fund with just your own $300,000?

Yes, but it meant that every trade I did would have to be for $300,000. I couldn't trade any smaller. I ran the hedge fund out of my kitchen. Morgan Stanley gave me a prime brokerage account for which I am forever grateful. It was one of the best and worst experiences in business I have ever had.

Sounds a bit Dickensian.

It was a fantastic learning experience, but I would have much preferred to read about it. Emotionally, the highs got lower, and the lows became incredibly low.

Specifically, what happened?

Let me give you the story of the first day.

You are really one for memorable first days.

On my first day, I did my first trade, and I made £37,000 or about $60,000 on my $300,000 cash. I walked out of the kitchen and said to my wife at the time, "I just made £37,000. It is going to be a success. I don't have to worry about the seed capital. If I can keep compounding like this, we'll be in great shape."

She said, "That is really good, but garbage collection is happening in 10 minutes. If you don't get the bins down to the bottom of the drive in time, we're going to miss it, and we'll have all the garbage in the garden for the next week."

I remember literally answering, "But I am a master of the universe."

She said, "Yes and you now have eight minutes to get the rubbish down to the bottom of the driveway."

I remember walking down the garden, carrying the garbage bags, and muttering to myself, "I am a fucking master of the fucking universe. I just made fucking £37,000, and I am carrying the fucking rubbish out." That was the high point of my experience the first time I ran a hedge fund. That was as good as it ever got.

What went wrong?

After that, I made some money and lost some money, and then—I don't know if I should go into this . . .

Don't worry, we can always take it out if it's a problem.

I worked very closely with a guy when I was at NatWest, and he really stitched me. He strongly recommended that I buy a stock, which I did buy. The next day, the stock had a big loss. I waited for a phone call from him, but it never came. Eventually, I called him and asked him what was going on with the stock he had recommended. He said he had been selling the stock all day. He just stitched me. That was a bad experience.

What do you mean he stitched you?

He recommended buying the stock, which I did. The next day he smashed the stock.

When you say "stitched you," you mean he set you up.

Yes. I thought he was a friend, but he wasn't a friend. Some people who you work with for years and think will support you will do nothing to help you, while other people you know in passing may be very helpful. It really taught me a lot about human nature and made me think again about whom you can and can't trust.

How much did you lose on that stock tip? Did you lose as much as you made on the big trade on the first day?

I lost more than that. The fund had been running a few months, and I was going to show a 10 percent loss as of the end of the month. There was a total disconnect between my feelings and reality. In my head, if I was down 10 percent, my business would be over. No one ever would give me money to manage. I had no perspective. I had no older person to put his hand on my shoulder and say, "Calm down. Just do the things that work and stop doing the things that don't." I can remember sitting at the kitchen table, my head in my hands, staring into an abyss. I put so much pressure on myself to make money every day. *I must make money. I must make money. I must make money.* And I was having a very hard time making money in the market. It felt like the market was kicking me around.

I woke up one morning around 4 A.M., lying in bed, feeling sick in my stomach, and thinking, *What is the market going to do to me today?* I closed the business that day. It was an incredibly tough experience. If only I had someone to give me perspective and say, "Slow down. You're not trying to make 500 percent. Stop thinking in absolute terms and start thinking in terms of percentages."

What did you do after you closed your fund?

I went to Nomura where I started a risk arbitrage business.

What was your approach to risk arbitrage?

Do fewer deals and be bigger. If you have a big enough balance sheet, buy enough shares to be sure you have enough votes. If you thought you needed 8 percent of shares to assure the approval of the merger plan, you might as well buy 15 percent because you knew the deal would be going through. Just be big. That was a very successful approach.

But you still have other risks in the deal going through like failure to get government approval.

I would tend to be big late in the deal when those other risks had been ticked off. All we were ever concerned about was the likelihood of the deal closing; the spread margins were secondary. Parents buying out subsidiaries were by far the best trade; there were no due diligence issues and you knew the deal would be going through.

Nomura ended badly for me because there was a change in management. The new guy in charge wasn't straight. He had a convertible book, and all he was doing was buying illiquid convertible bonds and every month-end pushing the price up. He was the market because he owned most of these issues. So all he had to do was buy a few hundred bonds every month to push the price up.

At one point, a trader from another department came to me for guidance because he was being asked to mismark the book.

Was he a subordinate?

He was subordinate to one of the other managers.

Why did he come to you?

Because I had a reputation for being straight. I told him to mark the book correctly, and I would deal with it. I went to the senior management and said they couldn't put pressure on this guy to mismark his book. He was a lowly trader. If it ever came out, it could ruin his career. I told them they had to leave the book marked correctly. I thought it was a cogent argument.

A week later, I was asked to leave because I was not a team player. I told them if they wanted to fire me that was fine, but they needed to pay me the percentage I was owed. They wanted me to resign first and then they would pay me afterwards. I asked them, "Do I have the word 'STUPID' written across my forehead?" I had two follow-up meetings with management. I didn't trust them, so I went to the meetings with a hidden tape recorder.

Eventually they fired me, and I sued them. It took three years for the case to go to trial, and it cost me £350,000 in legal expenses. If I had lost the case, it would have financially wiped me out. We went to court and won the case hands-down.

Did you use your recordings in the trial?

Oh, yes, and they were extremely useful. We furnished Nomura with the tape transcripts, but they still weren't prepared. At one point in the trial, one of their witnesses testified regarding some conversation.

The judge said, "There is a transcript; show me where he said that." He answered, "It's not there."

The judge said, "I'll cross out that section of your statement. What about the next section, would you like me to cross that out as well?"

The tape really helped me in terms of credibility because I had told the absolute truth, while they had lied. I got £1.35 million, which was equal to 15 percent of my profits; it should have been 20 percent. When I look back, even though I won the case, it was a bad decision to sue.

Why is that?

If I had spent the time it took for the litigation to drag out pursuing my own business, I would have made multiples of the £1.35 million settlement. It was a bad trade.

What did you do in those intervening years?

I literally built a house. I dug my own foundation. I did most of the work myself. I hired a builder to help with the things I couldn't do on my own.

What else occupied you during those three years besides building your own house?

I had my court case, and I was building a house. That occupied all my time.

Did you have any plans about what you were eventually going to do?

I didn't know what I was going to do, but I was finished with markets in the city. I was never going back.

Why? You had done very well in the markets.

Because I had such a terrible experience with people—the company politics, people lying. In my view, all I had ever done for any of my employers was make money. And yet, I didn't have much money. Either I didn't get paid properly, or even when I had a contract, I got screwed on that. I found the whole experience to be very discouraging.

How did you go from loving the markets, like it was a videogame you were being paid to play, to not even wanting to get a trading job?

That's an interesting question, isn't it? In 1986, I had gone to the city to make some money until I figured out what I wanted to do. I never worked it out. I still haven't worked it out.

Apparently, at some point, you did get back into the markets. How did that occur?

It was a bit of coincidence. I was going on a fishing trip in Venezuela with an old buddy from NatWest. I traveled via New York, and while I was there, I spoke to an old broker contact who advised me to speak to First New York Securities.[3] I met with the two guys who had set up the business; both of them at the time were in their sixties. They wanted me to come work for First New York Securities for a fixed percentage of the profits I made. Initially, I was reluctant because of all the negative experiences I had, but eventually they convinced me to come to New York for a few months to give it a try.

---

[3]For the sake of full disclosure, my son works at First New York Securities. Clark's connection with the firm came as a complete surprise to me during the interview.

After I had been there for a few months, the guy in charge said to me, "We have been talking about you. We decided you were a player."

I'm thinking, *Here it comes; I'm going to get screwed now.*

He continued, "We owe you a lot of money, but you have never mentioned it."

I said, "If I thought I needed a contract, I wouldn't be here. If you are telling me that I need one, I'll just go now, and you can just keep the money." Then in my poor attempt at humor I said, "And I am sure that if I fell under a bus, you would give money to my kids."

Later that day, two partners independently approached me with the same basic assurance. One of them said, "I want to assure you that if anything ever happened to you, I would personally make sure that your family got the money." [Clark is visibly moved by this recollection.]

You sound emotional about it, even to this day.

I am still getting emotional about it now because it was the first time that anyone had said anything like that to me. It really, really touched me.

What did they mean when they called you a "player"?

Because they owed me money, and I hadn't been asking where my money was. Since I hadn't mentioned it, they brought it up.

What kind of trading were you doing?

I was doing directional risk arbitrage.

What does that mean?

I might do the risk arbitrage, or I might not hedge, or I might go long both sides.[4] It depended on the situation. I was basically trading the companies in a merger event.

---

[4]In a standard stock-for-stock merger deal, risk arbitrage managers will buy the acquired company, which will trade at a discount to the announced share exchange ratio because of the risk that the deal might not go through, and hedge by selling the acquiring company. If the deal goes through, they will earn the discount. Clark might do the trade as a conventional arbitrage, or he might do outright trades in the companies involved in the merger.

When did you start your current fund, and what happened to your relationship with First New York Securities?

I set up my own asset management business in the U.K. and started an event-driven fund in 2001. I continued to manage First New York Securities money pari passu alongside with the fund, and I still do. I was also a de facto advisor to First New York Securities, but with my fund having grown to near $1 billion, I didn't want to maintain that commitment.

I met with the head of the firm in New York and told him I was too busy with my own fund to maintain my advisory role with First New York Securities. I said, "I will leave you with one bit of parting advice. You are too old. You're killing your own business. Get out."

He said, "I think you are right."

How did you think he was killing the business?

Like any entrepreneur who starts a business, he was holding on too tight. They have been doing proprietary trading for 25 years and have never had a losing year. Despite that track record, they have missed the entire growth in asset management. They have had no hedge fund business through the entire hedge fund era. He was getting too old to take risks, and he admitted it himself. In the end, I agreed to become a managing member of First New York Securities. The firm is very inefficiently run and has no technology. We need to make it more efficient and bring it into the twenty-first century. We need to start managing outside money and create a more valuable business. That is the plan.

What are your long-term goals?

I am still waiting to figure out what it is I want to do when I grow up. I am still waiting for the revelation. In some ways, it is quite depressing.

I don't understand. You have been very successful.

But what have I achieved? I haven't built anything.

How do you measure success? If it's monetary, by any reasonable definition, you have been more than successful. If it is

building a business, again by any reasonable definition, you have been successful. You are not going to invent a cure for cancer. If you want to impact the world, I guess you could give money away.

I give money away; that's what I do. I am still here because I couldn't figure out anything better to do at the time. It still feels like I'm waiting to work out what I should be doing.

Don't you feel that trading is what you were born to do?

Well, no. I have a view—and maybe it's a bit egotistical—that I can do anything I want to do. I'll go to the city to get a job as a trader. I will build a house. I'll take on a bank in litigation. I'll start a hedge fund.

If that's your perspective, then do whatever you want to do.

That's the problem.

You don't know what you want to do?

No. I can tell you that running a fund doesn't make me happy. I enjoy it, but I used to enjoy it a lot more than I do now.

Why is that?

Because it was a lot less complicated. I was just trading. Now it's running a business.

You're still searching for something.

Yes, there is still a hole there. I'm searching to be satisfied by something. Let me tell you the trouble with trading. There is no career in trading. You are only as good as your last trade, and that is it. You build nothing; you just trade. The day you stop trading, it's gone. So what you have spent doing for X hours every working day of your life has ended, and there is nothing left to show for it, except for money. You have to keep trading because you don't want to stop and look back. Because what have you done? You have built nothing. You have achieved nothing.

You get to the end of it and look back and wonder, *What have I accomplished?* I have a very nihilistic view of it, but that is the way I feel. I am still back at that point where I am a 17-year-old trying to decide what I want to do.

But somewhere along the line you went from having joy in this business to feeling unsatisfied. Do you know what caused that transition?

I am not sure, but it is probably from the point that I decided I was going to grow a business instead of just trading.

That almost sounds like it was when you started the hedge fund.

It probably was. The joy ended. Being a trader was fun, and you could walk away. But when you have a business, you can't walk away. So it becomes a prison in some ways, whereas being a trader was very free.

Ironically, you've taken on more business responsibility by becoming a managing member of First New York Securities. Where is the rationale in that?

The rationale is that there is a trade to be done.

The trade is to fix the company?

Yes. The trade is fix the company, be involved for a period, and get much more value for it. It's all very rational. I try to do rational things. Sometimes, you make rational decisions every step of the way and yet end up in a place that is very far from where you want to be. When I first came to First New York Securities, I said, "I don't want to manage anything. I just want to trade." And here we are.

It's very ironic. You said you didn't want to manage anything, and you ended up helping manage the company.

Yes, it is. I also constantly think that I am about to be found out, which is another personal driver.

What do you mean by "found out"?

A number of times in my career, I have thought that maybe I have just been lucky. Maybe I don't really know what I'm doing, and I have just bluffed my way through. Maybe I have just found a few trades that work, but I won't find any more trades that work, and I will be found out.

[I had overrun my meeting time allotment and Clark had to leave for another meeting. We decided that we would finish the interview on one of his trips to New York. Several months later I met with Clark at First New York Securities. After some casual conversation, he began talking about trading before I even asked a question.]

As a trader, you have to be honest with yourself. I have met many traders who have laid out a strategy on how they will be scale-down buyers. "I'll buy some at eight, and if it goes down, I will add at seven, six, and five." But if you are the type of person who will be puking his guts out if it goes to seven, let alone to six or lower, you shouldn't be buying at all at eight, or if you do, it should be 25 percent of the size. You have to train yourself to trade at a smaller size so that you trade within your emotional capacity. If you are really, really excited about a trade and swing the bat in a big way, and 10 minutes later the market moves against you, but you are the type of person who doesn't handle that type of volatility well, you will end up cutting your position and losing money, even if the trade was ultimately a big winner. We see this behavior in traders all the time. It is the size of the position you put on rather than the price at which you put it on that determines your ability to keep the position.

Your message then is that although traders focus almost entirely on where to enter a trade, in reality, the entry size is more important than the entry price because if the size is right, you are much more likely to stay with a winning trade.

One of the first lessons my first boss taught me was that price is irrelevant; it is all about controlling the size of your position. On a related point, liquidity is also very important. That is why when a merger deal breaks, we cut it straight away because you get a pocket of liquidity. It may be at a much lower level, but at least you have the liquidity. If you wait, the liquidity can dry up, and you will be left with an outsized position in what has become a directional trade.

Getting the size of a position wrong is a perfect example of a common trader mistake. What other mistakes have you seen traders typically make in the course of your career?

One of the things we have seen inside First New York Securities many times is traders coming from an information-rich environment, such as a big investment bank, to a trading house and finding that the information flow is all gone. It is like trading in a vacuum for them. We have seen guys with incredibly strong reputations, who have been trading actively for years in big size, and when they come here, they find they can't make any money, and maybe they even lose a little bit. It becomes a downward spiral. They trade smaller and smaller, and every dollar they lose becomes emotionally more and more important to them. They lose all perspective. Many of these traders never had a plan; they just responded to the stimuli around them. I tell them that they need to replace the information flow they previously had. I advise them to draw up a list of 20 contacts and phone them every day.

Does that work?

Well, they don't take the advice.

What other advice do you give them?

I have been through similar situations myself. I found it was critical to find things to involve yourself in. It is a very good thing to be busy when you are a prop trader because you don't want to have too much time to stare at the screen, particularly if your style of trading is to have only a limited number of positions on at one time. Once you have your positions on and are waiting for the market to do what it needs to do, what are you going to do in the interim? Coming back again to the investment bank world, they have meetings and all sorts of stuff going on that suck up time. Traders would all complain about the waste of time, but what it actually meant was that it limited the amount of time they were in front of their screens staring at their positions. You don't want to be sitting in front of your screen and staring at market prices for 12 hours a day. Staring at the price is not going to tell you very much. You will start to overprocess and overtrade.

I have found that one of the common denominators among successful traders is patience, particularly in regard to staying with good trades long enough—and that is true regardless of the time frame, even daytraders. I assume the more time you spend staring at the screen, the less patience you will have.

You will have less patience, and if you are in a negative loop, every downtick cuts you. You will feel physical pain with every tick the market goes against you.

It sounds like you have had that experience.

I have had several occasions in my career where I sat with my head in my hands, thinking, *I am never going to make a penny again. I am crap. I have always been crap. I have just been found out.* Even though you may have made money for 10 years, you can still get into that mind-set.

You had a knack for trading, but now it is gone. You lost it.

I lost it. I was never that good. It was just the market. Now the market is changed, and I don't know what to do. It is a horrible, horrible feeling.

When you do get into that type of phase, what do you do?

I have learned over the years that when you get into that mode, don't do anything. Discipline yourself not to trade for two weeks or whatever time period you choose. Take a holiday.

Does that work?

Oh, yeah, as long as you don't have any positions on when you go. You need to get out of everything. Then go away and forget about it. Now that takes time because what you will do for the first few days is torture yourself. I could have done this. I could have done that. But for me, after a few days, I can let it go. Once you let go, you can unwind. Then, when you come back, you have to set rules. You need to be able to say that you won't trade for, say, two weeks. You'll see trades that you are itching to do, but you need to have the discipline not to do them because, clearly, you are not in sync with the markets. Otherwise you wouldn't be where you are. When you feel you are ready to begin trading and see a trade that you really like, trade a fraction of the size you would normally trade. At least half the time, the trade may go your way initially, but then it will go against you because all you may be experiencing is a feel for the next few ticks.

[At this point, the president of First New York Securities ushers in my son, who works at the firm, saying, "I wanted to introduce a young man to you." (I had arrived at just the last minute for my scheduled meeting with Clark, so I did not get a chance to say hello to my son first.) We all chat for a few minutes, and they leave. Clark queries me a bit about my son. In describing the trading style he is gravitating toward, I mention that high volume is one of the things he looks for in trading setups.]

That is quite interesting because one of the things I did at Lehman when I was short on information was to filter for European stocks that had unusually large volume. Then I went through all the charts of those stocks to see if any were making interesting bottoms. I would then call my contacts and ask them what they knew about those specific stocks. That's how I started to find situations to trade. Volume is incredibly important. I have found it to be a very valuable indicator.

And still do?

Yes. If a stock has been bombed out, and there is a sudden jump in volume, it doesn't mean you should buy it straight away because it can go quiet again. But clearly, somebody is there beginning to buy. Then you watch for signs that the stock is resilient on down days in the market, suggesting there is underlying buying support for the stock, and you begin to nibble away at establishing a position. Sometimes, the stock will then see a day where all of a sudden it just gaps up, and you trade to catch that gap. You have to do some fundamental work to find out what is going on because you don't want to end up buying a stock that is headed for zero. Volume is just a way of identifying potentially interesting situations.

You talked earlier about advising traders on the need to call people. Can you think of examples where calling people led to information that was useful for trading?

You need to be willing to call people to get information. You need to ask the next question. You never know what you will find out that will be useful. For example, there was a merger deal that had to be approved by the FCC, and nothing was happening. In the meantime, the spread kept widening and widening, and we were getting more concerned about the position. We kept calling the FCC over and over again until one time, by luck, we got the secretary of one of the commissioners, who said, "Oh, that; it's on his desk ready to be signed, but he is away fishing this week."

Another time, we were on the phone with a banker regarding the funding for a deal. I kept asking him a question I knew he couldn't answer. I asked the same question in 10 different ways, knowing full well that he couldn't tell me whether the funding was done or not. After the call, I said, "Sell it now." There were so many things that would have been perfectly reasonable for him to say, but he didn't.

What could he have said?

Well, he couldn't say the funding was done or that it wasn't done, but he could have said that it was a work in progress or that they were confident.

What did he say?

All he said to each question was "I can't answer that question." If you don't make the phone call, if you don't ask the next question, you will never know.

Can you give me an example of a trade that illustrates your process?

A good example is our trade in Fiat in 2003. We made 20 percent in a month on that single transaction. At the time, the broad market was rallying sharply in a rebound from the preceding bear market. Fiat had a big rights issue.[5] At the same time, Deutsche Bank had announced that they would be disposing of their industrial holdings, and Fiat was one of their positions. Rather than exercise their rights, which would increase their position, Deutsche Bank decided to sell their rights. You had a situation where the market was going up, and while Fiat should have been going the same way, it was actually going down because of a big seller. And that seller was not driven by fundamentals, but rather by a desire to rebalance their portfolio to reduce industrial holdings. The rights were especially cheap because of the Deutsche Bank selling. We bought the rights, which effectively gave us a cheap call. Buying the Fiat rights was a trade where everything lined up. First, the market was very strong. Second, the stock was substantially underperforming the market and its sector for two technical reasons—there was a rights issue and a large seller for technical reasons that had nothing to do with the fundamentals. Third, the rights provided you with a way to put on a large position for a small capital outlay. Fourth, because Deutsche Bank was a large seller of rights and the stock was difficult to borrow, the rights were trading below their intrinsic value.

What advice do you give to people who want to be traders?

First, they need to make sure they understand their motivation. Not everyone who says that want to be a trader really does. Trading has this macho mystique. People will say they want to be a trader and won't

---

[5]A rights issue is one way a company can raise capital. Rights are issued to existing share-holders and allow them to purchase additional shares in proportion to their holdings, typically at a discount to the current market price, for a fixed period of time. Shareholders can either exercise their rights, buying additional shares at a discount, or sell their rights if they do not wish to purchase any additional shares. The intrinsic value is the difference between the market price and the price at which the rights can be exercised. If shares are available to borrow, rights will trade above the intrinsic price because otherwise, buying the rights and shorting the stock would provide a risk-free arbitrage.

admit to perhaps wanting to be an analyst, even if they would be happier as an analyst. They might even make more money as an analyst because they would be better at it.

You have seen a lot of traders. What are the characteristics of traders who succeed?

They all work hard. There is a First New York trader in New Zealand who trades international equities. He can't be awake 24 hours a day, but he seems to be.

Nearly all the successful traders I have known are one-trick ponies. They do one thing, and they do it very well. When they stray from that single focus, it often ends in disaster. In the hedge fund world, you will see traders who do one thing very well, make a lot of money at it, and then think, *This one thing is rather boring. I can do other things because I am a genius.* So they start doing other things. You had a number of great macro traders decide to branch into multistrategy funds. It didn't work too well in 2008 when they were all exposed. One well-known macro trader wrote to his investors in 2008 that he had made them money, but it was all the other managers in the fund, trading an assortment of strategies, who lost all the money. Well, you hired them. You gave them all the money. We have seen that again and again in hedge funds. Managers diversify away from their expertise because they have made a lot of money and think they can do anything.

What is it about some traders that drives them away from what they do well to do things they may not do well?

I think deep down inside they know they are one-trick ponies, and that one thing could end.

But successful traders who are one-trick ponies, when that trick stops, they learn another trick.

That is exactly what happens, but some traders will change while their one trick is still working and destroy it. You need to be a bit obsessive to do the same thing 10 hours a day. People who are obsessive can become very good traders.

Are there any other traits that distinguish the successful traders?

Really good traders are also capable of changing their mind in an instant. They can be dogmatic in their opinion and then immediately change it. *This market is going higher. It's absolutely going up. No, it's definitely going down.* If you can't do that, you will get caught in a position and be wiped out.

Can you think of a personal experience where you completely changed your mind in an instant?

A perfect example was when Euro Disney was listed in the U.S. many years ago. It was already listed in Europe, but Blue Sky laws required a waiting period before it could be listed in the U.S. I built up this large position in anticipation of a burst of retail demand that would emerge when it was listed in the U.S. On the first day it became available to U.S. retail investors, we had buy orders for millions of shares. That morning, I was already very long, but I put in buy orders to get more long. The market gapped higher on the opening and started racing away on the upside. We weren't getting filled on anything because there was so little for sale. The market was moving up in gaps with very little volume. In an instant, I completely switched my orders and started selling whatever I could.

What flipped you around?

I recognized in a moment of clarity that if I had reached a fever pitch, in trying to buy at any price, the moment the market turned, it would just head straight down.

And I assume it went down quickly?

It fell about 10 percent from that point that day, and it kept going down in the following days. Everyone had done the same thing. Everyone had come in long in anticipation of an influx of retail buy orders.

Was there a catalyst for your sudden change in sentiment?

Something clicked. I was hysterical. Before the 1987 crash, I was on a desk with experienced traders, and a rumor circulated that you had to buy this small stock called London and Overseas Freight. The stock had started the day at £.10 and I had bought it at £.12. The stock kept on going up all through the day, £.13, £.14, £.15, £.16 . . . . The guys on the desk who hadn't bought couldn't stand the pain of not being in, and they got long. And the stock just kept going higher and higher. Finally, one trader who had not bought the stock was on the squawk box to the floor saying, "Where is it now?"

The answer came back, "It's at 22."

I remember these words to this day. He said, "I don't care what I have to pay, just get me in!"

He got filled at £.23. It never traded higher, and it closed the day at £.12. The stock eventually went to nothing. It was just a microcosm of hysteria. It might have been my recognition of the same type of hysteria in myself years later that triggered my about-face in Euro Disney. I may have even said to the broker, "Just get me stock! Just get me stock!" And something clicked. I have been here before. I have seen this.

What explains the extremely low volatility of your track record versus most other event-driven funds?

You have to be able to cut your position. I'll never accept anybody saying they can't cut a position.

How did you manage to completely sidestep downside volatility in 2007 and 2008?

In 2007, we got rid of anything that was directional or long dated and put almost all our money in short duration risk arbitrage—deals that we felt were almost certain to close and that had very wide spreads because of the market volatility. The ability of these companies to close their transactions had not been degraded by what was happening in the world. The only risk I saw was that something might happen that would cause the prime brokers to change margin requirements, which would force us to liquidate. I thought the only way that would happen would be if there was some more major market distress. To hedge against this possibility, I bought out-of-the-money puts on the S&P and sold out-of-the-money calls to pay for the puts. If the market went sideways or up, we would do very well because of our core portfolio. If the market went down suddenly, we still felt our core portfolio would hold up, and the puts would provide protection against a change in margin requirements.

In 2008, the world had changed. Volatility quadrupled. I decided we should trade a fraction of what we used to trade. Most people didn't do that and got blown up.

Was there anything that triggered your cutting exposure?

We had a good month, then another very good month, and started the next month very strong. Then two days later, we were down for the month. And nothing had happened. I could just smell that we had to cut our positions. We took off 75 percent of our exposure.

So you didn't gradually cut your exposure in 2008?

Oh, no. I don't believe in this idea, *We will sell 25 percent of our position and then think about it.*

Is gut feel important to trading?

Absolutely. I have learned to trust my judgment. Gut feel is important, and you can trade off of it, but you need to have a set of rules that control your size and stop loss points.

What are the trading rules you live by?

If you wake up thinking about a position, it's too big.

Never stop asking questions. Speak to as many people as you can. Research every opposing opinion.

When everything lines up, you need to swing for it because in those situations, even if you are wrong, you probably won't be wrong by that much. But if the position starts behaving in a way you don't understand, you need to cut it because then you clearly don't know what is going on. The market is telling you that you don't know.

What is your philosophy about the markets?

The market is not about facts; it's all about people's opinions and positions. Consequently, anything can be at any price, any time.

Once you understand that, you realize that you need to have protective stops.

Any final words?

Your job as a trader is to make the line go from bottom left to top right. That's it. If the line goes down too much or too long, you were wrong. You can't argue that the market is wrong because it is your job to predict every move in the market. You had managers in 2008 who lost 50 percent, and in some cases even as much as 80 percent. Why? Because they couldn't accept they were wrong. They kept doing the math, and they kept saying they were right. They missed the point. Their math might have been right, but their job isn't to do the math; their job is to trade what is in front of them. You had guys saying they were right, the market was wrong, and that they had billions of dollars of embedded value in their portfolio. Their job isn't to create billions of dollars of embedded value; their job is to make the line go from bottom left to top right. Once you understand that is your job as a trader, you have to start protecting the direction of the line.

■ ■ ■

Clark's core advice to traders—do more of what works and less of what doesn't—sounds so commonsensical that it may seem almost unnecessary to state. But what is surprising is how many traders fail to adhere to this seemingly obvious principle. Examples abound. Some traders may be good at taking well-thought-out longer-term positions, but then also take short-term trades based on whims in which they have no edge. Other traders have effective systems, but get bored following a computerized approach and override their own system with discretionary decisions that degrade overall performance. There is no shortage of examples of traders deviating from what they do best, whether due to boredom, or a sense that if they are good in one type of trade, they should be good at other types of trades as well. Clark's message to traders is that they need to figure out exactly what they are best in and then focus on doing those trades.

Many traders may not even be fully aware of where they are making and losing money. One useful exercise traders can do is to analyze their past trades by segmenting winners and losers. Often, such analysis will reveal patterns with certain types of trades being predominant in either the winning or losing categories. If indeed you find that certain types of trades are making money and other types of trades are losing money, then as Clark advises: Do more of what works and less of what doesn't.

As a related point, Clark cautions traders against diversifying away from their expertise. Some traders succeed because they are good at doing one type of trade. This success can often encourage traders to expand into other areas in which they may not have any expertise or particular edge.

Traders focus almost entirely on where to enter a trade. In reality, the entry size is often more important than the entry price because if the size is too large, a trader will be more likely to exit a good trade on a meaningless adverse price move. The larger the position, the greater the danger that trading decisions will be driven by fear rather than by judgment and experience. According to Clark, one way of knowing your position is too large is if you wake up thinking about it. You also need to be sure that your methodology is consistent with your risk tolerance. For example, if your trade implementation strategy allows for building a three-unit position, but your natural risk tolerance is only one unit, you can easily end up panicking out of good positions because you are trading larger than your comfort level. Trading size needs to be kept small enough so that fear does not become the prevailing instinct guiding your judgment. As Clark says, you have to "trade within your emotional capacity."

Position size is important not only in avoiding trading too large, but also in trading larger when warranted. If everything lines up in a trade—a compelling reason why the trade should work, large potential relative to risk, high confidence in the position, and so on—then the trade should be put on in larger-than-normal size. Clark cites buying the Fiat rights below intrinsic value as an example of such a trade.

Traders also need to adjust position size in response to the changing market environment. If the market volatility increases dramatically, traders need to reduce their normal exposure levels correspondingly, or else their risk will dramatically increase. In 2008, Clark reduced his exposure levels by 75 percent in response to sharply increased volatility.

Flexibility is an essential quality to successful trading. It is important not to get attached to an idea and to always be willing to get out of a trade. Clark says that really good traders are capable of changing their mind in an instant if the price action is inconsistent with their trade hypothesis. They can be absolutely convinced the market is going higher one moment, and then be just as sure the market is going down in the next.

Virtually all traders experience periods when they are out of sync with the markets. When you are in a losing streak, you can't turn the situation around by trying harder. When trading is going badly, Clark's advice is to get out of everything and take a holiday. Liquidating positions will allow you to regain objectivity. You can't be objective if you are in the market. Taking a physical break will interrupt the negative downward spiral that can develop in a losing streak, as each loss further diminishes confidence. When you restart trading, trade smaller until you have regained confidence.

Beware of trades borne of euphoria. If you find yourself influenced by the market hysteria to get into a position, watch out! Clark recalls such as situation in Euro Disney where he recognized that his own irrationality in trying to add to his position in a sharply rallying stock was itself a warning signal. Once this realization hit, he switched from bidding to selling, just in time, as soon after, the stock reversed into a steep dive.

Clark considers staring at the screen all day as being counterproductive. He believes that watching every tick will lead to both selling good positions prematurely and overtrading. He advises traders to find something else (preferably productive) to occupy part of their time to avoid the pitfalls of watching the market too closely.

Clark believes traders need to monitor and control their equity to prevent any significant drawdown. "Your job as a trader," he says, "[is to] protect the direction of the [equity] line."

Chapter 10

Martin Taylor

The Tsar Has No Clothes

Most hedge fund managers seek to grow assets under management. Martin Taylor chose the reverse course. Ten years after launching his hedge fund with $20 million in seed capital and seeing his firm's assets under management balloon to over $7 billion, Taylor notified his investors that he was closing his fund in 12 months' time.[1] He made this announcement at a time when his hedge fund's net asset value (NAV) was within a hair of its all-time high and after having achieved a track record characterized by consistent outperformance. Taylor had decided that other considerations mattered more than maximizing earnings. He coordinated the closing of his original fund with the opening of a new fund that capped assets at less than one-quarter of the

---

[1]The fund documents required Taylor to give investors a 12-month notice before terminating the fund.

previous fund's size. A hedge manager voluntarily cutting his assets by more than 75 percent is a rarity, if not a singular event.

Martin Taylor may well have the best performance record in emerging markets. Between 1995 and early 2000, Taylor managed a long-only fund focused on East European equities. Then after a five-month hiatus, he launched a hedge fund, Nevsky Fund, in October 2000. Taylor named his fund after Alexander Nevsky, a thirteenth-century Russian hero who defended his country against outside invaders, and thus was not an objectionable figure to neighboring East European countries. Initially, the hedge fund continued to focus on East European equities, but by 2003, the investment scope broadened to global emerging markets. Across his entire track record (1995 to 2011), Taylor achieved an average annual compounded net return of over 27 percent, more than doubling the 12 percent return of the corresponding emerging markets index.[2] During its 11-year history, Taylor's hedge fund achieved an average annual compounded net return over 22 percent, more than doubling the corresponding 10 percent return of the HFRI Emerging Markets index.

Taylor achieved his substantially higher returns, while having much smaller drawdowns than both long-only and hedge fund emerging market indexes. He was the only long-only manager to avoid a loss in 1998. He also did extremely well during the 2000 to 2002 bear market, with his hedge fund up 27 percent annualized during that period. Taylor's only losing year was 2008, but even then his loss was less than one-third the long-only index decline and 40 percent of the hedge fund index loss.

I interviewed Taylor at his home in a suburb of London, which I reached on a pleasing walk from the train station, passing through the town park on a sunny, breezy Saturday morning in late April. We talked in the living room, sitting beneath a large English impressionistic painting, aptly named *Harvest Storm*. Taylor was dressed very casually in shorts and a T-shirt, ready to depart for the weekend as soon as we finished talking. His family had left for a trip to the grandparents about an hour into our conversation. To allow adequate time for our meeting, Taylor had graciously scheduled to leave later, planning to catch an

---

[2]MSCI Emerging Europe index 1995–2002 and MSCI Global Emerging Markets index 2003–2011.

afternoon train. I had estimated we would need at least three hours. Our conversation lasted more than five hours and could easily have carried on longer, but both Taylor and I were conscious of his delayed departure. One chunk of our conversation regarding Russia proved unusable, as Taylor capped that portion of his narrative by saying, "You know, you can't use any of that. Russia is not a country where you want to make enemies."

■ ■ ■

When did you first get interested in markets?

I came to it quite late, actually, and entirely by chance. I went to university during the booming 1980s. Everyone wanted to get a job in the city because that was where you made a lot of money.[3] But it didn't particularly interest me. I came from a left-wing background. My dad was a labor counselor for 35 years. For my parents, working in the city was anathema. It was all about rich capitalists ripping off the rest of the economy for no net gain to society. I graduated in 1990 in the middle of a pretty nasty recession.

With what degree?

History.

What were your career objectives at the time?

I didn't have any thoughts at all. After I graduated, I thought I would try my luck getting a job in Australia for a year or so, but unbeknownst to me, Australia was in an even worse recession than we were. I came back after six months and ended up finding a job as an accountant at PricewaterhouseCoopers.

Did you have any accounting background?

No, none at all.

---

[3]"The city" is a small historic section in central London that is the heart of the financial district.

I'm surprised that they would hire you without any accounting background.

I would look at it another way. People who choose to go for an accounting degree at the age of 17 have limited intellectual heft and imagination. If you are 17 and want to be an accountant, how sad is that? High-level auditing is more about opinion than nuts and bolts. So you don't necessarily want someone who just looks at nuts and bolts because they're not going to get the big picture. That is why I think the London accounting firms recruit people from across disciplines rather than just accounting majors.

How did you get your education in accounting?

The way it works in the U.K. is different from the way it does in the U.S. In the U.K., for a three-year period, you work full time and study in the evening, taking exams at the end of each year, and qualifying at the end of the period. The only difference if you have an accounting degree is that you get an automatic pass on the first year exam.

It doesn't sound like you had any particular desire to be an accountant, though.

My thinking was that as an accountant I would get to audit different businesses, which I thought might give me some ideas of what I wanted to do on a more permanent basis. By pure chance, I was assigned to a group that audited investment banks, stockbrokers, and asset managers. After Thatcher got elected in 1979 and the subsequent Big Bang reforms, the city was thought of as being the icon of achievement in the U.K. If you were a AAA student, that is where you would end up. I was expecting to meet all these smart people. My list of companies included a lot of highly regarded financial firms. What both fascinated and appalled me was here were all these people just out of university, making hundreds of thousands of pounds, while I'm making £12,000, and I thought 99 percent of them were just plain stupid. They were thick and arrogant, and yet they were all earning these staggering sums of money. I had an epiphany. I thought, *Hang on; it can't be all that difficult to make money if all these idiots are doing it.*

As an accounting student, if you interview a trader for an audit, they try to blind you with jargon. They hit you with lots of alphas, deltas, gammas, blah, blah, blah, in the hope you'll run away in 10 minutes because you can't understand anything they say. I hate failure, though, so I would make them take me through it. By doing that, I became fascinated by how markets work. Also, the 1 percent of traders who were smart were *really* smart. I've always loved politics and economics, and I enjoyed seeing how they impacted markets. And, on top of that, I realized I could actually make a lot of money by being a trader. I went from not being interested in the stock market at all to being fascinated by it.

I've always been quite tight and interested in saving my money. At the time, I was saving money to put down as a deposit on a house. It seems bizarre now, but I used that money to start trading options on the FTSE.

You started trading without any prior knowledge at all?

None whatsoever. At this stage, I had been reading the *Financial Times* every day for about 18 months. I also had been reading books on markets and traders, including your books.

Any books that were influential?

Actually, your books were very influential. I still reread them now and then.

Why did you decide to trade options on the FTSE index instead of trading stocks?

When you work for a large accounting firm, you are very limited in your ability to trade public securities because any firm they are working with is on a restricted list. That is why I never considered buying stocks in individual companies. I didn't want to be speaking to compliance every day. The stock index appealed to me because I thought that after following the market for 18 months, I would be quite good at predicting short-term price moves.

Why did you choose trading options on the index as opposed to trading the index itself?

Because by buying options, the downside is limited and the upside is unlimited. That sounded good to me.

On what basis were you making your market trading decisions?

It sounds so unbelievably naive now, but basically I did it on how overbought or oversold I thought the market was and what I thought the market direction should be based on my broad feelings on global macro. But, of course, although I didn't realize it then, what I knew about global macro at the time was pathetic.

How did you judge whether the market was overbought or oversold?

Again, it sounds pathetic, but I based it simply on whether the market was up a lot or down a lot. I can't really believe I'm saying this now. My thinking was something like, *The market has been down six days in a row. There was some bad economic news, but I think that should be in the price now. I'll buy some.*

So what happened?

I started out with £2,000, which was a lot of money to me then, and after six months my account was up to £10,000. I thought I was a bit of a genius. In those days, you could buy a house for £70,000, and a big deposit was 20 percent. So I almost had enough money to get a mortgage. As I made money, I got more and more confident, and I increased the position each time. Ultimately, I put on a position where I was completely wrong. I just held it, held it, held it, and sold it when my account was back down to £2,000. Over a five-day period, I lost everything that I had made over the prior six months.

So you had a mental stop point equivalent to your starting account level.

Absolutely. I was not going to allow myself to go into a loss. It's hard to explain, but because I had lost money that I never had in my hand, it didn't feel as bad. But if I had lost my savings, that would have been a catastrophe.

It's quite good that you had the discipline to get out because if you had stayed in, you probably would have lost all your money.

Oh, yes, in another two days I would have lost it all. The conclusions I drew from losing all my profits were: First, I didn't know what I was doing, and second, I really wanted to know what I should be doing. I also realized that trying to make money out of big macro moves was a mug's game. I thought that I would have a much better chance of beating the market if I focused on companies, which I obviously couldn't do as long as I stayed in my accounting job. I had always planned to resign once I qualified as an accountant, and that's what I did. I started applying for jobs three months before my three years were up, and I was very lucky to get a job as an analyst for Baring Asset Management.

I joined Barings as a junior equity analyst in their emerging markets team. I was assigned to the Eastern European group. At the time, 1994, the Eastern European markets were in their infancy. By the time I joined Barings, I had been following markets for three years. I had decided 18 months earlier that trading was something that I really wanted to do because I had finally found something that really excited me. I was extremely motivated and had done lots of study on my own on how to analyze companies.

My immediate boss, Rory, had an IQ that was way up there, and I learned a lot from him. His intellect, however, often got in the way of his investing. If he was bullish on a stock for 10 reasons, he could always think of nine reasons to be bearish, which would cloud his mind to such a degree that he would end up not buying it. Rory was the quintessential Englishman; he was very reserved. Rory's boss, Nancy, on the other hand, was a very extroverted, hard-driving American who was in charge of Barings's Eastern European investment group.

Here I was, covering these new markets that had just opened up, and my immediate boss was this reserved Englishman, and his boss was a high-energy American whose natural inclination was to give her staff a lot of responsibility and leeway. When I got excited about an idea to buy some company, I would go to Rory for approval, and after talking to him for a half an hour, he would find 10 reasons not to do the trade. More often than not, the stock would then go up. We all worked in close proximity. What started happening was that Nancy would over-hear the conversation and say to Rory, "That's rubbish. Why don't you let him do the trade?" Within a few months, Rory sort of gave up objecting to my ideas. What this meant was that about six months after joining the firm, I was running a chunk of the portfolio.

Several months later, the head of the whole global emerging markets department resigned, and Nancy was promoted to his position. That promotion meant that I was left with Rory to manage the Eastern European fund. Rory, in the meantime, was spending most of his time on an emerging market venture capital fund, which Nancy was also involved in. So 10 months after I had started with Barings, I had become the main day-to-day portfolio manager for the Eastern Euro-pean fund.

Did it seem odd to you that with less than one year of experience you were in charge of running a fund?

No, it didn't. Although I was doing the day-to-day portfolio manage-ment, I was still managing the fund with Rory. One thing that was very helpful was Rory's resilience. He was completely unflappable. His natural reluctance to take decisive action was a virtue when there was panic in the markets. I was very new to the job. During volatile periods, when it was all going wrong, he would counsel me, "Just calm down. This is what happens." Working with him allowed me to learn about volatility without making crass errors like selling at the lows or buying at the highs. Rory is the kind of person you would want with you in a battlefield. People would be dropping all around you, and Rory wouldn't have a hair out of place.

What happened to your fund during the Russian financial crisis of 1998?

I became unbelievably negative on Russia about a year before it blew up in August 1998. I was so bearish that I took my fund to 40 percent cash, which was unheard of for a long-only fund.

What made you so convinced about the bearish side?

The reason Russia didn't blow up earlier was because the money pulled out of Asia during the 1997 Asian crisis had to go somewhere. The money went into Eastern Europe and Latin America and created a mad bull market. But the way that I saw it, what was happening in Asia was the prototype for what would happen in Russia. There was a big disconnect between what I thought and what the market thought. The Asian crisis was caused by large current account deficits, which led to large borrowing and ultimately the crisis when the countries couldn't service their debt. When foreigners got scared, not only wouldn't they extend new money, but they started pulling their existing money out.

Based on the official numbers, Russia was running a current account surplus. So, superficially, it seemed quite different from Asia. The true measure of a balance of payments account is what happens to reserves. Even though Russia supposedly had this huge current account surplus and large capital inflows as people were throwing money at Russia, its reserves were going down instead of up.[4] Russia should have been running a balance of payments surplus of about 10 to 11 percent of GDP each year, but instead, reserves were going down. I thought that the reserves numbers were truthful because the Russian central bank couldn't lie about those without being found out quickly by comparing their data with that of other Central Banks. Where was the difference? The difference was that during the ineptitude of the Yeltsin government years, theft of company assets was pervasive. The numbers didn't add up. Something was very, very wrong.

Wasn't anyone else talking about the discrepancy in the balance of payments numbers?

No one at all outside of our team. It was almost surreal.

---

[4]It is an accounting tautology that the sum of the current account balance and the capital account balance is equal to the change in net reserves. Therefore, by definition, if a country has a current account surplus and a capital account surplus, its net reserves should increase by the sum of these surpluses.

How did you discover it?

It wasn't difficult. The facts spoke for themselves. All I had to do was confirm them by matching what I knew about the behavior of individual Russian companies on the ground with the reported capital and trade flow data. I then wrote a lengthy internal paper on it because colleagues thought I had to be exaggerating.

So what was the explanation?

Russian exports were massively overstated in cash terms. Most of the money from exported goods was being diverted to private Swiss accounts and never showed up in Russia. For example, a Russian mining company might export $100 million of raw materials and report the sale as $50 million. The missing $50 million would go to a private Swiss account, and $40 million of the reported $50 million would go to the same account and show up as a receivable—receivables that never quite made their way back into Russia. So only a fraction of reported export sales were actually received as cash payments in Russia. And what is the name for the difference between the $100 million of goods sold and $10 million of cash actually received in Russia? It is capital flight. So what you had was a massive black hole in the capital account.

So the owners of the companies were absconding with 90 percent of what they were selling? Was the theft really of that magnitude?

Yes, and across the entire Russian economy. Then you will ask me, "Why didn't the companies collapse?" They didn't collapse because they weren't paying their workers.

Well, how did the workers survive if they weren't being paid?

A lot of companies ran token systems. The workers would be paid tokens that could only be spent in the company store. It was very much like Victorian England. The workers had no choice because often the company would be the only employer in town. The company owned all the housing, the stores, the local football team, everything.

So basically the workers made just enough to pay for food and housing.

That's right, and there was no money spent on infrastructure, which deteriorated year after year.

How did the owners get the companies in the first place?

They got control through the voucher privatization scheme. Workers were given shares, or vouchers, in their own company. In the two years between the fall of the Soviet Union and the implementation of the voucher privatization program, managements of different companies were siphoning off funds from the money received for exports. They used this money to buy up vouchers from the workers. The workers had no idea what these vouchers were worth. Say, for illustration purposes, each voucher was worth $10; they would offer the workers $1 for them.[5] If a worker had 100 vouchers, that would be $100. The workers would say, "Really, you will offer me as much as $1 apiece!" Remember, the workers were extremely impoverished. After the Soviet Union fell, the whole welfare system broke down. A $100 for their book of vouchers was half their annual salary.

Weren't there any workers smart enough to hold onto their vouchers?

Those who were, let's just say, were encouraged to sell. So coming back to the Russian macro situation, it was clear to me that the same thing that happened to Asia was going to happen to Russia because Russia was living beyond its means. If you included the unreported massive capital flight, Russia had a huge balance of payments deficit. Russia was 40 percent of the Eastern European index benchmark. So I went to zero

---

[5]At the time, 95 percent of all financial transactions were carried out in USD by domestic Russians as they didn't consider the ruble a store of value, due to a combination of hyperinflation, wild swings, and rapid depreciation in the ruble's value. All share prices were also denominated in USD on the Moscow Stock Exchange. Basically, at that time, the USD was the effective domestic exchange rate in Russia, despite the authorities' attempts to enforce the contrary.

weighting for Russia, which for a long-only fund is an extraordinary thing to do.

What was the timing of your switch of the Russian allocation to cash?

I started selling our Russian holdings in October 1997.

Was there any catalyst for the timing?

The Russian equity market had more than tripled during the Asian crisis as investors fleeing Asia shoveled money into a country that was being touted by brokers as a post-Communist "miracle." Then came one day in October 1997 when there was a rumor about Yeltsin's failing health, and the market crashed 23 percent in a single session. Although I was disgusted by Russia at the time, I had been willing to stay in it as long as it kept going up. I wasn't going to argue with all the idiots who were buying Russia. If I had gotten out, and it kept going up, it could have been the end of my career. Remember, Russia was 40 percent of my benchmark.

Given what you understood about the true situation, weren't you concerned about an overnight collapse?

I was, but what I did was to be a bit underweight in Russia relative to the benchmark. So if it suddenly collapsed, I would still do better than the benchmark. The day the market collapsed, I felt physically sick because I was only underweight by about 3 percent, and this was a situation regarding which I had developed enormous conviction over the past nine months.

What did you do?

Well, the next day, the market fortuitously opened up nearly 30 percent. So with the compounding effect, the market was back to about even with its price before the previous day's break.

Why did it bounce back so much the next day?

The Yeltsin rumor was denied by the government, and people who had missed out on the Russian bull market suddenly saw the previous day's sharp correction as an amazing buying opportunity. I felt an enormous sense of relief. Within 10 minutes of the opening, I started aggressively selling off the Russian stocks in our portfolio. The market still finished that day up 24 percent, but the reason I was right to start selling that day was that the spell created by the senseless bull market had been broken by the previous day's price collapse. When markets are trending up strongly, and there is bad news, the bad news counts for nothing. But if there is a break that reminds people what it is like to lose money in equities, then suddenly the buying is not mindless anymore. People start looking at the fundamentals, and in this case I knew the fundamentals were very ugly indeed.

What happened after that day?

It started to slide. By February 1998, it was down 50 percent. Normally, it might seem to be a good idea to cover shorts, or in my case, reinstate long positions, after a decline of this magnitude. But I thought that the fundamentals remained extremely negative and that being long was a very bad idea. I was concerned that I might come under some pressure from my clients and colleagues to reinstate the Russian long exposure in the fund because of the market's large decline. So I wrote an internal analysis that detailed all the reasons why I thought the Russian market would still go much lower. In fact, it went down another 88 percent from that point.

The title of Taylor's paper, The Tsar Has No Clothes—*a title I obviously plagiarized for this chapter's heading—left little ambiguity as to the decisiveness of his opinion. Taylor's concluding comment was free of any qualifications and a particularly gutsy call keeping in mind that he was writing about a market that had already declined 50 percent in four months:* "Russia's problems are unlikely to be tackled until a serious ruble crisis jolts them out of their complacency. This leaves significant further downside for the equity market. We must remain underweight."

At the time I wrote the paper, there was still a perception that as a country with thousands of nuclear weapons, Russia was too big to be allowed to fail and risk anarchy. As a result, international hedge funds were very long GKOs, ruble-denominated T-bills, which were yielding 40 percent.

If short rates were 40 percent, there must have been real concern somewhere that Russia would default.

Of course there was; it was obvious. The inflation rate at the time was only about 10 percent. If you're getting paid a 30 percent real rate of return, it tells you that the country is about to go bust. The rate was so high because no one in Russia wanted to buy GKOs. The Russians knew perfectly well what was going on, and they put all their money in Switzerland. You have to look where the smart money is. In an emerging market, the smart money is domestic, not international.

Had the rate been extremely high even a year earlier?

Yes, and it had been steadily trending up.

So even as the short rate was moving up to stratospheric levels, Russian equities still went higher and then stayed at relatively high levels?

Yes, the market went up because there was a switching out of international money from Asian markets, which were much, much larger.

What was the catalyst that finally broke the Russian market?

In early summer 2008, Goldman Sachs managed the sale of about $25 billion of low-yielding, dollar-denominated, Russian sovereign 10-year Eurobonds to allow the Russian government to retire a similar amount of high-yielding GKOs. These Eurobonds started trading down from day one and then continued to fall steadily. Investors who had been persuaded to buy those bonds started seeing immediate large losses and were pretty upset. Foreign reserves, which were only about $20 billion to $25 billion at the time, should have doubled after the Goldman Sachs deal, making Russia safer and increasing the attractiveness of the Eurobonds, but they only increased by about $3 billion. This blatant anomaly forced international investors and the international media, after years and years of being in denial, to finally question the whole notion of the legitimacy of Russia's capital accounts data. Where was the cash going? It is likely that the money was received by senior government officials, divvied up, and then most of it went straight to Switzerland. There is a moment when the market realizes that the emperor has no clothes, and in Russia this was that moment.

How come you still had such a large loss in August 1998 if you were completely out of Russia?

Even though I was 40 percent in cash, the invested portion of my portfolio consisted of good companies with very high betas. Virtually every stock I owned had a beta of 1.5 or higher. Although I didn't have any of the crap in Russia that went down 95 percent, I did have stocks that went down 70 or 80 percent because they were widely owned, since they were good quality companies. The difference was that these companies continued to produce 30 percent earnings growth per year, which meant that as soon as the market stabilized, their prices shot back up. In contrast, the earnings of the Russian companies evaporated, and their prices never rebounded. Being 40 percent in cash allowed me to avoid being a seller during the August crash and made it possible for me to be a buyer in September after emerging market stocks had fallen sharply. As a result, when the market went back up, my portfolio rebounded with an insane beta. That is why I was able to finish 1998 slightly up, even though the index was down 30 percent.

Presumably, if you were right on your extreme bearish call on Russia, other emerging market stocks would go down as well. Why then wouldn't you have been in low-beta rather than high-beta stocks before the break?

Buying low-beta stocks is a common mistake investors make. Why would you ever want to own boring stocks? If the market goes down 40 percent for macro reasons, they'll go down 20 percent. Wouldn't you just rather own cash? And if the market goes up 50 percent, the boring stocks will go up only 10 percent. You have negatively asymmetric returns. It is what I call a pigeon-and-elephant trade—you eat like a pigeon and shit like an elephant. If you have a portfolio of boring stocks and want to make it produce equity-like returns, you have to leverage it up. If the portfolio then goes wrong, the loss is going to be massively asymmetric because of the leverage. I also think emerging market bonds are inherently unattractive. If all goes well, you get your coupon payment, but if the country defaults, you could lose all your money. So why would you ever bother?

Do you always have high-beta stocks?

Absolutely—high-beta stocks balanced by cash or shorts. That has been true ever since I was a long-only manager. Boring companies never have the opportunity for earnings growth. And I like earnings growth, even though I don't like paying up for it.

It seems like emerging market stock prices would be dominated by macro forces. How important is the individual stock selection?

There are so many things in macro that are inherently unpredictable. If you get 50 macro experts in a room, you will get 55 opinions. You can get much more knowledge and predictability about a company. We talk or meet with every company we own every few months. Over a period of years, you can build up a relatively good understanding of what the company does and their ability to execute new business plans. Therefore, you can have a much higher degree of confidence about the prospects for company performance than you can about the macro outlook. The type of trade in which you can get the confidence to take a big position and stay with it for years is therefore more likely to be company driven rather than macro driven.

Having said that, though, the macro outlook is still very important when making any given company investment decision. There are three things I like to see when I buy a stock: a favorable macro situation, a secular trend, and good company management. A good example of a trade with all three elements was our long position in the Russian mobile companies during 1999 to 2005, which was also one of the largest trades we ever had in Russia. The macro outlook was very favorable because the ruble had an 80 percent devaluation in 1998, which was coupled with a tremendous rebound in oil prices from their low of $12 in the same year. As a result of these two events, Russia went from an awful balance of payments deficit to an incredible balance of payments surplus. The resulting surge in foreign reserves led to a liquefaction of the Russian economy and the end of the nonpayments culture. People started getting paid real money. The resulting massive increase in purchasing power among ordinary people in Russia led to a strong secular trend supporting the trade: Mobile phone penetration was increasing annually by about 25 percent. Finally, I also liked the companies. They had good management teams who were happy to see you regularly. The companies were also transparent with very good accounting disclosure.

Why did you leave Barings?

Barings had a big marketing machine, and since I had outperformed the market by about 15 percent per year, the money was pouring into the fund like crazy. Having $2 billion in assets to invest in a tiny market, as East European equities were at the time, was insane. As investments into the fund increased, the negative impact of managing larger assets became more pronounced. I would have a good idea, put on about 25 percent of the position, and then the stock would run away because other people would hear what I was doing. It was just awful. I felt trapped. And I couldn't close the fund to new investors. At the same time, I was frustrated by not having the ability to go short. I would frequently see companies that I wanted to short as the tech bubble expanded, but I couldn't do anything because I was running a long-only fund. Also, I wasn't getting paid much, which is typical for a long-only institution. Even though I was probably accounting for as much as 30 percent of the firm's total P&L, I was being paid a trivial amount.

Putting these three things together—the negative impact of large assets on performance, the inability to go short, and the failure to financially benefit from my outperformance—by the middle of 1999, I realized that I wanted to run a hedge fund. However, I didn't want to start my own company and spend half my time being the CEO; I just wanted to be the CIO. So I joined Thames River, which is an umbrella company that provides the support structure for hedge funds. I went on the road in September 2000. Even though for the past six years, I had the best long-only emerging markets track record in the world by a wide margin, we raised only $20 million.

Why do you think that was?

There were multiple reasons. First, we were in the middle of a bear market. Second, I had only run a long-only fund, so some investors questioned my ability to run a long/short fund. Third, the fund was focused on emerging markets, which at the time were considered to be the Wild West of investing. Fourth, we initially couldn't approach any of my former clients at Barings for legal reasons.

What was the transition like going from long-only manager to long/short hedge fund manager?

We started the fund at the end of September 2000. There were various stocks I liked in Russia. I went only 40 percent net long, but the market was down about 20 percent that month, so I was down about 6 percent. Immediately I had investors calling saying, "You can't lose 6 percent in one month." I said, "Fine, if you don't like it, take your money away." For the second month, we had only $100,000 of new investment. All the people who said, "We can't come in on day one, but we will come in on day two," ran for the hills because I was down 6 percent in the first month. I stuck to my guns, and then I was up 8 percent in December, and we finished the quarter up 2 percent.

I always tell my new investors, "You will lose money investing with me at various points in the year, and it will always be unpleasant when it happens." This health warning is crucial so that investors have proper expectations. If someone comes to you and says they only invest in risky assets, but guarantee you limited downside volatility, they are either extraordinary geniuses—and there are probably only two of them on the planet—or they are liars. If you are investing in assets with an annualized volatility of 20 percent to 40 percent, you're inevitably going to take two or three decent hits to your NAV each year. And if you can't live with those hits because your clients are telling you that they can't live with monthly drawdowns, as soon as a position starts going against you a bit, you will sell it in a panic near the lows. You will then be psychologically impaired in regard to that position, which means you will never buy it back and will therefore miss out on any subsequent upside. Every year that the Nevsky fund has been running, we have had at least two intramonth losses of between 6 percent and 12 percent.

What is your normal net exposure range?

Between 20 percent net long to 110 percent net long. I believe that if you're trading very volatile instruments and you are completely out of the market when it reverses, then you will never get back in again. I will have some net long exposure even when I am bearish. For example, during the first quarter of 2009, even though I was still very bearish, I was 20 percent net long. As a result, when markets reversed to the upside in March, I didn't feel bad about buying more, since I had made some of the money on the rebound. It was mentally easy for me to double my net long exposure to 40 percent. If, on the other hand, I had been net short when the turn came, I would have been waiting for a pullback to cover my short, and the pullback never came.

But aren't there times when the market is so negative that it makes sense to be net short?

When the market is so bad that you think it is obvious that you should be net short, that's typically the time when it is all in the price and you should be buying. The people who annoy me the most are market strategists that work for brokers. They will recommend being aggressively overweight or being net short, and then they are wrong for two or three years. They are total bears or total bulls. And if they worked for a hedge fund, they would have had their capital wiped out many times over. Being in a position of running people's money, I can't take extreme positions and maintain my mental equilibrium. Managing money is real life, not some bullshit strategist fantasy world. When the market goes up, I try is capture 70 to 80 percent of the move, and when the market goes down, I try to lose only 30 or 40 percent of it.

Being dogmatic in market positioning is why a lot of hedge funds who did brilliantly in 2008, because they were short the entire year, then blew up in 2009.

[Taylor mentions a specific hedge fund manager.]

He is what I call a one-trick pony. I know he has a good track record, but I have no respect for him. He did one good trade: being short in 2008. But then he stayed short the following year when markets were up 40 percent to 50 percent, and by the end of the year, he was out of business. He did what market strategists do at a brokerage house, but he did it with client money. You can't do that. You have to always be pragmatic enough to move with the market. You always need to be facing in the right direction.

You started your hedge fund in the middle of a bear market. How did you manage to do so well in 2000 to 2002? [Taylor's hedge fund had an annualized return of 27 percent from its inception (October 2000) through 2002 compared with a return under 3 percent for the HFRI emerging markets hedge fund index and net losses for long-only emerging market indexes.]

In 1999, I underperformed because I was underweighting tech stocks and high beta bubbles in countries like Turkey, which I thought had no value at stupid investment multiples. Of course, that didn't stop them from going up a lot more. Avoiding the tech crash, though, was one of the reasons returns were so good in 2000 to 2002, as was being heavily invested in Russia, which was rising from the ashes thanks to the stimulative power of a very cheap ruble and firm oil prices.

Can you talk about 2008, which was your only losing year?

In 2008, emerging markets were down 54 percent, and I was down 17 percent, which is exactly in line with what I tell my investors—namely, in a bear market I expect to take 30 to 40 percent of the downside. I was very bullish at the end of 2007. We came into 2008 positioned 85 percent net long in high-beta stocks and 200 percent gross exposure. I was troubled, however, by widening credit spreads. It was reminiscent of August 2007 and suggested there were issues within the European banking sector. So I cut our exposure down to 40 percent net long. Aggressively selling down our positions in the first week of January was critical. We were actually up about 4 percent at midyear.

Help me out here. Why was cutting your long exposure sharply in early January beneficial? You were still net long and you were up for the first half-year. Logically then, wouldn't you then have been up even more if you didn't pare down your position?

A lot of the stocks we sold in early January were higher at the end of the second quarter, which would make our January sales look stupid, since we never went back to that 80 percent net exposure level. But I will tell you where you are wrong. If you remember, in late January, equity markets fell to new lows when the SocGen rogue trader position was discovered and unwound.[6] If we hadn't sold at the beginning of January, we would have sold at the bloody lows and would probably have been down 15 percent in January 2008 instead of only 5 percent. Not only would we have sold at the lows, but when the market then rallied in February and March, we wouldn't have had any position. Instead, because we had drastically cut our exposure in the first week of January, we were in a position to take advantage of the collapse later in the month. When the news about SocGen came out, I thought that was great because now I knew why the market has been down so much, and I was very comfortable buying into the weakness. If we had been nursing a 15 percent loss, we could never have taken the risk of buying on the break, even though it seemed like a great opportunity, because if we were wrong, we would be down another 10 percent and down 25 percent for the month. We would have been out of business.

What was the primary cause for the 2008 loss, which occurred during the second half of the year?

Our losses in the second half of 2008 came from our net long exposure. Although in the developed countries, GDP growth was flattening out and beginning to look ugly, in the emerging markets, everything was still booming. The earnings of all the companies in our portfolio were up sharply and valuations were very attractive. So whereas the fundamentals for developed markets suggested that you didn't want to have any exposure to anything, the fundamentals of the individual emerging market companies supported a strong net long posture. Given the contrast between attractive emerging market valuations and the high-risk global environment, we compromised with a moderate 40 percent net long exposure. After the Lehman collapse triggered major credit concerns, however, we reduced our exposure to 20 percent net long.

---

[6]The late January 2008 low coincided with Société Générale's liquidation of a rogue trader's massive long European stock index futures position.

Maintaining a 20 percent net long exposure instead of getting out completely helped us avoid getting whipsawed by the quick succession of extreme peaks and troughs in late 2008. During the fourth quarter of 2008, there were three rallies of approximately 15 percent to 20 percent that all ended up being followed by new lows. If I had dumped our entire position, then when the market rallied 15 percent to 20 percent, after it had been down nearly 40 percent, I might very well have thought, "Oh, my God, this is the turn," and jumped right back in again. Then when the market was back to a new low a few days later, I probably would have thought that I had been right to be out of the market in the first place and sold everything again. There would have been a danger of getting whipsawed on the subsequent short-lived sharp rallies as well. So while our net long exposure resulted in losses during the second half of 2008, ironically, we might have lost more if we had gone flat.

How did your investors respond to your first losing year?

We didn't have a single redemption until October 2008. From that point on, our fund was used as a cash machine because, given my golden rule of investing in only liquid securities, we were able to remain open for monthly dealing on an unchanged basis, despite the crisis, whereas most of our peers were in distress and had resorted to gating their funds.[7] Some of our fund-of-fund investors had all their capital withdrawn by their clients, so they had to sell everything. After having had no net redemptions for the first eight years of the fund, between October 2008 and March 2009, nearly half of the assets were redeemed. Bizarrely, though, within three months, all the money that had left came back. As

---

[7]Most hedge fund prospectuses contain a "gating" provision that allows the fund to curtail total investor redemptions beyond some specified amount (e.g., 10 percent of assets under management per quarter). If investor redemptions exceed the gate threshold, and the gate provision is enforced, then the hedge fund would only meet investor redemptions pro rata up to the specified maximum redemption level for that redemption period. The unmet portion of redemption requests would be filled pro rata in subsequent redemption periods within the same gate provisions, until redemptions were totally fulfilled. During the financial meltdown of late 2008 to early 2009, an unusually large number of hedge funds enforced gate provisions, as there were widespread investor redemptions due to the liquidity crunch and general market panic.

soon as markets stabilized, investors who had us on their watch lists for years, but were unable to invest because we were closed to new capital, stepped up to the plate, forcing us to close the fund once more.

Having been both a long-only fund and hedge fund manager, how would you compare the two?

Managing long-only money is really easy because if you are up more than the index, everyone loves you, since a huge majority of the managers, 85 percent or so, underperform the index. And even when you lose, as long as you are losing less in relative terms, people still love you. Whereas if you are a hedge fund manager, when the market is up, investors want you to perform like the market or better, and when the market is down, they want you to perform like cash.

Why do such a large percentage of long-only managers under-perform the index?

There are multiple reasons for it. First, management fees in emerging markets are relatively high—typically, 100 to 200 basis points. Second, the high volatility of emerging markets leads to a bias of managers making poor investment decisions, such as panicking out of positions near the bottom and jumping into positions near the top because they are afraid of missing the move. Third, the composition of the emerging market index changes frequently, which leads to a negative bias when managers sell a stock that has been dropped from the index and is under widespread selling pressure. Fourth, and perhaps most important, emerging markets tend to behave more irrationally than any other market because a large percentage of participants in these markets are local retail investors. These local investors will often make decisions based on reasons that you and I would not consider rational, such as rumors and conspiracy theories. I think if you took a poll among local emerging market investors, two or three times as many of them would think that the World Trade Center towers were brought down by the CIA rather than by Al Qaeda. When you are dealing with that kind of mind-set, you can get very badly burned investing just on fundamentals.

I thought that foreign investors were dominant in emerging markets.

The thundering herd of foreign investors that can shift huge amounts of money in and out of emerging markets are dominant around cycle turning points, but over longer periods, the key price moves are influenced by local investors and the rumor of the day. You can have a situation where you go short because there is terrible fundamental news on a company, and then the stock keeps on going up because of some wild, unfounded rumor that the son of the president is going to buy the company out.

Why then don't people invest directly into the index if such a large percentage of managers underperform the index?

There are several reasons why emerging market long-only funds have persisted despite their appalling performance. One key reason is marketing. Look at the Templeton emerging markets funds, for example, managed by Mark Mobius. Contrary to his media image as an emerging markets investment guru, he has in fact massively underperformed the index over the past 20 years. This fact hasn't stopped them raising tens of billions of dollars because he is always in the papers visiting and opining on emerging market companies and governments. The world of investment advisers is heavily influenced by media image so they suck their clients into this stuff.

Why do so many people continue to invest with him if the relative performance has been so bad?

Because they're not looking at relative performance. Emerging markets have gone up a lot over time. So if, for example, emerging markets are up an average of 10 percent per year, and he is up 6 percent per year, they are just looking at the fact that their investment is up.

Besides marketing, what other reasons are there for investors choosing long-only emerging market funds over emerging market indexes?

The other reason is that even index funds in emerging markets underperform the index because of high fees. Why would you buy a guaranteed loser? Marketing guys hold out the hope that maybe you will pick one of the funds that outperform the index.

Why did you recently decide to give back about three-quarters of your investor assets?

The type of trading around our core investment positions that I do to control risk in the portfolio is very time-consuming and burns a lot of heart muscle. It means that I have to work from five in the morning until nine at night every day. I start the morning with the Asian lunchtime and work through until the U.S. close. That's not very sane, is it? The $20 million that I started with in September 2000 had grown to $7.5 billion by February 2010, and that was with the hedge fund being closed for much of the period. We had $3.5 billion in the hedge fund and $4 billion in the long-only fund. I had started with three people, including myself, and the firm had grown to 35 people. So I ended up with a big team and lots of clients. It had all gotten very large and very time-consuming. I realized that if I continued the way I was going, I was eventually going to kill myself. Last February [2010], I decided to shrink my fund down to 20 percent of my former client base.

Was it a forced liquidation?

The only way we could reduce the number of our clients was to close the original fund and to simultaneously reopen a new fund, which is what we did. Last year, we gave our clients a one-year notice that the original fund would be closing. I wanted to give myself the flexibility to change my investment style.

Change it in what way?

In the original hedge fund, I had always committed to have at least 50 percent of my investments in emerging markets. If, for example, I didn't have any exposure to Asia, and Asia went mental, I would be afraid that my clients might sue me for incompetence. Whereas now, if I don't like Asia, and I want to get a bit more sleep in the morning, I can choose to not have any exposure in Asia and get up later.

What is the mandate of the current fund?

Basically, I can do anything that I like. I will still have material exposure in emerging markets, but the point is that I don't have to be in emerging markets. I'm also trying to get away from that tyranny in hedge funds: monthly performance. Previously, a large percentage of my clients were fund of funds who were driven by monthly data because a large percentage of their clients were driven by monthly data. You end up in this situation where you are obsessed with monthly returns, which can influence poor long-term investment decisions, even though it might make monthly returns look better.

In the new fund, we will still report monthly returns to clients, but instead of having a monthly newsletter, we will go to a quarterly newsletter. I am trying to stop caring about what my clients think. I want to continue to invest money the same way but have the freedom to take a longer view. For example, during the past two months, the performance of my core positions has just been awful—the market has gone up and they have gone down. But I feel I have the freedom to maintain a long-term investment focus rather than being overly concerned about the monthly relative performance.

Out of curiosity, what are these currently poor performing core positions?

My biggest position is Apple. The reason I like Apple is that it is a company that is almost solely analyzed by U.S. analysts who think that Apple has limited growth potential because of the large market share it already has in the U.S. They fail to appreciate that only 300 million people live in the U.S., and there are 6.7 billion people in the rest of the world. The market in which Apple has the highest approval rating is China, which is a market with 900 million mobile phone subscribers. And currently, how many iPhones have been sold in China? Three million. Their unique operating system and excellent hardware give Apple a barriers-to-entry advantage relative to their competitors. I believe over the next four years, Apple will inevitably repeat the success it has had in the U.S. on a global scale.

We forecast the earnings of every company we follow for three or four years out. I like to invest in companies that are cheap relative to their sector, but where we are forecasting earnings above consensus for the next few years. The catalyst I monitor for a stock to realize value is earnings surprise. In the case of Apple, we are forecasting earnings 50 or 60 percent above the street for the next three or four years. Although Apple is currently trading at 16 times forward prospective earnings for 2011, based on our forecasted level of earnings for 2014, it is only trading at 4.8 times earnings. Apple is one of the fastest-growing companies in the world, with one of the best management teams, trading at less than five times earnings based on our future earnings projections, and with $150 billion net cash by 2014, which is nearly half of its market cap. We currently have 20 percent of our portfolio in Apple.

Given all those bullish fundamentals, why hasn't Apple performed better?

One reason it is not performing at the moment is because it has gone up a lot, so investors think they can't buy it. But the main reason is that all that the analysts in the U.S. seem to be focused on is that the next iPhone may be delayed for a few months. They think that is bad. It is not bad at all. The reason Apple is so brilliant is because their execution is outstanding. Would they prefer if Apple came out with their next iPhone version early and did what RIMM [Research in Motion Ltd.] has done with the PlayBook, the new tablet they have for the Black-Berry, which is one of the most suicidal pieces of rubbish ever put out? RIMM will probably go bust in the next three or four years.

Why is that?

Because they keep on having incompetent product launches. For example, they're bringing out a new tablet, and you can't even use it for e-mail. And this is a product that is targeted for the corporate market! That is like producing a car with no engine or wheels. It is literally as bad as that. It shouldn't have come out for at least another year. The reason they rushed it to market, even though it is not ready, is that the Apple iPad 2 is such a big advance that it has helped Apple break into the corporate market. Now businesspeople are saying, I don't want my BlackBerry phone anymore; I want an iPhone. RIMM was worried that if they didn't come out with competition for the iPad 2, they would lose the corporate market. But what they have done is guarantee that they will lose the corporate market by undermining every company IT manager who argued for maintaining the BlackBerry over the iPhone. What RIMM has done is taken a knife and driven it through the heart of their business.

I interviewed Taylor on April 30, 2011. On the previous day, Apple had closed at $350 and RIMM at $49.By the time I was proofing this text in the production process less than 11 months later (March 19, 2012), Apple was at $601 and RIMM under $15.

How do you pick shorts?

Shorts are more difficult. On the long side, I like companies that are cheap relative to their sector, but where I expect positive earnings surprises during the next few years. So turning that around, ideally, I would like to go short companies that are expensive relative to their sector and where I expect profit warnings over the next few years. The problem is that these bad companies have the greatest risk of being takeover targets. The emerging markets are full of sectors where multinationals want exposure, and the only companies they can generally take over are bad companies. In emerging markets, in order to take over a company, you need to triangulate between the company, the government, and the regulator. It is much more difficult for a foreign firm to get government or regulator approval for a takeover of a local company that is doing well, or about to do well, because the authorities will fear being seen as "selling out" to foreigners. Whereas if it is a bad company, the government and regulators are much more likely to approve the acquisition because it will be seen as saving the company and saving jobs. You can be long a good stock at seven times earnings and short a bad stock at 15 times earnings, and some stupid foreign company comes along and pays a 50 percent premium to buy the bad company.

So how do you walk that tightrope when the companies you most want to short are the ones most vulnerable to a takeover?

Half to three-quarters of our shorts are stock index futures. So most of our net exposure adjustment is done through shorting markets rather than individual companies.

How do you manage the shorts that are individual companies given the takeover dilemma you detailed?

We only short bad companies that can't be taken over because they are owned by the government or their own pension fund. If the company is owned by the pension fund, it will never be sold because the workers will be afraid that the acquiring company would sack 20 percent of the labor force.

What percent of companies are owned by the government or pension funds?

In emerging markets, about one-third of all companies are government or pension fund owned.

What is your risk control process?

We are always in the most liquid securities. If we get it wrong, we get out immediately. We do a lot of research before we put on any trade. Not only do we forecast the earnings for a stock three or four years out, we also forecast the macro picture three or four years out as well.

Can you really forecast that far out?

Our macro views change quite regularly. You just have to be pragmatic. When you get it wrong, you need to get out immediately. I am wrong all the time. If I can be right 60 percent of the time, and when I am right I have some big winners, and when I am wrong, I staunch the losses quickly, I can make a lot of money.

Do you have any specific risk control rules?

We have never had and would never use any form of quantitative risk control because all quantitative risk control models use historical volatility. It is like driving by looking in the rearview mirror. If you use volatility as a guideline, and volatility suddenly increases, you will—Doh!—find that your risk was much greater than you thought, but by then you will already have been wiped out. That is exactly what happened to a lot of managers in 2008. We also never use stops.

So what do you do to manage risk instead?

It is common sense. There are multiple requirements for a trade to take place. Do we like the company? Is it cheap? Does it generate cash flow? Do we trust the management? Do I have confidence in my projections? Is the macro outlook favorable?

If a company meets all the criteria, then the next step is determining the appropriate position size. Given the degree of company and country risk, what do I think is the appropriate size position? If it is something very risky, a large position for me might be 1 percent to 5 percent of the portfolio. If it is a lower risk position in which I have very high confidence, the position could be as large as 20 percent of the portfolio, as is currently the case for Apple. I accept that if anything were to happen to Steve Jobs, the stock could go down 10 percent. That would be a 2 percent hit on my portfolio. I could live with that because I think the stock will triple over the next four years. If I have that big of a position in Apple, can I have another significant position in the same industry sector? No, I can't because a negative shock event or development might be one that impacts the entire sector rather than being Apple specific.

In controlling risk, it is also very important to have people in your team whose opinions you respect, who can push back at your ideas in a way that will make you stop, listen, and test your own views. My partner, Nick Barnes, is crucial to me in this regard.

Steve Jobs died about a half year after this interview. Although Apple stock moved lower in the weeks preceding his death, ironically, the stock moved higher after the event.

Is there any common denominator as to why your projections for a stock will differ from the market's perception?

Normally, it is because there is some kind of trend that I think is common sense but that the market does not appreciate because it is extrapolating history instead of looking forward. For example, Apple has never had any consequential sales in India or China, so the street assumption is that they never will, which is imbecilic. As another example, during the fourth quarter of last year, Apple sold 7.3 million iPads. The average street forecast for iPad sales this year is 29.5 million units. All they have done is take fourth-quarter sales of last year and annualize them. What they are failing to take into account is that Apple has revolutionized an existing product that was already way ahead of any competitor. Not only is it a much better product, but Steve Jobs decided to price it competitively instead of at a premium. Given Apple's economies of scale, no one else can even possibly compete. So we think they will sell 40 million iPads this year and 60 million next year. The street's forecast for next year is 40 million. It is not rocket science; it is just common sense.

Everything we have talked about has involved fundamental analysis. Does that imply that you don't use technical analysis at all?

Oh, no. Charts are very important. Once I have done the fundamental work and decided to buy a stock, I will first look at the chart before putting on a position. If the stock is very overbought, it won't stop me from buying, but I will start with a small position because there is a larger chance of a correction. If instead I put on the entire position and then the stock had a large correction, I would feel terrible. Say I really like a company and want to put 10 percent of the portfolio in it. If the stock is extremely overbought, then I might start with only a 1 percent position. If the stock just keeps on going up, then I am happy that I bought at least some. I will also be more willing to buy more because I bought part of the position at a lower price. Whereas, if I didn't initially buy anything because the stock was overbought, I would then never buy any of it, which would be a dreadful mistake.

Equally important, if I decide to buy a stock based on fundamentals and then look at the chart and see that it has massively underperformed relative to the market, I will check who has been selling the stock. Such price weakness might indicate that all our fundamental research is worthless because management has lied to us. I also use charts as an aid to adding to positions. If I am bullish on a stock but don't have a full position, and then the stock breaks out on the chart, I will then go to a full position because the breakout confirms that the market is now seeing the same thing I am seeing.

So you're basically using charts as a supplemental tool.

Yes, the core is always fundamental. There is, however, one exception where a trade might be initiated because of charts. If a stock is extremely oversold—say, the RSI is at a three-year low—it will get me to take a closer look at it.[8] Normally, if a stock is that brutalized, it means that whatever is killing it is probably already in the price. RSI doesn't work as an overbought indicator because stocks can remain overbought for a very long time. But a stock being extremely oversold is usually an acute phenomenon that lasts for only a few weeks.

So you're saying that RSI is only useful in one direction.

Correct, which is oversold. If the RSI is extremely oversold, I will then look at the fundamentals to see if whatever has caused the stock to be sold off that sharply is already discounted by the price. If it is, then I will buy.

Is your approach totally analysis driven, or does gut feel ever play a role?

Gut feel is actually crucial. If something isn't acting right, it is an indication that you need to go back and recheck the fundamentals. I currently have a partial short position in the IBEX, the Spanish stock index. I was thinking of substantially increasing my position. Then yesterday, several economic statistics were released. They were all awful, but the market went up. So I scurried away.

You covered your position?

No, I just didn't add to it because the algorithmic funds were clearly still in control of the market. It would be insane for me to have a large position because I could get destroyed before the market turns down. I have to wait before I short Spain aggressively. My gut feel was, "Ugh, this is not acting right." But I'm not going to cover my partial position because fundamentally I still think I am right.

What advice would you give to stock investors?

You have to be an expert in what you invest in. You need to understand why you are invested. If you don't understand why you are in a trade,

---

[8]The RSI stands for Relative Strength Index, which is a popular overbought/oversold indicator developed by J. Welles Wilder.

you won't understand when it is the right time to sell, which means you will only sell when the price action scares you. Most of the time when price action scares you, it is a buying opportunity, not a sell indicator.

What do you consider the worst trading mistake of your career?

My biggest mistake or pattern of mistakes was the way I traded the 2009 market.

I thought you had a big up year in 2009.

I was up 32 percent for the year, but I should have been up at least 45 to 50 percent. I am usually very good at riding big beta rallies. My failure to do so in 2009 caused me great angst at the time.

Why did you trade differently in 2009?

Normally, I let winners run and cut losers. In 2009, however, as a result of the posttraumatic effects of going through the September 2008 to February 2009 period—talking to clients who are going out of business and seeing 50 percent of your fund redeemed is all very wearing—I got into the habit of snatching quick 10 to 15 percent profits in individual positions. Most of these positions then went up another 35 to 40 percent. I consider my pattern of taking quick profits in 2009 a dreadful error that I think came about because I had lost a degree of confidence due to experiencing my first down year in 2008, even though the loss was consistent with the expected loss given the magnitude of the market decline. I was constantly worried that markets were about to turn down again, particularly in regard to all the new investors who came into the fund in the second quarter of 2009. I was painfully aware that these new investors did not have the cushion of my previous cumulative gains, and I worried about losing money for them. I was also more aware of my size in the market, as volumes did not recover to anywhere near precrisis levels, whereas the fund size was back to precrisis size by July 2009. I was concerned about being able to exit in a hurry if necessary. Basically, all these things made my trading more short term and hair trigger, which is absolutely not my style. Normally, if I like something, I stick with it.

I only stopped this damaging pattern in mid-2010 after I had given investors 12-month notice in March that the hedge fund was closing. This action had an immediate impact in reducing the size of the fund, as redemptions came through steadily. Also, by allowing and encouraging all investors, old and new, to exit at a high watermark, it made me feel that I had done right by all of them. After this point, I relaxed and returned to my former investment style.

■ ■ ■

In selecting emerging market equities, Taylor looks for three essential characteristics:

1. **Favorable macro outlook**—There are two key ways in which Taylor's macro assessment will influence the portfolio. First, Taylor will concentrate longs in countries with the most positive fundamentals. Second, the global macro outlook can influence the total portfolio net exposure. For example, in late 2008 to early 2009, the very negative global macro fundamentals kept net exposure significantly lower than it would have been based solely on the individual company fundamentals.

2. **Supportive secular trend**—Taylor looks for situations in which there is a strong fundamentally based secular trend that supports the trade. For example, the strong trend in increasing Russian mobile phone usage in the early 2000s was a key consideration that prompted Taylor to place a large and very profitable position in companies in this sector. As another example, Taylor's expectation that Apple's global market share of its products will trend steadily higher in coming years was the dominant reason why Apple was his largest holding at the time of this interview (April 2011).

3. **Good company**—Taylor looks for companies with attractive growth prospects priced at reasonable values relative to future expected earnings. He avoids what he calls "boring" companies (typically low-beta stocks) regardless of whether they are good values.

Investors often miss the best stocks because they can't bring themselves to buy a stock that has already gone up a lot. What matters is not how much a stock has gone up, but rather how well a stock is priced relative to its *future* prospects. Taylor's largest holding at the time of our interview, Apple, had already experienced a very large price advance— and indeed, it was the magnitude of this prior rise that kept many investors from buying the stock, despite its excellent fundamentals. As Taylor viewed it, however, the amount of the prior price gain was irrelevant because based on his earnings projections for Apple, the stock was actually very cheap, notwithstanding its seemingly lofty price.

It is important that your net exposure match your comfort level. For example, if you are uncomfortable being completely out of the market, then a flat position may actually be riskier than a modest long position because you will be much more likely to chase false rallies and get whipsawed. Taylor believes that having some long exposure during the highly volatile late 2008 to early 2009 period actually reduced his potential losses, even though the market declined. He reasons that if he had been out of the market completely, he would have been prone to being whipsawed by one or more of the period's false rallies, potentially losing more than he did with his modest net long exposure. The moral is that you have to know your net exposure comfort zone. For Taylor, the low end of this comfort zone is 20 percent net long.

As another example of the benefits of trading within a net exposure comfort zone, a smaller net exposure may yield better returns, *even if the market moves higher*. For example, although the market eventually rose to higher levels, by sharply reducing his net long exposure in early January 2008, Taylor was in a position to increase his long exposure following the price plunge later in that month. If he had stayed heavily net long, he might well have been forced to sell into the market weakness to reduce risk. The difference between being a buyer on market weakness instead of a potential seller more than offset the reduced returns implied by a lower net exposure for the period as a whole.

Although trying to tightly constrain monthly losses may seem like a prudent approach—and indeed is for many traders—for investors with a long-term perspective, a constraint of keeping monthly losses below some moderate threshold could be detrimental. Taylor believes that an obsession with monthly returns can adversely influence long-term investment decisions. If he is strongly convinced that a stock will move much higher over the long term, then in his view, cutting exposure on interim weakness to limit the depth of a monthly loss would be a mistake. Freeing himself from what he calls the "tyranny" of a monthly return focus was one of the main motivations behind Taylor's decision to return investor assets and restructure as a much smaller fund.

In my experience, it is usually a mistake for a manager to alter his investment decisions or investment process to better fit investor demands. Taylor acknowledges this same perspective when he states, "I am trying to stop caring about what my clients think."

Taylor believes the best opportunities are those where you can identify a potential trend that the market does not appreciate because it is extrapolating history instead of looking forward. For example, Taylor anticipates that a growing global market share will result in Apple's sales far exceeding prevailing projections. Therefore, whereas Apple seemed adequately priced based on current earnings (a forward prospective P/E of 16 at the time of the interview), it was screamingly cheap based on Taylor's estimate of earnings three years forward (a P/E under 5).

Investors often make the mistake of equating manager performance in a given year with manager skill. In some instances, more skilled managers will underperform because they refuse to participate in market bubbles. In fact, during market bubbles, the best performers are often the most imprudent rather than the most skilled managers. Taylor underperformed in 1999 because he thought it was ridiculous to buy tech stocks at their inflated price levels. This same investment decision, however, was one of the key reasons why he strongly outperformed in subsequent years when these stocks experienced an extended slide.

Chapter 11

Tom Claugus

A Change of Plans

T
homas Claugus had it all planned out. Financial security was very important. He would get a degree in a practical science and an MBA, a set of credentials he felt would ensure a successful career. And that is just what he did. After receiving a degree in chemical engineering, Claugus spent two years working in his chosen field and then interrupted his working career to attend Harvard Business School. After receiving his MBA, Claugus returned to his former company, Rohm & Haas, and worked his way up the corporate ladder. Within 15 years, he was manager of their European operations and thought to be in line to eventually become the firm's CEO. He had financial security. His career was on an upward trajectory. He loved his job and the people he worked with. It was all going exactly to plan except...

Claugus had another passion. He was also an avid stock investor who first became enticed by the stock market as a child. Claugus adhered to a discipline of living on only one-third of his income and investing the remainder. Through a combination of strong performance and the additional investment of his annual savings, his stock account grew steadily over the years. Eventually, Claugus found that he was earning more money from the stock account than from his executive position in the chemical industry. He decided to abandon his successful career to become a portfolio manager. He said it was the most difficult decision he ever made. His second thoughts about this decision and the vacillation that followed led to great personal angst as described in the interview.

Claugus has realized a 17 percent average annual compounded net return over a 19-year period. His audited personal account did even better, compounding at 33 percent gross during the seven years prior to the fund's launch. During the combined 26-year track record, Claugus had five losing years; two of them were very modest: 3 percent or less. The only significant negative years were 1991, when his account was down 12 percent, 2008 when the fund lost 25 percent, and 2011 when the fund was down nearly 9 percent. In each case, the subsequent year's gain more than doubled the loss (excluding 2011, for which the following year's return is unknown at this writing). For example, following the dismal 2008 performance, the fund was up 56 percent in 2009, its best year ever.

Claugus is a natural contrarian. He often lags badly when others are making easy money and soars when others are panicking. This mirror image investing experience was clearly evident in the final year of the tech bubble (1999) and its aftermath. Claugus actually had a small loss in 1999 when the S&P 500 was up 21 percent, but then scored large gains during the major bear market of 2000 to 2002. The one glaring exception in avoiding poor performance in a bear market was the financial meltdown of 2008 when Claugus lost money along with most everyone else.

Even when Claugus is doing well during strong equity market years, the source of profits may be counterintuitive. As a case in point, Claugus achieved an 18 percent annual compounded return during the 1990s (his fund launched in 1993), not by riding the steadily rising tide of stock prices, but by being net short throughout the period. Claugus's highly differentiated exposure levels (vis-à-vis most equity hedge funds) have been one of the characteristics, besides solid long-term returns, that have attracted investors, particularly those managing multifund portfolios. Claugus's hedge fund company, GMT, currently manages $5.0 billion in its onshore and offshore Bay Resource funds.

Claugus is based in Atlanta where I met him a decade earlier when giving a talk to a regional hedge fund group. I interviewed Claugus when he came to New York City to attend a conference. We met after the day's sessions were complete and found an empty meeting room where we could talk in relative privacy. We were periodically interrupted by a security guard who first came by to see who we were and then returned intermittently to see when we would be leaving.

■ ■ ■

When did you first get interested in the stock market?

My father invested in stocks. As a young boy I saw my father check the stock quote page of the paper every day. I was curious what he was doing, so I asked him about it. I think I bought my first stocks when I was nine years old.

How does a nine-year-old have money to buy stocks?

I had a paper route. One of my parents opened a custodian account for me.

Did your father help you pick stocks to buy?

No, he gave me an S&P stock guide. I leafed through it and found two local companies I recognized—Wheeling Pittsburgh Steel and McCrory, which was a five and dime chain store—so I bought them. Both companies eventually went bankrupt. I made a little money on Wheeling Pittsburgh Steel, but I held McCrory into bankruptcy.

My father was a product of the Depression, and he was scared to death of being poor again. Somehow—I don't know how he did it—he transferred that insecurity to me. From a very early age, I knew I wanted to be financially independent. That was very important to me. I remember when I was a freshman in college, I put together a 30-year financial plan outlining how I could save and invest my money. I calculated that by saving two-thirds of my income and earning 10 percent a year on my investments, I could be a millionaire by the time I was 53. The reason I picked chemical engineering was that I was good at math and chemistry, and engineering paid well. It was as simple as that. My whole goal was to make $12,000 a year. I almost switched to business several times during college.

Why didn't you?

I came from a family with a science background. My father was a veterinarian, one of his brothers was a heart surgeon, and the other brother was an engineer. It was sort of expected that I would major in science or engineering. Business was considered too easy. But I wasn't a very good engineer. I did well academically because I was dedicated and worked extremely hard. My father also scared me to death about how important it was to do well in school. When I went to college, he said, "Tom, you are going to feel like you're going to jail. You can go out Friday night or Saturday night, but you can't go out both, or else you won't get ahead." I really had in my mind that, at some point, I would study business. My plan was that I would get an MBA. I thought that if I could get both a chemical engineering degree and a business degree, then I could be a manager in a chemical company.

After my first two years of work, I decided to go to business school. I applied and got into Harvard. I got the impression from most of my classmates that their families were elated when they got into Harvard Business School. My father, however, was not happy at all when I got accepted. I was not even sure that I was going to go. Then word got out at my company that I had been accepted to Harvard Business School, and one of the vice presidents called and asked me out to lunch. I thought, *This guy never even acknowledged my existence, and now he calls to take me out to lunch just because I was accepted. Maybe I should go to this place after all.*

Your father was an educated guy; he was a veterinarian. Why was he so negative on your going to Harvard?

He was upset that I was leaving a job that was paying $15,800 to go back to school. My father was a very tough guy. He didn't start undergrad until his mid-twenties because he felt he had to stay home, work the family farm, and take care of his mother. My father measured almost everything in terms of money. During the summers, I would help my father on the farm, cutting timber and doing other stuff. He would take me down through the woods and teach me about trees. We came across this magnificent walnut tree. My father said with admiration, "Isn't this a beautiful tree? It's probably worth $3,000."

Not counting your dabbling with stocks as a child, when did you start investing in the stock market?

I never wanted to depend on my job for money. So I started investing from day one. From the start, I tried to give myself motivation to save money. My plan was to live on one-third of my income plus 3 percent of my net worth. The 3 percent of my net worth figure was based on the assumption that I could earn at least 10 percent a year. So, effectively, my plan was to live on one-third of all income.

When did you go from being a long-only investor to incorporating shorting as a key component of your investment strategy?

In 1986, I became concerned that the market was overpriced. I like risk. I like the excitement of being in the market. I knew I didn't have the discipline to stay out of the market, and I felt that stocks were too expensive, so I started shorting.

When in 1986?

In early 1986.

So you started shorting almost a year and a half too early. [The market didn't peak until August 1987.]

Yes, and a lot of times before the market cracks, the lower-quality stocks zoom. I remember being on the tennis courts with my friends in the summer of 1987 [he begins a tremulous laugh that betrays an undertone of pain], and I was losing so much money that I had to call my mother to get a loan to meet the margin call. She was the only one I could call. There is no way my dad would have loaned me the money.

Did you stay short all the way through until the crash?

I did.

So even though the market kept moving against you, you just...

I just hung in there.

You never second-guessed yourself?

Sure I did. In fact, when I was playing tennis that day, I told my buddies that I was a failure, and that I was going to lose all my money.

You were short during the crash of October 19, 1987. What stands out in your memory about that day?

As the market was crashing, I thought I could start putting on some longs to reduce my net short position. The trade I remember most is putting in an order to buy Mead Paper at 32, and I got a fill at 27—the market was collapsing that quickly.

Did you cover any of your shorts during the market freefall?

I don't believe I covered much because most of the stocks I was short were low quality, and I didn't think there was a need to cover them quickly. Instead of covering shorts, I started buying stocks that I really liked.

But some of the stocks you were short must have been down by 30 percent or more that day.

I was short these fly-by-night companies, some of which were probably manipulated. I think there were only two stocks that were up on October 19, 1987, and I was short one of them. It eventually cratered. I have always tried to be long and short in things that I really believed in for the longer term—situations in which I felt that the fundamental underpinnings of the company were completely different from the way it was being priced.

In 1987, you went from margin calls to windfall profits. Did the 1987 experience influence you in any way?

1987 was the first year I made more money in the market than I did in my job. That was an eye-opener for me. And every year after that, I made more money in the market than in my job.

How did you go from a career as a chemical engineer and the manager of European operations for a chemical company to being a portfolio manager?

If you had asked me a year before I left Rohm & Haas whether I would ever leave, I would have told you that I was there for the duration. My aspiration was to be CEO of Rohm & Haas. The reason I had been investing in the stock market up to that point was that I liked risk taking, and I wanted to be financially independent. I knew I couldn't reach my financial goals on my salary. I was cruising along on a pretty good path; my investments were working for me, and I was making more money on them than in my job. My net worth reached $1.6 million. I thought, *3 percent of $1.6 million is $48,000; I could live on that.* Once I had that realization, all of a sudden, the economic necessity to keep on working went away. Until that point, every time I asked myself, *When are you going to do what you want to do?* the answer would always be, *Later.* Did I really want to live in Philadelphia, which is where Rohm & Haas was located? Not really. The realization that I had the economic freedom to sustain a business for three to five years totally turned me upside down. I spent a year in terrible turmoil.

Turmoil in trying to decide what you wanted to do?

Yes. Ultimately, I decided to manage money like I manage my own money. I started a hedge fund in 1990 with $3 million; part of it was mine, and the rest was from friends and family.

What was the experience like managing a fund for the first time?

I went from regional director in Europe with everyone telling me how smart I was to managing a portfolio by myself out of my home. I felt a very low sense of self-worth. After nine months of this, I said to myself, *Claugus, you are a people person; you made a big mistake.*

What convinced you that you had made a mistake?

I think it was the loneliness. I had spent 17 years at Rohm & Haas. I missed my friends.

How had you done in terms of performance in those first nine months of managing the fund?

I was up in the first six months, but then I started giving money back. I think I was still up a little bit when I started to seriously question my decision to manage a fund.

Once I was unsure about what I wanted to do, I was afraid that if I continued on and lost money, I would feel a responsibility to make up the difference to my investors, and by reimbursing them, I could lose all the money I had saved up during the past 14 years.

Did you discover that managing money was different from what you had perceived it to be?

The responsibility of having other people's money really weighed on me. If you have a 10-year time horizon, you can make good decisions and make a lot of money. If you have a three-year time horizon, you could probably still do well. But if you have only a three-month time horizon, anything can happen.

Why did you think there was a three-month time horizon?

Because I started doubting whether I would continue.

Did you close the fund?

I did. I closed it at the end of the first year.

What finally prompted you to close the fund?

I had talked to my friends about how I felt. Rohm & Haas heard that I was unhappy being on my own and offered me a job. I decided to take the offer and close my fund.

How did you feel when you closed the fund?

Here was the most startling thing for me. I got the offer letter from Rohm & Haas around Christmastime. I'll never forget the sinking feeling I had when I read the letter. It was an offer to be regional director of Asia based in Hong Kong. I really had no desire to go to Asia.

Hadn't you discussed the details of your job before accepting the offer to come back?

I hadn't up to that point. They had basically said they would bring me back into a key job and that I would possibly still be in line to become CEO of Rohm & Haas. Basically, they desperately needed someone good in Asia. No one else who was qualified wanted to go. Their attitude was *Tom wants to come back. Perfect. He has to earn his way back, and we'll send him to Asia. It will be well perceived by the organization.* For them it was very clear.

I walked out to put the *for sale* sign in front of my house, and I just couldn't do it. One of my sons was a great gymnast; he was a state champion. So one of my concerns was: Where would my kids do their athletics? I had this terrible feeling about it. So I called the CEO of Rohm & Haas and said, "Do you mind if I go to Hong Kong and check it out first?" He said, "Sure, go to Hong Kong."

When I was at the airport in line for the flight, I was still not sure that I wanted to go. So I got out of line. Then I got back in line, and then back out again. I finally got on the plane.

What was your impression of Hong Kong?

Very crowded. I offered to donate a trampoline to the school, and they said they didn't have room for it [he laughs for a long time at this recollection]. I wasn't wild about it, but I decided I would go anyway. I tried to get myself psyched about going, but I just couldn't do it. I decided I needed to go back to Hong Kong to check it out again. It was a replay of my first visit. I spent five months trying to get myself to go to Hong Kong. I became depressed. I lost 45 pounds.

Boy, you really didn't want this job.

This was the first time in my life that I decided to do something mentally that was in conflict with my emotions. My body just stopped me in my tracks. I didn't realize it, but there was no way I could go to Hong Kong. Rohm & Haas had a coach who did assessments of managers to see if they had the right profile to be CEO. During this period, she was talking to me on the phone and asked me a number of questions. She said, "Tom, I think you are clinically depressed. You need to see a psychiatrist. You need to do it right away." She found me a doctor who placed me on antidepressants. Finally, I went to Rohm & Haas—I was probably down to about 135 pounds by that time, and I looked like death—and I told them that I couldn't take the job in Hong Kong.

When did you come out of your depression?

Very quickly after I turned the job down.

That did it?

That plus the antidepressants. I had a friend who had gone through depression, and as soon as he realized that I was going through depression myself, he gave me advice. He said, "Look Tom, here's what you have to do. I went through all this counseling, and all I can tell you is just get the drugs." After I had taken the antidepressant for about two weeks, the cloud lifted, and I could see again.

Was that the only episode of depression you had?

The only one.

Why do you think you had become clinically depressed? Was it primarily a matter of having to relocate to a place where you didn't want to go?

What put me into clinical depression was trying to force myself to go to Hong Kong when I didn't want to do it. But I didn't know for sure why I didn't want to do it.

What do you think now was the reason?

It was because I was giving up on my dream. In my heart, I really wanted to be on my own, and I hadn't taken it to completion.

Did you learn something from that whole experience?

Yes, it taught me the importance of having your emotional side lined up with your mental side for life-changing decisions.

What did you do after you turned down the job at Rohm & Haas?

I decided that my original plan to start a hedge fund was what I really wanted to do.

When did you start a new hedge fund?

In January 1993.

That is about a year and a half after you turned down the Rohm & Haas job. Why did you wait so long?

After my uncertainty the first time, I wanted to be sure of my decision the second time.

What about your concern about managing other people's money?

If I am 100 percent dedicated to managing your money, and I lose your money, I can look you in the eye and say, "I did my best," and I could be okay with that. If I am not 100 percent engaged, however, and I'm not even sure I want to be in the business, then managing other people's money is very hard. Once I was sure I wanted to manage money, it took away 80 percent of the angst.

It is the same reason we don't put up gates.[1] We had huge outflows in 2008 because we didn't have gates. Sure, I would have preferred to

---

[1]A *gate* is a legal provision contained in many hedge fund disclosure documents that permits the fund to implement a more restrictive redemption policy if a greater-than-specified percentage of assets are instructed to be redeemed on the same redemption date. An example of a gate would be a provision that investors as a group cannot redeem more than 10 percent of a fund's assets on any single redemption date. If investor redemptions exceed this threshold, they would be fulfilled pro rata of a 10 percent total. Unfilled redemptions would be carried forward to subsequent redemption periods until completely fulfilled.

reduce investor withdrawals, and as it turned out, investors would have been far better off if they didn't redeem in 2008. People do things that are not in their best interest. But there is a big difference between their making their own decision and my telling them what is in their best interest. If investors want to redeem, and I say they can't because there is a gate, and then I lose their money, that is a way different feeling than losing money for investors who have reached their own decision to stay in the fund.

How did you find the experience of working alone the second time around?

I enjoyed it.

What changed?

Just time. I got used to working alone. And I love investing.

What is your investment philosophy?

I am a reversion-to-the-mean thinker. We use standard deviation bands to define extreme readings.[2] For example, here is a chart of the S&P based on data going back to 1932. (I didn't want to use the run-up to the Depression and the early years of the Depression because I thought it would distort the data.) Using a 95 percent confidence band, the low is currently at 895 and the high is at 2,522. The argument is that you would have your maximum long position at the lower band and your maximum short position at the upper band.

But obviously, there are times where you can stay beyond the bands for a long period.

That's where we will lose money. For example, here is the tech bubble when we were net short, and the market kept going up.

---

[2]Specifically, Claugus derives the best-fit regression line for the log of prices using all data back to 1932 and then calculates the 95 percent confidence interval—the two equidistant lines parallel to the best-fit line that encompass 95 percent of all the months.

How would your exposure vary based on the market's position relative to the extreme bands?

At the lower band, we would be 130 percent long and 20 percent short. At the midpoint, we would be 100 percent long and 50 percent short. We are 50 percent net long at the midpoint rather than neutral because of the long-term secular uptrend in stock prices. At the upper band, we would be 90 percent short and 20 percent long, or 70 percent net short. Our net exposure will increase as the market goes down and decrease as the market goes up. We do similar calculations using the Nasdaq and Russell 2000 indexes and then derive a composite target exposure based on the relation between current prices and the price bands in all three indexes.

What are the other elements of your investment approach besides a reversion-to-the-mean adjustment in your portfolio net exposure?

After determining the portfolio net exposure, we do a similar analysis by sector, trying to identify sectors that are cheap and sectors that are expensive.

I assume that you favor longs in sectors that are cheap and shorts in sectors that are expensive. Are there exceptions?

All the time. The relative valuations are only a guideline. It is critical to also examine the specific fundamentals. For example, Brazil may show up as being expensive, but the fundamentals are very good, so I don't want to be short.

The next part of our analysis is figuring out why a sector or stock is expensive or cheap, and do we see something that is going to change that? That is where we spend 90 percent of our time. I look for anomalies. When I screen quarterly earnings, I look for quarterly earnings that are up more than 50 percent or down more than 30 percent. For example, recently, the earnings for Rock Tenn, a paper company, were up huge. So I tried to figure out why.

What was the reason?

The paper stocks had been cheap for four or five years. I had been looking for a reason to buy them, but it is not a great business, and I couldn't come up with one. But over time, there were two things that had happened. First, no one had built any capacity for years because the business was so bad. Second, there was consolidation. As a result of these factors, there was an inflection point; the pricing power had shifted in favor of the suppliers. It is easier to turn down business when capacity is running at over 90 percent than when it is running at 60 percent. I didn't necessarily want to own paper companies long term, but I wanted to own them then. That is why we bought Rock Tenn.

What happened with that position?

We still hold it, although we have traded around the position. It is up over 50 percent from where we originally bought it.

With the security guard coming in with increasing frequency and Claugus tired after a long day, we decided we would continue our interview the next day. I met Claugus the following day at the conference during lunch break. Against my better judgment and prior experience, I agreed to continue our conversation over lunch in the hotel restaurant, which grew steadily noisier as the interview progressed. Deciphering the resulting taped conversation through the background din was a job worthy of the FBI. After repeated listenings with the sound turned up to uncomfortably loud levels, I was able to make out most of our conversation. It is the absolute last time I ever do an interview over a meal.

I checked your net exposures and was surprised to see that you were only modestly short near the end of the tech bubble. Wouldn't your long-term valuation model have indicated a more decisive net short position at that juncture? Surely, the market must have been near the upper part of the valuation range at that point.

We were supposed to be more heavily net short. Our target exposure for the fourth quarter of 1999 was 70 percent net short. However, we were losing money so fast that we had to back off our position. Every day, I would come in and we would be down another 1 percent. It got to the point where I said, "I may be right, but I have to shrink the portfolio." What I did was that for every 1 percent the portfolio lost, I reduced the exposure by 2 percent. As a result, instead of being 70 percent short, we went into the fourth quarter of 1999 at 70 percent short and 50 percent long, or only 20 percent net short.

I thought I might replace some of the shorts once the market broke, but I didn't have the guts. I have people tell me all the time that I should short stocks after they break. All I can tell you is that if you didn't short the stock when it was 80, psychologically, it is very difficult to sell it when it's 50.

Do you have specific risk management rules?

For many people, risk control means that they have a plan for what they will do if something goes very wrong. I try to avoid getting into that situation in the first place. Our defining moment of a survival threat is being down more than 7 percent in a month and not knowing why. If you look at the history of our fund, you will find that 90 percent of the monthly returns were between +7 percent and −7 percent. So as long as a monthly loss is less than 7 percent, we are still in a normal range. If a loss exceeds 7 percent, it indicates that something is wrong. If I can figure out what is wrong, then I might not change anything. If I can't figure out what is wrong, then I have to reduce the exposure.

So once you are down 7 percent for the month, you just play defense?

No, not necessarily. We were down big in September 2008. I started taking off exposure, but I was selling stock at what I considered ridiculous prices. It just felt wrong. So I stopped. Losing money on the long side is different from losing it on the short side.

Because on the long side there is a limit to how low prices can go, but on the short side, the risk is open-ended?

It's not only that. It's also different from the client's perspective. During the fourth quarter of 1999, when the market was skyrocketing and I was net short, I was losing my ass at the same time most other hedge funds were making a ton of money. When your investors look around, and you're losing money, while everyone else is making money, they are much more likely to pull their investment. Being short in a rising market is very difficult from an investor relations standpoint. In 2008, we were losing money, but so was everyone else. It's a lot easier to keep your capital base in that type of scenario.

It sounds like your risk management process is very discretionary. It depends on your trusting yourself to act when losses are beginning to get more extreme than usual.

Yes, it is very hard. We spend a lot of effort to avoid getting into that type of situation in the first place. You want to design a portfolio that will survive a 150-foot tidal wave. The number one risk factor for me is leverage. At the extreme levels, our net exposure is usually less than the net exposure of a typical mutual fund. One of the reasons I didn't take more exposure off in 2008 was that I was only about 75 percent net long. Virtually every mutual fund on the planet is close to 100 percent long. So what is the big deal?

With the benefit of hindsight, do you believe you made any mistakes in 1999?

I did make one change to the process because of the 1999 experience. I previously used a 90 percent confidence interval to define the extremes at which I would go to a maximum net long or short position in the portfolio. As a result of the 1999 experience, I widened the band to 95 percent. Part of the judgment factor is how much risk you want to take at the extremes because the market can keep going. The problem I had in 1999 was that I went to a maximum short position too early.

But in terms of stock selection, I don't think we did anything wrong. At the start of 2000, I was trying to figure out what went wrong in 1999. I have what I call my Evel Knievel screen. These are companies that are trying to jump the Grand Canyon and probably won't make it. There are only two conditions for the screen. First, the company is trading at more than five times book value. Second, the company is losing money. My job is to figure out which stocks won't make it across the Grand Canyon and then go short those stocks.

At the time, the Internet business model was to get share on the net. It didn't make a difference how much money you lost doing it, as long as you increased your share. In fact, if you lost a lot of money, it meant you were being aggressive. Normally, when I do my Evel Knievel screen, I get maybe 60 or so companies. At the end of 1999, I had 180 names. And out of these 180 names, about two-thirds of them had doubled in price during the prior quarter. I thought to myself, *There is nothing you can do; these are the best shorts on the planet.* I ultimately concluded that I would go short those types of stocks again because 99 times out of a 100, I am going to make money. So it would be wrong for me to change my approach because of the 1999 experience.

So you concluded that you didn't really do anything wrong.

That's right. Just because you made money doesn't mean you were right, and just because you lost money doesn't mean you were wrong. It is all a matter of probabilities. If you take a bet that has an 80 percent probability of winning, and you lose, it doesn't mean it was a wrong choice.

I totally agree. A big mistake investors make is that they judge whether a decision was right based solely on the outcome. There is a lot of randomness in the outcome. The same set of conditions can lead to different outcomes. If you played 2008 all over again, the same set of initial conditions would sometimes lead to the market bottoming sooner and sometimes lead to a depression. My take on it is that whether a trading decision was right or wrong is not a matter of whether you won or lost, but rather whether you would make the same decision all over again if faced with the same facts (assuming you have a profitable process).

2008 was the first time you had a significant loss at the same time the equity markets and other hedge fund managers were down sharply. What was different in 2008?

It all goes back to our net exposure indicator. If the current indicator value is in the lower quartile—that is, price valuations are low—we will be significantly long. If the market then drops sharply, we will lose money just like everyone else. If, however, the market breaks sharply when the indicator is in the upper quartile, then we will significantly outperform.

I noticed that you were net short for most of the bull market of the late 1990s, and yet you did very well. How did you manage to achieve strong returns being net short in a sharply rising market?

Stock picking. When the market sells off really hard, as happened in late 2008 to early 2009, it is usually a matter of liquidity. There's no place to hide in a liquidity sell-off; people sell everything because they have to, not because they want to. The reverse rarely happens on the upside. People don't run out and buy everything. There are always some stocks that are going down. The interesting thing is that shorts are actually easier to find than longs. It is easier to spot a broken company than a good company. It is easier to identify bad management than good management.

In September 2011, about nine months after I had interviewed Claugus, I called him with additional questions.

You are currently 85 percent net long. That seems to be a relatively high long exposure given the current concerns about the U.S. economy and the stability of the European Union. What makes you so bullish?

The net exposure is primarily determined by the mean reversion model, but I don't think the economy is as bad as the media is portraying it. We track a number of basic indicators to get a feel for the real economy. For example, rail traffic is up 2 percent for the year, and truck traffic is up 4 percent, which are not figures indicative of a contraction. Load factors on airlines are pretty good as well. RevPAR [revenue per available room] for hotels is up 7 percent. These are basic indicators you can look at that tell you the economy is just not that bad. Although we still have to work through some of the housing bubble excess, I don't expect construction and housing starts to fall much from here because they are already so low they have almost nowhere to go but up.

That's the most optimistic assessment I've heard about the U.S. economy from anyone.

I wouldn't say I am optimistic. If you look at the current numbers, I think it is very difficult to argue that the U.S. economy is in trouble. But if you look at the budget and trade deficits and government spending, the situation is out of control. We clearly need to rein in government spending, and when that happens, it is likely to slow the economy. It is like a household that has been living off their credit cards and has to start paying back their debts.

So even though the current economy may be okay, if we have this contraction looming, doesn't that act as a counterbalance to your bullish argument?

Exactly, and that is why I brought it up. Here I am fairly long stocks, and if I look over my shoulder, I see this huge storm cloud, and I don't know when it is going to hit. It could be in six months; it could be in six years. In Europe, the markets are already disciplining the governments. Eventually, the same thing will happen in the U.S. if we don't take actions beforehand. And, so far, the politicians have shown no ability to either cut costs or raise revenues in anticipation of the growing debt problem. Politicians only respond to a crisis when they have someone to blame—either the market, or the bankers, or anybody but themselves—and then they will act. The Western world has a huge debt problem and is managing it very poorly.

So where does that leave you? On the one hand, you have all these indicators that tell you the economy is better than most people think it is, while on the other hand, you have this storm cloud that when it hits will presumably take the market down sharply, at least initially.

We are trying to focus on industries and companies that will do okay, regardless of the economy, and on international economies that we expect will continue to do well.

**What kind of companies would be more immune to a contrac-
tion in the economy?**

Companies that offer solutions to problems. One example is Celanese.
They are working on a process to produce ethanol from natural gas at
much lower costs. If they can take cheap natural gas and turn it into
ethanol and undercut the current price of ethanol, and possibly even
gasoline, they would be able to capture a share of the huge fuel market,
regardless of what the economy is doing.

**Which countries are you focusing on that you believe have the
best long-term prospects?**

China is one, but with the caveat that centrally run economies generally
don't do well. We like Indonesia. Fifteen years ago, they were a basket
case, but now, they have a sound budget, exports are growing, and the
economy has been doing well for several years. We also like Brazil,
Singapore, and Colombia.

Colombia? That is not one I would have expected on the list.

Ten years ago, you couldn't drill a well in Colombia because you would
get shot. The FARC was all over the place. Now the government will
actually base military personnel at drilling operations. The Putumayo
Basin is largely unexplored because people couldn't get in there before
the last four or five years. In the past three years, Colombia's oil production has shot up from 600,000 barrels per day to 950,000 barrels per
day, and I think it will continue to grow rapidly. The same thing is true
for other industries as well, such as agriculture. The changed security
situation in Colombia is sparking a complete rebirth of the Colombian
economy.

**What percent of your portfolio is in emerging markets versus
developed countries?**

Right now, it's at about 30 percent and growing, which is as high as it
has ever been.

How do you pick stocks? Can you provide an example that illustrates your thinking process?

I can use one of our current largest positions, which is United Airlines, as an example. The conventional wisdom is that airlines are a terrible investment and that you never want to own them. In fact, Warren Buffett says that he has a full-time employee whose only job is to keep him from ever buying another airline again.

My son has a similar line. He asks, "How do you become a millionaire?" Answer: "Start with a billion and buy an airline."

There are many reasons why airlines are widely considered to be poor investments. They are capital intensive; they are people intensive; they are difficult to manage; they have to rely on an inefficient government air traffic control system; and if, despite all of that, they ever manage to make money, the unions start asking for more wages, so they don't make money then, either.

That's a persuasive "bullish" argument. So why is United Airlines one of your largest long positions?

It is a controversial call, but that is how you make money when you are right. My view is that the lack of profitability in airlines has its origins back in the days when airlines were regulated. Regulation fostered the proliferation of airlines because prices were protected, and it also resulted in very high cost structures. When the airlines were deregulated, the legacy carriers, who had very high cost structures, had to compete with newcomers, such as Southwest Airlines, who had a much lower cost structure because they had not been exposed to years and years of a pricing umbrella, which encouraged inefficiency.

Two things happened that changed the investment outlook for airlines. First, with the exception of American Airlines, all the major carriers went through bankruptcy, which allowed them to restructure their costs. Second, the industry has been able to merge down to three major players: United, Delta, and American. Among the three, I think that United has the best route structure. United, along with its partners, controls approximately 50 percent of the flights from the U.S. to Asia and 40 percent of the flights to Europe. I believe that going forward, United can get their operating margin up to about 10 percent, which isn't that great, but it is fabulous for an airline. It would give United $6 per share earning power. At the current price of $20, earnings at that level would imply a P/E ratio of only 3.3. I am not willing to put a large multiple on United, but even a multiple of only 8 to 10 would imply that I have a chance of doubling to tripling my money in the stock.

Can you give me another trade example that illustrates how you pick stocks?

One thing I try to do is find oil companies whose price reflects only current production without accounting for ongoing exploration programs that have the potential to significantly increase future production. It is a way of essentially getting free optionality. For example, we are long Petrominerales, a Colombian oil and gas company that currently produces about 40,000 barrels per day. The optionality in the trade is that Petrominerales has 600,000 acres leased in the same region as their current producing wells, and they have a number of rigs drilling new wells there, but the market is not pricing in any of this potential additional production. The best time to enter this type of trade is after a disappointment. Petrominerales also has assets in Peru, and recently, one of its competitors drilled a dry hole in Peru, which caused all the oil companies in the region to sell off sharply. We used this price break as an opportunity to buy the stock.

Another good example of this trade concept is Canadian Natural Resources. We took a large position in this stock when they announced a new oil sands project, which had the potential to generate $1 billion a year in cash flow. Even though it was obvious and clear that this production would be coming on stream, the market didn't assign any value to it. What tends to happen is that people who use fundamental screens, such as price to cash flow and other metrics, will not pick these stocks because the potential future revenue does not show up in the statistics.

Does the type of trade idea illustrated by this example apply only to oil producers or does it have broader applicability?

The broader idea is getting optionality from a business opportunity that is not producing current revenues, but has the potential to produce future revenues—a concept that would apply to other industries as well. For example, in recent years, Apple was frequently priced at the value of their existing products without pricing in the potential for future revenues on new products, despite their consistent record of innovation.

Sometimes the future opportunity may relate to asset values rather than increased cash flow. For example, one of our holdings is a company called Paramount Resources, which acquires land that has the potential for oil or gas exploration. They will identify interesting geological situations, lease the land, and just wait. They will sell the land once the area becomes discovered by oil companies who start drilling exploratory wells in the vicinity. If you looked at Paramount's numbers, you would never buy the stock; it always looks expensive because they are capturing the resource, but are not developing it themselves. So its true value never shows up in the numbers. You have to be willing to look at their acreage and figure out what it's really worth from an asset basis rather than a cash flow basis.

Any other examples of companies with free optionality?

Celanese, which I mentioned before, is currently trading at only 10 or 11 times earnings, and they have a new process for making ethanol that could be a complete game changer for them. I don't think the market is attaching much, if any, value to this process because it hasn't gone into production. The first plant is scheduled to come on stream at the end of next year. I often find that the market won't pay anything for production potential that is more than a year away.

As another example, we had a substantial long position in emerging market wireless during the past five years. Some developed countries have cell phone penetration rates greater than 100 percent (some people have more than one cell phone). The simple idea that drove this investment was the expectation that the emerging market penetration rate, which at the time was about 60 percent for the sector, would approach closer to developed market rates because the utility of cell phones was so high.

The general principle is that we look for future revenue generation that can be reasonably anticipated but that is not reflected by the current market price. This idea is probably the single most important concept in our stock selection process.

■ ■ ■

There is an important lesson provided by Claugus that is both specific to
the stock market and also has general implications for all investors: Vary
exposure based on opportunity. In terms of stock investing, Claugus will
vary his net exposure between theoretical extremes at 70 percent net
short and 110 percent net long, depending on the placement of current
prices within the price band that contains 95 percent of all price
observations. When stock prices are near the low end of the long-term
price band, Claugus will hold a maximum long position. Conversely,
when prices are near the upper end of the band, he will hold a maximum short position. Varying the net exposure based on the prevailing
opportunity provides for substantial improvement over an investment
approach that maintains net exposure within a narrow range.

One of Claugus's major themes in selecting individual stocks is
looking for companies that will benefit from a future development that
is not being priced into the current market. The source of the
improvement can take many forms including anticipated new sources of
production, new technology, an expected increase in asset values, and
so on. Claugus says that if a revenue source is more than a year away,
the market will often fail to assign any significant value to it. Claugus
views these trades as providing free optionality—you pay a fair value for
the stock based on the prevailing statistic only, but get the upside of the
anticipated favorable development (e.g., new source of production) for
free. Fundamental screens will fail to identify these stocks because the
source of the bullish potential is not at all reflected in current statistics.

A common error that traders make is to judge whether a trading
decision was right—or wrong—based on the outcome. If I offer you 2:1
odds on a fair coin toss, and you take the bet and lose, it may be a losing
bet, but it is still a correct bet because, on balance, making the same
decision repeatedly will be very profitable. Similarly, a losing trade can
still reflect a correct trading decision. Claugus lost money in shorting
what he terms "Evel Knievel" stocks in late 1999. But these trades were
not mistakes because Claugus has found that shorting these companies is
a winning strategy. There is no way of knowing a priori which individual trade is likely to be a winner. Traders need to accept that a certain
percentage of good trades will lose money. As long as a profitable

strategy is implemented according to plan, a trade loss does not imply a trading mistake.

On the flip side, a winning trade can still be a poor trading decision. For example, if someone went long Internet stocks at the beginning of January 2000 and liquidated at the end of February 2000, in terms of outcome, it would be a brilliant trade. But it would be a horrible trade in terms of making the same trading decision over and over again under similar circumstances. The market happened to top in early March, but it could just as easily have topped in early January. Even though the specific trade would have been profitable, if the same trading decision were made over and over again under similar circumstances, the net outcome would often be a large loss.

Trading is a matter of probabilities. Any trading strategy, no matter how effective, will be wrong a certain percentage of the time. Traders often confuse the concepts of winning and losing traders with good and bad trades. A good trade can lose money, and a bad trade can make money. A good trade follows a process that will be profitable (at an acceptable risk) if repeated multiple times, although it can lose money on any individual trade. A bad trade follows a process that will lose money if repeated multiple times, but may make money on any individual trade. As an analogous example, a winning slot machine wager is still a bad bet because if repeated multiple times, it has a high probability of losing money.

Chapter 12

Joe Vidich

Harvesting Losses

Typically, the managers I select for interviews are managers that I either know or locate through networking. Joe Vidich is one of the exceptions. I found him by searching a hedge fund database, looking for funds with exceptionally high return/risk performance. The Manalapan fund, which was launched in May 2001 and managed by Joe Vidich, stood out for its impressive performance statistics. I had never heard of either the fund or the manager.

For the 10-plus years since the fund's inception, Vidich has averaged an annualized compounded net return of 18 percent (24 percent gross return) with a maximum drawdown of only 8 percent. This modest maximum drawdown is exceptional for an equity hedge fund during 2001 to 2011, a time period that included two massive bear markets. Vidich has tremendously outperformed his sector. During the corresponding time period, the HFR Equity Hedge index was up only 4 percent annualized with a maximum drawdown of nearly

29 percent—less than one-quarter of Manalapan's return with nearly four times the drawdown. And the index understates the average maximum drawdown because of the smoothing effect of diversification. Reflecting the combination of strong returns and moderate losses, the Gain to Pain ratio of the Manalapan fund is a very high 2.4. (See Appendix A for an explanation of the Gain to Pain ratio.)

I originally met with Nick Davidge, the managing director who runs the business operations for Manalapan. At the time, I was living in Martha's Vineyard, and, conveniently, Davidge was visiting Cape Cod. I took the ferry over and joined him for a waterside lunch on a pleasant summer day. Davidge explained how he became a principal of Manalapan. Davidge was the founder of a company that provided order routing software to market makers, and Joe Vidich was one of his clients. Davidge recalled, "What struck me about Joe when I first met him was that he was an intellectual who was also a trader." Through this association, Davidge became aware of Vidich's trading skills, particularly the effective way Vidich combined his longer-term investment themes with his reading of market sentiment in individual names. When Vidich launched his fund years later, Davidge was one of the first investors. After Davidge sold his company, he joined Vidich as a partner in Manalapan.

Vidich combines longer-term investments with short-term trading that provides supplemental returns. For the investment portion of the portfolio, Vidich begins by formulating a big picture of the economy and the stock market. Next, Vidich looks for themes that drive him to sectors and subsectors. As a final step, Vidich does fundamental analysis and observes trading activity to select the best individual stocks within the targeted sectors. Vidich's timing in entering and exiting these positions is heavily influenced by what he calls his assessment of senti-ment—price action relative to events. Vidich or his analysts listen to about 300 conference calls every quarter. The market action following these conference calls can provide Vidich with important clues. For example, if a company reports generally bullish news in its conference call, and the next day the market is up, but the stock is down, Vidich would view this price action as a bearish indicator.

Before starting his fund, Vidich spent a dozen years as a market maker and proprietary trader for various small brokerage firms. Vidich explains that since the order flow from retail investors is heavily long biased, the market maker is by definition a short trader. For every buy order a market maker fills, he has to trade out of the resulting short position. Vidich feels that because of his many years of experience as a market maker, his trading skills are most finely developed on the short side. Even though long-term investment themes and position trades are core to Vidich's investment approach, he is an extremely active trader. The turnover for the fund is approximately 20X of which about 15X is on the short side. Vidich's net exposure varies widely, and has ranged between 80 percent net long to 37 percent net short.

Vidich's firm, Manalapan Oracle Capital Management, is located in a small town in central New Jersey. Vidich is an amateur artist, and Manalapan's offices can double as an art gallery, as his paintings adorn every wall. His style ranges between postimpressionism and abstract, with some paintings having one foot in each camp. Vidich says he is not technically proficient—and indeed his paintings that include animal figures have a primitive style—but he has a strong sense of color. There are clear influences of Gauguin and Van Gogh in his work. (Interested readers can view a selection of his paintings at www.easthurley.com.) Vidich says that he began painting many years ago as a way to relax. The more stress in his life, the more he paints. He was particularly prolific the year he divorced.

Vidich seems to enjoy whatever he is doing, whether it is trading or being interviewed. He has a loud, booming laugh, which was triggered often in our interview, as he was clearly amused by his recollections.

■ ■ ■

[Vidich opened our conversation by asking why I had selected him for an interview.]

Why you? That's relatively easy. In terms of return/risk, in the 10 years you have been running this fund, you have generated better numbers than 99 percent of the managers out there, and that is exactly what I'm looking for. How did you first get involved in stocks?

I got into the stock market because my brother's friend who was a stockbroker was going to India to see his guru and needed someone to sit at his desk for a month to simply answer the phone. I had just graduated college and wasn't doing anything yet, so I said I would do it.

What did you do when there was a phone call from a client who wanted to place an order?

I gave it to the guy next to me. I wasn't registered, so I couldn't do anything. I eventually did get registered as a stockbroker with the same firm.

What degree did you graduate with?

I had a master's of international business from the Columbia School of International Affairs. Almost all the people I graduated with went to work for international banks, who were hiring big at the time, or the foreign service. I had no interest in working for a corporation.

Did you actually look for a job after you received your master's?

My kids say, "Dad, you never even tried looking for a job." And, in a sense, they are right. I did go for a number of interviews with banks after I graduated, but I just felt I wasn't the right person to get into that environment. There was something holding me back from being interested.

What appealed to you about being a stockbroker?

It was the high energy.

Had you learned anything by the time you became registered as a stockbroker?

I had a friend who had been trading stocks since he was a kid. After I became a stockbroker, he told me, "Joe, you don't know anything." But I had a lot of enthusiasm. He was right, though, I didn't know anything. I was probably dangerous to my customers. I was literally following the firm's research, but if you work for a firm that has bad ideas, you don't have a chance.

When did you begin trading?

I am not a cold caller. It's not in me to call someone up and try to solicit business. I am not a salesman. Never have been; never will be. I'm, actually, the exact opposite. I never made much in commissions, but then my three best accounts all disappeared for different reasons. An old-time trader I knew advised me that I should ask my boss permission to trade my own account. I took his advice and went to my boss and said, "Can I set up my own trading account because I really don't have any other income?" [He laughs harder and louder than usual at this recollection.] He offered me a deal to set up my own account with the authority to carry up to $30,000 in positions overnight, providing I put up $2,000 of my own money. I would be allowed to keep any profits, and the firm would keep all the commissions. That sounded like a good deal to me. I did okay, averaging about $4,000 a month.

Any trades stand out from that time period?

One of the brokers in the office kept touting this stock ERLY industries. So I finally bought some. When I bought the stock, it was 7½ bid, 7¾ offered. I didn't realize that the stock frequently traded at a one dollar spread [another hearty laugh]. So right after I bought it at 7¾, all of a sudden it was 6¾ bid. I only had $2,000 in the account, and I had bought 2,000 shares. That meant if I tried getting out of the stock, my equity would be wiped out. I was stuck in that stock for about two weeks. Finally, the bid came back to 7½, and I took my loss immediately. I didn't care. It was such a thin stock that I was just happy to get out.

In those early days, what did you learn about trading that was useful?

I learned that it is always better to do your own work and get your own information because then you will have more confidence. If you listen to someone else to get into a trade and things go bad, then you have to listen to that person again to get you out. I have a real antipathy toward outside research analysts calling us with trading ideas because if you follow their advice to get into a trade, then you have to wait for their advice to get out, and things can change. The price could be down 10 percent or 15 percent before they call you again.

What else did you learn?

I learned that low-priced stocks can be terrible or great. You have to look at the valuation of the company. Chrysler was a penny stock. Global Marine traded for one dollar, and went to $90. A few years ago, some of the best companies in America traded down to a few dollars. Dow Chemical traded for $5. Now it is back to $38. Why did it trade down to $5? Because everyone was afraid. People seeing their money disappear started redeeming their mutual fund and hedge fund investments. Faced with liquidations, mutual fund and hedge fund managers had no choice but to liquidate, regardless of the price. The downmove became a self-fulfilling trend until something changed. When that change occurred, there was tremendous upside in the various names. There are times when fear dominates. Those are the times you have to be a buyer. Those are the times of great opportunity.

Anything else?

I learned the danger in selling expensive stocks just because they are overpriced and buying value stocks just because they are underpriced. Pricey stocks are always 30 percent pricier than they should be because people are willing to own them at 30 percent above what they should own them at. A good growth stock is always overvalued, and a lousy company is always undervalued. That is the danger of buying value stocks. Until you get the turn where the market recognizes an improvement in the business model, they are always going to be undervalued. If you are going to short a growth stock because it is 30 percent overvalued, it is going to grow for the next five years always being 30 percent overvalued—until it finally breaks, and by that time, you are probably not going to be there.

Why do you believe you have done so well?

One reason that I have done well is the evolution of information flow in the marketplace. When the SEC adopted fair disclosure in 2000, it meant that company conference calls had to be open to everyone. Information could no longer be controlled by the large brokerage firms who then funneled it out to the public. I am not an expert on everything. When you listen to a conference call, you hear what the analysts' questions are, and the analysts generally know a lot more about the company than I do. When analysts key in on certain things, it tells you what they think is important.

Can you give me examples of conference calls you listened to that directly led to trades?

We shorted Citigroup at $48 in 2008 before it crashed. Why did we go short? The earnings report had come out for Citigroup, and the stock was down $2. That was a really big move for Citigroup. So I decided to listen to the conference call. I understood banks in terms of their basic business, but I didn't understand anything that was said about CDOs or anything else to do with mortgage-backed securitizations. But the key thing I realized from the call was that not a single analyst understood it, either. You could tell from their questions that they didn't know what was going on, and confusion is opportunity. So I went short the stock.

Any other examples?

A number of years ago when we were long a lot of coal stocks, one of the coal company conference calls mentioned that they had to place large orders for coal cars because they just didn't have enough cars to meet all the demand. I immediately checked a number of companies that manufactured coal cars and noticed they were all generally flatlining in price. We knew at least one large coal company was going to be a major buyer, but this fact was not reflected at all in the price. So we went long Trinity Industries, which was one of the manufacturers of coal cars. If Trinity had been up dramatically, then maybe the impending increase in the demand for coal cars would already have been priced in, but you could tell from the flat price action that it was not priced in.

As another example, in 2007 and 2008, I listened to a number of conference calls with coal, oil, and natural gas companies in which they indicated that they would be deferring their capital expenditures. What do you do then? You go out and look for companies that are in the capital equipment space selling to those industries because you know their orders are going to slow down. There is a definite opportunity to short those names.

In sharp contrast to most long/short funds who experienced significant losses in 2008, you had a very good year. How did you achieve those results?

We were short mortgage lenders and a lot of the bank stocks. I listened to the Countrywide conference calls every quarter. I remember Mozilla, the CEO, saying that because Wall Street was getting into the business in a major way, the spreads were being cut more and more, and therefore they had to take greater and greater risks. At the same time, default rates had begun to rise. It was clear that the housing bubble couldn't be sustained and that companies like Countrywide and Washington Mutual were good shorts. I didn't know they would go down as much as they did, but I knew there was no way they would be going higher. I didn't necessarily understand the intricacies of the mortgage securitizations, but I realized that the banks were heavily leveraged in this product. On top of that, when politicians are making statements that certain banks deserve to fail, why would anyone want to own bank stocks? I had seen it all before. I had seen a number of big banks go to zero during the S&L crisis. I had seen insiders at these banks buying on the way down. Even they were caught by the greater trend, which they didn't see.

Besides being short banks and mortgage lenders, what other trades accounted for your 2008 gains?

Energy stocks were a major winner for us in 2008. During the first half of the year, we made money on the long side. Then prices started going way beyond what we thought was reasonable, so we scaled out of our position. When prices went up even more, we started going net short. When energy stock prices broke after the reversal in crude oil, we switched back to the long side around the time when crude had fallen back to the $90 level, which it turned out was way too early. But then we realized that things were getting worse and worse, so we took our losses on the longs, went back short, and played the trend down.

Also, we had a lot of days when the market opened up sharply higher and closed sharply lower. One thing that I learned as a trader is that if the market [Dow] moves up 400 points in the morning, you usually don't go much further. Every time there was a big rally, we would put our shorts on, and on a selloff, we would cover the shorts.

[Nick Davidge who has been sitting in for the interview interjects.] I annualized our turnover for the second half of 2008, and it was 23X of which 21X was in trades initiated as shorts.

When did you transition from a net bearish bias in late 2008 back to a bullish bias?

We went long after Obama was elected. There was tremendous disenchantment with the Bush administration at that point. They had lost confidence across the board, including a lot of the business community. Obama was talking about policies to get the economy going. He was going to spend money. He was going to save the states, which were going down big-time. No matter what you think of the policies, they were throwing money back into the system, which was bullish. In early 2009, we started looking around for the best business models and balance sheets we could buy. We were looking for stocks with the lowest financial risk—companies that did not need to refinance debt and could ride out a prolonged, deep recession. We went long a bunch of the no-debt retailers who had lots of cash and had gotten crushed—stocks like Gap, which was an $11 stock with $5 in cash and over $1 in earnings. We bought Shaw, which had $12 in cash and had fallen all the way to $18.

Are there mistakes you learned from as a trader?

As an equity trader, I learned the short-selling lessons relatively early. There is no high for a concept stock. It is always better to be long before they have already moved a lot than to try to figure out where to go short.

What are examples of concept stocks?

The Internet stocks in the 1990s and biotech stocks in the late 1990s to early 2000s.

How about a current example?

The cloud computing companies. When P/E multiples get to 50, 60, or 70, you are in the realm of concept stocks.

I understand that you do both position trading and short-term trading. Is there something about the way prices move intraday that is helpful in short-term trading?

Yes. Do you know what happens in a bull market? Prices open up lower and then go up for the rest of the day. In a bear market, they open up higher and go down for the rest of the day. When you get to the end of a bull market, prices start opening up higher. Prices behave that way because in the first half hour it is only the fools that are trading [pause] or people who are very smart.

Sounds like a dangerous combination. Why is there a tendency to open counter to the prevailing trend?

When the market closes near the high of the move, there will be some traders who want to sell near the high, and they will be sellers on the next day's opening.

Are there any other useful short-term patterns?

If there is bearish news before the opening and the market does not trade down much during the first hour, it indicates that the smart money is not selling and that the dip is a buying opportunity.

Do you use sentiment indicators in your trading?

CNBC is my sentiment indicator. [He laughs loudly.] It's the best sentiment indicator, and it's free.

How do you judge sentiment?

I judge it based on how the stock moves. If everyone is bearish because that's what CNBC says, that is public sentiment, but if the stock gaps higher after a conference call, that's the market sentiment. What matters is the market sentiment, not public sentiment. I try to drown out public sentiment, except if public sentiment is so heavily one-sided...

How do you judge that?

You watch CNBC.

What is your opinion on stop orders?

They are for fools.

Do you want to expound?

If you want to ensure that you get the low of the day, use a stop. People tend to place their stops near the same price level—usually at a new recent low. If the low for a stock during the past year has been 30, there will be a lot of stops placed just below 30. If the market trades down to 30, the stops will be hit, and since there will usually be a lack of buy orders at the new lows, prices will gap lower. If we like a stock, we will sometimes try to place our buy orders one-half point below where we believe the stops are.

If you have a stop order in the market, it means that one price will dictate the outcome. That is a bad concept. You can, however, use mental stops, which are essentially evaluation points. If the stock is down, say, 15 percent, you should evaluate why it is down 15 percent, but you shouldn't automatically sell it there. Stop orders may be okay for some public investors, but not for professionals. Stop orders are an outrageously poor way to manage risk.

What is the right way to manage risk?

The right way to manage risk is to monitor your positions and to have a mental point at which you reevaluate the position. The amount of room you would allow till that point would be different for different stocks. Every stock has its own risk profile. Some stocks could go down 50 percent, and it wouldn't necessarily mean anything. But for a stock like Coca-Cola, you should be reevaluating if it moves 5 percent against you.

Don't ever consider yourself right. The hardest thing is to sell on the way down. It's emotionally difficult because you believe you're right or that you will eventually be right. The best way I have found to do it is to begin by selling 20 percent of the position. That doesn't hurt, and if the stock comes back, I can still say I was right. If the stock goes lower, I can also say I was right because at least I sold 20 percent of the stock higher.

Is that what you typically do—scale out of a position?

Yes, I scale out, and I also scale in. The idea is don't try to be 100 percent right.

So the message is if you can't take the loss, take a little bit of a loss.

That way you will never be completely wrong, and you can reassess the situation if the market goes lower. It is all about keeping the portfolio from weighing you down. Sometimes, though, it is best to just liquidate the entire position. It's a good idea to harvest your losses because it forces you to revisit the trade. If you are in the trade, you are always defending it. Liquidating forces you to reevaluate the trade relative to other opportunities. You sold the position. Do you really want to buy it back? Or would you rather put the money in this other idea, which looks a lot better right now?

[Vidich has to take a break from the interview to check on the markets. I take the opportunity to speak to Davidge, who has been sitting in on the interview and probably understands Vidich's approach better than anyone else. Davidge begins by giving his own take of Vidich's methodology.]

One of the key characteristics of Joe's trading is his willingness and ability to gradually take losses. Joe's comments about the emotional benefits of taking losses incrementally can give you an insight into how he manages portfolio exposure.

One point of our conversation that I was particularly confused about was Joe's comments about sentiment.

There are two types of sentiment. There is the popular sentiment, as it might be expressed in the media, and then there is the sentiment that is expressed by the market. When Joe talks about sentiment, he is referring to how the market responds to external events. What is the news? What is the price action? That is what generates his view of the markets. A stock being down after a good earnings report would be an example of negative sentiment. That is how Joe thinks about sentiment.

I was confused because most people use the word sentiment to refer to some measure of how bullish or bearish the public is. In the popular usage, bullish sentiment is bearish, whereas the way Joe uses the term, bullish sentiment—a more positive response to market news than expected—is bullish.

The use of sentiment as a contrary indicator reminds me of a funny story. In 1999, a longtime friend of mine visited me in my New York office. He is a brilliant guy. He went to Harvard, got a PhD at Penn, and ended up doing work on semantics, artificial intelligence, and computer language.

I asked him, "So, Bill, what are you doing with your investments these days?"

He answered, "I am 100 percent in tech stocks."

I said, "Wow, do you really think that is a prudent place to be?"

"Well," he said, "I have a lot of expenses, and I need the extra return."

I thought to myself, *If that is the way other people are thinking and acting, we are really in trouble. This is all going to end very badly.* That friend, as brilliant as he is, has always been wrong about stocks, and I've used him as a contrary indicator.

[Vidich returns after about 20 minutes, and we continue the interview.]

What are examples of market response reflecting positive or negative sentiment?

Just recently, Rockwell Automation (ROK) raised guidance for the year, and the stock is down $9. What does that tell you? It tells you even though earnings are currently increasing, smart investors—there are a lot smarter guys out there than I am—are anticipating a major inflection point in earnings in the next few months.

Nick had mentioned that you had another portfolio manager working for you last year. I wonder what that experience taught you.

It taught me that I didn't need him [another hearty laugh]. Everyone has a different perspective. The person we hired to be a portfolio assistant had an investment style that was completely different from mine. He approached stocks from a business school perspective, looking for the best business models and best companies. That is okay, but he didn't have the courage to average down into a position. Also, the stocks that he followed were not the stocks that I followed. As the head portfolio manager, I am also the risk manager and have to follow all the positions. He was hired to help me save time, but I was spending more time following his positions, which interfered with following my own positions. Training someone to think like I do about the markets, which is more like a stream of consciousness, is very difficult. It is totally different from the way they learn to think in business school.

What are the trading rules you live by?

It is really important to manage your emotional attachment to losses and gains. You want to limit your size in any position so that fear does not become the prevailing instinct guiding your judgment. Everyone will have a different level. It also depends on what kind of stock it is. A 10 percent position might be perfectly okay for a large-cap stock, while a 3 percent position in a highflying mid-cap stock, which has frequent 30 percent swings, might be far too risky.

Why do most people fail at trading?

To be successful in the markets, you have to be willing to change your opinion. Most people are not willing to change their opinion. You have to be humble about your ideas.

What other mistakes do people make in trading?

Most people are more afraid of making money than losing money.

What do you mean by that?

There is no real reason to sell a stock just because it's up 20 percent.

I would argue that when people sell a stock when it's up 20 percent, it's not because they are afraid of making money, but because they are afraid of losing what they made.

Maybe you are right. They're afraid of losing money. But they are only afraid of losing gains. If the stock is down 20 percent, they are not going to sell it. What they are really afraid of is not being right. That is why they won't sell it when it's down 20 percent—because that would confirm they were wrong.

Recently, my analyst in Texas, who is very good, called me about one of our positions that was up. He said, "We should probably sell some."

"And why?" I asked him.

"Because we should probably lock some profits in."

"And why?" I asked again.

He didn't have a good reason. He wanted to sell to justify his idea and lock in gains on his recommendation. But that is his own world. It has nothing to do with where the stock is going.

We had another position that was initially profitable, but then sold off when all the analysts downgraded the stock three days before the earnings report. I thought they must all know something negative and that we should be selling the stock. My analyst couldn't understand why I would want to sell the stock then—right after it had given back all the gains we had made. I wanted to get out because I thought the stock was going lower, and it did. The decision had nothing to do with where we bought the stock or what the current price was.

What personal characteristics do you believe you have that allowed you to succeed in this business?

The willingness to take losses and understand that I may not be right.

Do you use objectives on your trades?

I have points where I will reevaluate, but it's a moving target. Also, I try not to sell on the way up; I try to sell on the way down.

So, if you buy a stock at 40 that you think would be fully priced at 80 . . .

I would sell it at 75 on the way down rather than at 80 because I might be giving up much more on the upside than the difference in selling it a little bit lower.

Four months later, after listening to all the tapes of our interview, I felt that a number of important questions had either been unasked or answered unsatisfactorily. I conducted a follow-up interview by phone. By the time of this call (July 29, 2011), Vidich had switched from bullish to bearish. In the week immediately following this call, equities plunged, experiencing their largest single-week decline since the 2008 market meltdown.

When I interviewed you a few months ago, you were quite bullish. Now, you are bearish. What changed?

Part of it was the recent resolution of the debt-ceiling impasse, in which the entire reduction of future deficits was based on spending cutbacks without any increase in revenues.[1] Spending cutbacks, which primarily impact lower- and middle-class consumers, will have a much greater drag on the economy than increases in revenues for higher income earners. The Tea Party has also put Obama in a corner in clearly making it impossible for him to implement any further stimulus if the economy needs it.

What else turned you bearish?

We are seeing an increasing number of companies whose operating margins are beginning to contract as their input costs increase, and those costs can't be passed on to the consumer.

---

[1]In the summer of 2011, Republicans refused to vote for an increase in the debt ceiling without commensurate spending cuts. President Obama had originally insisted on a package that also included some revenue increases, but ultimately agreed to a spending-cuts-only deal to avoid the looming possibility of the U.S. government running out of money to pay its bills—a prospect the Tea Party segment of the Republican Party clearly seemed willing, and, in some cases, even eager, to accept.

Anything else?

When you listen to numerous conference calls in which the executives are worried about the current economic environment, that sentiment translates into a real impact on business.

So the way you interpret sentiment, negative sentiment is bearish rather than bullish.

There is a big difference between informed sentiment, like CEOs, and investor sentiment. Investor sentiment, however, is usually wrong, at least over the longer term.

How do you judge investor sentiment?

One way is by listening to my own investors. When I start hearing the same comments from a number of my investors, it is a good reflection of what everyone is thinking.

For example?

When the retail stocks were getting hammered last year, my investors were all asking, "Why would you want to own any retail stocks?" Of course, that was exactly the right time to own them. That was the bottom of the retail sector.

Now that you have switched from net long to net short, what would get you long again?

Buying. If all of a sudden stocks stopped going down on bad news that would be a positive sign.

You did extraordinarily well in 1999 and then had an even more amazing 2000. [Vidich managed a very small fund before starting the current fund. This fund, which started in October 1999, made 87 percent in the fourth quarter of 1999 and 147 percent in 2000.] You obviously had to shift from being

extremely bullish in 1999 to extremely bearish in 2000. How did you manage to time this transition so well?

I didn't switch from being a bull to a bear. First, I switched from being a bull to being hedged because the stocks I was long were up by so much. Once I was hedged, I was protecting my profits, and I began to notice that I was making all my money on the shorts. As more information came out, I realized that I should be selling my longs and keeping my shorts.

Do you use charts?

Charts are extremely important. One of the best patterns is when a stock goes sideways for a long time in a narrow range and then has a sudden, sharp upmove on large volume. That type of price action is a wake-up call that something is probably going on, and you need to look at it. Also, sometimes whatever is going on with that stock will also have implications for other stocks in the same sector. It can be an important clue.

Does any trade stand out as your most painful experience?

If you are diversified enough, then no single trade is particularly painful. The critical risk controls are being diversified and cutting your exposure when you don't understand what the markets are doing and why you are wrong.

Has that happened recently?

I was long Google at an average price of about $550. It kept going lower, and I couldn't understand why. Finally, I just got out at $505. It went down to about $480, and then it abruptly reversed, surging above $600 in a matter of weeks. Psychologically, that is extremely painful, but you have to be willing to take your hit. Even when you are wrong in taking your hit, it cleans the slate, and cleaning the slate can be very therapeutic. If you don't clean your slate, you will end up keeping your losers. Some stocks with losses will come back, and you will sell those, but the ones that don't come back, you will end up keeping. Getting out sometimes right before a stock turns is the price you pay to keep your losses under control.

■ ■ ■

It is a common dilemma faced by traders. The market is moving against your position. You are well aware of the dangers of an unconstrained loss. But you also still believe in your position and are worried about throwing in the towel just before the market turns. You are frozen in indecision. Vidich offers a perspective that provides a solution. "Don't try to be 100 percent right," he says. Instead of making an all-or-nothing decision, when Vidich is faced with a losing position, he will often begin by liquidating part of the position. Taking a partial loss is much easier than liquidating the entire position. It allows the trader to act rather than procrastinate. If the position continues to move against Vidich, he will liquidate some more. In this way, a losing position is gradually reduced (and eventually entirely liquidated if it doesn't turn around), mitigating the damage. The next time you are undecided between liquidating a losing position and gritting your teeth and riding it out, remember that there is a third alternative: partial liquidation.

A common mistake made by traders is that they let their greed influence position sizing beyond their comfort level. Why put on a 5 percent position when you can put on a 10 percent position and double the profits? The problem is that the larger the position, the greater the danger that trading decisions will be driven by fear rather than by judgment and experience. Vidich stresses, "Limit your size in any position so that fear does not become the prevailing instinct guiding your judgment."

Flexibility is a key characteristic of superior traders. Vidich is a long-term bull in the energy markets, but he doesn't let this view interfere with making the right trading decision. In 2008, when prices moved excessively on the upside, Vidich gradually transitioned from net long to net short. In the subsequent collapse in crude oil, Vidich repositioned himself back on the long side of energy equities once crude had fallen to about $90. But he soon realized that the changing fundamentals and market sentiment implied lower prices and reversed back to the short side. Crude oil prices and energy equities subsequently collapsed. Vidich's flexibility in changing his trading opinion turned a potential major loss into a large winner.

Don't make trading decisions based on where you bought (or sold) a stock. The market doesn't care where you entered your position. When Vidich felt a stock that had just fallen all the way back to where he had bought it was going lower, he just got out, not letting his entry level affect the trading decision.

It you are going to control your losses, there will be times when you will get out just before the market turns around. Get used to it. This frustrating experience is an unavoidable consequence of effective risk management. Vidich's discipline in "harvesting his losses" has made it possible for him to keep his maximum drawdown to single digits for over a decade and through two major bear markets. This impressive risk control, though, could only be achieved because Vidich was willing to accept the fact that he would sometimes end up liquidating losing positions right before they reversed dramatically, as had just happened to him in his long Google position.

Chapter 13

Kevin Daly

Who Is Warren Buffett?

"Who is Warren Buffett?" is what Kevin Daly thought when queried about the famous investor in an initial job interview in 1983. Finding the answer to this question directly led to the investment methodology Daly employed throughout his career. True to Buffett's investment philosophy, Daly seeks out companies that are selling well below the intrinsic value of their business. He has been extremely successful in applying this methodology.

After 15 years of writing equity research and "eating his own cooking" in his personal stock account, which grew steadily in value with the exception of a losing year in 1994, Daly launched his own fund in 1999. In the 12 years he has been running the fund, Daly has realized an average annual compounded gross return of 20.8 percent (16.4 percent net). Although Daly does some shorting, it plays a relatively minor role, usually accounting for less than 10 percent of assets under management. In this context, Daly's investment approach is closer to a

long-only fund—although he will periodically hold significant percentages of cash—than to a long/short hedge fund. Since inception,
Daly has earned a cumulative gross return of 872 percent (514 percent
after management and incentive fees) compared with only a 68 percent
contemporaneous return for the Russell 2000 (the most comparable
index given Daly's smaller cap focus) and a negative 9 percent return for
the S&P 500.

The ability to generate substantial returns with a near long-only
approach in an equity market that has gone essentially sideways over the
long term tells only part of the story. Perhaps the most impressive aspect
of Daly's performance has been his control of losses. Although the
equity market witnessed two huge bear phases in which stock indexes
were more than halved, Daly's maximum drawdown from an equity
peak to equity low has been only 10.3 percent. Even more impressive in
terms of risk control, with the exception of November 2000 when he
lost 6 percent, all his other monthly losses have been under 4 percent.
Daly's Gain to Pain ratio based on net returns is a very high 3.2. (See
Appendix A for an explanation of the Gain to Pain ratio.)

Daly earned a civil engineering degree at the University of Berkeley,
but well before he graduated, he realized that he had no interest in his
chosen field of study. He was bothered by the lack of creativity in the
process. The answers to any specific problem were prescribed. If you
knew the formulas, you would plug in the numbers, get the answer, and
move on to the next problem. There was a sameness about it that was
unappealing to Daly. After graduating, he enrolled in the University of
San Francisco's MBA program, thinking that a career in business might
provide him with the variety he sought.

Daly's first job—and as it turned out only job prior to launching his
hedge fund—was with Hoefer & Arnett, a boutique brokerage and
investment-banking firm. He was originally hired as a broker, but this
quickly morphed into a research position. Originally, Daly was the only
research analyst, but as the firm grew and other analysts were hired, he
became the research director. His Five Corners fund was originally
launched within the firm.

It is probably more accurate to think of Daly as a private investor
than a hedge fund manager. The hedge fund is essentially the private

account he would be running if he were on his own, with a structure that allows other investors to co-invest. Daly accounted for about one-third of the invested assets when the fund launched, and still accounts for about the same percentage today. He runs the fund as a solo operation from his home office. Daly is quite happy with this simple structure, and he is downright reluctant to put any effort into raising assets for his fund, as it might necessitate expanding beyond a one-man business. He is loath to complicate what he considers the perfect current arrangement. Daly is a man whose work and hobby are the same. If Daly were retired, I believe his life would be totally unchanged. He would, no doubt, still be spending his day managing his stock account, which would be indistinguishable from the current fund. He would be doing the exact same research and investment management he is doing now.

Daly is tall, trim, and very fit looking. He regularly mountain bikes—his other main hobby besides investing—in the steep hills that sit behind his house. One of the trail junctions—Five Corners—is the origin of his fund's name (Five Corners Partners, LP). I interviewed Daly in the comfortable living room of his home in the exurbs of San Francisco. He was relaxed and low key. I could see him remaining unfazed and sedate even in panic markets.

■ ■ ■

How did you get started in the financial industry?

My first interview after graduating business school was at a small regional investment bank. I was interviewed by Alan Hoefer, who was one of the firm's three partners. During the interview, he asked me if I had ever heard of Warren Buffett. "No," I answered. "Well, what are they teaching you in business school these days?" he asked. It was a long interview, and I didn't think I did particularly well. I took mental notes, and after the interview I started doing my own research. I got Buffett's annual letters. I read up on the companies Hoefer had mentioned in the interview. Weeks went by, and I didn't hear back from him. I assumed that was it.

Why did you think you did poorly in the interview?

Well, for starters, I didn't even know who Buffett was.

It reminds me of my first interview after graduate school. I had a degree in economics, but they taught you nothing about the markets. The interview was for a job opening as a commodity research analyst. The research director asked me if I knew anything about commodities. "Not really," I said, "something like gold." My answer was so bad that I still remember it after all these years. Fortunately, I still got the job because I wrote my way into it. The story about your interview strikes a familiar chord. You come out of an academic background with good credentials, but you know absolutely nothing, and can't answer the simplest question in a job interview.

Exactly, that is where I found myself. The prior summer, I took a break after graduating business school to travel through Europe. While traveling, I bumped into a friend of mine who I knew from Berkeley. He had gone to business school at USC, while I went to business school at USF. We got together after we returned. We started talking about our job searches, and by coincidence, it turned out we had both interviewed for the same job. He told me they had hired someone else from Berkeley; neither one of us got the job.

They never gave you the courtesy of a call to tell you that someone else got the job?

No, they didn't, but it turned out the other person was hired as an investment banker, which was not the position I had interviewed for. After I got back, I called Hoefer and said, "I'm going to be in the Burlingame area next week," which was a complete lie. "Do you mind if I stop by to say hello again?" Hoefer said it was fine for me to come by.

I went in and ended up having lunch with Bob Arnett, who was the other founding partner in the firm. At lunch, I was talking a lot about Buffett and the companies Hoefer & Arnett were invested in because at that point I felt well-versed enough to hold my own on these topics. At one point in our conversation, Arnett looked at me and said, "Are you telling me all of this because you are interested in it or because you think it's what I want to hear?"

"A little bit of both," I answered.

The next week I got an offer from them to be a broker.

Were you concerned that it was a sales position?

I didn't care; I just wanted to get my foot in the door. It was a very small firm. I hoped that if I applied myself, I wouldn't be stuck as a broker. As it turned out, I was only a broker for about two months.

Once you started there, what did they have you do?

They had me cold calling.

Was it difficult?

Yes, it was very difficult. Some of the people on my call list were dead.

Did you get any accounts?

No, I didn't get any.

Were you getting frustrated?

Yes, I didn't like it at all. After about two months, I started writing research on my own. I covered companies that were not well followed on Wall Street, which gave us greater access to managers in the large mutual fund companies. Our focus was on value. Both Hoefer and Arnett taught me to look at companies from the perspective of what would a rational businessman pay for the company if he was writing a check today. One interesting aspect of the business for me was that unlike the large brokerage firms that had a salesman between the analysts and clients, we wrote and sold our own research. This structure gave me the opportunity to meet with some of the major mutual fund managers, such as John Templeton, Chuck Royce, and Bob Rodriguez, who were clients.

I guess these funds directed commission business to you in exchange for the research ideas.

Exactly.

Did you learn anything from these clients?

By coincidence, I was in New York at the time of the 1987 crash. In doing my manager visits on that day, I saw three very different responses to the crash. Some guys, when I walked into their office, they were almost catatonic. All they could do was stare at the screen, watching the market evaporate in front of them. They couldn't buy, and they couldn't sell. They would apologize for not being able to take the meeting, and I completely understood. I saw other clients who were selling in panic mode. Then I saw Chuck Royce who took our meeting as if nothing were happening. He sat in an office that had a glass screen divider between him and his trading desk. Each time I finished discussing an idea, he would slide the glass window open and tell one of his traders to buy 50,000 shares. He wasn't afraid to keep buying. The way he responded taught me that you have to stay focused on the value of a business and see past exogenous crises events. Stocks get cheaper than fair value. It may be painful to buy into a panic over the short run, but over the long run, it can pay off if you are buying stocks well below their value.

What prompted you to start a hedge fund?

I had been doing research for 15 years, and I thought I was pretty good at it. I had also been investing in the ideas that I was recommending all along. Starting a hedge fund seemed like a natural outgrowth of what I had already been doing. Also, I was able to start the fund within my own firm. I launched the fund in 1999 with $3 million; one third was my own money, and Chuck Royce and friends and family accounted for the rest. When I started the fund, it was right in the middle of the Internet craze. I found some good value names in that space.

How could you possibly have found value in Internet stocks in 1999?

I found fiber-optic businesses that were buried inside of larger companies. You could buy some of these companies for P/Es as low as 11 or 12 and effectively get a free call on the fiber optic portion of their business, which was not reflected in the price. One example was Newport Corporation, which was primarily known as a company that produced test and measurement equipment for the semiconductor industry. When

I purchased it in 1999 at the presplit price of $14 per share, it was trading around 11 times next year's earnings, had a nice balance sheet, and was very capably managed. What most investors didn't realize at the time was that the company contained a division, accounting for a quarter of total sales, that produced products used in the fiber optic component manufacturing process. In other words, they made products that helped build the "information superhighway." As fiber optic networks were built out, Newport's little division benefited. Sales increased by 80 percent in 2000, and the share price rose even faster. In 2000, I began taking profits in the 30s, thinking that at those levels the stock had reached intrinsic value. I sold the last of my shares around $100, at which point I thought the stock was grossly overvalued. I failed to appreciate that in a market where Internet stocks with little or even no earnings and minuscule revenues could magically levitate to stratospheric levels based on silly metrics like sales per engineer, there was no telling how high a "real company" like Newport could go. Later that year, the stock eventually topped out at $570 per share!

I have tried to do that type of investing throughout the fund's life—looking for companies that are somewhat obscure, not covered by Wall Street, or have a niche business inside the company that no one is focusing on. I use the smallness of the fund to my advantage. I can go down to smaller cap values that the larger funds can't look at.

What cap range do you focus on?

I am pretty agnostic in terms of capitalization levels. I can go big or small. It is really value that drives my interest. My focus is on buying a company at a discount to intrinsic value, which can be measured in a lot of different ways depending on the business. Market cap is not a factor.

Since you are agnostic about market cap, you must have a very large investment universe.

About 10,000 stocks.

How do you select stocks from such a large list?

I use Compustat and Zacks to screen their lists of U.S. and Canadian stocks.

What metrics do you use to screen for stocks that may be of interest?

The accounting for financial companies is quite different from that of nonfinancial companies, so I use different screens for each. For nonfinancial companies, I use some of the following:

- *Enterprise value/EBITDA*—Enterprise value (EV) is equal to the company's market cap (the number of shares outstanding times the share price) plus all long-term liabilities (debt and preferred stock outstanding, as well as underfunded pension funds) minus cash. The enterprise value is the amount one would have to pay to acquire the entire business. EBITDA, earnings before interest, taxes, depreciation, and amortization, is a measure of the amount of cash flow the business produces annually. The ratio measures what you are paying relative to what you are getting. I look for companies trading at low multiples of EBITDA.
- *Price to free cash flow*—FCF is the money a company has left over after it has paid all expenses and made capital investments. It can be used to pay dividends, repurchase shares, or make acquisitions. The aim is to find businesses selling at low multiples of FCF.
- *P/E ratio*—The current price per share divided by the forecasted earnings. The lower the ratio the better.
- *EV/EBIT (cap rate)*—This ratio is a twist on the EV/EBITDA metric. However, instead of EBITDA we used EBIT, earnings before interest and taxes but *after* deducting depreciation and amortization. At my old firm, Hoefer & Arnett, we used to call EV/EBIT a "cap rate," similar to a cap rate used to value real estate. We used to argue, why buy a piece of commercial real estate with a 6 percent cap rate or a bond with a 7 percent yield if you could buy a business like Macy's with a 20 percent cap rate?

For financial companies and banks, I use some of the following:

- *Price/tangible book value*—The tangible book value (TBV) is equal to the book value minus intangible assets, such as patents and goodwill. Assuming the loans on a bank's balance sheet have been appropriately accounted for—a big assumption considering the events in the financial industry over the past several years—a bank trading around its TBV would represent the value at which one could theoretically liquidate the bank. The TBV per share, therefore, might provide somewhat of a floor for a bank's value.

- *P/E ratio*
- *Tangible common equity/total assets*—This ratio provides a measure of a bank's capital adequacy. The more tangible common equity, the less leverage is employed and the "safer" the bank is.

How many stock names do you end up with after your run your screens?

About 200. I also come up with company ideas by reading and talking to friends in the industry.

What do you read regularly that is helpful?

I read the *Wall Street Journal, Barron's,* and a number of subscription based newsletters including the *Wall Street Transcript, Dick Davis Investment Digest, Grant's Interest Rate Observer, Value Investor Insight, Santangel's Review,* and *Form4Oracle,* which provides data on insider sales and purchases. I also use two members' only websites that share investment ideas: Value Investors Club[1] and SumZero. Two other useful websites are Vickers Stock Research, which tracks institutional holdings of individual stocks, and Thompson Reuters, which both aggregates brokerage firm research and provides transcripts of company presentations at conferences and quarterly earnings calls. These transcripts can be particularly useful. I will often read through a transcript more than once looking for upbeat or downbeat comments, or signs of evasiveness. Finally, I review SEC Filings (10Ks, 10Qs, and Proxy Statements) and FDIC Bank Call Reports.

How do you go from a list of possible investment candidates— your screen lists supplemented by the ideas garnered by reading and networking—to selecting actual investments?

Then the real work begins, which is the qualitative assessment.

---

[1]The Value Investors Club is discussed in detail in Chapter 15.

What do you look for in the qualitative assessment?

The first thing, is it an easily understandable business. I focus on companies I am familiar with—what Warren Buffett calls investing within a "circle of competence." I avoid difficult to understand industries with short and unpredictable product life cycles, such as biotechnology and high technology.

I look for good businesses. A good business is one that provides a necessary service or product and has a balance sheet and cash flow that can sustain it through difficult periods. I also look for companies that other companies might like to acquire due to their market share, intellectual property, distribution network, or real estate value.

After I have identified a company to research, I will then begin to read through any Wall Street research I can find, especially initiation reports—the reports produced by analysts when they first begin coverage on a company—even if the report is somewhat dated. I find these reports provide great background on a company and the industry it competes in. Frequently, these reports include some background on the company's competitors, as well as tables that compare the company's profitability versus its competitors.

Several years ago, I found a company, Insurance Auto Auctions (IAAI), in this manner. I had been reading a research report on Copart (CPRT), a competitor of IAAI's, and found a table near the end of the report that compared CPRT's margins with IAAI's. There was a huge disparity between the two. Both companies acquired wrecked cars from insurance companies, stored them on their lots, and then auctioned them off live or through the Internet to buyers including salvage yards and auto body shops. Although both companies did the exact same thing, IAAI's margins were much lower. After meeting with management and doing some research, I couldn't figure out any reason why IAAI's margins shouldn't increase towards CPRT's levels. In addition, the stock could be purchased for just over five times forward EBITDA and at better than a 10 percent free cash flow yield. I began to purchase the stock around $15 per share, buying all the way up to $22 per share. Within a year, a buyout firm, Kelso, Inc., bought the company at $28.25 per share.

The general principle is that when there are major discrepancies between similar companies, the profit potential can result in a takeover or be realized by the market. Then when the stock reaches a reasonable valuation, you sell it and move on to the next investment.

Good ideas don't come that often. But the wider you cast your net through reading, screening, and speaking with others, the greater the likelihood that you will succeed in finding good ideas.

Can you think of a trade that didn't work that provided a learning lesson?

In late 2006, I bought Horizon Lines, which was a Jones Act container shipping company operating vessels primarily between Hawaii, Alaska, Puerto Rico, and the U.S. mainland. Under the Jones Act, all vessels transporting cargo between covered U.S. ports must be built in the U.S., registered under the U.S. flag, manned by predominantly U.S. crews, and owned and operated by U.S.-organized companies that are controlled and 75 percent owned by U.S. citizens. As one can imagine, the Jones Act creates a significant barrier to entry in these shipping lanes, and as a result, Horizon Lines had a substantial share of the market. On the negative side, though, the company also had its share of debt and a number of older vessels that needed to be replaced. My thinking at the time was that I was investing in a company that had a significant moat around it and that it would generate a lot of free cash flow, enabling it to deleverage. I started buying shares in the mid-20s, and in 2007, the stock reached the mid-30s. However, it was about this time that Horizon Lines' shipping volumes began to weaken, which caused the share price to decline, as did renewed market unease over the company's need to replace its older ships. I became concerned about the Horizon Lines' ability to generate a meaningful amount of free cash flow, and without it, I was afraid the company's debt load could sink it. Fortunately, I got out above my average cost, and in the process, I learned another valuable lesson about the danger of investing in overleveraged companies. The stock today trades at 24 cents per share!

I assume the best value opportunities arise in the most extreme bear markets. If you identify a stock as a buy in that type of market environment, how do you handle the timing of entry?

No bells sound when things get better. I'll never forget speaking with the CFO of Measurement Specialties during the downturn that began in late 2008. A large part of their sales was to auto OEMs. When car sales in the U.S. and around the world plummeted, Measurement's customers chose to draw down their inventories instead of ordering from them and other auto suppliers. As a result, the CFO told me that the phone didn't ring for about a month; their auto customers just went quiet. Unless I assumed that no one was going to buy a car again, I knew that this situation had to change at some point. The company had earned $1.20 a share in 2007. I began buying stock at $3.79 per share in April 2009 and bought it all the way up through the $7s. I sold most of my stock in the $14s in early 2010, which was nearly triple my average entry price, but still far too early—the stock eventually reached a peak of $38.98 in mid-2011.

Many value stocks stay undervalued for a long time. How do you avoid the value trap?

Lots of companies screen as being "cheap." I think that it's easy to avoid value traps. The trick is to stay away from companies that can't grow their cash flow and increase intrinsic value. If I think the business is a "melting ice cube" like newspapers, yellow pages, and video rentals, to name a few bad businesses, then I won't invest in it, no matter how cheap it is. Conversely, if I invest in a business that can be purchased at a discount to its intrinsic value, and that value is growing, then all I have to do is wait and be patient. As Buffett says, "Time is the enemy of the poor business and the friend of the great business."

Do you hold stocks for a long time?

It depends on valuation. As long as the share price doesn't get too far ahead of a company's intrinsic value, I will maintain the investment.

What has been your average exposure?

I'm mostly long. Typically, my longs are between 30 and 90 percent. My shorts are usually less than 10 percent.

How have you managed to keep your losses so small with such a long-biased exposure, given that we have had two huge bear markets since you've been running the fund?

I watch various economic statistics, including more esoteric data such as weekly rail car loadings. When the data points to a slowdown, I might reduce my exposure. If I am concerned enough, I may even move to almost all cash. This attention to economic indicators helped me in 2002 and in 2008. Although in 2010, the same cautionary approach cut my profits. I sold a number of stocks on the notion that the economy was in trouble, and then the Fed initiated QE2 [that is, a second phase of quantitative easing], and stocks took off. I was up 13.3 percent net in 2010, but I would have been up a lot more if I hadn't liquidated in response to my concerns about the economy. I have no regrets, though, because I'd rather miss an opportunity than lose money.

During the long bear market in 2000 to 2002, did you have low exposure the whole time?

I had very low exposure, and I was very patient.

How low?

I was almost 90 percent in cash.

For the whole bear market?

For most of it.

When did you cut back your exposure dramatically?

Around the end of the first quarter of 2000.

That's right at the beginning of the bear market. What prompted that timing?

It was mostly a matter of valuations being very stretched.

When did you get back into the market?

In late 2000. I thought we had a pretty good washout and valuations were more compelling. Then in November 2000, I had my worst month ever. I lost 6 percent, and I went back to mostly cash.

Was it just the large monthly loss that got you back on the sidelines?

I think so. I don't like losing money.

How long did you stay mostly in cash?

Probably till early 2003.

What was the all-clear sign for you?

It was a combination of the compression in valuations and signs that the economy was improving. I was hearing from a number of companies that business was picking up.

What was your experience in the 2008 bear market?

I took my exposure down, but not nearly as much as in 2000. I was approximately 60 to 70 percent cash.

Did you have any emotional response to the market meltdown?

I try to keep emotions in check. Having a lot of emotion about investing doesn't do you any good.

I guess you had pared down to a point of comfort.

I just kept on doing my research and focusing on what I knew worked, which is valuation. Certainly in that time period, I also wanted companies with good balance sheets.

You have been very successful in keeping your losses small. Is there more to it than just going to cash when the environment is uncertain?

It's also the type of companies that I buy—companies with good balance sheets and solid free cash flow. I'm always trying to buy a dollar's worth of assets for 50 cents, which helps limit the downside.

How do you decide where to get out of a position?

It's valuation driven. I wait till the stock is fair valued.

Do you ever hold profitable positions beyond what you consider fair valuation?

No. I made a lot of mistakes doing that over the years. For example, holding onto a position for a full year for tax reasons, and then giving up profits I would have locked in. You want to stay true to the investment process. When I buy a stock, I identify the difference between what I think it is worth and the stock price. Once the share price closes the gap, I sell all or most of it—I sometimes hold on to a small residual position—and move on to the next investment. That might take a year, or it might take a month.

What personal characteristics have allowed you to be successful?

I try to stay as unemotional as possible when things go against me.

What is your advice about investing in stocks?

You need to always keep in mind that stocks are units of ownership in a business. If you buy a stock at a good valuation, and the price goes down, unless something has changed with the business or business outlook, you should stay the course, or possibly even buy more. Conversely, don't get carried away if the stock goes up. You should use the same valuation discipline to decide where you're going to sell. If the stock reaches what you think is fair value, take your profits and go on to the next one.

Wouldn't staying the course, let alone buying more, be a dangerous prescription if we are in a bear market?

That's different. I was talking about price fluctuations in a single stock. I know how to analyze companies. I don't know how to analyze the economy.

Why do you think you are managing so little money when your return/risk is better than most equity hedge fund managers?

That's an easy question to answer. I'm a lousy marketer. I have never actively marketed the fund. I prefer to look for good investments as opposed to new investors. Also, at my current level, I can make a decent living without the headaches that come with building a larger firm. When I was on the sell-side, I used to be responsible for hiring and supervising analysts, and I never enjoyed that quite as much as looking for companies to invest in.

■ ■ ■

Claude Debussy said, "Music is the space between the notes." Analogously, the space between investments—the times one is out of the market—can be critical to successful investing. Despite being primarily a net long equity investor, Daly achieved cumulative gross returns in excess of 800 percent during a 12-year period when the broad equity market indexes were essentially flat. How did he do it? Well, of course, superior stock selection was an important component, but it is not the entire answer. Not being invested (that is, being primarily in cash) during negative environments is the other part of the answer. By not participating in the market at the wrong times, Daly sidestepped most of the large drawdowns in equities during two major bear markets—a crucial factor that underlies the large growth in his equity. Sometimes, being out of the market may be nearly as important to success as the investments made. Whether you are a value investor, as Daly is, or use some totally different investment or trading approach, the critical lesson is that it is important not to be involved in the market when the opportunities are not there.

A corollary to the ability to be out of the market is the importance of patience to successful investing. You need patience to stay on the sidelines when the environment is adverse to your approach or when opportunities are lacking or suboptimal. Think of the patience it required for Daly to remain largely in cash for well over two years in the prolonged 2000 to 2002 bear market.

Daly's stock investing methodology and philosophy can be summarized as follows:

- Stick to businesses you understand.
- Find companies in those businesses that are undervalued vis-à-vis the pertinent metrics or similar competitors.
- Take profits when prices move up to fair valuation levels.
- Sail into a cash harbor when the market seas turn stormy.
- Stick to the basic process, and never take flyers.
- Treat investments as a business, not as a gamble.

Daly has one important edge that is also shared by virtually every reader of this book: small asset size. Daly manages only $50 million, which is small by fund manager standards. This smaller size allows Daly to range broadly across the capitalization spectrum, including companies that would be too small to trade if he were managing several hundred million dollars, let alone billions of dollars. Some of the best opportunities have come in these smaller cap issues. Daly fully understands the advantage of managing smaller assets, which is one reason why he has made virtually no effort to raise additional assets. Individual investors may feel they are at a major disadvantage to large hedge fund managers, but they actually have an important advantage: Their small trading size allows them to move in and out of positions, even less liquid equities, with virtually no market impact.

The larger the assets, the more difficult it is for a manager to enter and liquidate positions without incurring significant slippage costs. Also, as the assets managed grow, the universe of possible opportunities shrinks. For large hedge fund managers, many markets and securities cannot be traded, simply because the size at which they could trade these markets and still have adequate liquidity is too small to have much impact on their portfolio, and hence not worth the bother. Although some managers have been able to maintain performance with large assets under management, I have also seen many managers who did very well while trading smaller asset levels, but then experienced significant performance deterioration when they allowed their assets to grow beyond the optimal level for their methodology. For managers, the discipline to turn down additional investor assets when they believe it would impede their performance is an important element in longer-term success.

Chapter 14

Jimmy Balodimas

Stepping in Front of Freight Trains

J immy Balodimas breaks all the rules. He sells into uptrends and buys into downtrends. He adds to losers and cuts his winners short. He is a predominant short in a market that is up the majority of days.[1] By any of the standard guidelines for trading success, Balodimas shouldn't survive in the markets, let alone thrive. Yet he is one of the most successful traders at First New York Securities, the prop trading firm at which he began his career 15 years ago, and he has never had a losing year.

I first interviewed Balodimas on February 22, 2011, a day in which the equity markets were down sharply in a selloff that ostensibly was triggered by the uprising in Libya, which led to a sharp rally in oil prices

---

[1]Balodimas does short-term trading of equities. Using the S&P 500 as a benchmark, during the 1990s and 2000s—the decades in which Balodimas traded—the market was up 53 percent of the days. Source: Crestmont Research (www.CrestmontResearch.com).

and market concerns over a disruption in oil supplies. The Libyan upheaval was part of the domino effect of Mideast unrest that began with the overthrow of the Tunisian dictatorship a month earlier. This down day in the stock market followed a three-month period in which the price advance in equities had been so unrelenting that neither the S&P 500 nor the Nasdaq index was able to go more than five days without setting new highs in the ongoing bull market that had begun two years earlier. The current month had been particularly brutal for shorts, as the market reached new highs almost daily, never taking more than three days to do so. Balodimas had been net short throughout this move. Watching the succession of near daily highs, Balodimas commented to his trading assistant, "This is like the tech bubble, only with real stocks."

Balodimas's trading assistant was my son, Zachary Schwager. It was Zachary who made me aware of Balodimas and his incredible trading skill. Zachary was amazed at how Balodimas could be short a rising market and still generate profits—more profits, in fact, than many other traders in the firm on the right side of the market. Describing his boss, Zachary said, "Jimmy has zero fear. If he ever has a small position, it is either because he was right on the trade right away or because the market has not yet moved against him. He has the same even emotional response whether he is up or down for the day."

I caught Balodimas on a very good day for him—a day he had just made back more than his entire loss for the month-to-date. But had I not known he was short, I would never have guessed it from his laid-back demeanor. There was no sign of the excitement or euphoria many traders would have expressed after such a rapid favorable reversal in the markets. I am sure if I had come one trading day earlier when his equity was setting a new low for the month, Balodimas would have been equally even-keeled.

I had arrived about 25 minutes before the close, expecting to silently observe Balodimas from the sidelines. In my e-mail to him the previous day, I indicated I might arrive a bit before the close, but that, of course, I would not expect to begin the interview until after the close. I was aware that Balodimas was an active trader, and I did not want to get in the way. Immediately after I arrived, Balodimas began talking—the interview had begun before I realized it had. Balodimas made no further trades while I was there. I had assumed this absence of activity was because Balodimas had already placed all his intended trades for the day. Zachary, however, later informed that Balodimas had stopped trading simply because I was there. Not surprisingly, given the market's largest daily decline in many months, it had been an active day. "We placed about 500 trades before you came," Zachary said, "and if you were not there, we probably would have done a lot more. That's just the way Jimmy is. If people are there, he will pay attention to them and not the market." Chalk up another one for rules broken.

I interviewed Balodimas at his trading desk with his six trading screens, a sea of red quotes, as a backdrop. I found the room uncomfortably warm, but Balodimas was dressed in a heavy sweater.

■ ■ ■

You have been short this market?

It has felt to me like the market was ready to come down for some time. Even though I held that view, I have tried to maintain some level of discipline, recognizing the market was quite strong. I was still net short every day, but until this month by only about 5 to 10 million. That is the type of number that I can manage to not get hurt by too much even if the market is up 1 percent or 2 percent for the day.

But you are more heavily short now?

Yes, coming in to today, I was 15-million long and 41-million short. I got a lot bigger on Friday afternoon.

For almost any other trader, that would sound like a strange statement. To put it into context, last Friday was a day after a long string of days in which the market was up almost every day, with no corrections along the way. The close was near the high of the week, the high of the month, and for that matter, the highest level in recent years.

Something was happening last week that seemed different from the rally before then. The market had been grinding steadily higher, but the fact that it was so easy for the market to go up last week, let me know that something was up. Thursday, the market rallied sharply after being weak in the morning. Then Friday, the market got really strong again near the close. The market was moving up like there was no supply. Coming on top of the large gains we had in the past four months, I thought, *Now, the market is getting stronger? Now?* [He says this emphasizing the repeated "now" in a tone of incredulity at the sheer preposterousness of this price action—a tone that communicates, "Give me a break," without saying the words.] The move felt fluffy to me, and I honor all the senses I get. It just seemed like a logical place for me to get more short. I try to formulate my own ideas by listening to what the market is saying. Sentiment is one of my big clues as to what is happening.

How do you judge sentiment?

There are lots of different ways to gauge it. I watch TV. I read the paper. I listen to what people at the firm are saying. People are afraid to short. "I'm not shorting any more stock; I'm tired of losing money." I heard that last week.

I don't have the speed I used to have. I am not a sniper anymore. I used to be like lightning; always moving. I don't move as fast anymore. There are things I do differently now. That's part of my evolution. Maybe I am a bit early, but if I am early, I don't get bigger just because I think I'm right. There are a lot of things that I have changed. Even though the market has been straight up this year, I'm still net ahead. I have made more money than most guys who've been net long for our firm.

How can you still be ahead when you have been wrong on the market?

I have some kind of knack for it. I don't know exactly what the knack is. Maybe it's being comfortable in situations where everyone is nervous. I always take some money off the table when the market is in my favor. Regardless of whether it is a lot or a little bit. Even if the market is down only ½ percent or 1 percent and I think the market should be 10 percent lower, I'm still taking money off. That saves me a lot of money, because when the market rallies, I have a smaller position. That is a habit I have had since day one. I always take money off the table when it's in my favor. Always, always, always.

But this past month, the market has hardly been down.

It's been very limited. I have been short an average of about 15 to 25 million this month. I have probably taken about 20 percent of that position off every morning that we were down in the first 30 minutes. Whatever is red—it doesn't make a difference what the symbol is, or whether the stock is down only fifty cents or a dollar—I am taking some off. It is almost mechanical. It is sort of like my internal program that I do regardless of what the news is. If the market then goes up again, I am reselling the same 20 percent of my short at prices that are maybe 3 percent higher than where I covered. So the average share price on my shorts goes up. But it is a lot of work. Going along with whatever the market is doing doesn't make sense to me, and I have to honor that. I have made money every year in my career. Even though my system is flawed—I'm not entirely disciplined and I give myself too much leeway—it has still worked for me.

How did you develop your trading style?

My firm has always given me a lot of latitude, which allowed me to stretch my boundaries. While it was uncomfortable, it helped me learn how to make and lose money without being scared of doing either. I learned by trading a lot all the time. I traded more than anyone else at the firm. That is how I got my feel for stocks. I really felt them. I felt, *Oh, something has changed. I don't know what it is, but something has changed.* I really trusted that feeling. What was interesting to me early in my career was that I would get a thought about what would happen, and then be surprised when it did happen. It always appeared on the screen to me. It always showed itself to me. A stock reveals itself to me when something changes.

How do you see it?

It's a sense I've developed, and I have learned to trust that sense. I think I have spent as much time in front of screens watching the nature of stocks as anyone else in the business. Because I have watched these same symbols for almost 15 years, they almost take on a life of their own.

Can you give me an example of what you mean by sense?

I'll give you a great example. Tyco went from being one of the favorites on Wall Street to one of the Wall Street disasters in a very short order of time. I started buying at $34, and in a few days it went straight down to $18. My average price was around $23. I was long 750,000 shares and down about $5 million on the trade. I remember my boss coming over to my desk and asking, "Jimmy, what are you doing?" I said, "Don, I'll take care of it. I know what I am doing." No one was talking, because everyone knew the size of my position. I took over the entire desk position on the stock.

Even though the stock was collapsing, I really believed, "This is my opportunity." I don't remember the exact price, but I said to myself if it went below that price, I would have to start liquidating. It literally traded right at that price and stopped going down. At that point, I had a sense that something had changed. I didn't sell a share until the price was $1.50 above my average price, which happened that same day. I sold one-third of my position that day, and the next day I sold the rest of the position about three or four dollars higher. Then it went straight down again. I ended up having the biggest month of my career.

The stock always seems to reveal itself to me, especially when I have a large position and I'm watching it closely. What I have learned to recognize over my career is that I don't have to be early because I almost always see it. Maybe it's my lack of discipline that gets me in early. I want to be in early just in case I don't see it, but yet I've always seen it when it changes. It's a feeling; it's a sense. I think, *Why did I go early again? Here is my signal.* I don't get it every time for every stock, but I get it pretty often.

Tyco ultimately went even lower. What gave you the confidence to buy it when you did?

It was just a feeling.

Was it sentiment related?

It was completely sentiment related. It was the velocity of the fall that got my interest. The price move from $27 to $18 probably happened in about two hours' time. That was when I bought a lot more, knowing that this was an all-out panic and an opportunity.

If it had gone below your price, would you have scaled out of the position or liquidated it all?

I never buy or sell anything at the market because I'm wrong and have to get out. I have never done that in my career. I'll begin to work out of the position, and if I see it turn around, I'll get back in again, thinking that I was right all along.

So you have never had a position that made you cry uncle?

I have a lot of positions that made me cry uncle, but I don't capitulate.

[Zach speaking] Jimmy never panics. When we had the "flash crash," his first question was, "Is there something wrong with the data?" It took him about a minute to realize the price quotes weren't wrong, and he went long everything right there.

[Jimmy continues] I don't let myself panic. Even if I don't know what's going on, I'm not going to sell. I might lose 5 percent more trying to find out what is going on, but I'm not going to make a decision because other people are choosing to make a decision out of emotion. I'm not going to be *that* guy.

There was one exception, though. I had to throw in the towel on my short position in homebuilders.

Was it a good decision that you covered your short position?

Yes, I was much too early.

When did you get bearish on the current market?

I remember in September [2010] saying to Zach, "Wow, the market is going up here. I should be long stocks." After the market rallied,

I started going net short in October, and then at the end of the month, the market started to rally really hard. In November, I realized I had to adjust my position. Instead of covering my shorts, I started buying a lot more longs in value stocks, which started to catch in November and December, and that helped me a lot. In December, I made back most of the money I lost in October and November.

But you were still net short?

Yes, I haven't been net long since September.

Even though you thought the market was going higher?

Because it didn't make sense to me that it was going higher. So I just reduced my short exposure by buying longs. The way I looked at it, the more the market went up, the more right my short was going to be. The more it went up, the more money smart people would take off the table. Smart guys always sell when the market is going up. That's how they make money.

I'm not trying to prove I'm right. I'm not trying to prove the market is stupid. I just like making money. There are so many guys I've seen in my career who do something just because someone else is doing it. That is a way of getting beat up. I believe I have as good a sense as anybody in the market. I trust that sense, and it has served me well.

Was that sense there from the beginning?

Yes, that sense was there early on.

Do you think it is innate?

Yes, part of it is innate; there's no question about it. My goal is to one day be able to match up my trades with my sense that it's ready to happen right now and to only invest at those times. For me, mastery would be knowing that I don't have to be early, and all I have to do is wait for when I see it because I almost always see it.

If you usually see it when the time is right, why do you frequently initiate the trade before you get that feeling? Wouldn't it work out better if you waited until you had that

strong conviction that now is the time, rather than anticipating the trend change before that point?

One hundred percent. No question about it. Sometimes I am the adult in the seat, and sometimes I am the child. If I am the child, he just wants to be involved. I am not a computer, and I have my flaws. Sometimes I just want to be involved, and I get in instead of waiting until I see, "Oh, there it is." It's a lack of discipline that I have been contending with my whole career. Even though my track record would indicate otherwise, I still have some lack of trust in my process. I still want to be in the market early, just in case I don't see it.

So even though you usually get a strong sense when the market is ready to move, you almost trade like you don't have that skill. Does that make sense to you?

It's worked in that I have improved my discipline. I don't allow myself to get bigger if I am wrong early. Even though I think I am right, I won't necessarily short more because it is higher. When I was younger, I would get bigger just because the market was going up. Now, I'll wait till I get that sense that the market is ready to move before I get bigger.

When did you first get interested in the stock market?

My very first influence was probably seeing the movie *Wall Street* in high school. In my senior year of high school, I worked for a stockbroker who was also the branch manager. In Williams College, I took a one-month course taught by Simon Long on trading and capital markets. Simon was trading for Bear Stearns at the time. He had a trading setup at his home, and I would go there almost every day. Simon was a really smart guy and a bit eccentric. He just loved talking about the markets. He really brought the markets to life for me. Also, I wanted to make money.

Was it the money that appealed to you in the movie *Wall Street*?

It was more the action that appealed to me. I'm a high-energy guy. I thought that trading perfectly fit my personality. My desire to make money was more influenced by my parents being immigrants who worked very hard. Those were my key influences. There wasn't much more to it. After college, all my friends went into banking, but I knew I wanted to be a trader. Even though I didn't know exactly what it was, I knew it was what I wanted to do. I interviewed with some larger firms like UBS and Société Générale, and then one of my friends told me about a small firm called First New York Securities. I interviewed there and Don Ehrenberg hired me.

Do you know what got you the job?

I don't know what got me the job, but several years after I had started with the firm, I brought my mother in to meet Don. In their sit-down conversation, Don told her, "I don't know what you did to your son, but I never had anybody work so hard." I knew I wanted it more than anybody else. There was no way I was not going to make it. I always had that competitive drive, whether it was getting into a top college, or competing in college sports.

What did you learn about trading at First New York Securities?

I was an assistant for a year; same as Zach is. I learned how to follow positions and a daily P&L. I was fascinated by how the stock market moved and how money was being made.

What was the trading style of the trader you worked for?

Eric had a style similar to the style I have: Buy companies when they are out of favor and sell companies when everybody loves them.

It sounds like you came into this business as a contrarian.

I was introduced to that style of trading very early on, and it made complete sense with the way I looked at the world. Fidelity and the other behemoths that run massive amounts of public money are only buying what's good at the time. They're never going in there when Apple is dislocated or Exxon is dislocated. They're always selling then. The smart guys are always on the other side. That's the game on Wall Street. I'm not complaining.

How much did they start you out with?

I don't remember the exact amount, but I remember that I made $350,000 in my first year, $800,000 in my second, over $1 million in my third, and I never looked back.

Do you ever use fundamentals?

No, never. There was a three-year period when I had fundamental analysts working for me, but I found it very difficult to match up their views with my timing. I trusted my own work much more. It was a distraction. Fundamentals were not something I wanted to commit more time to. I wanted to spend my time mastering my discipline and focusing on what was going on with me emotionally that was causing me to make certain choices. That is where the real curiosity was for me. Trading is a great mirror into myself. It doesn't make any difference how much money I lose or make; I am not going to be sad or happy.

What did you do to be successful from the start?

I was totally focused on trading. Nothing else mattered. Not my health; not my relationships.

What was the first time you took a large loss?

I was short homebuilders during their big rally. I felt something was wrong. I didn't understand what was going on. Eventually, it became obvious that momentum hedge fund buying was driving the market. For the first time, I began doubting if I knew what I was doing. I lost about $7 million in one month. Losing such a large amount of money in such a short period of time opened the door to allow other questions to come into my life. That is when I started focusing on my health. I remember thinking, *This is going to take me a year to make back.* I made that money back in about two or three months. I don't remember how I did it.

What made you so bearish on homebuilders at the time?

I remember at that time people flipping houses and making money immediately. It felt very unreal to me. It was the way people talked about the homebuilding sector. It was a new paradigm. Every time I have had a major concept, I have eventually been right, but sometimes I am too early.

I assume you were also negative on technology in 1999?

Yes. It's always driven by the nature of how something is advancing. It never made sense to me how something can move so much in such a short period of time. It didn't make sense that everybody had it wrong before then, and all of a sudden there is a whole new way of looking at it. Intuitively, it didn't feel right, and I honor that intuition.

Given your style of anticipating tops, how did you avoid disaster during the Internet bubble when it was commonplace for stocks in that sector to go up tenfold or more?

I traded the technology stocks rather than the Internet stocks, but they still had crazy moves.

Were you early?

Absolutely, but what was different in those days was that even if a stock was in a big upmove, you could get an opening where the stock was down $4, and then it would go back up. But because the stock would open sharply lower, it would give you the opportunity to take money off the table, and then you would have dry gunpowder. What has changed in the last five to eight years with hedge funds becoming the main players is that there are far fewer pullbacks. Now, you can't be too early. The last two years [April 2009 to March 2011] have devastated the shorts as much as any other time I have seen, even including the Internet bubble.

Has that forced you to change your style at all?

Absolutely. It has forced me to rely more on the trust that I will see the transition point so I don't have to be so early.

How were you positioned when the stock market topped in March 2000?

I was short, but I didn't pressure the short. As it was going down, I was covering.

So you were taking money off the table as the market went down.

Yes, but I was shorting the early rallies.

But you didn't continue to play the downtrend in the tech stocks, which lasted for 2½ years?

I didn't milk the downmove. I am not a milker. For me it was a question of "What's next?" There is never a shortage of themes. The market is always creating minibubbles. There is so much opportunity all the time that you never have to get yourself into trouble. You never have to be early. But I always have an inner conflict. There are certain periods where I get more obstinate because I think I'm right. I am more rigid than I would like to be. I think I am an exceptional trader, but sometimes I let my strong beliefs get in the way. I am working on letting go of my beliefs and be the trader I can be.

But the beliefs get you on the right side of the market.

The beliefs have always kept me making money and not playing the short-term moves that I don't really trust. The markets are such a greater fool's game. I don't want to be the greater fool. There is clearly ego there.

I understand why you may not want to play the momentum trade when it is contrary to your beliefs. But why not wait on the sidelines until you get the sense that the time is right?

[Zach interjects.] Jimmy has this amazing execution. There are days when the market is up 5 or 10 handles and Jimmy may be $10 million short, and he will still finish up for the day. And I can see that if he had not done any executions, he would be down $150,000 for the day. But instead he'll end up being up $30,000 for the day just by constantly trading in and out. We did 520 orders today. So when Jimmy is short and the market is up, he is not necessarily losing.

[Jimmy speaking again.] That's the point. Regardless of my belief that the market will fall apart, even when the market gives me just a 1 percent or 2 percent move, I'm still taking chips off the table. That way of trading explains a lot more of why I have made money in my career. It was not so much about my being right on the direction of the market as it was that when they were giving me money, I was always taking it, on a daily basis.

So even though today was only the first day of a downmove, you still took money off the table?

I took half of my capital off today. If the market bounces, I will short the rebound for sure.

If the market bounces, that's easy—you just replace the shorts you covered. But what if the downtrend you were anticipating continues tomorrow?

If it's lower, then I will just be buying back more stock. I don't mind if I miss a move down because the market will always have a move that I can re-enter if I really feel like it. I am never afraid of missing anything. The market is always providing opportunities.

So it doesn't bother you if you end up getting back in at a worse price than you got out.

All I think about is making money; not being right.

[Zach speaking to Jimmy.] Something that you said that always made sense to me is, "I never need to make money in a stock where I lost it."

[Jimmy continues.] Early in my career, I had more of a tie to stocks. Now, I couldn't care less where I am making money. I don't have any vendettas [a long pause] anymore [he laughs].

But you used to?

Yes, for sure.

How did you learn to give it up?

I just got tired of fighting. Losing all that money being short home-builders was the biggest blessing because it led to me looking at my life in a different way. Why am I making life so much harder on myself? It could be so much easier. There is something wrong when I start feeling that uncomfortable. Whereas before I would dig in my heels, I'm not willing to go there anymore. Now, when a trade feels painful, I start reducing my exposure. I am much more sensitive and conscious about how I am feeling. If a position doesn't feel right, I will make the shift. I can't sit with that feeling very long anymore.

What is a recent example of when you had that type of feeling that something was wrong?

October [2010]. The markets were starting to accelerate up, and I was losing a lot of money. Even though the market had been going up for a year and a half, it shifted into a higher gear. I didn't like the way the market felt.

You sound like you are a natural short.

I am a natural short because there is a hype, a marketing campaign that is always at work to get people to be long stock, and it's unnatural. It's an energy that can't always be maintained.

The trading approach you have described—a strategy of selling stocks when they are up and buying stocks when they are down—hardly sounds like a recipe for success. In fact, it is easy to imagine how the approach could be disastrous. So obviously there is more to what you are doing. Can you put some color on it? How do you do what you do? Can you provide some specific examples of how you pick and time your trades?

I divide stocks into those that I'm looking to buy and those that I'm looking to sell. Then I recognize when those buys or sells show up in a way that suggests there is a possibility for an accelerated move in a short period of time.

How do you recognize that point?

Something changes. The chart could change. Something could happen within the group. There is something always changing, where clues are given to me along the way, that shows me it's time. For example, Goodyear was one of the stocks on my buy list. The other auto parts stocks had broken out a while ago, but Goodyear was lagging. We had been watching it for a long time. Then about two weeks ago, there was a day before the earnings report when the volume was huge and the price was picking up. I said, "I think this is our spot. Goodyear is ready." I had been watching it for six months. I always had a small position in it because the other auto parts stocks had phenomenal moves. I thought that Goodyear should catch a bid at some point. When I saw something change, I knew the stock was ready.

What changed—volume?

The volume was incredible on an up day. I knew that one day, I would see a change, and that was it. I believe that sense, and I went long.

Any other examples?

[He scans his trade pad and then brings up a chart on one of the screens.] Here's another example: Dollar General. We bought it right around here. [He points to the chart at a spot after a sharp downtrend with the price having fallen to near the low end of a longer-term price base.]

What was the rationale for that trade?

Retail stocks were going up. We were looking for some value in retail. The stock had sold off seven points in a month and a half.

What is this big upside gap? [I refer to a price move on the chart that occurred a little over a week after the trade entry.]

There was a takeover.

Once the takeover was announced, did you get out?

Absolutely. It was a 15 percent move.

[Balodimas continues to bring up price charts.]

MU [Micron Technology]. We had been long all along, but we got much bigger on this day here where the stock was up a lot and broke out of a band. Although it had a big move up that day, it was still in the trading range it had been in for a few years. [The stock had broken out of the trading band of the past few months, but was still within a broader long-term trading range.] So, I wasn't chasing the stock. I felt comfortable with it.

I wouldn't feel comfortable with something like this. [He brings up the chart for FFIV, a cloud computing company.] I would never buy that stock. [The chart shows a long, nearly unbroken uptrend, followed by a huge downside gap not far from the high, and then a rebound about two-thirds of the way back to the high.] This is a stock I would short. Tomorrow, if the market is up, I will probably be a seller.

Why specifically are you so negative on this chart?

It is a broken stock. It broke on big volume. The indexes have made new highs, and the stock can't get above its 50-day moving average. All the investors had been riding the stock all the way up. Although cloud computing is a great story, it is overplayed. Current prices way outstrip any growth potential for the next few years. Analysts are talking about 2015 numbers. It's ridiculous. No one knows what is going to happen four years out. It's difficult enough to forecast the next quarter. The rhetoric buildup is always a similar pattern.

Here is another one. Amazon broke down here, and I went short on this day. [The Amazon chart is another long-term uptrend with a big downside gap that occurs not far below the high. The day Balodimas points to is on a subsequent partial rebound back toward the high.]

Why were you bearish on Amazon?

Because of the chart. The price had almost doubled in a year. The big volume on this down day showed me the turn was for real. I didn't go short that day because the market was down $20. I waited until the market rebounded above the 50-day moving average. Amazon still went up another $12, but then I doubled up near the high [the rebound high was in the vicinity of the previous high] because I still thought I was right, and I did okay.

Here is Chipotle—a wild stock.

[I look at the chart, and it is another large uptrend.] If I look at a stock, and it's in a large uptrend, I know you will be talking about the short side.

The short side, right. I got caught in this whole thing. [Balodimas points to the last segment of an accelerated uptrend.]

You stayed short the whole way?

The whole way. We doubled up here. [Balodimas points to a spot on the chart closer to the high of the upmove.] So we brought our average price way up.

So you doubled up into a deep losing position?

Into a deep losing position, but knowing it's Chipotle. They sell tacos! It's not like it's some new technology company. I'm not going to be that scared of it. The tacos may be really good, but the stock has gone from $140 to $270 in three months. Really? I don't care how good the tacos are. I got out here. [He points to a retracement on the chart.] So I recovered about three-quarters of the loss.

You seem to do a lot of selling into uptrends.

Yes, but I am always buying it back on the dips. And you hope to get lucky sometimes and get a big down day. That just happened to me in cotton. I was short the cotton ETF, and on these two days I lost $200,000. [He points to a chart with another big uptrend with a near vertical upmove on the last two days of the advance.] I was short 7,500 shares, and on this day I added another 22,000 shares. [He points to the high day of the move.] I saw there was huge volume. I said, "This is a squeeze. I don't care what's going on in Egypt. The stock has doubled. I should take my shot here." Call it luck. Call it what you want. The stock was down 12 percent the next day. I ended up making net $100,000 on the trade. It was La La Land. The ETF could easily have been up another $10 on the next day. That's where the chutzpah comes in. When no one else wants to do it, sometimes there is great opportunity.

There are days like today when the cash register rings. But it seems like your trading style is one that must place you in discomfort on most days.

Yes, because the market is up more days than it is down, and I would guess that in my career, I have been short about 75 percent of the time. But I wouldn't say it's discomfort. It's pretty much of the routine.

It seems like the only time you are with the trend is when you are betting on a reversal and then the market turns around.

I am good at catching the early part of the trend. I'm trying to learn how to catch the middle part of the trend better. I am never there for the last three innings—the capitulatory phase.

The interview has carried on for three hours, and Balodimas's energy seems to be flagging. I suggest that perhaps it might be best to finish the interview in a second meeting. Balodimas readily agrees. I return about three months later (May 24, 2011). I begin our second conversation with a line of questions about parts of his strategy that just don't make sense to me.

It seems to me that what you are really skilled at is trading around a position. In fact, you are so good at it that you often make money on a position even when the longer-term trend is against you. It's like you are really good going up the stairs quickly, but you are often going up the down escalator. Wouldn't your performance improve going up the up escalator? If you traded around a position going with the trend, instead of against the trend, wouldn't you do even better?

Here is a good example of why I don't have any trust in doing that. Recently, silver had an historic run on the upside. I had been eyeing silver for six months. Technically, it was in a bullish pattern. In commodities, more so than in any other asset class, most traders trade the trend. Nevertheless, I thought the market was a short. I watched the market for six months until I thought, *It's time to sell this thing*.

Did anything happen on that day?

It had a reversal, but it was the buildup up to that point that was important. The silver price had nearly tripled in just over a year. The precious metals markets were spooked by the University of Texas taking delivery on $1 billion of physical gold. There was news on TV every day about inflation. I am seeing all of this and thinking that they are really pushing the story very hard. It felt like everybody was buying silver. Those are the opportunities I look for. I went short the silver ETF. The prior price move up had already been parabolic, and then the rally became even more vertical. There was real money being put to work in silver. If you saw the amount of volume trading in those last four days of the upmove, it was clear that it wasn't retail investors. It was institutions saying they had to be there. The big volume told me that supply was coming into the market. I doubled up during that rally. The market made a new high, and within three days I was down $4 million on the trade. It was already Cuckooland before that rally, and I knew the market was an even better short, but I had already used up all my ammunition. I wasn't willing to bet my year and have to make back $8 million if the market had another move like it just had over the past few days. It wasn't worth it to me to put myself in that position. The market then sold off to about my average price, and I covered the position. On balance, I probably about broke even, and then the market quickly dropped down to $32 from its high near $49.

But you had covered the whole position.

Yes, because I was tired. I may not have made money on that trade because I got too big a few days too early, but my point is that my way of looking at the world is right. You had every expert tell you how much silver was worth, and yet it went down from $49 to $32 in the biggest market selloff in over 30 years. I went maximum short within four days of the market top. I trust my radar as to what is really happening in the market. So, when you ask me if I should change my style, maybe I should be more flexible, but I don't have the trust to buy a market in a trend, the way I trust my instincts on a trade.

I wasn't asking you why you didn't buy silver at \$30 or \$35. I understand that totally. And, actually, if you tried doing that, I think it would turn out badly because it is so counter to everything you believe in. But, I'm asking you something different. Earlier in the upmove, there is a point when you think that this market is eventually going to set up for a good short, but you only watch it because you think the trend still has a way to run. At that earlier juncture, why not participate on the long side until you think the market is getting closer to a point where it is a sale? In other words, I am talking about going long well before the market becomes parabolic, let alone vertical.

I am good at catching the turning points, but I'm not good at staying in a market when the street gets behind it. I'm always early. But the analysts and the people who run most of the money on Wall Street are never going to put their necks out there. They're waiting for the trend to be really intact, and they are trying to catch that middle portion of the trend, which is the juiciest part of the ride. I catch the first part of the trend, which is the hardest part. I am getting better at extending it, but I am not there for as much of the ride as I should be.

Here is what I don't get. It seems that in all the price moves where the market is in Cuckooland, as you term it, once the market finally breaks, it usually keeps on going. Why participate in only the first few weeks of the new trend when these types of markets will run at least six months to a year or longer once they turn? Why trade only the first price break from the highs? After you get out, why not reenter from the short side on a bounce? The very fact that you committed to a major short position is itself an indication that when the market does break, it is likely to carry on for some time and some distance. If you went back and checked those trades where you took a maximum position,

anticipating a major market reversal, I would bet that in every case, the market kept on going after it finally broke.

That's 100 percent true. I understand that, and yet I don't have the patience to sit there every day with the same positions. The next level down is something that I don't have the trust to stay with.

But that trust should come from your own prior conviction to put on a maximum position before the market turned. The very fact that you were in that trade is itself a great indicator that the trend will likely continue in the other direction once the market has broken. You have this great indicator—not an indicator on a chart, but an internal radar—that identifies potential major market turning points. You also have a talent for trading in and out of a position. Why not combine those skills? Take, for example, the commodity peak in 2008. You anticipated that top, went short in the last stage of the rally, and then took your profits on the first break after the highs. Why not at that point say, "This market was way overdone. It's going to keep going down for a while. I'm going to get back short on a rally." Then you would be trading both in sync with your original prognostication and with the trend. And if you combine that positional bias with your skill in trading in and out of the market, you would open up a whole source of additional profit potential that you are leaving on the table. It seems to me to be such an obvious thing to do. It seems like the opportunity that you haven't taken is tailor-made for your set of skills. It's like you are currently trading with two hands tied behind your back. You are trading these ideas when the trend is strongly against you, but once the market turns and the trend is in your direction, you go on and do something else.

Look, Jack, I know that, and I want to have those types of trades because I'm right there. What part of my thought process is shutting out those trades? I don't know. Maybe I am just comfortable being comfortable, and trading with the trend would require me being uncomfortable. The part of the price move where everyone is freaking out and my boss is freaking out is where I am at ease. I am very comfortable when panic has set in because I know then, "I got them. They're trapped."

That's ironic because what you consider comfortable—selling into a near vertical rally—is exactly what most people would find highly uncomfortable.

Maybe that is where the fun of it is for me. And yet, where I am making most of my money is in the short-term trading around my positions.

That's exactly my point! Why not put the two together? Why not combine that short-term trading with positions that are in line with your original directional call after the market has confirmed the turn you expected? I am not suggesting you give up doing any trades you do. All I am saying is why not add that other component? When you have that really strong feeling and then the market does break, the odds are that the trend will continue for a while.

It always does. Those huge opportunities in my career were probably $50 million trades, but I took all the risk and maybe only made $3 million when just a few weeks later it would have been a $10 million profit, and a few months later $25 million. I hope in my career I will make those trades sometimes. I know I will have the opportunity.

Do stock upgrades or downgrades figure into your trading?

Generally, the stocks that I am short are being upgraded, and the stocks that I am long are being downgraded. That's how Wall Street works. They're always pushing it when things are great, and they're always selling it when things are bad. They don't impact my trading.

Do you still see yourself trading 10 years from now?

I think trading will always be part of me, but I don't think it will be a 9 to 4 thing.

But ironically, the very style that has brought you success— continuously trading in and out of positions—almost by

definition seems to necessitate your sitting in front of the screen all day.

So far, yes. But even in the last two years—and Zach can attest to this—I will step away from the screen to go to meetings. That is a way of bridging myself to a world that doesn't have me only in front of my screens.

What are your goals?

I want to continue to learn. I want to be a great businessman. I am involved in a lot of other businesses—outside investments that I have made.

What other businesses are you involved in?

Video games, clean tech, movie postproduction, and health care.

How does trading fit into it?

Trading is my source of funds.

How do you see your trading evolving over time?

I really can't imagine myself sitting in front of the screens for the rest of my life.

Wouldn't it be hard to step away from something that you are so good at?

I started stepping away part time and doing other things four years ago. It has been a slow process because trading is something I am good at, and it comes relatively easy to me. But sitting in front of screens is very limiting when there are so many other things that interest me. This was my first job. I want to let go of the shackles. I know there is so much more of life that I can experience and engage in, but the only way I can do that is by stepping away.

■ ■ ■

I feel this interview should contain the type of warning that accompanies TV footage of dangerous stunts: "Don't try this at home." The truth is that Balodimas's style is so highly individualistic, so dependent on innate talent, and so poorly attuned to most traders that, as a generalization, they would be better off doing the exact opposite than trying to emulate his approach. Of all the traders I have ever interviewed for any of the Market Wizard books, none has provided a more difficult role model from which to draw lessons applicable to most traders. There are, however, three lessons that can be drawn from Balodimas's story that do have more general applicability without potential lethal side effects:

- **The need to adapt**—While the commonality of human nature provides elements of consistency in market behavior across time, markets also change, and successful traders adapt to that change. In the case of Balodimas, he noticed that the much greater level of market participation by hedge funds was resulting in smoother price moves for individual stocks and far fewer pullbacks, particularly intraday. This structural change in the market made it more difficult for Balodimas to offset losses from being too early in a position with profits from trading around the position. It became more important not to be too early on trades. Balodimas responded by keeping positions smaller until there was a market change that gave him a high degree of confidence that a turning point was imminent. Even though very few readers will be able to relate to Balodimas's trading strategy, the idea that trading methods need to be adapted to changing market conditions is an important concept that can be applied to each trader's specific approach.
- **Trading around a position**—A key element in Balodimas's trading success is adjusting position size counter to market fluctuations. For example, if he is short, he will reduce his position on price breaks and rebuild the position on rallies. Balodimas is so skillful at trading around positions that he's often able to generate net profits even when the net price movement of a stock over time is counter to his position. Although Balodimas's timing for this type of trading is an innate skill that cannot be translated and one that few traders will be able to match, many traders may nevertheless find that trading around a position improves performance and makes it easier

to hold onto winning trades. As a simple example, assume you are long a stock at 50, looking for a long-term objective of 76, and expecting near-term resistance in the vicinity of 62. Given these assumptions, you might choose to reduce long exposure on an advance to the 61 to 63 zone, looking to reinstate the full position on a pullback. The potential drawback is that a retracement to the reentry level may fail to occur, in which case profits will be realized on a smaller position. On the positive side, if the liquidated portion of the position is reentered at a better price, total profits will be enhanced, and perhaps even more importantly, the ability to hold the position will be improved. Whether trading around positions is net beneficial or detrimental will be highly contingent on the individual trader. It will not necessarily be a good fit for all traders, but some traders may find it a highly useful approach.

- **Avoid euphoria**—Even though it has worked well for Balodimas for a long time, the last thing I would advise traders to do would be to sell into panic rallies. Very few traders will possess the innate timing skill and emotional stamina to pull this off successfully, and the cost of being wrong can be extreme. Still, for those who are on the right side of a market that accelerates into a parabolic move, it may well make sense to take partial or total profits while the market is in a panic state, rather than waiting for a reversal, which in these types of markets can be both abrupt and extreme when it does come. In short, if you are long a market that you would be petrified to sell, it may not be a bad idea to get smaller or get out.

Some readers will finish this chapter and think, "Balodimas has just been lucky. You can't trade that way and get away with it. He will eventually step on a land mine." Well, Balodimas has stepped on a land mine—many, in fact—but it hasn't stopped his consistent forward momentum. Think about it. Balodimas averages hundreds of trades a day and has been trading for 15 years through multiple bull and bear market phases. What are the odds of consistent superior performance with this frequency of trading on the basis of luck alone? Such an outcome would border on statistical impossibility.

As successful as Balodimas has been, from my objective perspective, it seemed that he wasn't applying his methodology to its full potential.

Specifically, the markets he anticipates will be major tops and bottoms invariably trend for a long time once they reverse. Yet despite this consistent pattern and his skill in identifying these major turning points before they happen, he only trades a small part of the ensuing trend. It seemed obvious to me that he could further improve his performance by simply trading these markets for a much longer time—a conclusion with which he agreed. The point is that even the best traders may not be executing their strategies in the best way. Any trader that has an edge, as Balodimas clearly does, should consider whether the trading methodology being employed is best aligned with that edge.

I am frequently asked whether becoming a Market Wizard is a matter of innate talent or hard work. My standard answer is to use a running analogy. As intimidating as the task may seem to those physically unconditioned, most people can run a marathon given sufficient training and dedication. But only the small minority born with the right physical characteristics will ever be able to run a 2:15 (men) or 2:30 (women) time, regardless of how hard they work. The analogy for trading is that similar to running a marathon, proficiency is achievable with hard work, but performing at an elite level requires some degree of innate talent. Balodimas provides a good example. Sure, he was extremely dedicated to succeeding as a trader and willing to work long hours with full focus on trading, but his level of trading success was only possible because he has some innate skill, some inner radar, that gives him a sense of what markets will do. I don't care how devoted someone is to trading or how many hours they are willing to watch trading screens, the reality is that this type of skill will be out of reach for most people.

There is no single true path to trading success. On the contrary, the trading methodologies employed by the Market Wizards are extraordinarily varied. The trading approaches used are not merely different, but in the case of someone like Jimmy Balodimas, the trading methodology may be closer to a mirror image of what other traders do than bearing any similarity. Aspiring traders need to understand that the quest is not a matter of finding that one approach that unlocks the secrets of market success, but rather finding an approach that fits their personality. Jimmy Balodimas has found an approach that works for him because it fits his personality—independent, competitive, contrarian, and very comfortable with risk. The same approach, however, would be potentially disastrous for most other traders who would have very different comfort levels in trading style. Over the years, I have received many inquiries that read something like the following:

Dear Mr. Schwager,

　　I wonder whether you know of any traders who are looking for apprentices. I'm willing to work long hours without pay to be able to learn from one of the Market Wizards.

This type of query reflects a misdirected quest. You cannot succeed in the markets by copying someone else's approach because the odds are remote that their method will fit your personality. The answer lies not in copying someone else's method, but in finding your own.

Chapter 15

Joel Greenblatt

The Magic Formula

J oel Greenblatt's name came up several times when I called hedge fund managers I knew for their recommendations on who I should consider including in a new *Market Wizards* book. One manager said, "He wrote this book, *You Can Be a Stock Market Genius.*" Responding to my muffled groan, he said, "Yeah, I know, the title, but it's really a great book. I think that book got a lot of hedge fund managers in the business." I subsequently read the book and found it covered the esoteric subject of special situation trading (spinoffs, mergers, restructurings, rights offerings, stub stocks, warrants, etc.) with surprising conciseness, clarity, and even a sense of humor.

In the appendix, Greenblatt provided the track record for his fund, Gotham Capital. The record began in 1985 and stopped abruptly in 1994. The average annualized compounded return was exactly 50.0 percent (before incentive fees). The outperformance was remarkably consistent. The lowest annual return during the entire 10-year period was positive 28.5 percent. It was one of the best track records I had ever seen. Why, I wondered, would anyone close a fund that was doing so remarkably well? Since it was clear from his books that Greenblatt remained active in the markets, I couldn't even guess at a plausible explanation for closing the fund. The answer, it turned out, was both logical and obvious (once you knew it). Greenblatt closed his fund precisely because it did so well. Assets had grown to the point where they were impeding returns, so Greenblatt decided to return all investor money. Greenblatt, along with Rob Goldstein, his partner since 1989, continued to trade the Gotham Capital account with their own capital for more than another decade, using the same concentrated portfolio of special situation trades as they did in the fund—the types of trades Greenblatt detailed in *You Can Be a Stock Market Genius*. The returns for this proprietary account are not available. Off the record, Greenblatt did tell me the average return for the account subsequent to the return of investor money. Let's just say that Gotham continued to do extremely well (far better than the vast majority of hedge funds), although not approaching the lofty average return of the terminated fund.

Greenblatt's second book, *The Little Book That Beats the Market*—the man is not timid when it comes to titles—grew out of a research project. In 2003, he hired a programmer to test how two key metrics that together were representative of his investment selection criteria—picking companies that were cheap and good—actually performed in the markets. Greenblatt used *earnings yield* to represent cheapness and *return on capital* to represent goodness.[1] The two measures were combined in a single ranking that worked even better than Greenblatt and Goldstein expected. Greenblatt named this combined ranking indicator the *Magic Formula*, a name that implicitly pokes fun at the hype accompanying market indicators, but also acknowledges the surprising efficacy of the measure (as empirically demonstrated). In fact, Greenblatt and Goldstein were so impressed with the Magic Formula that they set up an eponymous website to use it as the basis for managing stock portfolios.

---

[1]Greenblatt's definitions of these terms are different from their most common definitions and are fully detailed later in this chapter.

The success of the initial research project led to a major expansion of the research endeavor in which Gotham spent "tens of millions" to develop and test a more sophisticated construction and application of value indicators. The proprietary indicators used were conceptually similar to the magic formula, but were considerably more complex and yielded more accurate measures of value. The results were so good that the partners shifted Gotham's money management methodology from a concentrated special situations focus to a diversified systematic value approach. The new diversified approach also had much greater capacity, effectively removing the reason that had prompted the return of investor capital in the original Gotham fund. In 2009, Gotham returned to the world of money management, launching two long/short funds, one large cap and one small-to-mid cap. So 15 years after having returned investor money and believing himself to be permanently out of the money management business, Greenblatt, in coordination with Goldstein and a team of 10 research analysts, found himself once again managing investor money based on the same core principles. This time, however, the trading was based on a diversified, systematic methodology instead of the original approach, which yielded a concentrated portfolio of value and special situation stocks.

Greenblatt and his team at Gotham next applied the systematic value approach to the task of constructing value-weighted indexes, which appeared to substantially outperform all existing types of equity indexes. Gotham has launched several funds and separately traded managed accounts trading these new generation value-weighted indexes, in both U.S. equities and international equities, with the funds segmented by cap size. The funds trading these new generation indexes provide mutual fund and institutional equity index investors with a seemingly much better investment alternative. This new investment vehicle is the big secret in Greenblatt's third book, *The Big Secret for the Small Investor*. Greenblatt believes that it's just a matter of time before other mutual funds begin copying this innovative approach, but that Gotham's proprietary research capabilities and process should continue to provide superior performance versus competitors.

■ ■ ■

When you were young, did you have any idea what you wanted to do with your life?

Probably not. I had a better idea of what I didn't want to do. I got an MBA, and then went to law school, primarily because I didn't want to get an investment banking job working 90 to a 100 hours a week. But I dropped out after one year when I realized I had no interest in being a lawyer.

What got you interested in the stock market?

In my junior year in college, I read an article in *Forbes* about Ben Graham. A lightbulb went off, and I started reading everything I could find on Ben Graham. In college, we were taught the efficient market hypothesis, which wasn't very appealing to me. The theory didn't coincide logically with what I saw going on in the market. There were lots of stocks that doubled or halved during the course of one year. The premise that these stocks were efficiently priced at all of the prices between their highs and lows seemed implausible to me. When I read Graham, I thought to myself, *That is so logical; stocks fluctuate around fair value over time.*

Did you have any interest in the market before that point?

I had an interest in horse racing and dog racing more than in the stock market.

Did you go to the track?

I went to the track when I could get in, usually the dog track because they weren't very stern about keeping you from sneaking in.

Did you have any methodology in betting?

Unfortunately, I didn't. I'll never forget my first big bet. One time, I went to the track with my cousin, and I found a dog who had run 12 seconds faster than all the other dogs but, for some inexplicable reason, the odds against him were 99 to 1. That seemed like a great bet to me. I didn't know why the other gamblers were so stupid. The dog finished dead last. After the race, I found out that the dog had run 12 seconds faster at a much shorter distance and that this was his first time running a longer distance. That experience taught me a quick lesson that I had to do more research.

When did you first start investing in stocks?

After I read about Ben Graham and before going off to law school, I started a fund buying what Graham called *net nets*, stocks trading below their liquidation value. I did a study on stocks selling below their liquidation value, which eventually turned into my master's thesis. I worked with two of my friends from business school, Richard Pzena and Bruce Newberg. We didn't have money for a database. The university library had the S&P stock guides for the past 10 years or so. We manually collected the data from the guides. We only looked at about 15 percent of the stock universe because it was pretty mind numbing getting the data by hand. At the time, the University of Pennsylvania had a DEC10 computer, which was about four times the size of this room, and probably had less power than today's smart phone. Richard was pretty good with computers. We put all our data into the computer and found that Graham's formula, which he had written about many years earlier, still worked extremely well. The portfolios we put together using Graham's principles did much better than the indexes. The study got published in the *Journal of Portfolio Management* in the summer of 1981. Before going off to law school, I started a fund to buy stocks selling below their liquidation value with $250,000 that I had raised from my father's friends.

How long did you manage that fund?

For about two to three years. When I had my first full-time job, it was suggested to me that it was not appropriate to keep the fund running.

How did the fund do?

It made 44 percent cumulatively.

Since you had gotten off to such a good start with the fund, did you consider the possibility of building that into a career instead of getting a job?

I thought I had more to learn. It was a good experience managing other people's money and knowing what that felt like.

What was your first investment based job?

After my first and only year at law school, I took a summer job trading options at Bear Stearns.

Did you know anything about options at that point?

No, I ended up doing forward conversions, which are a riskless arbitrage.[2] The idea was to put on these arbitrage trades and earn 18 to 19 percent annualized.

The option market was that inefficient at the time?

No, interest rates were that high at the time. I think the arbitrage added about 5 percent to 6 percent to the risk-free rate. Frankly, the trading was kind of mechanical. At the time, you didn't have the option prices on the screen in front of you. I had to run to the other side of floor to get a printout of option prices to see what options were setting up attractively relative to the stock. Then I would run back to my desk to try to execute the trade. Although it was interesting learning about options, by the end of the summer, I knew that I had no interest in trading options for a living.

What did you do after the summer job?

I got a job as an analyst for a startup risk arbitrage firm called Halcyon Investments. There were three partners, and I was the only analyst. They

---

[2]A forward conversion consists of a long stock position hedged with a synthetic short position (short call/long put at same strike and expiration). If the synthetic short position can be implemented at a net credit premium, it provides a locked-in, risk-free profit.

offered me $22,000, which was about half the going rate for MBAs at the time. I jumped at it because I loved the idea of being the only analyst in a startup firm. I thought I could learn a lot.

Wasn't the fact that you had no experience at all in merger arbitrage an impediment to getting the job?

Well, at $22,000, they clearly weren't willing to spend much money and weren't looking for an experienced analyst. I hoped they were just looking for someone with potential.

What year was this?

I started December 1981.

Ironically, you began your career right before a major bottom in the stock market.

It was interesting. At that time, not many people were looking to go to Wall Street because the market hadn't gone up for 13 years.

What were your experiences in your first job?

At the time, merger arbitrage was the Wild West. There were great inefficiencies and plenty of opportunities, so that even a pedestrian year might be a 60 percent to 80 percent return.

Was this just doing plain vanilla merger arbitrage?

We did do straight risk arbitrage, and there were wide spreads available. But I was never that attracted to the risk/reward in risk arbitrage. In the Ben Graham approach, if you pay a cheap price for something, you have asymmetric returns on the upside because you can't lose that much, but you still have large profit potential. Risk arbitrage is exactly the opposite. In risk arbitrage you're trying to make $1 or $2 if the merger goes through, but risking $10 or $20 if the deal breaks. Instinctively, I didn't like those odds, even though, on average, if you had a lot of deals, it paid off well. I was always attracted to the periphery of risk arbitrage, such as hostile deals, meaning another bidder was coming in, or deals where there were interesting pieces of paper being offered instead of cash.

The fact that I understood options because of my summer job at Bear Stearns was also very helpful. In risk arbitrage, timing is very important. When is the deal going to close? If you have some edge in answering that question, you could gain leverage by using options that expire at a certain time. Also, by knowing the price at which a deal was going to close, you could find opportunities in options, which were critically dependent on price and which might be mispriced because the merger distorted the normal probability distribution assumption implicit in option prices. You could also use options to hedge deals that might break. There were so many interesting combinations.

Did you get involved in other event-driven types of trades as well?

We did some at Halcyon, but when I started out on my own, I was very attracted to special situation trades where there was something going on in the business and the usual rules didn't apply. It might be a spinoff, or a new piece of paper being issued, or a recapitalization, or a two-tiered tender offer—situations that the typical Wall Street analyst was not equipped to evaluate. I liked complicated situations. If there was a 400-page document to read, I was attracted to analyzing the deal because I knew most other people wouldn't read it.

How did you go from your job as an analyst at Halcyon to starting your own fund?

One of my friends, Bruce Newberg, who was one of the co-authors for the paper we wrote for the *Journal of Portfolio Management*, worked for Mike Milken. One day after I had been at Halcyon for about three years, I was talking to Bruce on the phone and happened to mention that if I could raise several million, I would go out on my own. Bruce called me back the next day and said, "Mike said fine." Milken ended up offering to invest twice what I had asked for, but I only wanted to start with $7 million. I had been trading my own account while I was at Halcyon and making over 100 percent a year. I wanted to make sure I could run the fund the same way as my personal account, and I didn't want to start off too large.

Can you give me an example of the types of trades you did in your original fund, which had a special situations focus?

One interesting example was a Marriott spinoff. Marriott got caught in the real estate downdraft of the early 1990s. Marriott's primary business was hotel management, and they got stuck owning a lot of the underlying hotels, which they usually try to sell off. So they spun off the hotels and the debt that accompanied the hotels into a new company, Host Marriott, and kept the good business, Marriott International. The main business—the hotel management—was actually a Buffett type of business, and it was being relieved of all of its debt. So it was a very clever transaction. But what I was most attracted to was what I call the *toxic waste* of the transaction, Host Marriott, which was the heavily leveraged, out-of-favor part of the business that no one wanted at the time.

What attracted you to it?

The first thing that attracted me to it was that it was clearly unwanted by anyone who could read either the newspaper or a balance sheet. I thought no one else was going to pay any attention to it because it looked so ugly, so it might be fertile ground for me to explore. Also, I thought institutions would likely sell off their shares in the spinoff because it represented only 10 to 15 percent of the original company and would probably be too small a cap size for them to hold. The spinoff was also in a different business. Most people investing in the parent, Marriott International, were interested in the hotel management business, so they would discard Host Marriott, which was in a different business, hotel ownership. The lack of new buying interest and the likelihood that many of the Marriott shareholders would sell off their shares in the spinoff meant that there was a good chance that Host Marriott would end up being undervalued. It certainly meant it was worth taking a close look at.

So what did you find?

I found that insiders had a large stake in the spinoff. The guy who masterminded the spinoff was actually going to run the "bad business."

It didn't make sense that he would choose to go with the spinoff if it was really as bad as the press reports made it sound. Also, the Marriott family was retaining 25 percent ownership in Host Marriott.

I also discovered that Host Marriott provided tremendous leverage. It was expected to trade at about $3 to $5 per share with debt of about $20 to $25. For illustration, assuming a share price of $5 and a debt of $25 would imply the assets of the new company would be worth about $30. The low share price relative to the company value meant a 15 percent increase in value of the assets would nearly double the value of the stock. Of course, leverage could work the other way, but the upside potential was lopsided relative to the downside risk—the stock can't go below zero. Also, given the large insider ownership, I didn't think it was likely that the deal would be structured for Host Marriott to fail. In addition, the deal required that Marriott International, the "good" Marriott, extend a $600 million line of credit to Host Marriott.

What ultimately happened?

As expected, most institutions dumped their shares at a low price. The stock then nearly tripled in four months.

Can you give me another example of a special situations trade that illustrates your approach?

In the early 1990s, Wells Fargo, which had an excellent long-term, consistent fee-generating business, came under a lot of pressure because of its high concentration of commercial real estate loans in California, at a time when California was in the midst of a deep real estate recession. There was a possibility, although unlikely, that the real estate downturn could be so severe that Wells Fargo would go through all its equity before investors could get the benefit of their long-term fee generation. If it survived, though, the stock would likely be much higher than its current depressed price of $80, which reflected the prevailing concerns. The way I looked at the risk/reward of the stock was that it was a binary situation: The stock would go down $80 if Wells Fargo went out of business and up $80 if it didn't. But by buying LEAPS with more than two years until expiration instead of the stock, I could turn that 1:1 risk/reward into a 1:5 risk/reward. If the bank survived, the stock should be a double, and I would make five times my money on the options, but if it failed, I would lose only the cost of the options. I thought the odds were much better than 50/50 that the bank would survive, so the stock was a buy. But in terms of risk/reward, the options were an even better buy. The stock did end up more than doubling before the options expired.

How long did you continue to trade the same general strategy as you did in the hedge fund after returning money to investors in 1995?

For about 10 years. Then we gradually transitioned to investing using a systematic value approach.

Why the change?

It wasn't a change in investment principles. I have always been a value investor. The Gotham Capital fund and Gotham Capital subsequent to returning outside capital held a concentrated portfolio of both straight value positions—that is, value positions without an obvious catalyst—and positions in special situations, which are more catalyst-driven trades. The transition to what we're doing now came about because I always wanted to test the principles I had been teaching and using to manage money. In 2003, Rob Goldstein and I hired a skilled computer programmer so that we could backtest some of the key measures we look at when we evaluate a company. The first metric we tested was based on Ben Graham's principle of buying cheap.

How did you define cheap?

There are a lot of ways of measuring cheapness. We used the *earnings yield*, which we defined as the ratio of *earnings before interest and taxes* (EBIT) to *enterprise value*.

In his book The Little Book That Beats the Market, *Greenblatt provided the following explanation of earnings yield:*

> *Earnings yield was measured by calculating the ratio of pre-tax operating earnings (EBIT) to enterprise value (market value of equity + net*

interest-bearing debt). This ratio was used rather than the more commonly used P/E ratio (price/earnings ratio) or E/P ratio (earnings/price ratio) for several reasons. The basic idea behind the concept of earnings yield is simply to figure out how much a business earns relative to the purchase price of the business.

Enterprise value was used instead of merely the price of equity (i.e., total market capitalization, *share price multiplied by shares outstanding) because enterprise value takes into account both the price paid for an equity stake in a business as well as the debt financing used by a company to help generate operating earnings. By using EBIT (which looks at actual operating earnings before interest expenses and taxes) and comparing it to enterprise value, we can calculate the pre-tax earnings yield on the full purchase price of the business (i.e., pre-tax operating earnings relative to the price of equity plus any debt assumed). This allows us to put companies with different levels of debt and different tax rates on equal footing when comparing earnings yields.*

For example, in the case of an office building purchased for $1 million with an $800,000 mortgage and $200,000 in equity, the price of equity is $200,000 but the enterprise value is $1 million. If the building generates EBIT (earnings before interest and taxes) of $100,000, then EBIT/EV or the pre-tax earnings yield would be 10 percent ($100,000/$1,000,000). However, the use of debt can greatly skew the apparent returns from the purchase of these same assets when only the price of equity is considered. Assuming an interest rate of 6 percent on an $800,000 mortgage and a 40 percent corporate tax rate, the pre-tax earnings yield on our equity purchase price of $200,000 would appear to be 26 percent. As debt levels change, this pre-tax earnings yield on equity would keep changing, yet the $1 million cost of the building and the $100,000 EBIT generated by that building would remain unchanged. In other words, P/E and E/P are greatly influenced by changes in debt levels and tax rates, while EBIT/EV is not.[3]

[3]Excerpt from *The Little Book That Beats the Market* by Joel Greenblatt (Hoboken, NJ: John Wiley & Sons, 2006). Reprinted with permission of John Wiley & Sons.

We looked at the 2,500 largest companies in the U.S. In the first test, we ranked the stocks based on the EBIT/EV ratio. We used Compustat's Point-in-Time database, which is the actual data that was available as of any given past date, so there is no look-ahead bias. That database starts in 1988, so we started our test from that date.

The twist that Warren Buffett put on Graham's method was that it is nice to buy cheap businesses, but if you can buy a good business cheap, that is even better. One of the metrics Buffett used to decide whether a company was a good business was *return on tangible capital*. In the book, I used an example of Jason's Gum Shop, which costs $400,000 to set up each store including inventory, displays, and other costs, and every year that store throws off $200,000 in profits, which is a 50 percent return on capital. Then I compared it to another business called Just Broccoli, which also cost $400,000 to open a new store, but every year that store throws off only $10,000 in profit, or a 2.5 percent return on capital. Clearly a business that can return 50 percent on capital is better than a business that can return only 2.5 percent on capital. Another way to look at it is that every business needs fixed assets and working capital to be in business, and the relevant question is *How efficiently does it turn its fixed assets and working capital into profits?* So the second metric we used in our test was return on tangible capital.

In his book The Little Book That Beats the Market, *Greenblatt provided the following definition and explanation of return on capital:*

> Return on capital was measured by calculating the ratio of pretax operating earnings (EBIT) to tangible capital employed (net working capital + net fixed assets). *This ratio was used rather than the more commonly used ratios of return on equity (ROE, earnings/equity) or return on assets (ROA, earnings/assets) for several reasons.*
>
> EBIT (earnings before interest and taxes) *was used in place of reported earnings because companies operate with different levels of debt and different tax rates. Using operating earnings before interest and taxes, or EBIT, allowed us to view and compare the operating earnings of different companies without the distortions arising from differences in tax rates and debt levels. For each company, it was then possible to*

compare actual earnings from operations (EBIT) to the cost of the assets used to produce those earnings (tangible capital employed).

Net working capital + net fixed assets (or tangible capital employed) was used in place of total assets (used in an ROA calculation) or equity (used in an ROE calculation). The idea here was to figure out how much capital is actually needed to conduct the company's business. Net working capital was used because the company has to fund its receivables and inventory (excess cash not needed to conduct the business was excluded from this calculation) but does not have to lay out money for its payables, as these are effectively an interest-free loan (short-term interest-bearing debt was excluded from current liabilities for this calculation). In addition to working capital requirements, a company must also fund the purchase of fixed assets necessary to conduct its business, such as real estate, plant, and equipment. The depreciated net cost of these fixed assets was then added to the net working capital requirements already calculated to arrive at an estimate for tangible capital employed.[4]

We took the same 2,500 companies and ranked them on their return on capital. We then combined the two rankings—one based on the earnings yield and the other on return on capital. Effectively, we equally weighted these two measures by adding the two rankings, which gave us the best combination of cheap and good. If a company ranked number one based on earnings yield and 250 based on return on capital, its combined rank value would be 251. We weren't looking for the cheapest companies, and we weren't looking for the best companies. We were looking for the best combination of cheap and good companies. In the book, I called this combined ranking the *Magic Formula*.

During the 23 years of our backtest, using the Magic Formula to choose a portfolio of the top 30 names from the 1,000 largest capitalization stocks would have approximately doubled the return of the S&P 500 (19.7 percent versus 9.5 percent). (Selecting portfolios from the

---

[4]Excerpt from *The Little Book That Beats the Market* by Joel Greenblatt (Hoboken, NJ: John Wiley & Sons, 2006). Reprinted with permission of John Wiley & Sons.

2,500 largest companies would have had an even larger outperformance, but would have required holding less liquid smaller cap stocks.) The decade of the 2000s was particularly interesting. During 2000 to 2009, the formula still managed to deliver an average annualized return of 13.5 percent, even though the S&P 500 was down nearly 1 percent per year during the same period.

The power of value investing flies in the face of anything taught in academics. Value is the way stocks are eventually priced. It requires the perspective of patience because the market will eventually gravitate toward value.

We also divided the formula rankings into deciles with 250 stocks in each decile. Then we held those stocks for a year and looked at how each of the deciles did. We repeated this process each month, stepping through time. Each month, we had a new set of rankings, and we assumed we held those portfolios (one for each decile) for one year. We did that for every month in the last 23 years, beginning with the first month of the Compustat Point-in-Time database. It turned out that Decile 1 beat Decile 2, 2 beat 3, 3 beat 4, and so on all the way down through Decile 10, which consisted of bad businesses that were nonetheless expensive. There was a huge spread between Decile 1 and Decile 10: Decile 1 averaged more than 15 percent a year, while Decile 10 lost an average of 0.2 percent per year.

Since there is such consistency in the relative performance between deciles, wouldn't buying Decile 1 stocks and selling Decile 10 stocks provide an even a better return/risk strategy than simply buying Decile 1 stocks?

My students and hundreds of e-mails asked the exact same question you just did. The typical comment was, "I have a great idea, Joel. Why don't you simply buy Decile 1 and short Decile 10? You'll make more than 15 percent a year, and you won't have any market risk." There's just one problem with this strategy: Sometime in the year 2000, your shorts would have gone up so much more than your longs that you would have lost 100 percent of your money.

This observation illustrates a very important point. If I wrote a book about a strategy that worked every month, or even every year, everyone would start using it, and it would stop working. Value investing doesn't always work. The market doesn't always agree with you. Over time, value is roughly the way the market prices stocks, but over the short term, which sometimes can be as long as two or three years, there are periods when it doesn't work. And that is a very good thing. The fact that our value approach doesn't work over periods of time is precisely the reason why it continues to work over the long term. Our formula forces you to buy out-of-favor companies, stocks that no one who reads a newspaper would think of buying, and hold a portfolio consisting of these stocks that, at times, may underperform the market for as long as two or three years. Most people can't stick with a strategy like that. After one or two years of underperformance, and usually less, they will abandon the strategy, probably switching to a strategy that has done well in recent years.

It is very difficult to follow a value approach unless you have sufficient confidence in it. In my books and in my classes, I spend a lot of time trying to get people to understand that in aggregate we are buying above-average companies at below-average prices. If that approach makes sense to you, then you will have the confidence to stick with the strategy over the long term, even when it's not working. You will give it a chance to work. But the only way you will stick with something that is not working is by understanding what you are doing.

When we got our results showing a perfect ordering of the 10 deciles, my partner Rob Goldstein and I looked at each other and said, "This is pretty interesting." We got these stellar results without trying very hard. We thought that by making further refinements, we might want to manage our own money using a systematic value approach. We now have 10 analysts and go through the income statement, balance sheet, and cash flow statement of each of the companies in our universe, and we figure out what real cash flow is and what real assets and liabilities look like based on the way we analyze companies. We have built our own database for over 4,000 U.S. and foreign stocks.

Forward-looking estimates?

No, we are still looking backward.

How much does this more complex analysis add vis-à-vis the Magic Formula you presented in your book?

If you are building a diversified portfolio from the entire universe of stocks we follow, it is quite helpful to be using the right numbers, although a diversified group of at least 20 or 30 stocks following either method does quite well.

As good as the systematic value approach works, it still doesn't reach the level of returns you achieved using a concentrated special situations approach in your original fund and the account that you continued to trade, using the same methodology, after you returned investor money.

That's true, but when you have only six to eight main positions, and one or two of them don't work out, you're not very happy. Using our current systematic value approach, we can put together long/short portfolios with hundreds of names on the long side and hundreds of names on the short side that can earn 15 to 20 percent per year, which compounds very nicely with much less volatility than a portfolio of six to eight names. If I were starting all over again, I would probably still do it the same way I originally did. But now that I am investing a larger sum of money, I prefer compounding at a good return without assuming the greater volatility that comes with high concentration, even if it means forgoing some extra return. Given this investment preference, the systematic value approach is very appealing. One approach is not better than the other; they are just different. It is an evolution, not a change in process. We have just systematized the same principles we always used to make money. That is what has stayed the same. We are just doing it in a more diversified, methodical way and taking advantage of our team of analysts.

I suppose your current approach can also handle a lot more money.

It can, although that was not the original objective. Our main goal was trying to reduce volatility. People don't fully appreciate the importance of not losing money. Negative compounding is very difficult to overcome. If you lose 50 percent of your money, you have to make 100 percent to recover the loss. If you have more volatile returns, that volatility can result in larger losses that are more difficult to make up. If, however, you have a more diversified long/short portfolio, you have a smoother ride and the opportunity to compound your money very well.

When we started this research, Rob and I didn't know that it would yield an investment strategy that we would want to work on full time. The research showed that our approach worked even better than we expected and that it could be applied effectively to portfolios with hundreds of holdings. These findings led to our launching several long/short funds, as well as several funds with index-like diversification.

Just before you said that you would have gone broke being short the bottom decile and being long the top decile. What are you doing differently in your long/short funds to avoid that trap?

Rob and I directly manage the risk. Although we have a team of six smart technology guys who help us—all smarter than I am—none have any financial background. We purposely picked people who didn't have a financial background because Rob and I wanted to be the portfolio managers. We wanted to create the best portfolio of our longs and shorts subject to various constraints. We wanted to manage our betas on the long and short side. We wanted to limit our concentration in any specific industry group and limit our exposure in any single stock. We have a widely diversified portfolio. In our small-cap portfolio, the largest long position is around 0.6 percent of equity, and the largest short position is even smaller.

How are your long-only equity indexes different from existing indexes?

Most investors have bad choices. Seventy percent of mutual fund managers underperform the market over time, as measured by the S&P 500, primarily because of their fees that reduce the total return. You might think you could do better by trying to find managers among the

30 percent that outperform the market. The problem, however, is that there is no correlation between those who did well in the past 3, 5, or 10 years and those who continue to do well in the future.

Since investors can't predict which 30 percent of the managers will do better than the market, the obvious conclusion is to simply go with an index fund, which has lower cost and is tax efficient. And that makes some sense. But it turns out that most popular indexes, such as the S&P 500 and Russell indexes, are very inefficient because they are market capitalization weighted. In a market capitalization weighted index, the higher the price of a stock, the larger the percentage of the index it will represent. Therefore, by definition, a market capitalization weighted index will automatically own too much of the overpriced stocks and too few of the bargain-priced ones. Of course, equally weighted indexes will also include plenty of valuation errors, but since all stocks are weighted equally, these errors will be random in contrast to the systematic errors inherent in market capitalization weighting.

The way you can tell how much capitalization weighting costs investors is to compare these indexes to equal weighted indexes of the same stocks. Based on the returns during the past 40 years, equal weighting has beat market capitalization weighting by about 2 percent per year. One problem with equal weighting is that stock number 500 is much smaller than stock number 1, and if too many people try to do equal weighting, the amount of buying in the smaller stocks would distort their prices. Additionally, because prices are always changing, there are more transaction costs in maintaining an equal weighted index. Because of these problems, Rob Arnott came up with a fundamentally based index (the RAFI FTSE index), which weights companies based on the size of their sales, book value, cash flow, and dividends rather than their market capitalization. Because the weighting factors used in the index are correlated to company market capitalization, larger market capitalization companies will account for a larger percentage of the total index. And since price is not involved, errors are also random, similar to an equal weighted index, and the index performs about 2 percent better than capitalization weighted indexes.

So the fundamentally based index does about as well as an equal weighted index, but it can handle more money.

That is exactly right. We thought we could provide significant additional improvement by creating an index that allocated more money to cheaper stocks. All the existing value indexes, such as the Russell value indexes, are capitalization weighted. For example, the Russell 1000 value index will take a subset of the Russell 1000 companies (usually 650 stocks) that have the lowest price-to-book ratios and whatever other value factors they look at, but then they weight those stocks by market capitalization. In contrast, we are placing more weight on the cheaper companies, which is quite a different thing. We have found that by constructing an index this way, we could create an index that, over the past 20 years, would have beaten the S&P 500 by an average of 7 percent per year with the same beta and volatility.

In addition to indexes, we have put together more select funds with around 100 of the cheapest stocks, also weighted by cheapness. What is interesting is that in the first six months of this year, our Value Select fund, which invests in U.S. equities, was number one in its category out of about 1,300 funds, and our Select International fund was the single worst fund in its category out of about 400 funds. We were both the very best and the very worst following the exact same strategy in different markets, and I found that fascinating.

What is the implication of that?

The Value Select fund, which was the best-performing fund in its category, beat the market by only 5 percent, while the Select International fund, which was the worst performing fund in its category, underperformed the market by only 5 percent. It tells you that no one was really picking stocks. If we can be number one out of 1,300 by outperforming by only 5 percent, and the last place fund out of about 400 in another category by underperforming by only 5 percent, it means that almost everyone must be index hugging.

You run both large and small cap funds. Do you believe there is more opportunity in small cap stocks?

Although I don't believe the *small cap anomaly* exists within the Russell 3000, I do still think it is very important to look in the small-cap universe because lesser-followed companies are more likely to be misvalued.[5] Those misvaluations can consist of both undervaluations and overvaluations, so there may not be any directional bias on average. But that does not take away from the fact that the small-cap sector may be a particularly fertile ground to look for undervalued stocks because it is less followed.

What is the story behind the Value Investors Club you started?

In 1999, we had one of the best ideas I had seen in a long time in our portfolio. We thought we were one of the few investment firms on the street to have uncovered this opportunity. One of my partners, John Petry, had found a posting on a Yahoo message board that had precisely analyzed the same situation that we thought we were such geniuses to have figured out. It was a complicated capital structure with lots of interesting parts. If you analyzed it correctly, you found it was a company that was trading at half its cash value with a good business attached to it. But it was very hidden. Yet here was someone on a Yahoo message board who had nailed it. John and I had the same reaction, *Well, apparently, there is intelligent life out there.* We agreed that it would be interesting to put together a group of these guys who would share ideas with each other.

We came up with the idea of prequalifying people to join the group. I had been teaching at Columbia for a number of years. The only way you could join was to submit an investment write-up on a specific company that would have received an A+ in my class at Columbia. Perhaps only two or three students in my class achieve this grade each year—and they are a group of pretty smart people. So we really set the bar quite high.

Who would judge whether the original submission was good enough to warrant entry into the club?

Back then, I did, along with my partner, John Petry, who co-founded the club with me.

---

[5]The *small cap anomaly* refers to the premise that smaller cap stocks have a higher return than large cap stocks over the long run.

How many people are part of the club?

We limit it to 250 members.

You must get a ton of submissions from people who want to join the club.

We do. A lot of them are good, but we are looking for the great ones.

But how do you find time to go through them?

Originally, I helped, but now a board consisting of John Petry and a number of managers who we are close with handle that job. The people on the board are anonymous; we are the only ones who know who they are.

Has the club been a good source of ideas over time?

Yes, and one of the nice benefits has been that we have met incredibly talented people. We even helped some of them start their own funds. The people we backed are not big names. They are simply people who are passionate about investing. Most of them have chosen to run smaller amounts of money and get higher rates of return rather than build a big business.

So a lot of the members are hedge fund managers?

We originally wanted individuals. Actually, the first person who inspired this idea, the one who had posted his analysis of a complicated trade on a Yahoo message board, had a job working in a supermarket. He is a brilliant guy, and he is now working as an analyst. The people in the club have varied backgrounds. Although we had envisioned it as a club for individual investors, it quickly attracted a lot of professionals who wanted to share in the ideas. About half of the 250 members in the club are professional managers.

Once people are accepted into the Value Investors Club, do they still continue to post new ideas? What is the incentive for them to do so?

There are no membership fees, but we require each member to submit two idea write-ups per year and to assign a rating to 20 other ideas. If you are willing to share your best ideas, then you can stay in; if you're not, you are asked to leave.

Is the website only visible to the 250 club members?

Right now, for teaching purposes and to attract talent, we do allow nonmembers to have access to posted ideas with a 90-day lag or access with a 45-day lag if they register. Since the ideas are value-based, many of them are still timely even after these lags.

What are the three biggest mistakes investors make?

First, succumbing to emotions. They tend to make investment decisions based on an emotional response to price action or what they read in the papers or hear on the news. Second, investing without knowledge. If you can't value a company, you have no basis on which to invest. Valuing a company is pretty hard, and probably no more than 1 percent or 2 percent of investors have the ability to properly value companies. You can't buy companies for a lot less than they are worth unless you can figure out what they are worth in the first place. Third, placing too much weight on the recent past performance of managers.

We inadvertently created an interesting experiment that vividly demonstrated the impact of investor errors. After I wrote *The Little Book That Beats the Market*, we set up a website called magicformulainvesting. com. At the time, I wasn't planning on managing outside capital, but many investors who read the book asked for help in executing the strategy. Since I had always been fascinated by the idea of a benevolent brokerage firm that allowed people to pick their own stocks from a limited list of preselected names based on "value," we teamed up with Blake Darcy, who had founded DLJ Direct, to set up that type of brokerage firm. Investors were also be encouraged to pick at least 20 or 30 stocks so they got the average instead of being overly dependent on a few stocks. Blake suggested that we also add a checkbox that allowed investors to choose the option of having us manage the portfolio rather than picking the stocks themselves. Less than 10 percent of the people decided to choose my original idea of doing it themselves, and over 90 percent just checked the box for us to do it for them.

We tracked how the individual investors who managed their own portfolios from the exact same list of stocks did versus the automatic portfolios we constructed. The self-managed accounts underperformed the "professionally" managed accounts by over 25 percent in the first two years. I thought that was fascinating. We had effectively created a control group experiment. Here are the people who did it themselves, and here are the people who did it automatically. Both groups had the same principles and the exact same list of stocks, but letting investors make their own decisions destroyed all the outperformance.

Why did they do so much worse?

There are a number of reasons that are probably common to most individual investors. They took their exposure down when the market fell. They tended to sell when individual stocks or their portfolios as a whole underperformed. They did much worse than random in selecting the stocks from our prescreened list, probably because by avoiding the stocks that were particularly painful to own, they missed some of the biggest winners.

What was your worst mistake?

We found a business, Key3Media, that had a great return on tangible capital employed and great operating leverage. It was a trade show company that used to run COMDEX, the largest technology trade show. They would rent space in Las Vegas for their shows at $2 per square foot and rerent it for $62. The company was an impending spinoff that was part of Ziff-Davis. Because of a special situation that allowed us to create long exposure in the stock at $3 per share before the spinoff, which was a very cheap price, we took a 10 percent position in it. Several months later, it IPO'd at $6 per share, giving us a quick double on the stock. Within a few more months, the stock price doubled from the IPO level. So at that point, this single stock had quadrupled from our entry-level price and grown to about 40 percent of our portfolio. The business started to falter a little, but the worst loss came when the company made a large acquisition two days before 9/11. After 9/11, people stopped traveling. The operating leverage of renting space at $2 and rerenting it at $62 worked in reverse when they couldn't rerent the space. Their profits went down almost dollar for dollar with the decline in revenues. In addition, they had leveraged up to make their acquisition. By the time we completely liquidated our position, we had lost back all our profits and then some.

So what are the lessons of that experience?

Stuff happens. Don't fall in love with any position. Always keep a large margin of safety, even if you're playing with house money. Even though the stock was still at a discount to what I thought it was worth right before 9/11, it obviously was a much less attractive value than it was before it had quadrupled, and we probably should have taken some profits. Also, operating leverage works both ways. To quote Howard Marks, "Experience is what you got when you didn't get what you wanted."

How do you measure risk?

As a value investor, I look at risk of loss over the long term. Given my margin of safety, how much could I lose if I hold the stock for two or three years, even if I am wrong in my expectations? I don't look at the stock's volatility in the last three months, which doesn't have much meaning for me at all. I think volatility is so widely used as a risk metric simply because it is easy to measure, not because it is a good gauge of risk of permanent loss of capital. Downside volatility is merely one aspect of risk, not necessarily the most important, while upside volatility isn't much of a risk at all—unless you are short.

What course do you teach?

I teach at Columbia Business School. The first four years, I taught a course called Security Analysis, and for the past 12 years, I have taught a course called Value and Special Situation Investing. They are not that different.

What do you teach your students?

Buffett said if he were to teach a business class, he would teach two things: how to value a business and how to think about stock prices. That's what I do. In the first lecture of the course, I point out that, although they are all very smart, and there are many other good business schools in the country whose students are also very smart, most MBAs who get involved in the markets will fail. I explain that therefore it can't be intelligence that is the defining reason why someone is successful in the markets. I think the difference between those who succeed and those that fail is how they think about the market. Everyone is bombarded every day with price movements, explanations for those price movements, macro events, and lots of other information. You need a methodology to cut through all that information and see things as they are. It all comes back to the way Graham looked at the market. Over the short term, prices fluctuate due to emotion, but over the long term, they come back to value. Value investing is figuring out what a business is worth and paying a lot less.

I promise my students that if they do good valuation work, the market will agree with them; I just don't tell them when. It could be a few weeks, a few months, or even a few years. But generally, if you have done good valuation work, 98 percent of the time, two or three years is enough time for the market to agree with you. That is a very powerful concept. It gives you patience. Of course, if you do poor valuation work, you can get into trouble. But if you stick to things you understand well, do good valuation work, give yourself a wide margin of safety, and have confidence in your work, eventually, you will end up doing quite well.

For many businesses, though, it may be very hard to predict what their future growth rate and normalized earnings will be. My students sometimes ask, "What do you do for a company that is in a competitive industry, or technology is causing major changes, or new products are coming out, or some other circumstance makes it very difficult to estimate what future earnings might be?" I tell them to just skip that company and find a company that they can analyze. It is very important to know what you don't know. As Warren Buffett says, "There are no called strikes on Wall Street." You can watch as many pitches as you want, and only swing when everything sets up your way.

Another important point I try to teach my students is that you have to consider not only what your opportunity set is right now, but also what opportunities you may be forgoing later by investing now. If your opportunity set is not that great right now, maybe you should wait another 6 to 12 months before becoming fully invested. Otherwise, if you invest all your capital now based on the current opportunity set, you may not have that money available for a better opportunity in the future, or you might have to sell what you buy now at a lower price to free up the money. That is why I always assume that my minimum bogie is at least a 6 percent return, even if interest rates are near zero, as they are now. Moreover, I have to beat 6 percent by a measurable amount because the assumption is that the 6 percent is risk-free. So I wouldn't take 8 percent, unless I have high confidence that it will grow over time. I need a "margin of safety," as Graham would say. I compare normalized earnings to the risk-free rate or 6 percent, whichever is higher. My opportunity set is not only what my choices are right now, but also what I think my choices might be at some time in the foreseeable future.

What has been your experience with investors?

Back in 1988, a few years after I started Gotham Capital, one of the earliest fund of funds became an investor. At the time, we were sending only quarterly letters to our investors. The fund of funds said, "We have to report to our investors more often; can we get monthly numbers?" I agreed. The first month they were invested, we were up 1.1 percent, which I thought was pretty good. But I got a call from the head of the fund of funds who said, "You know, we have a lot of investments with firms like yours, and, on average, they were up 1.2 percent last month. To what do you attribute your underperformance?"

I sit on several multibillion-dollar investment boards. I know from direct experience that after four or five quarters of outperformance by one manager and underperformance by another manager, the natural response is, "One guy knows what he's doing, and the other guy doesn't." Not referencing the boards I am involved with, statistics demonstrate that money follows performance, meaning most allocators just chase who did well recently. It is hard to resist this temptation because you are getting all this data, and you have a fiduciary responsibility to try to do a good job. The world has become much more institutionalized over the last 25 years since that early fund of funds invested with us. There is much more number crunching and short-term performance monitoring by institutions, and time horizons have continually shortened.

What are the implications of that?

Since time horizons have shortened, the advantage of taking a longer-term investment horizon has increased. You would think that with the increased availability of databases, the explosion of computing power, the availability of the Internet, and a lot of really smart math guys getting involved in the financial markets, any factors that have done well over the last 20 years would tend to degrade over time. In fact, the valuation metrics that we use, which are longer term and require a willingness to wait for them to work, have actually gotten stronger. And the reason for that is that the institutionalization of the market has shortened time horizons—it has reduced the window of time managers have to out-perform. Most managers can't wait for two years for an investment to work. They have to perform now. Their institutional and individual clients appear to demand it through their money flows. That is why companies that are not expected to do as well in the next year or two as they did in the recent past, or companies that are subject to near-term uncertainty, are systematically underpriced. Even if a manager knows that he should be looking longer term, his investors pressure him for performance over the near term.

All the statistics say that money chases the guy who did well last year and leaves the guy who didn't do well last year. And the subsequent performance is actually worse for the guy who did well last year. If you look at the past 3-, 5-, and 10-year returns of managers, there is no correlation between those who did well in those prior periods and those who do well in the subsequent 3, 5, and 10 years. Returns, however, are what allocators normally rely on to make decisions. If you are an allo-cator, you typically don't know the thought process that went into each investment decision. All you get to see are the results. The problem is that the past results are very misleading in terms of who is going to do better in the future.

One reason for the lack of correlation between past and future performance is that if investors chase good performers, the managers with better recent performance will attract more capital, and it is harder to run more money. As Warren Buffett said, "A fat wallet is the enemy of good investment returns." It is very difficult to have a lot of great ideas. If investors keep piling in money, then those managers have to do something with the money, and they may be forced to do some things differently than when they had less money.

There is one recent study that looked at the returns of managers during the 2000 to 2009 period. The study showed that 97 percent of the top quartile managers for the decade spent at least three years in the bottom half of managers. More surprisingly, 79 percent of the top quartile managers for the decade spent at least three years in the bottom quartile, and nearly half of them spent at least three years in the bottom decile. You know that investors didn't stick with the managers in the bottom quartile, let alone the bottom decile. Yet those were the managers that ended up with the best record for the entire period.

Here is another interesting statistic. The single best-performing mutual fund for the entire decade was up 18 percent a year, on average, during a period when the market was flat, yet the average investor in that fund lost 8 percent. That is because every time the fund did well, people piled in, and every time it underperformed, people redeemed. The timing of the money flows was so bad that investors, on average, turned a fund that was making 18 percent a year into a losing investment. I think that says it all. Institutions make the same mistakes as smaller investors.

Capital allocators should be looking at the process—how does the manager go about picking stocks and managing the portfolio—not returns, which have no predictive value. Only if you really believe in the process do you have some chance of picking a manager who will outperform in the future. It is probably just as difficult to pick a good manager as it is to pick a good stock.

Do you believe that in the long-only world, periodic underperformance is almost a natural characteristic of betterperforming managers over the long run?

That's an interesting question. What I would say is that to beat the market, you have to do something different from the market. And if you are going to do something different, sometimes you will underperform significantly. For example, if you are a value investor, there will be times when the market will be responding to factors such as emotion and momentum where a value approach might perform poorly.

How did you get involved in education reform?

I am a capitalist, but one of the things that makes capitalism an equitable system is when everyone has a fair chance. The way the system is structured, though, most children in need don't have access to a good education. If you are looking for leverage in philanthropy—that is, you want to get the most bang for your buck—education is one of the best ways to achieve that goal.

I started out by backing a seventh-grade class on Long Island that was in a very high-needs community. I visited the class a number of times, and it became quite clear that many of the kids were four or five grades behind in reading and math. This particular charity was helping the kids after school and a little bit before school, but the kids were wasting most of the school day because they were so far behind. After doing this for a few years, I went to the head of the program, Dr. Gerry House, and said that I would like to start with kindergarten or first grade to get to the kids before they fell so far behind. She said that it was a good idea, but that their mandate was to work with middle school and high school kids.

At Dr. House's recommendation, I then ended up hooking up with Dr. Robert Slavin of Johns Hopkins, who was probably the number one education researcher in the country at the time, and he had put together a program in reading and math for kindergarten and first grade students. I looked at the statistics for the program, and while it did achieve significant results, only about 50 percent to 60 percent of the students were at grade level. The program is called *Success for All*. I asked Dr. Slavin, "How could you truly get success for all? Would more money help?" He said, "Of course, if it is spent in the right way."

I went back to the same school in which I had backed the seventh-grade class and told the superintendent, "Give me an elementary school, and I will spend money until all the kids can read." He turned me down. After some other failed efforts, I finally found a school in Queens that was interested, and we started the program there for K to 5. In the second year of the program, they won an award for being one of the most improved schools in the state.

How much were you spending per child?

$1,000/year per child.

That's all! What was the essence of the program?

We provided tutoring in math and English, using tutors that were trained in the Success for All program. We also had professionals who monitored the kids so that anyone who needed help would get it. We couldn't hire the tutors through the public school system because of all the red tape. So I just ended up providing them for free. Because I had so much trouble navigating through the bureaucracy of the public school system, I met with Joel Klein.[6] He suggested that I should consider opening a charter school, which would give us the flexibility to hire our own teachers.

In 2006, John Petry and I started a single charter school based on the business model that it would serve as a prototype that could be expanded to other schools if it were successful. We designed the program from the beginning so that it could be replicated. We hired Eva Moskowitz, who is amazing, to run the program. Eva has now opened nine charter schools, with four more scheduled to start next year.

What kind of results have you had so far?

Because of New York State law, you have to start charter schools small. We started with grades K and 1, and then added a grade each year. Under New York law, if we started any larger, we would automatically be unionized. It's a law the unions have helped pass to handicap the growth of charter schools. Since testing grades are grades three through

---

[6]Reform-minded Chancellor of the New York City Department of Education.

eight, only four of our schools have reached testing grade so far. The four schools that were tested last year beat Scarsdale, Great Neck, and all the top school districts in the state.

Where were these four schools?

The schools were all in Harlem.

With the success you've had, don't you face the problem of too many parents trying to get their kids into your school relative to the space you have?

The only way to get into a charter school is through a lottery, and we have about nine kids applying for every spot.

What did you think of the film *Waiting for Superman*?

Harlem Success was actually one of the schools profiled in the movie. There was also another excellent documentary, *The Lottery*, which focused solely on Harlem Success.

Do you think there is some hope that your program may help change the way government-run schools operate?

I think eventually it will. K–12 education in the United States is a $600 billion business, and philanthropy can't be the answer. All that philanthropy can do is to show the way. Charter schools are public schools, but they are independently run. Eva and her team have shown that it's not the kids' fault. We have the same kids as the publicly run schools. We get them by lottery. And it's not that the parents don't care; they do. It's not because there is not enough money; we actually run our schools for less money per student. So the bottom line is that we have the same kids, same parents, and less money. If our charter schools can continue to demonstrate success, it will hopefully remove the main excuses for why publicly run schools are unsuccessful. I am not suggesting that it is an easy job; it is an incredibly tough job. But the current system is not run well, and there are a lot of impediments to success in the system. Our goal is that there will be incentives for the public schools to adopt the things that we have done that have worked.

Have you seen any impact at all on the political side of things?

Lots of educators and legislators have visited our network's schools, and I think they have been flabbergasted. That's a great start. As we show more years of success, and because our goal is to share everything we are doing, I think we will have an influence.

Given the poor state of the current U.S. educational system, are you then optimistic that your efforts and similar efforts by others will lead to a meaningful improvement in the system within, say, the next 10 years?

That is the goal, but I also believe it will. We will play our small part, but there are plenty of other people following similar models. We share the intellectual property of anything we do that works, and we steal liberally from the most successful charter schools that work. The relevant question is not how well the average charter school performs, but rather whether some charter schools perform much better. The goal is finding those models that work and rolling them out in size. It is just like capitalism in general. You want to find winners and reproduce those.

But do you believe logic and results can overcome the political obstacles of the special interests?

Unfortunately, at the moment, the teachers union protests every new school we try to open because they don't want the competition. The teachers union's plan is to kill us with 1,000 cuts, which means opposing us every step of the way. If we can survive that onslaught, and we are still here in 10 years, which I think we will be, then the effect should be huge. If Eva can replicate the success they have had so far in 30 or 40 schools, it will help change the discussion. I think a lot has already been changed.

Have any politicians embraced what you're doing?

Although I have my disagreements with President Obama on a number of economic issues, for a Democrat, I think he has been very progressive on the education issue. The Democrats have generally been in the pocket of the teachers unions. President Obama has gone against his party's general stance and has embraced reform. I give him a lot of credit for doing that. The Race to the Top program was helpful in supporting charter schools in New York State by incentivizing states if they adopted pro-reform policies.

■ ■ ■

About a week after I interviewed Greenblatt, I sat in on his class in the Columbia Business School. On this particular day, Greenblatt had invited a guest lecturer and used the first half of the session to answer student questions. The premise of the Q&A format was that Greenblatt would answer the questions as he thought Warren Buffett would. Since Greenblatt's investment philosophy is so closely aligned to Buffett's, his students were continually confused whether he was answering a question as Buffett or as himself, although in many cases, it probably didn't make much difference. Below is a sampling of some of Greenblatt's comments in that class:

- My oldest son, who is a senior in college, is studying to be an opera singer. About half a year ago, he said to me, "Hey Dad, I'm probably going to be starving for the next five to six years, so maybe I should learn something about investing, too." I started teaching him in June. Stock prices have been crazy since then. He said everything I told him he would experience happened during his first five months he was watching the market. One of the stocks he picked at $16 went down to $9 dollars, then up to $18, and then back to $16 again. The business did not change at all during that period, yet the stock price changed significantly. Everybody says, "There are too many people looking at stocks; there are no more opportunities." There are plenty of opportunities.
- You are setting yourself up for failure if you invest differently than you want to in order to please investors.
- Manage your own account if you can. There is nothing like actually doing it and learning what it is like when you lose money and finding out what your emotions are when you are doing well and not doing well.
- Buffett said, "Time is the enemy of the poor business and the friend of the great business."

- One of the reasons why looking at return on capital is important is that it keeps you out of the value traps.
- When Rich Pzena was here he talked about Computer Associates. He told the story about how he called up their top 12 customers. They all said that they hated the company. They hated the product; they hated the service; they hated everything about it. He then asked them if their top competitor offered their software and services for free, would they switch? All 12 said something to the effect, "Are you crazy? We can't switch. We can't close our business for a few days to switch to a competitor." That is an example of a sticky type of business.

■ ■ ■

Greenblatt provides three critical lessons about value investing:

1. Value investing works.
2. Value investing doesn't work all the time.
3. Item 2 is one of the reasons why Item 1 is true.

Investing in good businesses that are priced cheap—Greenblatt's approach modeled after Buffett—will outperform the market over the longer term. This value edge does not go away because the periods of underperformance using a value approach can be long enough (a few years) and severe enough to discourage investors from sticking with the approach. Although many managers may realize the merit of value investing, they too will have trouble using such an approach because of the shortening of investor time horizons in tolerating subpar performance. The fact that institutions have become increasingly likely to redeem investments from managers who turn in below-average performance for periods as short as one year, let alone two years, means that managers who stick to a value approach risk losing substantial assets at some point. The inability of so many investors and managers to invest with a long-term horizon creates the opportunity for *time arbitrage*—an edge in an investing approach that requires the commitment to long-term holding periods.

Greenblatt believes the efficient market hypothesis provides an inaccurate model of how the market really works. Greenblatt's view is that although the market will eventually trade at fair value, a price that would be consistent with the efficient market hypothesis, in the interim, which can sometimes be as long as years, stocks can deviate substantially from their fair value. According to Greenblatt, a more appropriate model is that prices trade around fair value, but broad deviations occur because of wide swings in investor emotions. Greenblatt invokes Benjamin Graham's famous metaphor of Mr. Market, a hypothetical business partner, subject to erratic moods, who is willing to sell shares to you or buy shares from you. As Greenblatt describes it in *The Little Book That Beats the Market*:

> *Sometimes Mr. Market is in such a good mood that he names a price that is much higher than the true worth of the business. On such days, it probably would make sense for you to sell Mr. Market your share of the business. On other days, he is in such a poor mood that he names a very low price for the business. On those days, you may want to take advantage of Mr. Market's crazy offer to sell you shares at such a low price and to buy Mr. Market's share of the business.*

You don't have to trade. Greenblatt advises that investors should wait for the right opportunity and the right time. Referencing Warren Buffett's comment, "There are no called strikes on Wall Street," Greenblatt says, "You can watch as many pitches as you want, and only swing when everything sets up your way."

Greenblatt believes that one of the biggest mistakes investors make is using past performance as the guide for selecting managers. Greenblatt cites empirical evidence demonstrating that there is no meaningful correlation between past and future manager performance rankings. He recommends selecting managers based on their investment process rather than their returns.

Since past performance is not predictive, Greenblatt believes that, on average, stock indexes are a better investment choice than mutual funds because of their lower fees and more tax-efficient structure. Despite these advantages, Greenblatt views most popular stock indexes as being structurally flawed. The most popular indexes, such as the SP500 and Russell indexes, are capitalization weighted, which means that the more overvalued a stock becomes, the greater the allocation, and the more undervalued, the lower the allocation—the exact reverse of what would be desirable. Equal-weighted indexes avoid this problem and add about 2 percent per year to the return of capitalization-weighted indexes. Greenblatt believes that a value-*weighted* index (not to be confused with a capitalization-weighted value index) can add significant additional improvement and may provide the most attractive long-only equity investment alternative for investors.

Greenblatt's trade in Wells Fargo illustrates the concept that options can be substantially underpriced in situations in which the fundamentals dictate a greater-than-normal chance of either a large gain or a large loss—that is, a binary outcome scenario.[7] In this particular trade, there was uncertainty whether Wells Fargo would survive a severe real estate downturn. If they did, however, its fee income suggested a far higher price. This binary outlook made a long-term long options position, which had almost as much upside potential on a very large move, but limited risk, a particularly attractive trade. The broader lesson is that options are primarily priced off of mathematical models that do not take account of specific fundamentals. If you can identify a situation where the fundamentals suggest that a large move up, or down, or in either direction is more likely than normal, options may provide a very attractive risk/reward trade.

Although it is not a lesson that is relevant to most investors, it can be critical to managers: Guard against letting assets grow to the point where size impedes performance. Given the spectacular track record of the first 10 years of Gotham Capital, Greenblatt could easily have grown his fund by multiples, collecting hefty management fees in the process. Instead, he chose to return all assets to investors to keep the money under management (his own and that of his partners) small enough so that it did not interfere with the ability to execute the strategy or impede performance.

---

[7]The same trading concept also figures prominently in Chapter 7.

Conclusion

40 Market Wizard Lessons

1. There Is No Holy Grail in Trading

Many traders mistakenly believe that there is some single solution to defining market behavior. Not only is there no single solution to the markets, but those solutions that do exist are continually changing. The range of the methods used by the traders interviewed in this book, some of which are even polar opposites, is a testament to the diversity of possible approaches. There are a multitude of ways to be successful in the markets, albeit they are all hard to find and achieve.

2. Find a Trading Method That Fits Your Personality

Traders must find a methodology that fits their own beliefs and talents. A sound methodology that is successful for one trader can be a poor fit and a losing strategy for another trader. O'Shea lucidly expressed this concept in answer to the question of whether trading skill could be taught:

> *If I try to teach you what I do, you will fail because you are not me. If you hang around me, you will observe what I do, and you may pick up some good habits. But there are a lot of things you will want to do differently. A good friend of mine, who sat next to me for several years, is now managing lots of money at another hedge fund and doing very well. But he is not the same as me. What he learned was not to become me. He became something else. He became him.*

3. Trade Within Your Comfort Zone

If a position is too large, the trader will be prone to exit good trades on inconsequential corrections because fear will dominate the decision process. As Clark advises, you have to "trade within your emotional capacity." Similarly, Vidich warns, "Limit your size in any position so that fear does not become the prevailing instinct guiding your judgment." In this sense, a smaller net exposure may actually yield better returns, *even if the market ultimately moves in the favorable direction*. For example, Taylor came into 2008 with a large net long exposure in high beta stocks in an increasingly risky market. Uncomfortable with the level of his exposure, Taylor sharply reduced his positions in early January. When the market subsequently plunged later in the month, he was well positioned to increase his long exposure. Had Taylor remained heavily net long, he might instead have been forced to sell into the market weakness to reduce risk, thereby missing out in fully participating in the subsequent rebound.

4. Flexibility Is an Essential Quality for Trading Success

Highly skilled traders will not only liquidate their positions if they believe they made a mistake, but will actually reverse those positions. In

April 2009, O'Shea was pessimistic about the financial outlook, but the market behavior was telling him that he was wrong. He formulated an alternative hypothesis that seemed to fit the price action—that is, the markets were seeing the beginning of an Asia-led economic recovery. Staying with his original market expectation would have been costly, as both equity and commodity markets embarked on a multiyear rally. O'Shea's flexibility in recognizing that his original premise was wrong and his ability to reverse his trading posture turned a potentially disastrous year into a winning one. As another example, Mai's best trade of 2011 came from shorting dry bulk shippers, a trade idea that, ironically, originated with the premise that these companies represented a buying opportunity. However, when in doing his research Mai realized that he was not only wrong, but that he had it exactly backward, he reversed his original trading plan. Clark emphasizes that good traders can change their minds in an instant. They can be absolutely convinced the market is going higher one moment and just as convinced it is going lower in the next.

5. The Need to Adapt

It would be nice to believe that if you can find a trading methodology that works and also have the discipline to apply it consistently, then trading success is assured. Unfortunately, the real world is a bit more difficult. Markets change, and strategies that work may eventually deteriorate. Good traders need to be vigilant to the possibility that a once reliable approach may lose its efficacy or even become a losing strategy due to changing market conditions. For example, Thorp was able to maintain the strong return/risk of his statistical arbitrage approach by continually adapting it. By the time he got to the third iteration, the original system had significantly degraded. Platt, whose firm BlueCrest trades both discretionary and systematic strategies, believes that systematic approaches must continually be revised or else they will degrade. He describes the process as "a research war." Balodimas had to adapt a less aggressive posture in positioning against ongoing trends once he realized that the growing participation of hedge funds was resulting in smoother and more prolonged market trends. Had he not responded to the changing market environment, his previous successful approach would likely have led to large losses.

6. Don't Confuse the Concepts of Winning and Losing Trades with Good and Bad Trades

A good trade can lose money, and a bad trade can make money. Even the best trading processes will lose a certain percentage of the time. There is no way of knowing a priori which individual trade will make money. As long as a trade adhered to a process with a positive edge, it is a good trade, regardless of whether it wins or loses, because if similar trades are repeated multiple times, they will come out ahead. Conversely, a trade that is taken as a gamble is a bad trade regardless of whether it wins or loses because over time such trades will lose money.

7. Do More of What Works and Less of What Doesn't

This core advice offered by Clark may sound obvious, but the reality is that many traders violate this principle. It is quite common for a trader to be good at one type of trade, but to degrade performance by also engaging in trades without any clear edge, whether due to boredom or other reasons. Clark's message is that traders need to figure out what they are best at and then focus their attention on those types of trades.

8. If You Are Out of Sync with the Markets, Trying Harder Won't Help

When trading is going badly, trying harder is often likely to make matters even worse. If you are in a losing streak, the best action may be to step away from the markets. Clark advises that the best way to handle a losing streak is to liquidate everything and take a vacation. A physical break can serve to interrupt the downward spiral and loss of confidence that can develop during losing periods. Clark further advises that when trading is resumed, the size should be kept small until confidence is regained.

9. The Road to Success Is Paved with Mistakes

Dalio strongly believes that learning from mistakes is essential to improvement and ultimate success. Each mistake, if recognized and acted on, provides an opportunity for improving a trading approach. Most traders would benefit by writing down each mistake, the implied lesson, and the intended change in the trading process. Such a trading log can be periodically reviewed for reinforcement. Trading mistakes cannot be avoided, but repeating the same mistakes can be, and doing so is often the difference between success and failure.

10. Wait for High-Conviction Trades

Having the patience to wait for high expected value trades greatly enhances the return/risk of individual trades. Mai, for example, is perfectly content to stay on the sidelines and do absolutely nothing until there is a trade opportunity that meets his guidelines. Greenblatt makes the point that for longer-term investors, placing suboptimal positions may tie up capital that could be applied to more attractive opportunities that arise in the future or require liquidating such positions at a loss to free up capital.

11. Trade Because of Perceived Opportunity, Not Out of the Desire to Make Money

Toward the end of 2010, out of a desire to reach his minimum profit target for the year, Benedict took marginal trades he otherwise would not have taken. These trades resulted in net losses and, as a consequence, Benedict ended up even further from his intended target. Trading to make money is always a bad idea. Traders should only take a trade when the market provides an opportunity as defined by their own individual strategy.

12. The Importance of Doing Nothing

For some traders, the discipline and patience to do nothing when the environment is unfavorable or opportunities are lacking is a crucial element in their success. For example, despite making minimal use of short positions, Daly achieved cumulative gross returns in excess of 800 percent during a 12-year period when the broad equity markets were essentially flat. In part, he accomplished this feat by having the discipline to remain largely in cash during negative environments, which allowed him to sidestep large drawdowns during two major bear markets. The lesson is that if conditions are not right, or the return/risk is not sufficiently favorable, don't do anything. Beware of taking dubious trades out of impatience.

13. How a Trade Is Implemented Can Be More Important Than the Trade Itself

A good example of this principle was provided by the way O'Shea traded his assumption that the bubble had burst in equities following the initial break from the March 2000 peak. He did not consider short positions in Nasdaq because of the danger of treacherous bear market rallies. Instead, O'Shea implemented his trade idea via a long bond position, reasoning that a bear market in equities implied that most assets would recede from inflated levels, which would lead to an economic slowdown and lower interest rates. Even though the stock market ultimately went much lower, if O'Shea had implemented his idea through a short stock index position, there is a high likelihood that he would have been stopped out by the 40 percent rebound in the Nasdaq index during the summer of 2000. In contrast, the long bond position, which he had implemented instead of going short the equity index, witnessed a fairly smooth uptrend. The trade was highly successful, not because the underlying premise was correct, which it was, but rather because of the way the trade was implemented. If O'Shea had gone short the stock index instead, he would have been correct on his call, but most likely would have lost money by being stopped out during the steep bear market rally in equities.

14. Trading Around a Position Can Be Beneficial

Most traders tend to view trades as a two-step process: a decision when to enter and a decision when to exit. It may be better to view trading as a dynamic rather than static process between entry and exit points. The basic idea is that as a trade moves in the intended direction, the position exposure would be gradually reduced. The larger the move and the closer the market gets to a target objective, the more the position would be reduced. After reducing exposure in this manner, the position would be reinstated on a market correction. Any time the market retraced to a correction reentry point, a net profit would be generated that otherwise would not have been realized. The choppier the market, the more excess profits trading around the position will generate. Even a trade in which the market fails to move in the intended direction on balance could still be profitable as a result of gains generated by lightening the total position on favorable trend moves and reinstating liquidated portions of the position on corrections. This strategy will also reduce the chances of being knocked out of a favorable position on a market correction because if the position has already been reduced, the correction will have less impact and may even be desired to reinstate the liquidated portion of the position. The only time this strategy will have a net adverse impact is if the market keeps on going in the intended direction without ever retracing to correction reentry levels. This negative outcome, however, simply means that the original trade was profitable, but that total profits are smaller than they would have been otherwise. In a nutshell, trading around a position will generate extra profits and increase the chances of staying with good trades at the expense of sometimes giving up a portion of profits on trades that move smoothly in the intended direction. For Balodimas, trading around a position is a critical ingredient in his overall trading success. Not infrequently, it even allows him to be profitable on trades where he's wrong.

15. Position Size Can Be More Important Than the Entry Price

Too many traders focus only on the entry price and pay insufficient attention to the size of the position. Trading too large can result in good trades being liquidated at a loss because of fear. On the other hand, trading larger than normal when the profit potential appears to be much greater than the risk is one of the key ways in which many of the Market Wizards achieve superior returns. Trading smaller, or not at all, for lower probability trades and larger for higher probability trades can even transform a losing strategy into a winning one. For example, by varying the bet size based on perceived probabilities, Thorp was able to transform the negative edge in Blackjack into a positive edge. An analogous principle would apply to a trading strategy in which it was possible to identify higher and lower probability trades.

16. Determining the Trade Size

What is the optimal trade size? There is a mathematically precise answer: The Kelly criterion (described in Chapter 6) will provide a higher cumulative return over the long run than any other strategy for determining trade size. The problem, however, is that the Kelly criterion assumes that the probability of winning and the ratio of the amount won to the amount lost per wager are precisely known. Although this assumption is valid for games of chance, in trading, the probability of winning is unknown and, at best, can only be estimated. If win/loss probabilities can be reasonably estimated, then the Kelly criterion can provide a starting point for determining trade size. Thorp recommends trading only half the Kelly amount (assuming win/loss probabilities can be estimated) because the penalty for overestimating the correct trade size is severe and because most people would find the volatility implied by the full Kelly amount too high for their comfort level. If win/loss probabilities can't be reasonably estimated, then the Kelly criterion can't be used.

17. Vary Market Exposure Based on Opportunities

Exposure levels and even the direction of exposure should vary based on opportunities and perceived relative value. For example, depending on whether stock prices appear to be cheaply or expensively priced, Claugus will vary his net exposure range from 110 percent long to 70 percent short. Varying the exposure based on opportunity can lead to significantly improved performance results.

18. Seek an Asymmetric Return/Risk Profile

Mai structures his trades to be *right skewed*—that is, the maximum loss is limited, but the upside is open-ended. One common way of achieving this type of return/risk profile is by being a selective buyer of options— buying options when there is a perceived greater-than-normal proba- bility of a large price move. O'Shea is another trader who structures almost all of his trades to be right skewed. Some of the trades he uses to achieve this return/risk profile include long options, long credit default swap (CDS) protection, and long T-bill/short Eurodollar (TED) spreads—all trades in which the maximum loss is constrained. Platt achieves right-skewed asymmetry at the portfolio level through the risk control process, which strictly limits each trader's maximum loss from the starting allocation each year, but does not raise the risk cutoff level if the trader generates profits during the year. In this way, the portfolio maximum loss is tightly curtailed, but the upside potential is open-ended.

19. Beware of Trades Borne of Euphoria

Caution against placing impulsive trades influenced by being caught up in market hysteria. Excessive euphoria in the market should be seen as a cautionary flag of a potential impending reversal.

20. If You Are on the Right Side of Euphoria or Panic, Lighten Up

Parabolic price moves in either direction tend to end abruptly and sharply. If you are fortunate enough to be on the right side of a market in which the price move turns near vertical, consider scaling out of the position while the trend is still moving in your direction. If you would be petrified to be on the other side of the market, that is probably a good sign that you should be lightening your position.

21. Staring at the Screen All Day Can Be Expensive

Clark believes that watching every tick can lead to both overtrading and an increased chance of liquidating good positions. He advises finding a more productive use of time to avoid the pitfalls of watching the market too closely.

22. Just Because You've Heard It 100 Times Doesn't Make It Less Important: Risk Control Is Critical

Many of the traders interviewed are more concerned about not losing money than making money. Risk control strategies mentioned by the traders included the following:

- **Risk limits on individual trades**—Many of the traders interviewed will risk only a small percentage of assets under management on any single trade. Ramsey, for example, only risks a loss of about 0.1 percent on any individual trade. Although such a close stop is probably too extreme (or perhaps even inadvisable) for most traders to adopt, the general concept of using a relatively close stop at trade inception, while allowing a wider stop relative to prevailing prices after a profit margin has been established, is an effective risk management approach that could work well for many traders.

- **Exposure reduction thresholds**—Despite achieving double-digit returns and managing assets in double-digit billions, the BlueCrest discretionary strategy has contained its worst drawdown to under 5 percent in more than a decade of trading through many volatile markets. The key to this amazing feat of risk management has been the firm's exposure reduction rules. BlueCrest's CEO, Michael Platt, restricts himself and other discretionary traders at the firm to a loss limit of 3 percent (from the starting allocation) before the exposure allocation is cut in half. A loss of another 3 percent leads to the removal of the trader's entire allocation. These rigid controls severely limit the loss any trader can realize from a starting allocation. The rules encourage traders to be extremely conservative in their risk-taking at the start of each year. As traders register gains, however, they can increase their risk levels because the original exposure reduction thresholds remain unchanged for the year. In this manner, upside potential is open-ended, while downside risk is severely curtailed. Barring huge overnight gaps in the market, larger losses can only occur through the surrender of year-to-date profits rather than losses of original capital. Benedict utilizes a similar risk management philosophy. Any time he approaches a 2.5 percent loss in any given month, he significantly reduces net exposure and continues to trade in smaller size until the loss is recovered. In this manner, he severely constrains his potential loss in any given month.

- **Position size adjustments for changes in volatility**—As examples of this approach, in 2008, both Woodriff and Clark cut their exposure levels by approximately a factor of four in response to the steep increase in volatility.
- **Trade-dependent risk controls**—Some trades are inherently risk-constrained, whereas other trades have open-ended risk. In recognition of these differences, uniform risk controls across all trades may not be appropriate. For example, when Thorp implemented arbitrage trades that had a well-defined maximum theoretical risk, he did not consider reducing exposure if the position went against him. In contrast, when he employed a trend-following strategy, in which the trades were directional and the risk was open-ended, he made exposure reduction on drawdowns part of the methodology.

23. Don't Try to Be 100 Percent Right

Almost every trader has had the experience of the market moving against a position sufficiently to raise significant concern regarding the potential additional loss, while still believing the position is correct. Staying in the trade risks an uncomfortably large loss, but liquidating the trade risks abandoning a good position at nearly the worst possible point. In such circumstances, Vidich advises that instead of making an all-or-nothing decision, traders should liquidate part of the position. Taking a partial loss is much easier than liquidating the entire position and will avoid the possibility of riding the entire position for a large loss. It will also preserve the potential for a partial recovery if the market turns around.

24. Protective Stops Need to Be Consistent with the Trade Analysis

O'Shea explains that too many traders set stops based on their pain threshold rather than as points that disprove their trade premise. Because traders can't stand the pain of a larger loss, they tend to set stops too close—that is, at a point at which they would still believe in the trade. Consequently, there is a tendency for some traders to try to repeatedly reenter a trade after being stopped out, potentially leading to multiple losses, which cumulatively can be larger than the single loss that would have occurred with a wider stop originally set at a meaningful level. O'Shea advises that traders should first decide at what price they would believe their trade is wrong and then set the stop accordingly. If the implied loss to this stop point is uncomfortably large, then the position size should be reduced commensurately. Using this approach, if the market reaches the stop point, it will be consistent with demonstrating that the original trade idea was wrong.

25. Constraining Monthly Losses Is Only a Good Idea if It Is Consistent with the Trading Strategy

Although tightly constraining monthly losses is a prudent action for many traders, for investors with a long-term perspective, monthly loss constraints can be detrimental. Taylor, for example, believes that if he has a strong conviction that a stock will move much higher over the long term, then cutting exposure on interim weakness to limit the depth of a monthly loss would be a mistake. Similarly, Greenblatt asserts that value investors must maintain a longer-term perspective and not be swayed by interim losses, providing the fundamentals haven't changed. For longer-term investors, such as Taylor and Greenblatt, monthly loss constraints would be in conflict with their strategy.

26. The Power of Diversification

Dalio calls diversification the "Holy Grail of investing." He points out that if assets are truly uncorrelated, diversification could improve return/ risk by as much as a factor of 5:1.

27. Correlation Can Be Misleading

Although being cognizant of correlation between different markets is crucial to avoiding excessive risk, it is important to understand that correlation measures *past* price relationships. It is only relevant if there is reason to believe that the past correlation is a reasonable proxy for future correlation. Some market correlations are stable, but others can vary widely and even change sign. For example, stocks and bonds sometimes move in the same direction and sometimes move inversely. If correlation is used during such a transition period, it can be worse than no information at all because it can lead to the exact wrong conclusions about future price relationships and risk.

28. The Price Action in Related Markets Can Sometimes Provide Important Trading Clues

For some traders, such as Benedict and Ramsey, the interaction of price movements in related markets is a critical input in their trade decision process. Although the price action in other markets can be important, there are no set rules in how such price action should be interpreted. Sometimes, one market may tend to lead another. In other situations, two markets may move in tandem, but then begin to move independently, a price behavior change that may provide price directional clues. As an example, after years of correlated price movement, in early September 2011, equity prices rallied, but commodity prices weakened. Ramsey read the failure of commodity prices to respond to equity market strength as a signal of impending weakness. During the second half of September, commodity prices and commodity-influenced currencies plunged.

29. Markets Behave Differently in Different Environments

Any analysis of fundamental factors that assumes a static relationship between economic variables and market prices will be doomed to failure because markets behave differently in different environments. As Dalio points out, the same fundamental conditions and government actions will have different price consequences in a deleveraging environment than in a recession.

30. Pay Attention to How the Market Responds to News

A counter-to-anticipated response to market news may be more meaningful than the news item itself. Platt recalls a trade in which there was a continuing stream of adverse news. He repeatedly expected to lose money after each news item, and yet the market did not move against him. Platt read the inability of the market to respond to the news as confirmation of his trade idea, and he quadrupled his position, turning it into one of his biggest winners ever.

31. Major Fundamental Events May Often Be Followed by Counterintuitive Price Movements

Dalio recalls two such critical events in his early trading career. The U.S. abandonment of the gold standard in 1971 was followed by a huge market rally, as was the Mexican default in 1982. There are two explanations for this type of seemingly paradoxical price behavior. First, such major events are often fully anticipated and discounted, or even overdiscounted. Second, a major bearish fundamental development may spur government actions that can often have a greater market impact than the event itself.

32. Situations Characterized by the Potential for a Widely Divergent Binary Outcome Can Often Provide Excellent Buying Opportunities in Options

Option prices are primarily determined by models that assume that large price movements are unlikely. In circumstances when the fundamentals suggest a significant potential for either a large price gain or a large price loss, option prices often fail to reflect the abnormally large probability of such outsized price movements. Examples of this principle include Greenblatt's option trade in Wells Fargo and Mai's option trade in Capital One.

33. A Stock Can Be Well-Priced Even if It Has Already Gone Up a Lot

Many traders miss participating in the best opportunities because they can't bring themselves to buy a stock or market that has already seen a large upmove. What matters, however, is not how much a stock has gone up, but rather how well a stock is priced relative to its *future* prospects. For example, Taylor's largest holding at the time of our interview, Apple, had already experienced a large price advance—and indeed, this prior large price gain kept many investors from buying the stock, despite its excellent fundamentals. But in Taylor's opinion, the amount of the prior price gain was irrelevant because based on his earnings projections, the stock was still priced cheap.

34. Don't Make Trading Decisions Based on Where You Bought (or Sold) a Stock

The market doesn't care where you entered your position. When Vidich felt that a stock that had just fallen all the way back to where he had bought it was going lower, he just got out, not letting his entry level affect the trading decision.

35. Potential New Revenue Sources That Are More Than a Year Out May Not Be Reflected in the Current Stock Price

Claugus likes to look for situations where a company will recognize new revenue sources one or more years out because such future potential earnings are frequently not adequately discounted, or discounted at all, by the current stock price.

36. Value Investing Works

Greenblatt has demonstrated that value investing works both through a long career as a highly successful trader using value principles and through rigorous computer-based research. The catch is that although value investing works over the long term, there are times when it works poorly. However, as Greenblatt points out, this periodic underperformance is actually the reason why value investing is able to maintain its edge. If it' worked all the time, it would attract enough followers so the edge would disappear. Given the inherent long-term character of the efficacy of this approach, value investors need to have a similar long-term perspective to avoid inconsistencies between their methodology and trading decisions.

37. The Efficient Market Hypothesis Provides an Inaccurate Model of How the Market Really Works

Prices are not always near fair value. Sometimes, prices will be much too high based on the prevailing information, and sometimes they will be much too low. Greenblatt quotes the metaphor originally used by Benjamin Graham, in which he compares the market to a highly erratic business partner who is sometimes willing to sell shares to you at absurdly low prices and sometimes willing to buy shares from you at ridiculously high prices. The trader should take advantage of these bouts of emotional irrationality by the market. Of course, the corollary is that the value investor will typically be a seller during periods of market euphoria and a buyer during market panics. To be able to hold fundamentally justified value positions through market panics, the value investor needs to maintain a long-term perspective.

38. It Is Usually a Mistake for a Manager to Alter Investment Decisions or the Investment Process to Better Fit Investor Demands

Greenblatt tells his students, "You are setting yourself up for failure if you invest differently than you want to in order to please investors." Taylor acknowledges this same perspective when he states, "I am trying to stop caring about what my clients think."

39. Volatility and Risk Are Not Synonymous

Low volatility does not imply low risk and high volatility does not imply high risk. Investments subject to sporadic large risks may exhibit low volatility if a risk event is not present in the existing track record. For example, the strategy of selling out-of-the-money options can exhibit low volatility if there are no large, abrupt price moves, but is at risk of asymptotically increasing losses in the event of a sudden, steep selloff. On the other hand, traders such as Mai will exhibit high volatility because of occasional very large gains—not a factor that most investors would associate with risk or even consider undesirable—but will have strictly curtailed risk because of the asymmetric structure of their trades. So some strategies, such as option selling, can have both low volatility and large, open-ended risk, and some strategies, such as Mai's, can have both high volatility and constrained risk.

40. It Is a Mistake to Select Managers Based Solely on Past Performance

Greenblatt cites various empirical studies demonstrating that the past performance of managers has no predictive value regarding their future performance. So the single factor that overwhelmingly determines how investors choose their investments—that is, past returns—has no efficacy. Greenblatt advises choosing managers based on their process rather than past returns.

As a related point, investors often make the mistake of equating manager performance in a given year with manager skill. Sometimes, more skilled managers will underperform because they refuse to participate in market bubbles. The best performers during such periods are often the most imprudent rather than the most skilled managers. Taylor underperformed in 1999 because he thought it was ridiculous to buy tech stocks at their inflated price levels. This same investment decision, however, was instrumental to his large outperformance in subsequent years when these stocks witnessed a prolonged, massive decline. In this sense, past performance can sometimes even be an inverse indicator.

Epilogue

I am often asked by readers how doing the *Market Wizards* interviews affected my own trading. The interview and writing process has helped solidify in my own mind the principles that are important to trading success. At times, it has also had a very specific influence. A great example occurred last summer. At the time, the stock market was approaching the high end of a long-term trading range, and for a variety of reasons, I expected the rally to fail and was positioned on the short side of stock index futures. Then the government released an extremely bearish employment report. It was so negative that commentators couldn't even cite one offsetting bullish consideration, as they usually do. The market initially sold off sharply in response—"Perfect," I thought of my trade—but by the end of the day, it nearly recovered the entire loss, ending the week near the recent high. From the perspective of a short, this was terrible price action. I thought I was in trouble. I was prepared to cover most of my position when the market opened on Sunday night. On Sunday night, however, the market opened lower. I immediately thought of Marty Schwartz's advice in my first *Market Wizards* book: "If you're very nervous about a position overnight, and especially over the weekend, and you're able to get out at a much better price than you thought when the market trades, you're usually better off staying with the position." I did, and Schwartz's insight saved me a lot of money, as the market proceeded to move sharply lower in the ensuing weeks.

Each trader must draw personal insights from these interviews. What is important will very much depend on your own trading style. But I believe all traders, regardless of their approach, can draw important lessons from the advice and comments of the traders interviewed. The relevant interviews and advice will just be different for each reader. As one personal example, I think my interview of Jimmy Balodimas, whose basic approach is radically different from my own, influenced me to trade more around positions—that is, to treat trades as more of a dynamic rather than static process—an aspect of his approach more in tune with my own natural inclinations. Balodimas's comment that "I always take some money off the table when the market is in my favor" resonated in my mind to beneficial effect, as some of my trades that went nowhere ended up generating net profits.

Over the years, many people have told me that reading the original *Market Wizards* books changed their careers and changed their lives. I have been told this both by professional managers and by numerous attendees at my conference talks. I never know whether this life-changing impact is for the better. One time, a physician told me that he dropped his career to become a trader after reading my book, and I actually felt guilty about having deprived the world of a doctor in exchange for one more trader. Ironically, one of the people whose lives was changed by the *Market Wizards* books was my own son, Zachary, who also had a direct impact on the content of this book. Here, too, I don't know whether the change will be for the better or worse, and will never know because the proverbial road not taken remains forever unseen. I thought it was appropriate to end with his personal reflections on the message and influence of this book and its predecessors as offering a view from the perspective of someone discovering and entering the world of trading.

Jack Schwager

■ ■ ■

The *Market Wizard* series has come to shape a great deal of my life, more than I could have ever anticipated.

I was 8 years old. It was "bring your child to work" day. I loved my dad's office. It was full of things that I was not supposed to touch. Better yet, he had a secretary with a large bowl of candy and apparently no inhibitions about increasing my chances for an early onset of diabetes. I was off in the corner disassembling my father's coffee machine when he called me over for a game. The rules of the game were simple. He would cycle through charts; it was my job to guess whether the chart's next move was going to be up or down. It wouldn't be until much later in my life that I would find out that this wasn't a game at all. It was an experiment. My father has, and still holds, a theory that some individuals are naturally gifted traders who have an instinctive ability to recognize and predict visual price patterns. Five charts into the game, he was able to conclude that I was not one of these individuals. It would be years before I would look at another chart.

In my junior year of high school, I would meet my first Market Wizard, John Bender. I had suggested to my father that we take a trip before I left for college. My dad is always game for an adventure. Several years earlier he had disappeared on a hike up Mount Temple in the Canadian Rockies. Instead of the simple day hike he told us he was departing on, he came back 12 hours later with frostbite, having decided to summit the mountain instead. I thought it best that we go someplace warm this time. John Bender had just retired from trading and used his gains to buy up thousands of acres of Costa Rican rain forest. He invited us to stay at a guesthouse on the reserve.

We arranged for an SUV to drive us four hours from San Jose up to John's reserve in the rain forest. Our car made its way up a winding, single-lane dirt road, at the top of which was a clearing with two heavily armed men. John's reserve was patrolled by guards to prevent poaching. The property had three residences (one under construction) set on a large, grassy plateau. One was the existing main house, in which John resided with his wife, Ann, while they built their spectacular, multilevel, 360-degree-view dream house on the edge of the plateau. We settled into the third dwelling, the guesthouse, and agreed to meet John for a drink once we unpacked.

John was sitting on his lightly landscaped porch, overlooking the rain forest below, beers in hand. We talked for hours as the sun set over the edge of the rain forest. John led most of the conversation. He had lots of energy, as if he had so much to say and had just been waiting for the right person to talk to. The conversation ranged from the paradoxes presented by quantum physics experiments to John's particular disgust for one fund manager, who he insisted was a fraud. I wouldn't hear that manager's name again for nine years, when the financial crisis exposed what John had known all along: Bernie Madoff was a fraud.

College was quickly approaching. I went down to my dad's office to seek his advice on a major. It's quite embarrassing to say, but at this point, I had still not read *Market Wizards*. I had no involvement with the markets, and my father was never one to push anyone toward his own desires. I told him I wanted to be a doctor. I remember his response very clearly: "I don't think that's a very good fit." My dad will always give you the truth, beginning his sentence with an awkward chuckle to hide his discomfort when his candor requires imparting an opinion he knows you don't want to hear. I didn't take his advice immediately, but it wasn't long into my first year of college when I realized he had been right. I am more of a creative type, and being a doctor was probably not a good fit. I switched to film school in New York.

To help spark my interest in investing, my father had given me a $500 Ameritrade account. I found a few recommendations online and bought three stocks. Two of my stocks continued to climb higher; the third, CSX, hovered in a range somewhere between $30 and $40. I called my dad. I was ready to impress him with my insight. Having noted the stock's trading pattern, I told him that I planned to sell it near $40 and then buy it back near $30. He was not impressed. He chuckled and said, "Yeah, people do that." Two years later my account was up over two thousand dollars. I recognized I knew remarkably little about the stock market and assumed that I had probably just been lucky. I liquidated my portfolio and bought a film camera.

My father was coming to New York to give a talk at a trading expo. He extended an invitation to me, which I cautiously accepted. I pulled out my only collared shirt from the bottom of the closet and made my way to the Hilton Times Square. Everybody was wearing suits, and I instantly felt uncomfortable. My mother, whom my dad refers to as his best long-term trade, was already seated. I walked over and sat next to her. She greeted me with one of her favorite comments: "You're such a handsome boy, but nobody would ever know by the way you are dressed." The room filled up, and my dad walked up to the podium. Everyone seemed extremely excited to hear what he had to say. I sank into my seat and hoped I would understand enough so that I could say something nice to him when it was over. I didn't know this moment would change the course of my life.

My dad began to speak. I waited for his words to drift beyond my realm of comprehension, but that moment never came. Einstein once said, "Any intelligent fool can make things bigger, more complex, and more violent. It takes a touch of genius—and a lot of courage—to move in the opposite direction." My father has always had the ability and desire to take complex ideas and boil them down to their simplest forms. His talk was based on the important lessons he had uncovered in his interviews with the world's top traders. Three key insights resonated with me, and changed my previous conceptions about trading.

1. *Trading is not reserved for the world's most elite.* The traders he interviewed came from various backgrounds. There was no correlation between trading success and school or prior occupation. The commonality of the traders was traced to hard work and determination, and their desire to unlock the puzzle of the market. They all shared an aspiration to avoid the psychological impediments that prevented most people from winning in the markets.

2. *Trading is not just a science, but also an art.* Even those traders who use a purely systematic approach to tackling the markets are still engaged in creative thinking. None of the traders he discussed stepped into an already working formula; nobody was handed a blueprint. Their success was built on the backbone of their ability to discover what others overlooked.

3. *There is no single right way to make money.* Those who succeed do so because they find what works for them. Trying to replicate someone else's method almost always results in failure. All successful traders have their own methodology, an approach that makes sense to them and that they are comfortable with.

The talk concluded with a question-and-answer session. To my surprise, the industry professionals had some questions very similar to my own. I realized then that there was not as much that divided us as I had originally assumed. We all wanted to know and understand more, including my own father, as this desire was what had set him out on his quest to interview these Market Wizards many years earlier.

I have had the honor of getting to work with my dad on this book, which is not meant to imply that I have done much at all. I have simply had the privilege of sharing my impressions and suggestions after reading each chapter as he completed them. The amount of work that my father puts into these books is just incredible. I was amazed at the time it takes to go through the many hours of tapes to formulate a chapter. People often tell my dad he is a great interviewer, to which he frequently replies, "I am a horrible interviewer, but I am an excellent editor." Of course, only the latter half of that statement is true. My dad has a natural ability to pull the best out of anybody. He manages to ask all the questions you can think of and then all the ones he can think of. Working with my dad on this book has been one of the greatest learning experiences of my life.

Beyond this book, I am quite pleased to say that this won't be the last time I am able to pick my dad's brain for market knowledge. After watching him speak at the trading expo, I dropped out of film school and went off the get my bachelor's degree in finance. I now work as a junior trader at First New York Securities. I have no idea what the future holds for me, or whether I will be successful at trading in the long run, but I do know that the knowledge I have gained from this experience will serve me wherever life takes me.

A couple of months ago, I was out for happy hour with a few associates. One of them asked me, "Do you feel that because of your dad you have a lot to live up to as a trader?" to which I replied, "It would be far easier to be as successful as my dad in trading than to be as successful as he is on a human level. My dad is one of the kindest, humblest, and most generous people I have ever come across. I would much rather be as great a person as he is than to be as successful as he is."

Zachary Schwager

APPENDIX A

The Gain to Pain Ratio

Most people tend to focus only on return. As I see it, as a performance measure, return is only meaningful relative to how much risk was required to get it. You could always get a higher return simply by using leverage; that doesn't mean it represents better performance. One statistic I particularly like is what I call the Gain to Pain ratio. I define the Gain to Pain ratio (GPR) as the sum of all monthly returns divided by the absolute value of the sum of all monthly losses.[1]

---

[1]The Gain to Pain Ratio (GPR) is a performance statistic I have been using for many years. I am not aware of any prior use of this statistic, although the term is sometimes used as a generic reference for return/risk measures or a return/drawdown measure. The GPR is similar to the "profit factor," which is a commonly used statistic in evaluating trading systems. The profit factor is defined as the sum of all profitable trades divided by the absolute value of the sum of all losing trades. The profit factor is applied to trades, whereas the GPR is applied to interval (e.g., monthly) returns. Algebraically, it can easily be shown that if the profit factor calculation were applied to monthly returns, the profit factor would equal GPR $+ 1$ and would provide the same performance ordering as the GPR. For quantitatively oriented readers familiar with the Omega function, note that the Omega function evaluated at zero is also equal to GPR $+ 1$.

This performance measure indicates the ratio of cumulative net gain to the cumulative loss realized to achieve that gain. For example, a GPR of 1.0 would imply that, on average, an investor would experience an equal amount of monthly losses to the *net* amount gained. If the average return per year is 12 percent (arithmetic, not compounded), the average amount of monthly losses per year would also sum to 12 percent. The GPR penalizes all losses in proportion to their size. Upside volatility, however, is beneficial because it only impacts the return portion of the ratio. In contrast, the Sharpe ratio—the most widely used return/risk measure—penalizes upside volatility. As a rough guideline, for liquid strategies, any GPR above 1.0 is very good, and a GPR above 1.5 is excellent.

APPENDIX B

Options—Understanding the Basics*

T here are two basic types of options: calls and puts. The purchase of a *call option* provides the buyer with the right—but not the obligation—to purchase the underlying item at a specified price, called the *strike* or *exercise* price, at any time up to and including the *expiration date*. A *put option* provides the buyer with the right—but not the obligation—to sell the underlying item at the strike price at any time prior to expiration. (Note, therefore, that buying a put is a *bearish* trade, while selling a put is a *bullish* trade.) The price of an option is called a *premium*. As an example of an option, an IBM April 130 call gives the purchaser the right to buy 100 shares of IBM at $130 per share at any time during the life of the option.

The buyer of a call seeks to profit from an anticipated price rise by locking in a specified purchase price. The call buyer's maximum possible loss will be equal to the dollar amount of the premium paid for the

---

*This appendix was originally published in *Market Wizards* (1989).

option. This maximum loss would occur on an option held until expiration if the strike price was above the prevailing market price. For example, if IBM was trading at \$125 when the 130 option expired, the option would expire worthless. If at expiration, the price of the underlying market was above the strike price, the option would have some value and would hence be exercised. However, if the difference between the market price and the strike price was less than the premium paid for the option, the net result of the trade would still be a loss. In order for a call buyer to realize a net profit, the difference between the market price and the strike price would have to exceed the premium paid when the call was purchased (after adjusting for commission cost). The higher the market price, the greater the resulting profit.

The buyer of a put seeks to profit from an anticipated price decline by locking in a sales price. Like the call buyer, the maximum possible loss is limited to the dollar amount of the premium paid for the option. In the case of a put held until expiration, the trade would show a net profit if the strike price exceeded the market price by an amount greater than the premium of the put at purchase (after adjusting for commission cost).

Whereas the buyer of a call or put has limited risk and unlimited potential gain, the reverse is true for the seller. The option seller (often called the *writer*) receives the dollar value of the premium in return for undertaking the obligation to assume an opposite position *at the strike price* if an option is exercised. For example, if a call is exercised, the seller must assume a short position in the underlying market at the strike price (since by exercising the call, the buyer assumes a long position at that price).

The seller of a call seeks to profit from an anticipated sideways to modestly declining market. In such a situation, the premium earned by selling a call provides the most attractive trading opportunity. However, if the trader expected a large price decline, he would usually be better off going short the underlying market or buying a put—trades with open-ended profit potential. In a similar fashion, the seller of a put seeks to profit from an anticipated sideways to modestly rising market.

Some novices have trouble understanding why a trader would not always prefer the buy side of the option (call or put, depending on market opinion), since such a trade has unlimited potential and limited risk. Such confusion reflects the failure to take probability into account. Although the option seller's theoretical risk is unlimited, the price levels that have the greatest probability of occurrence (i.e., prices in the vicinity of the market price when the option trade occurs) would result in a net gain to the option seller. Roughly speaking, the option buyer accepts a large probability of a small loss in return for a small probability of a large gain, whereas the option seller accepts a small probability of a large loss in exchange for a large probability of a small gain. In an efficient market, neither the consistent option buyer nor the consistent option seller should have any significant advantage over the long run.

The option premium consists of two components: intrinsic value plus time value. The *intrinsic value* of a call option is the amount by which the current market price is above the strike price. (The intrinsic value of a put option is the amount by which the current market price is below the strike price.) In effect, the intrinsic value is that part of the premium that could be realized if the option were exercised at the current market price. The intrinsic value serves as a floor price for an option. Why? Because if the premium were less than the intrinsic value, a trader could buy and exercise the option and immediately offset the resulting market position, thereby realizing a net gain (assuming that the trader covers at least transaction costs).

Options that have intrinsic value (i.e., calls with strike prices below the market price and puts with strike prices above the market price) are said to be *in-the-money*. Options that have no intrinsic value are called *out-of-the-money* options. Options with a strike price closest to the market price are called *at-the-money* options.

An out-of-the-money option, which by definition has an intrinsic value equal to zero, will still have some value because of the possibility that the market price will move beyond the strike price prior to the expiration date. An in-the-money option will have a value greater than the intrinsic value because a position in the option will be preferred to a position in the underlying market. Why? Because both the option and the market position will gain equally in the event of a favorable price movement, but the option's maximum loss is limited. The portion of the premium that exceeds the intrinsic value is called the *time value*.

The three most important factors that influence an option's time value are:

1. *Relationship between the strike and market price*—Deeply out-of-the-money options will have little time value since it is unlikely that the market price will move to the strike price—or beyond—prior to expiration. Deeply in-the-money options have little time value, because these options offer positions very similar to the underlying market—both will gain and lose equivalent amounts for all but an extremely adverse price move. In other words, for a deeply in-the-money option, the fact that risk is limited is not worth very much, because the strike price is so far from the prevailing market price.

2. *Time remaining until expiration*—The more time remaining until expiration, the greater the value of the option. This is true because a longer life span increases the probability of the intrinsic value increasing by any specified amount prior to expiration.

3. *Volatility*—Time value will vary directly with the estimated *volatility* [a measure of the degree of price variability] of the underlying market for the remaining life span of the option. This relationship is a result of the fact that greater volatility raises the probability of the intrinsic value increasing by any specified amount prior to expiration. In other words, the greater the volatility, the greater the probable price range of the market.

Although volatility is an extremely important factor in the determination of option premium values, it should be stressed that the future volatility of a market is never precisely known until after the fact. (In contrast, the time remaining until expiration and the relationship between the current market price and the strike price can be exactly specified at any juncture.) Thus, volatility must always be estimated on the basis of *historical volatility* data. The future volatility estimate implied by market prices (i.e., option premiums), which may be higher or lower than the historical volatility, is called the *implied volatility*.

About the Author

Mr. Schwager is a recognized industry expert in futures and hedge funds and the author of a number of widely acclaimed financial books. He is currently the co-portfolio manager for the ADM Investor Services Diversified Strategies Fund, a portfolio of futures and FX managed accounts. He is also an advisor to Marketopper, an India-based quantitative trading firm, supervising a major project that will adapt their trading technology to trade a global futures portfolio.

Previously, Mr. Schwager was a partner in the Fortune Group, a London-based hedge fund advisory firm, acquired by the Close Brothers Group. His previous experience also includes 22 years as director of futures research for some of Wall Street's leading firms and 10 years as the co-principal of a CTA.

Mr. Schwager has written extensively on the futures industry and great traders in all financial markets. He is perhaps best known for his best-selling series of interviews with the greatest hedge fund managers of the last two decades: *Market Wizards* (1989, new edition 2012), *The New Market Wizards* (1992), and *Stock Market Wizards* (2001). Mr. Schwager's first book, *A Complete Guide to the Futures Markets* (1984), is considered to be one of the classic reference works in the field. He later revised and expanded this original work into the three-volume series *Schwager on*

Futures, consisting of *Fundamental Analysis* (1995), *Technical Analysis* (1996), and *Managed Trading* (1996). He is also the author of *Getting Started in Technical Analysis* (1999), part of John Wiley & Sons' popular *Getting Started* series.

Mr. Schwager is a frequent seminar speaker and has lectured on a range of analytical topics including the characteristics of great traders, investment fallacies, hedge fund portfolios, managed accounts, technical analysis, and trading system evaluation. He holds a BA in Economics from Brooklyn College (1970) and an MA in Economics from Brown University (1971).

Index

Abstract factor analysis, 203–204
ABX Index, 248–252
Adapting, 447, 491–492
Airlines, 379
All Weather fund (Bridgewater), 49
Altria, 231–233, 234
Amazon, 439–440
Apple, 348–350, 357, 358, 381
Arnett, Bob, 408–409
Asset-backed securities (ABSs), 244. *See also*
   Mortgage-backed securities (MBSs);
   Subprime mortgages/bonds
Asymmetric strategies, 223–259, 497

Baccarat system, 186–187
Balodimas, Jimmy, 423–450, 491,
   495, 508
Bamberger, Gerry, 200–204
Banyan Equity Management, 78, 80, 100.
   See also Benedict, Larry
Baring Asset Management,
   329–330, 339
Beat the Dealer (Thorp), 184

Beat the Market (Kassouf and Thorp), 163,
   164, 189, 190
Bender, John, 509–510
Benedict, Larry, 77–101, 493, 501
Berkshire Hathaway, 211
Betting systems, 170–180. *See also* Gambling
The Big Secret for the Small Investor
   (Greenblatt), 453
The Big Short (Lewis), 223, 226
Blackjack system, 181–186, 218–219
Black-Scholes option-pricing model, 163,
   164, 191–192
Blue button, 289–290
BlueCrest. *See* Platt, Michael
Blue Ridge Trading, 131, 135, 136
Brazilian interest-rate trade, 235–236, 258
Breakouts, 123–124
Bridgewater, 47–49. *See also* Dalio, Ray
   All Weather Fund, 49
   culture at, 59, 70
   Principles, 51
   Pure Alpha fund, 48–49
   trading processes and system, 60–64

Bubbles:
  Colm O'Shea on, 13–24, 44, 494
  dot-com, 30–31, 33, 43–44, 372–373,
    410–411, 434
  financial bubble of 2005–2007, 14–24 (*see
    also* Subprime mortgages/bonds)
  gold, 34–35
  housing, 392
  predicting turnaround, 21
Buffett, Warren, 210–211, 463, 484
Burry, Michael, 248
Business cycle, 74

Call option. *See* Options
Canadian Natural Resources, 380
Capital One, 233–234
Cap rate, 412
Carry currencies, 14
Casino (film), 184
Casino games. *See* Gambling
Catalyst theory, 21
Category-based thinking, 49
Celanese, 378, 381
Chinese coal market, 253–255
Chipotle, 440
Citigroup, 391
Clark, Steve, 287–321, 490, 491, 492, 498,
  499
Claugus, Thomas, 359–383, 496
Collateralized debt obligations (CDOs),
  227, 245–252
Commissions, 113–114
Commodity Trading Advisors (CTAs), 36,
  104, 113–114, 129–131, 147. *See also*
  Ramsey, Scott; Woodriff, Jaffray
Company conference calls, 390–391
The Complete Turtle Trader (Covel), 266, 269
Computer strategies, early, 172–173
Concept stocks, 393–394
Constraining monthly losses, 500
Contrarian investing, 126, 138, 360, 432
Convertible bond arbitrage, 193
Copart (CPRT), 414–415
Cornwall Capital, 223–225

Corporate bonds, 23–24
Correlation, 57–58, 70–71, 96–100, 125,
  258–259, 276, 501
Countertrend vs. trend methodologies, 130
Credit default swaps (CDSs), 23–24
Credit expansion/deleveraging cycle, 73–74
Credit spreads, 23–24

Dalio, Ray, 47–66, 493, 500, 502
  Holy Grail of investing, 56–57
  template for understanding economies,
    72–74
Daly, Kevin, 405–422
Data mining, 144, 151–153
Davidge, Nick, 386, 396
Deleveraging cycles, 73–74
Delta hedging, 191, 193
Delta neutral hedging, 191
Depression gauge, 65–66
Discretionary trading, 61–62, 117–118, 262,
  269, 271, 283. *See also* Benedict, Larry;
  Platt, Michael; Ramsey, Scott
Diversification, 56–57, 70–71, 146,
  264–265, 402, 453, 467–468, 500
Dollar General, 438
Dot-com bubble, 30–31, 33, 43–44,
  372–373, 410–411, 434
Drawdowns, 60–61, 121
Drexel, 165
Dynamic delta hedging, 191

Earnings yield, 452, 461–462
Eastern European markets. *See* Taylor,
  Martin
EBIT, 412, 461–464
EBITDA, 412
Economics, teaching of, 8
Education reform, 480–484
Efficient market hypothesis (EMH),
  161–162, 217, 486, 504
Electronic trading, changes brought about
  by, 90–92
Emerging markets funds, 345–348, 356, 378
Enterprise value (EV), 412, 461–462

Entry size, 320
Equal-weighted indexes, 487
Euphoria, avoiding, 448, 497
Eurobonds, 336
Euro Disney, 316
European debt crisis of 2011, 12–13, 280–281
European sovereign debt, 38
Exchange Rate Mechanism (ERM), 11
Exiting trades, 120–121

False breakouts, 123–124
Fibonacci retracements, 119
Financial bubble of 2005–2007, 14–24. See also Subprime mortgages/bonds
Financial crisis beginning in 2007, 43
    Colm O'Shea on, 18–28
    determining start of, 17–18
    Michael Platt on, 270–273
    Steve Clark on, 317–318
First New York Securities, 304–306, 423. See also Balodimas, Jimmy
Fiscal policy, 66–69
Five Corners Partners, LP, 407
Five-phase cycle, 74–76
Flexibility, 321, 490–491
Forward conversions, 456
Forward pricing, 258
Free cash flow (FCF), 412
Free markets, 156
Fundamental analysis, 114–117, 353–354, 386. See also Taylor, Martin
Fund asset size, 421–422
Fund capacity, 154–155
Futures traders. See Commodity Trading Advisors (CTAs)

Gain to Pain ratio, 225, 262, 288, 386, 406, 513–514
Gambling, 32, 170–173
    baccarat system, 186–187
    blackjack system, 163, 170–171, 173–175, 181–186, 195–198, 218–219, 496

compared to investing, 218–219
    roulette system, 163, 169, 175–179, 181, 186, 218
Gate provision, 273, 344
Gating, 369–370
Geismar, Michael, 133
Gerard, Ralph, 210–211
Giuliani, Rudolph, 165
Gold, 34–35, 124
Goldman Sachs, 336
Goldstein, Rob, 452, 468
Goodyear, 438
Google, 402
Gotham Capital, 451–452, 453. See also Greenblatt, Joel
Graham, Ben, 454
Grantham, Jeremy, 239
Great Depression, 167–168
Greenblatt, Joel, 451–487, 493, 500, 503, 504
    on education reform, 480–484
    Magic Formula, 452, 464
    Value and Special Situation Investing course, 475–477
    Value Investors Club, 471–473

Halcyon Investments, 456
Hand, Eddie, 185
Hedge funds, 216
    Banyan Equity Management, 78, 80, 100 (see also Benedict, Larry)
    Baring Asset Management, 329–330, 339
    BlueCrest (see Platt, Michael)
    Bridgewater (see Dalio, Ray)
    Denali Asset Management (see Ramsey, Scott)
    Gotham Capital, 451–452, 453 (see also Greenblatt, Joel)
    LTCM (Long Term Capital Management), 16–17
    Manalapan Oracle Capital Management, 385–387 (see also Vidich, Joe)
    Nevsky Fund, 324, 340 (see also Taylor, Martin)

Hedge funds (*continued*)
Omni Global Fund (*see* Clark, Steve)
Princeton Newport Partners (PNP)
(*see* Thorp, Edward)
Ridgeline Partners, 166
High-conviction trades, 243, 256
Hockett, Ben, 224
Horizon Lines, 415
Host Marriott, 459–460
House, Gerry, 480
Housing bubble, 392. *See also* Financial
bubble of 2005–2007

Insurance Auto Auctions (IAAI), 414–415
Intrinsic value, 517
Investment misconceptions, 257–259
Investors, pleasing, 340, 345, 358,
484, 505

James, Bill, 136–137, 149
Jones, Paul Tudor, 141–142

Kassouf, Sheen, 163, 164, 189
Kellogg, Peter, 93
Kelly criterion, 194–198, 214, 220–221
Key3Media, 474–475
Keynes, John Maynard, 9–10
Kimmell, Emmanuel, 182–183
Klein, Joel, 481
Kovner, Bruce, 210

LEAPS, 460–461
Ledley, Charlie, 224
Lehman Brothers, 294, 295
Lewis, Michael, 226–227
Liquidity vs. solvency, 25
The Little Book That Beats the Market
(Greenblatt), 452, 463, 486
Long, Simon, 431
Long Term Capital Management (LTCM),
16–17
Long-term cycles, 69
LTCM (Long Term Capital Management),
16–17

Macro outlook, 338
Madoff, Bernard, 16, 163, 214–217, 510
Mai, Jamie, 223–259, 491, 493, 503, 505
Brazilian interest-rate trade,
235–236, 258
investment strategy pillars, 255–256
subprime mortgages/bonds, 244–252
Manager selection, 479, 486, 505
Manalapan Oracle Capital Management,
385–387
Market behavior, 502
Marriott, 459–460
Mean reversion, 142, 147–148, 156,
370–371
Measurement Specialties, 416
Merger arbitrage, 457
Micron Technology, 439
Milken, Michael, 165, 458
Mistakes, learning from, 50–51, 493
Mobius, Mark, 346
Monthly returns, 348, 357–358
Mortgage-backed securities (MBSs),
246–247. *See also* Subprime mortgages/
bonds
Moscowitz, Eva, 481

Net exposure indicator, 375–376
Net exposure ranges, 340–341, 357,
370–371
Net working capital, 464
Nevsky Fund, 324, 340
Newberg, Bruce, 458
Newport Corporation, 411–412
New revenue sources, 503–504
News, market response to, 502
9/11, 93–94
Nomura, 301–303
Normal distribution assumption, 257

Obama, Barack, 484
October 1987 crash, 22, 83–85, 138,
268–269, 290–293, 363–365, 410
Omni Global Fund, 287
Optionality, free, 380–382

Options, 191–192, 226, 231, 232–242
  carry currencies, 14
  vs. CDSs, 24
  overview of, 515–518
O'Shea, Colm, 3–45, 490, 491, 494, 497, 500
OTC (over-the-counter) markets, 156
Overnight index swap (OIS), 272

Paramount Resources, 381
P/E ratio, 412
Performance, correlation between past and
  future, 478–480, 486, 505
Petrominerales, 380
Petry, John, 473, 481
Planet Money (radio show), 226
Platinum, 124
Platt, Michael, 261–284, 498, 502
Position size, 320–321, 495–496
Princeton Newport Partners (PNP), 162,
  164–166, 192–193, 197, 204–207
Productivity growth, 72
Pure Alpha fund, 48–49
Put option. *See* Options

QE2 (quantitative easing), 123
Quadrant conceptualization, 49–50
Quantitative Foundation, 144–145
Quantitative Investment Management
  (QIM), 134–135, 144–145

Ramsey, Scott, 103–127, 498, 501
Random Character of Stock Prices (Cootner),
  191
Recessions vs. deleveragings, 73–74
Regan, James, 164–165, 204–206
Related market price actions, 501
Relative Strength Index (RSI), 119, 354
Reminiscenses of a Stock Operator, 7–8
Research in Motion Ltd. (RIMM), 349–350
Return on capital, 452, 463–464
Reversal vs. correction, 36
Ridgeline Partners, 166
Rights issues, 314
Risk and volatility, 259

Risk arbitrage, 301, 305, 457–458
Risk management, 78, 118, 127, 498–499
  Edward Thorp, 213–214
  Jaffray Woodriff, 155–156
  Joe Vidich, 395–396
  Larry Benedict, 100–101
  Martin Taylor, 351–352
  Michael Platt, 274–276
  Thomas Claugus, 373
Risk vs. volatility, 505
RMH Warrants and Low Price Stock Survey
  (Fried), 189
Rock Tenn, 371–372
Rohm & Haas, 365–367
Roulette system, 163, 169, 175–179, 181,
  186, 218
Russian financial crisis of 1998, 330–339

Schwager, Zachary, 424, 429, 435–436,
  508–512
Schwartz, Marty, 92–93, 507
Secondary variables, 148–149, 151
Sentiment, 394–395, 397, 401, 426, 429
Seykota, Ed, 95
Shannon, Claude, 174–180, 195
Sharpe ratio, 225
Shaw, David, 150, 208
Short-term trading, 394
Silver, 36–37, 441–442
Singer, Paul, 246
Slavin, Robert, 480
Société Générale, 343
Solvency vs. liquidity, 25
Soros, George, 11, 28
South Korean stock market, 252–253
Soviet Union. *See* Russian financial crisis of
  1998
Spear, Leeds & Kellogg (SLK), 77–78,
  92–93
Specialists, 86–87
Special situation investing, 231, 451, 458,
  459–461, 467
Spinoffs, 459. *See also* Special situation
  investing

Static hedging, 191
Statistical arbitrage strategy, 166, 199–204,
    207–208, 220
Statistical prediction, 144–145
Sticky businesses, 485
Stops, 41–42, 120, 395, 500
Subprime mortgages/bonds, 224, 244–252
Systematic trend-following strategy,
    264–266, 273, 284
Systematic value approach, 461–471

TABX index, 251–252
Tangible book value (TBV), 412–413
Tangible common equity, 413
Taylor, Martin, 323–358, 490, 500,
    503, 505
Technical Analysis (Edwards and McGee), 188
Technology bubble, 434. *See also* Dot-com
    bubble
TED spread, 25
Thames River Capital Management,
    339–340
Thorp, Edward, 161–221, 496, 499
    firsts achieved by, 163
    gambling experiments and strategies,
        170–187, 218–219
    option pricing model, 191–192
    statistical arbitrage strategy, 199–204, 220
    warrant pricing model, 189–191, 192
Time arbitrage, 485
Time horizons, 366, 477–478
Time value, 517–518
Trade implementation, 5, 23, 28–29, 494
Traders, hiring, 276–279
Trade size, 496. *See also* Kelly criterion
Trading around a position, 441, 445,
    447–448, 495
Trading book rules, 32
Trading pits, changes since electronic
    trading, 90–92

Trading rules vs. guidelines, 39–40
Trading style development, 39–40,
    449–450, 490
Trend following, 142, 147–148, 210–214,
    264–266, 273, 284
Trend-neutral model, 149
Trend vs. countertrend methodologies, 130
Trinity Industries, 391
200-day moving average, 119
Tyco, 428

Value and Special Situation Investing
    course, 475–477
Value at Risk (VAR), 40–41
Value investing, 465–466, 485, 504
Value Investors Club, 471–473
Value-weighted indexes, 487
Vidich, Joe, 385–404, 490, 500
Volatility, 518
Volatility assumption, 258–259
Volatility vs. risk, 505

Warburg Securities, 294
Warrants, 163–164, 166, 189–190,
    192, 206
Weighted indexes, 487
Wells Fargo, 460–461, 487
Williams, Greyson, 134
Wolfe, Tom, 182
Woodriff, Jaffray, 129–158, 499
    on data mining, 151–153
    on fund capacity, 154–155
    statistical prediction research, 144–145
Woodriff Trading, 131–132
Worst of option, 237

XLP index, 239–240

You Can Be a Stock Market Genius
    (Greenblatt), 451